# MARTIN BUBER

# Martin Buber

## *A Life of Faith and Dissent*

PAUL MENDES-FLOHR

Yale

UNIVERSITY
PRESS

New Haven and London

Yale University Press books may be purchased in quantity for educational,
business, or promotional use. For information, please e-mail sales.press@yale.edu
(U.S. office) or sales@yaleup.co.uk (U.K. office).

Set in Janson Oldstyle type by Tseng Information Systems, Inc.
Printed in the United States of America.

Library of Congress Control Number: 2018956107
ISBN 978-0-300-15304-0 (hardcover : alk. paper)

A catalogue record for this book is available from the British Library.

This paper meets the requirements of ANSI/NISO Z39.48-1992
(Permanence of Paper).

10 9 8 7 6 5 4 3 2 1

*Frontispiece:* Martin Buber in his Jerusalem study, 1963.
Courtesy of the Martin Buber Literary Estate.

For Rita, our children, and our grandchildren—
and my students, past and present

# CONTENTS

# CONTENTS

# INTRODUCTION

I am unfortunately a complicated
and difficult subject.
—Martin Buber

COMMENTING ON her own intellectual biography, Hannah Arendt noted, "I do not believe there is any thought process without personal experience. Every thought is an afterthought, that is, a reflection on some matter or event."[1] Correlating thought with experience, however, is a fraught endeavor—experiences are multilayered and often contradictory, and some experiences that may have left their imprint on one's thought are "not truly known" or are "gladly forgotten."[2] The task of the biographer, then, is to determine which experiences have any bearing on the intellectual and personal development of the principal protagonist of his or her narrative, but to do so while exercising due caution even when reading written records, especially those of the subject. A text may have an "implied author" who is not identical with its actual author; the way a text is written and received may project an image of the author that differs from his or her "true" or full personality, or represents only part of it. Moreover, as Saul Bellow candidly acknowledged, given all the revisions and fine-tuning that go into a work, the author often appears substantially different in writing from the way he or she is in "real life."[3]

All these challenges are certainly faced by any biographer of Martin Buber. Writing did not come easily to him; as he once confessed to an impatient editor of one of his collections of essays in English, "I want you to know for once and all that I am not a literary man. Writing is not my job but my duty, a terribly severe one. When I write I do it under a terrible strain."[4] He would write numerous drafts and continually revise his works from edition to edition, deleting whole passages and re-writing others. While Buber did not always alert the reader of subsequent editions about his revisions, his biographer can consider them hints at possible biographical shifts and intellectual adjustments.

The biographer, as Janet Malcolm observed in her study of Sylvia Plath, is (and I would add, should be) inevitably haunted by an "epistemological insecurity."[5] The story a biographer tells is by its very nature interpretive. When assembling facts and evaluating their biographical significance, the biographer often selects those that support the narrative he or she has constructed, in order to provide a coherent story line.

To minimize the inevitable tendentiousness of the narrative I have constructed, I sought to take my clues from Buber himself. The story I tell about his life and thought is shaped by what he relates primarily in his correspondence—the Martin Buber Archive at the National Library of Israel contains over fifty thousand letters between Buber and hundreds of correspondents—as well as in parenthetical autobiographical comments scattered throughout his writings. He also often wrote poetry in response to given events and experiences, of which very little was published.[6] Toward the end of his life, he wrote a short essay of "autobiographical fragments," which he introduced by noting: "It cannot be a question here of recounting my personal life . . . but solely of rendering an account of some moments that my backward glance lets rise to the surface, moments that have exercised a decisive influence on the nature and direction of my thinking."[7]

If one were to write his biography, Buber hence insisted, it should be focused on his thought, taking into account those constitutive moments: "My philosophy," he wrote, "serves an experience, a perceived attitude that it has established to make communicable. I was not permitted to reach out beyond my experiences, and I never wished to do so. I witnessed for experience and appealed to experience. The experience for which I witnessed is, naturally, a limited one. But it is not to be understood as a 'subjective' one. . . . I say to him who listens to me: 'It is your experience.' . . . I must say it once again: I have no teaching. I only point to something . . . in reality that had not or had too little been seen. I take him who listens to me by the hand and lead him to the window. I open the window and point to what is outside."[8]

Buber was, accordingly, wary of any biography that tried to probe the psychological sources of his ideas and his writings, thereby reducing them—and him—to a subjective, idiosyncratic, and thus speculative reading. In reply to an American doctoral student who was writing a comparative psychological biography of Buber and Kierkegaard, Buber protested:

> I do not like at all to deal with my person as a "subject," and I do not think myself at all obliged to do so. I am not interested in the world being interested in my person. I want to influence the world, but I do not want it to feel itself influ-

enced by "Me." I am, if I may say so, commissioned to show men some realities, and I try to do it as adequately as possible. To reflect on why I have been commissioned or why in the course of my life I have become more apt to show what I have to show, and so on, has not only no attraction for me but even no sense. There are men who want to explain themselves to the world; Kierkegaard did; I do not. I do not even want to explain myself to myself.[9]

Buber's views on this issue were multilayered. He once wrote to Franz Rosenzweig that in order to understand why he had rejected traditional Jewish observance, "I would have had to tell you about the internal and even external history of my own youth."[10] Still, he would point out, his own struggle with the traditional Judaism in which he was raised resonated with that of his generation of Jews, especially those who also hailed from eastern Europe. Many of his experiences and attitudes should therefore not be considered idiosyncratic or distinctively personal, but representative of those shared by many of his contemporaries—expressions of the complex lived question, born of Jewry's passage into the modern world, of how to continue to identify as Jews.

The story I have chosen to tell about Buber, then, coheres with Edward Said's conception of identity as "the animating principle of biography." The biographer seeks to understand a life in a way that reinforces, consolidates, and clarifies "a core identity, identical not only with itself, but in a sense with the history of a period in which it existed and flourished."[11] To characterize the identity and the set of questions that exercised Buber throughout his life and determined the course of his intellectual biography, I have drawn on the distinction between what Arthur A. Cohen called "the natural and [the] supernatural Jew."[12] The "supernatural Jew" is beholden to the timeless religious vocation of the Jewish people as defined by the (divinely revealed) Torah and rabbinic tradition; the "natural Jew" is subject to the vagaries of history and social circumstance. In traditional Jewish society, the quotidian interests of the natural Jew had been subordinate to Israel's supernatural calling. But with the Emancipation, the opening of the gates of the ghetto, and access to new social and economic opportunities, the natural Jew gained preeminence—and the attendant struggle against anti-Semitism and for full political equality often led to an eclipse of the supernatural Jew.

As his life and thought evolved, Buber's overarching concern was to reintegrate the natural and supernatural Jew. While unfailingly attentive to Jewish struggles for political and social dignity, he insisted that the politics of the natural Jew, particularly as expressed in Zionism, should be guided by the foundational ethical and spiritual principles of the supernatural Jew. He elaborated these principles under the rubric of biblical humanism (and alternatively, Hebrew humanism), portraying them as sustained by a dialectical balance between the particular and the universal. A Jew's uncompromised fidelity to the Jewish people, Buber held, need not undermine his or her abiding cosmopolitan and transnational commitments, and vice versa. In his essay "Hasidism and Modern Man," he eloquently affirmed this conviction: "It has often been suggested to me that I should liberate this teaching [of Hasidism] from its 'confessional limitations,' as people like to put it, and proclaim it as an unfettered teaching of mankind. Taking such a 'universal' path would be for me but arbitrariness. In order to speak to the world what I have heard I am not bound to step into the street. I may remain standing at the door of my ancestral house: here too the word [resonant with universal significance] that is uttered does not go astray."[13]

The challenge of aligning and balancing particular and universal responsibility marks the trajectory of Buber's intellectual biography. He continually renegotiated the relationship between them, eschewing all ideologically sealed positions. This struck Hannah Arendt as an uncommon virtue; upon visiting Buber in his advanced age, she was taken by his openness to different perspectives: "He is genuinely curious—desires to know and understand the world. In his near-eightieth year, he is more lively and receptive than all the opinionated dogmatists and know-it-alls. He has a definite sovereignty that pleases me."[14] Buber himself once remarked, "To be old is a glorious thing when one has not unlearned what it means to begin."[15]

Buber believed that he first found in the music of Bach his resolve to resist all-too-easy simplifications. As a twenty-year-old student at the University of Leipzig, he often attended the Bach concerts at the city's famed Saint Thomas Church. He remarked about these concerts: "It would be fruitless for me to undertake to say, indeed, I cannot even make clear to myself—in what way Bach had influenced my thinking. [But] the ground-tone of my life was obviously modified in some manner and through that my thinking as well."[16] Listening to Bach's polyphonic and contrapuntal music, he wrote, "slowly, waveringly, there grew [within me] insight into the problematic reality of human existence and into the fragile possibility of doing justice to it. Bach helped me."[17] His experience with Bach's music cast new light on what he came to view as a kind of sophomoric hero worship of the nineteenth-century socialist Ferdinand Lassale, of whose writings Buber had been enamored. He wrote: "I had admired [Lassale's] spiritual passion and his readiness, in personal as in public life, to stake his existence. What was problematic in his nature went unnoticed; it did not even concern me."[18]

In this autobiographical confession, I hear a caveat to avoid a hagiographic or simplistic account of Buber's own life and thought. Buber had his foibles, as all of us have. Scarred by the wounds of a troubled childhood, he was at times narcissistic and self-absorbed, and was often pilloried for what some perceived to be behavior inconsistent with his own demanding principles.

Anecdotes abound, particularly in the Yishuv (the Zionist community of Mandatory Palestine) and later in the State of Israel, about Buber's failure to be a truly dialogical, "I-Thou" kind of person. To be sure, anecdotes are epistemically ambiguous, for "Peter's opinions of Paul very often tell us more about Peter than about Paul."[19] Nevertheless, it is clear that Buber was not a perfect human being—although he was perfectly human.

Buber was a contested figure. He evoked passionate, often conflicting opinions about his person and thought. The late editor of the Israeli daily *Haaretz* Gershom Schocken recalls taking a walk with the Hebrew novelist and lifelong friend of Buber Shmuel Yosef Agnon, during which they discussed the prevailing controversies in Israel about Buber. "Agnon abruptly stopped, looked, and said: I would like to tell you something. There are people about whom you must once decide whether you love or hate them. I decided to love Buber."[20]

# MARTIN BUBER

# 1

A Motherless Child

AN APOCRYPHAL STORY relates that when Martin Buber walked the streets of Jerusalem, children would run after him, screaming *Elohim, Elohim* (God, God). He would slowly turn around, gently stroke his silken white beard, smile, and obligingly say, "Yes!" Buber was of course not divine, nor did he fancy himself to be a prophet, notwithstanding his biblical countenance. He had, in fact, first grown his famous beard in order to cover up an embarrassing twisted lower lip, an injury caused by the use of faulty obstetric forceps during his birth. Photos from his early twenties show him with a mustache grown over the injured lip; a luxuriant beard soon followed, providing what he undoubtedly believed was more effective camouflage.[1]

The deformed lip was not his only scar from childhood. When he was three years old, his parents suddenly separated, his mother running off without bidding him farewell. He recalled rushing to a window of his family's second-story apartment on

Vienna's Franz-Josefs-Kai overlooking the Danau river canal. From the small balcony outside the stately French window, he tried desperately to catch his mother's attention, but she disappeared over the horizon without looking back. The bewildered Martin was soon sent to live with his paternal grandparents in Lemberg (in Polish Lwów; today, Lviv, Ukraine), at that time the administrative capital of the Austrian-Hungarian province of Galicia, a largely Polish region that had been annexed by the Habsburg monarchy in 1772. Adele and Salomon Buber, who would raise Martin until he was fourteen, generally refrained from discussing intimate interpersonal matters. Neither said a word to Martin about his parents' separation; the fate of his mother, who had eloped with a Russian officer (Buber's parents' marriage was eventually annulled by a rabbinic court); or when he might see his mother again. (As he recalled eight decades later, "And I was too timid to ask.") When four-year-old Martin impulsively asked a neighbor' daughter what he hesitated to ask his grandparents, the older girl made it clear that a reunion was unlikely. "I can still hear her voice as she said, in a matter of-fact way, 'No, your mother is not coming back any more.'" Stunned by the bluntness of this reply, he finally accepted the desertion of his mother. "I wanted to see my mother. And the impossibility of this gave me an infinite sense of deprivation and loss."[2]

Recalling at the end of his life this painful exchange with his neighbor's daughter, Buber mused, "Whatever I have learned in the course of my life about the meaning of meeting and dialogue between people springs from that moment when I was four."[3] That moment was echoed in words he addressed to the German-Jewish community shortly after Hitler's seizure of power: "Children experience what happens and keep silent, but in the night they groan in their dreams, awaken, and stare into the darkness. The world has become unreliable. . . . It is up to us to make the world reliable again for children. It depends on us whether we can say to them and to ourselves, 'Don't worry, Mother is here.'"[4] The highly autobiographical nature of this statement is highlighted in a 1922 letter to Franz Rosenzweig. Commenting on the existential significance of the biblical psalms, he wrote: "For me, the psalms have always kept that sense of physical intimacy they had in my childhood (a motherless childhood, one spent dreaming of my living but inaccessibly remote mother): 'You have put friend and neighbor far from me' [Psalms 88:19]."[5]

The enduring imprint of his yearning to be reunited with his "inaccessibly remote mother" was poignantly expressed in an early love letter to his future wife, Paula: "Your letters are the only source of strength I have. . . . They are absolutely the only thing [that sustains me]. Aside from these letters, perhaps also the thought that there is a mother in you, [and] my faith in that. . . . Now I know: ever and always I have been seeking my mother."[6] Nearly twenty years later, while addressing a young man on the occasion of his bar mitzvah, he contrasted the voluntary act of faith of devoting oneself to God with one's whole being to the bond a child has with his or her mother, "whether one wishes it or not."[7]

The longing for the maternal embrace that would never happen led Martin at the age of thirteen to coin a "private term," *Vergegnung*—a mismeeting, "a-meeting-that-had-gone-wrong," or a meeting that had not taken place as one had hoped.[8] As he matured, he realized it "was something that concerned not only me, but all human beings."[9] More than thirty years later, with the publication of *I and Thou* in 1923, which introduced his philosophy of dialogue, he would probe the existential and religious meaning of *Begegnung*, meeting—the interpersonal encounter between individuals that occurs in an atmosphere of mutual trust: "Alles wirkliche Leben ist Begegnung" (All real life is meeting).[10] Buber's call to engage the world—our life with others—in dialogue also recognized the painful truth of how difficult it is to achieve, how often life's journey is filled with mismeetings and the failure of I-Thou encounters to take place. Alert to the fragility of human relationships, he spoke of the ideological and psychological "armor" we humans invariably wear to protect ourselves from such mismeetings.

From the perspective of his own experience, Buber was sensitive to the vulnerability of others, and to the pain we so often inflict on one another by what the nineteenth-century French novelist Jules-Amédée Barbey d'Aurevilly called "civilized crimes"—interpersonal "crimes that society commits daily, in secret and unpunished, with downright fascinating frequency and frivolity," although "they appear to be negligible crimes because no blood is spilled and the carnage takes place within the bounds of feeling and custom." Such "civilized crimes" are often as hurtful as the ones that society recognizes as violations of civil and criminal law.[11] The failure to truly meet another who signals, even if only indirectly, their need for a response of real presence (that is, an I-Thou encounter) was, for Buber, a civilized crime. "The human person," Buber observed, "feels himself exposed by nature—as an unwanted child is exposed—and at the same time a person isolated in the midst of the tumultuous human world."[12]

Aware of the emotional rupture that their three-year-old grandson had experienced in the wake of his mother's abrupt departure, Martin's grandparents pampered him and tried to protect him from any possible harm. Consequently, he rarely played with other children. As his son Rafael explained—with ironic sympathy—his father's lack of understanding for his own children, "my father did not have a 'normal' childhood; he never played dodge-ball on the street or broke a neighbor's window."[13] Until the age of ten—when he was enrolled in a Polish gymnasium—he did not to go to school at all, but was tutored at home. The emphasis was on languages and literature; he received private lessons in English, French, and German, as well as in traditional Jewish subjects. His grandfather Salomon Buber, an observant and learned Jew, taught him Hebrew and the fundamentals of classical Judaism. His principal teacher in rabbinic literature, however, was his great-uncle, his grandfather's younger brother Rabbi Zev Wolf (Wilhelm) Buber, a Talmud scholar who was renowned for his novel interpretations of rabbinic law.[14]

In the summers, Martin would frequently spend a week or so with his great-uncle in Delatyn, a bucolic town at the foothills of the Carpathian Mountains, along the Pruth River, and a favorite summer destination of East Galician Jewry, especially of many leading Hasidic rabbis. Since Zev Buber rented only a small apartment at the edge of the surrounding forest, Martin would stay at the home of one of his uncle's friends. In the summer of 1899, he shared a room with Moshe Hayyim Ephraim Bloch, who was three years younger. Bloch, a yeshiva student, would take long walks with Martin in the forest, and noted his love of nature — as well as an inscrutable sadness, reflected in moments of silence that would interrupt their conversations.[15]

Since Bloch had yet to master German, they likely spoke in Yiddish, one of Martin's primary languages. As a young adult, his correspondence with his grandfather was largely in Yiddish.[16] His grandmother would write to him in German, but most often in Hebrew script. A daughter of strictly orthodox parents, Adele (Udel) Buber (née Weiser) had learned German surreptitiously, violating the traditional Jewish prohibition of reading "alien" literature. But once she married the twenty-year-old Salomon Buber at age seventeen, she was able to pursue her passion for German literature openly.

Martin credited his grandmother with his love of reading. She was the one who initially exposed him to spoken German, though because she had largely acquired it through reading, her German missed many of the nuances and spontaneity of informal speech.[17] It was only when he began university studies in Vienna that Martin gained his first real exposure to German as it was spoken by native speakers. In the city of his birth, he was drawn to the famous Burgtheater, which he often attended daily. "There, by men who were called actors," he recalled, "the German language was *spoken*. In the books that I had read the signs were indicated; here for the first time did they become the sounds that were meant. That was a great instruction. . . . [Here] for the first time was the primordial gold of speech poured into the laps of heirs *who made no pains to earn it*."[18]

The eighteen-year-old Buber resolved to make every effort to acquire a relationship to German as it was spoken by those for whom it was a mother tongue. "Two decades passed before . . . I struggled through to the strict service of the word and earned the heritage with as much difficulty as if I had never . . . possessed it."[19] That it was German as spoken in the theater that inspired him may have unconsciously connected Martin with his mother, who was an actress. Both his friends and his critics noted that there was something theatrical in his speech—he spoke slowly and with precise, even dramatic, enunciation. (His deliberate manner of speaking also might have been to compensate for a slight speech defect due to his deformed lip.)[20] Martin's wife, Paula (née Winkler), would help him in his effort to master spoken German. A native German speaker, Paula, born into a pious Catholic family in Munich, was an accomplished writer. She would later publish novels under the masculine pen name Georg Munk and take an active part in her husband's literary work.[21] Until her death in 1958, Martin would regularly consult with her on matters of grammar and style.[22]

The two first met during the fall semester of 1899 at the University of Zurich. A vivacious, intellectually engaged, independent young woman, Paula attracted attention not only because she was one of the few female students at the university, but also, and especially, because of her bohemian, exotic flair.

Paula had been a member of a mystical colony in south Tyrol led by Omar al-Raschid Bey, a gray-bearded patriarch dressed in Bedouin robes who was regarded by his disciples as a charismatic, otherworldly sage.[23] A Jew by birth who had converted to Islam, al-Raschid Bey enchanted his followers—including young aspiring poets and philosophers—with the "wisdom of the Orient," a highly syncretistic mixture of Islamic, Indian, Buddhist, and other mystical teachings.[24]

In his memoirs, the philosopher Theodor Lessing, also a disciple of al-Raschid Bey, relates how many of his followers were taken with Paula, "the only beautiful woman in the small colony."[25] She had first come to Zurich with al-Raschid Bey to study Sanskrit and Indian religions at his behest (while his disconcerted wife, Helene, stayed in Munich).[26] Soon after she ended their amorous relationship, Paula met Martin at a seminar in German literature, and their romance began at a dance party in the Alps that lasted until the early hours of the morning. Some observers found it incomprehensible that she was drawn to the diminutive, slightly built Buber—he was barely five foot two—who was also younger than her by seven months.[27]

Their relationship yielded a child, Rafael, born on July 9, 1900. Although Buber was initially distraught to learn that Paula was pregnant, their next child, Eva, was born less than a year later, on July 3, 1901. Fearing that his grandparents would view having children out of wedlock with a non-Jewish woman as a double sin, Buber did not tell them about the relationship or the children's births. It was only in January 1907, after his grandfather had passed away on December 28, 1906, that Paula converted to Judaism. She married Martin the following April in a civil ceremony in Friedenau, then a suburb of Berlin.[28] Shortly thereafter, Martin told his grandmother about his relationship with Paula, and of their two children.

In his memoirs, composed in the twilight of his nearly ninety years, Martin wrote warmly of his grandmother, while mentioning his grandfather only in passing. Forty years earlier, he had written at greater length about his grandfather, but in the context of relating that in his youth Martin had been alienated from Judaism, despite growing up in the home of this famed and devoted scholar of rabbinic literature and fastidiously observant Jew. As long as Buber lived with his grandparents he was, as he himself put it, well rooted in Judaism, at least externally, but even then, "many questions and doubts jogged about in me."[29] This festering discomfort with Jewish religious practice came to full expression at age fourteen, when he left his grandparents' home to live with his father, who had recently remarried. In his father's home, he stopped putting on tefillin or observing other traditional Jewish rituals and practices.[30] If he went to synagogue, it was to Lemberg's liberal congregation, of which his father was a member. It was only then, as he later reported, that he was "exposed to 'liberal' influences in [his] religious education."[31]

Martin seems never to have developed the intimate relationship with his grandfather that he had with his grandmother, Adele. The warmth and admiration with which he writes of her in his memoirs is reflected in their correspondence. The letters he received from his grandfather, however, are invariably curt, and often strike a critical tone. In a Yiddish letter of June 18, 1906, Salomon asks his grandson why he does not write and acknowledge his letters to him: "even in Frankfurt or Berlin one can find ten minutes to write."[32]

Notwithstanding his apparent distance from his grandfather, Martin would share many of his traits.[33] Salomon was something of a workaholic, as Martin himself would become.[34] An immensely prolific scholar and a man of extraordinary wealth, Salomon was also an exceedingly generous patron of other scholars who were less well off. Salomon's unique position in European Jewry as a scholar and philanthropist (who supported many Jewish as well as non-Jewish causes) was eulogized in an obituary published in the London *Jewish Chronicle* on January 4, 1907. It delineated both his vast range of financial interests and his extensive involvement in municipal and communal affairs and philanthropy, then stated: "It will amaze some to learn that [Salomon] Buber was beyond question the most prolific man of Jewish letters of his time. His published works constitute of themselves a library; his unpublished writings fill many shelves. Buber was, in the rabbinic phrase, privileged to be placed at two tables—wealth and wisdom."[35] The Buber family traced its origins to Meir Isaac Katzenellenbogen, chief rabbi of Padua, Italy, whose other descendants include Karl Marx and Abraham Joshua Heschel. The family was more directly related, however, to Rabbi Benjamin Aaron ben Abraham Slonik, author of *Mas'at Benjamin,* one of the most authoritative and popular works of rabbinic legal responsa for generations of Polish and German Jewry, first published in Kraków in 1633 (with innumerable subsequent printings).[36] Slonik's great-grandson and Salomon's father, Rabbi Isaiah Abraham Buber, was renowned as a Talmud scholar whose success in business allowed him to fund generously various institutions serving the poor as well as to found a hospital in Lemberg. Despite a heavy April rainfall, thousands attended his funeral, at which he was eulogized by the leading rabbis of the city. His sons, led by Salomon, pledged a significant sum for the establishment of a new hospital in his memory as well as money to maintain the old hospital founded by their father.[37]

The Buber family was, in a nutshell, among the Galician Jewish intellectual and financial elite.[38] It was thus not surprising that in Jewish circles, Martin was known and greeted as Salomon Buber's grandson. In a letter to his grandmother, he noted with a palpable measure of chagrin that "whenever I meet with Zionists I am asked about Grandpa, his health, his work, and so on; I have yet to be introduced to someone who does not ask me about my relationship to Salomon Buber."[39] He was determined to forge his own identity, albeit with his grand-father's endorsement. In a letter to his grandparents on the occasion of his grandfather's seventy-third birthday, he begins with uncharacteristic affection and admiration for his grand-father: "When I think of your dear face, I have trouble fighting back my tears — tears of warmest reverence," and by expressing the hope that "your vibrant kindness, which so often brought me comfort and joy and steadfastness, will be preserved for me for a long, long time." He then continues with an appeal that his grandfather approve the path he had chosen. Although Zionist activity might not have been what his grandfather had envisioned for his grandson, Martin writes reassuringly, it too would serve the objective of securing the future of the Jewish people:

> I can show my gratitude and my love in no better way than by emulating your example — *in my own fields* — and by placing my own life, as you have done, in the service of the Jewish people. You have mined and refined treasures from the cul-ture of the Jewish past; I, who am young and still long more for action than for knowledge, want to help forge the Jew-ish future. But we are both ruled by the spirit of the eternal people, and in this sense I think I can say that I intend to carry on your life's work.[40]

This indirect appeal for reconciliation with his grandfather may have also been prompted by a hope to ease Salomon's and Adele's misgivings about his pursuing a university educa-tion with no concrete professional objective; there are hints of those concerns in their correspondence. An obituary for Martin's father, Carl, that appeared in a Polish Jewish news-paper in Lemberg notes that Adele Buber had forbidden her own son from pursuing his studies beyond high school. "She feared that Karol [Carl] Buber of blessed memory wished to continue his studies in secular schools, and might thus enter the world of secular sciences and conventions, so remote from Jewish tradition." Giving up his dream of studying medicine, Carl submitted to "his parents' desire" and "set out for a journey across Europe in order to study the silk textile industry." After mastering that industry, he expanded his business interests to mining phosphates and mineral oil, and later became "one of the leading experts in the economy of agriculture."[41] Given this history, Carl Buber may well have supported his son's decision to pursue a university education so that Martin might achieve what Carl had been denied.

Knowing that Martin had two children out of wedlock with a non-Jewish woman would surely have confirmed his grandparents' fears that secular studies would lead him astray. As the birthday letter to his grandfather indicates, Martin hoped that his affiliation with Zionism (first adopted while spending the winter semester of 1897–1898 at the University of Leipzig) would reassure his grandparents. At stake was not only their approval, but also the allowance he received from them, which he desperately needed. At the time he wrote the letter to his grandfather, Paula was already pregnant with their first child.

It was only when Martin began to devote himself to the study of Hasidism that he seems to have earned the approval of his grandfather, who would send him editions of Hasidic works unavailable in Germany. A few weeks prior to his death in 1906, Salomon received a copy of his grandson's first anthology of Hasidic lore, *Die Geschichten des Rabbi Nachman* (The tales of Rabbi Nachman), whose dedication signals their reconciliation: "To my grandfather, Salomon Buber, the last of the great scholars of the old-style Haskalah, I dedicate this work of Hasidism with reverential respect and love."[42] ("Old-style Haskalah" refers to eastern European followers of the Jewish Enlightenment, largely self-taught scholars who maintained to various degrees a fidelity to religious tradition and practice while also affirming the intellectual and cultural standards of educated Europe.) But Martin's father—who had consciously distanced himself from his parents' religious commitments by joining Lemberg's German-speaking liberal synagogue, and had tried to discourage his son from attending with his grandfather a Hasidic *Klaus* (prayer room)—found Martin's interest in Hasidism pointless. In a letter congratulating Martin on his thirtieth birthday, Carl beseeched him to turn to more important and "useful" topics: "I would be happy," he wrote, "were you to give up this Hasidic and Zohar stuff, for they could only have a mentally debasing and pernicious effect. It is a pity to devote your talents to such a fruitless subject, and to waste so much time and effort [on something] so utterly useless for yourself and the world."[43]

Undeterred by his father's disapproval, Martin's interest in Hasidism gained momentum, not least because of Paula's enthusiastic support. In fact, it was she, a student of Indian religions, who first evoked his interest in mysticism; before they met, his intellectual focus had been on philosophy, psychology, art history, and literature. She also lent her support for his engagement with Zionism. Several months after the birth of their second child, she wrote him, "I am growing toward your cause; you must and will see that. It will be mine and also that of our children."[44] In another letter, she declared, "I have a new desire, I must tell you this, because I previously did not have it: I would like to be active with you in the cause of Zionism—no, I will be. I have the feeling that I can and must do something for it."[45] She poetically expressed her growing embrace of her beloved's cause in an article in *Die Welt*, the Zionist weekly founded by Theodor Herzl, entitled "Reflections of a Philo-Zionist": "How I love you, people of affliction! How strong your heart is and how young it has remained! No, you shall not become another, you shall not sink in the confusion of alien peoples. . . . In being different lies all your beauty, all happiness and joy of earth. Remain your own! . . . How I love you, you people of all peoples, how I bless you."[46] In a long letter composed more than two years earlier, she related to Buber a heated exchange she had with a Jewish opponent of Zionism. In response to his denunciation of Zionism as a parochial cause, she argued that loving humanity and seeking broad horizons should not be confused with the bland homogenization of cultures that could result from a dogmatically cosmopolitan outlook:

> Our attitudes toward each other ought above all to be "person to person"—not "Frenchman to German," not "Jew to Christian," and perhaps less of "man to woman." So, as one says in Sanskrit, *tatntvam asi*. Simply: That you are. But what does that mean? Are we to blur all distinctions, obliterate all contradictions, for that reason? What for? In order to be able to deal more easily with our humanity? Would we, indeed, then be able to deal more easily with it? Do we love most what is least different from us? Do we love most what is most polished, flattest? Are not the contradictions [of human existence] the highest and ultimate and finest stimulants to life? . . . Why do we cry out against the modern school? We do so because it forces genius and fool into a single mold—so that a hybrid results; indeed, because it violates the soul. Are nations not also individualities? Don't peoples (*Völker*) have souls? Must we kill the souls of peoples so that the earth will be inhabited solely by individual human beings? Doesn't that really come down to the oft-decried ethnic stew?[47]

Paula's passionate endorsement of Zionism and love of the Jewish people served to shape, or at least strengthen, Martin's own fundamental commitments, as well as his resolve to walk what he would call the "narrow bridge" between allegiance to the Jewish people and an unyielding solidarity with all his fellow human beings.

Martin thus found in Paula not only the mother figure he longed for, but also a soul mate; they were bonded by both romantic love and their enduring intellectual and spiritual compatibility. Acknowledging that bond, they would lovingly address one another as "Mowgli," the child in Rudyard Kipling's *Jungle Book*. Raised with a pack of wolves, Mowgli exemplified the unity of spirit and nature. On the occasion of his fiftieth birthday, Martin wrote a poem, "Am Tag der Rückschau" (On the day of looking back) dedicated to "P.B.," in which he reminisced on his life thus far with the woman who had taught him to see spirit and nature as one:

> Then both spirit and world become open to me,
> The lies burst, and what was, was enough
> You brought it about that I behold, —
> Brought about, you only lived,
> You element and woman,
> Soul and nature![48]

The integration of soul and nature, of the transcendent and the everyday, would be the overarching theme of Buber's lifework.

# 2

## Herald of a Jewish Renaissance

THE ANNULMENT by a rabbinic court of Carl Buber's marriage to Martin's mother allowed him to remarry. At the age of fourteen, Martin would thus leave the home of his grandparents to join his father and stepmother. To soften the transition for his son, Carl purchased in Lemberg a stately townhouse across the square from the regional parliament. As perhaps Carl feared, Martin had difficulty accepting a "substitute" mother, and continued to spend as much time as possible at the home of his grandmother. Before leaving Lemberg in the autumn of 1896 to commence his university studies in Vienna, the eighteen-year-old Buber observed from the balcony of his father's home an anti-Semitic demonstration, indicative of a harsh political reality that awaited him upon moving from a provincial city at the eastern edge of the Austrian-Hungarian empire to the Habsburg metropolis.

At the University of Vienna, Martin would register for

courses in philosophy, psychology, literature, and art history—but it was the city's vibrant culture, particularly its theater and literature, that especially engaged the freshman's passionate intellectual interests. Within just a few months of arriving in the city of his birth, he published a series of four essays in Polish in a Warsaw literary journal on Vienna's avant-garde poets and writers.

This four-part series, "On Viennese Literature," marked Buber's literary debut. In these essays, Buber displayed already the extraordinary erudition and multicultural horizons that would characterize his writings over the next seven decades.[1] Though still a teenager, he drew on his wide reading of works in German, Polish, French, and Italian to present and compare four leading poets of the so-called Young Vienna: Hermann Bahr, Hugo von Hofmannsthal, Peter Altenberg, and Arthur Schnitzler. "In all of them," he observed with the confidence of a mature scholar, "is found that delightful, purely Viennese synthesis of lightness, melancholy, and reverie one finds in the waltzes of Strauss, the paintings of Makart, the comedies of Raimund, and the sculpture of Tilgner. In each of these is found the typically Viennese lack of the heroic, revolutionary element. They speak of working to create an individualistic, distinctive Viennese culture, but in reality they merely make the existing culture aware of itself."[2]

As represented by these poets, Viennese modernism, Buber argued, ultimately amounted to a superficial, even decadent individualism, devoid of any truly heroic, revolutionary self-expression. This indictment reflects the clear influence of Nietzsche on Buber. As Buber would later report to Ahron Eliasberg, a cousin through marriage whom he met and befriended when they both attended the University of Leipzig for the winter semester 1897–1898, he had two or three years earlier been "a passionate Nietzschean, but now I see him just . . ."[3]

What Buber meant by this "just" (*nur noch*), he had articulated a few months earlier in an unpublished German essay, pointedly titled "Zarathustra." Writing in an autobiographical voice, he recounts that at age sixteen he had come across Nietzsche's *The Birth of Tragedy*. "This book made me a disciple of Nietzsche, a sick disciple"—"sick" because he accepted Nietzsche's message uncritically.[4] Accordingly, the essay "Zarathustra" is "the history of an illness, and its recovery and redemption [from it]."[5] Nietzsche greatly appealed to the young Buber's discontent with the world he then inhabited: Buber felt "a raging hatred of the entire nauseating atmosphere in which I lived, a wrathful aversion against the official morality, the official education, the conventional smiles, whining, and chatter."[6] And Nietzsche's celebration of Wagner in *The Birth of Tragedy* led Buber to regard the composer as the "apotheosis" of the new anti-bourgeois individual.[7] In his self-described naïveté, the teenage Buber became a devoted Wagnerian as well. When he later read Nietzsche's critique of Wagner, he at first felt deeply betrayed by what he perceived as Nietzsche's undermining of his own worldview. But through reading Nietzsche's *Thus Spoke Zarathustra*, he wrote, he came to understand that Nietzsche's teachings were not meant to be taken as doctrine, but rather as a poetic demand for a radical skepticism about all systems—including his own thinking: "One of Nietzsche's principal objectives is . . . the awakening of mistrust of all and everything, of even of his own words, and silence. . . . Not the Superman-fantasy, but the arduous way to truth is Nietzsche's true, great idealism."[8]

In a rhetorical gesture of directly addressing Nietzsche, who at the time was still alive, Buber confesses: "This was my illness. I did not believe in you, but rather I believed you" (*nicht glaubte ich an dich, ich glaubte dir*)—that is, he had followed Nietzsche's teachings as doctrine, but not Nietzsche's personal example of an unyielding quest for intellectual integrity.[9]

The sixteen-year-old Buber was so taken by his new understanding of Nietzsche that he undertook to render *Thus Spoke*

*Zarathustra* into Polish, though he soon learned that a prominent Polish poet had already signed a contract to translate it, obliging the young Buber to give up the project. (Years later, a former classmate at the Polish gymnasium in Lemberg recalled that Buber would appear each day in class with a copy of Nietzsche's *Zarathustra* in hand.)[10] Although over the years he would modify his view of Nietzsche, Buber remained at bottom an apostle of Zarathustra and his life-affirming journey toward self-mastery, toward freedom from the dictates of arbitrary authority. This impulse would ultimately and decisively inform Buber's unique brand of religious anarchism, informed by his teaching that a life of genuine dialogical encounter with God is not determined by traditionally prescribed ritual practices and theological doctrine.

Buber's reference in his essay "Zarathustra" to his own "raging hatred of the nauseating atmosphere" of his youth, while it may have been the hyperbole of a newly minted Nietzschean, nevertheless expressed his genuine disaffection with what he perceived to be the imperious, rule-driven values of his upbringing.[11] An aversion to the ethical and educational ethos of his youth helps explain why, during his initial years as a university student, he maintained a studied disinterest in religious subjects generally, and Judaism specifically. In his essay on Young Vienna, he did not mention, even parenthetically, that two of the four poets he discussed (Altenberg and Schnitzler) were Jewish, and a third, von Hofmannstahl, was of Jewish ancestry. His cousin Ahron Eliasberg observed that Buber, in fact, demonstrated a "typical Jewish anti-Semitism," frequently referring to other Jews derisively as *echt jüdisch* (truly Jewish). Not surprisingly, Zionism had yet to speak to him. Eliasberg, who had a subscription to *Die Welt*—the principal organ of the World Zionist Organization—sought unsuccessfully to interest his cousin in the newly founded movement.[12]

Buber was at the time drawn to Polish nationalism. He actively participated in a secret conference of Polish students living in the Austrian-Hungarian empire, which he addressed to rousing applause.[13] Indeed, years earlier his attachment to Polish liberal nationalism was already apparent, when he spoke at a friend's bar mitzvah.[14] The *haftarah*, the portion from the Book of Prophets that Buber read during the service, included Micah 5:6: "The remnant of Jacob shall be / In the midst of the many peoples / Like dew from the Lord / Like droplets on grass." Drawing on a poem by the Polish Romantic and patriotic poet Adam Mickiewicz, "Ode to Youth," the fourteen-year-old Buber interpreted this passage as referring to the promise of true "eternal youth," not of the body but of the spirit. Noting that spiritual youth is ultimately sustained by love, the precocious Buber cited Victor Hugo, in French of course: "C'est Dieu qui met l'amour au bout de toute chose, l'amour en qui tout vit, l'amour en quie tout pose. L'amour, c'est la vie" (It was God who put love into everything, everything lives because of love, everything is based on love. Love is life) — meaning love toward all humanity, even one's enemies. At fourteen, his thinking foreshadowed the credo that would shape his mature philosophical and political vision. This humanistic impulse was already clear even in the speech at his own bar mitzvah, held (apparently at the behest of his father) at Lemberg's German-speaking liberal synagogue (Deutsche-israelitisches Bethaus).[15] Young Martin reflected on the meaning of the haftarah he read from the prophet Hosea (2:1–22). Addressing his father and grandparents, Buber focused his reflections on the prophet's appeal for *tzedek*, a core biblical concept that, although usually translated as "justice" or "righteousness," he rendered as "virtue" (*Tugend*). This allowed him to marshal the poem "Die Worte des Glaubens" by the German poet Friedrich Schiller, which includes the lines:

And Virtue—it is no meaningless sound;
Can be practiced each day if we trouble;
As much as we tend to go stumbling around,
Toward paradise, too, can we struggle.
And what no logician's logic can see,
The child-like mind sees obviously.[16]

While both speeches (at his own and at his friend's bar mitz-vahs) make extensive reference to traditional Jewish sources, particularly the Hebrew Bible and *siddur* (prayer book), in the second address he did not hesitate to evoke a teaching from the New Testament. In addressing his friend in Polish, he alluded to a famous passage in 1 Corinthians 13:13, and urged him "to let three words guide you on the path [of eternal youth], words that guide the Polish nation: Hope, Love, and Faith."[17]

The young Buber's wide learning and intellectual acumen soon became legendary, especially in family circles. Word of his scholastic achievements circulated in the family, likely including the report that at his high school matriculation exam in Greek, he was questioned about one of Sophocles' choruses—to which he replied by citing the entire song by heart in Greek.[18] When Ahron Eliasberg first met Buber, he was primed to greet him as a budding genius—and he was not disappointed. Much to his dismay, however, Eliasberg, who like his cousin was raised in the orthodox Jewish tradition, found Buber far less knowl-edgeable about Judaism than one would have expected of the grandson of Salomon Buber.[19] Eliasberg attributed what he re-garded as his cousin's poor "Jewish education" to his "bour-geois" upbringing, by which he apparently meant a neglect of Talmudic study. Although Buber had studied the Talmud with his great-uncle, he seems have suppressed that learning.[20] He had, however, acquired and retained a good knowledge of the Hebrew language and Bible, the classical commentaries (likely including midrash), and apparently also the Mishnah.[21] He was also said to have known the traditional Hebrew prayer book by heart.[22]

Buber was clearly drawn to German and Polish culture. Shortly before his bar mitzvah, he enrolled in the Franz Josef gymnasium in Lemberg. Years later, he would remember this school (named in honor of the Habsburg emperor and at which the language of instruction was Polish) as a microcosm of the Austrian-Hungarian empire — that its multiethnic and cultural tapestry was woven of contradictory strands:

> The language of instruction and social intercourse [at the Franz Josef Gymnasium] was Polish, but the atmosphere was that . . . which prevailed or seemed to prevail among the peoples of the Austrian-Hungarian empire: "mutual tolerance without mutual understanding." The majority of the students were Poles; a small minority were Jews. Individually, they got along well with one another, but as members of cultural groups they knew almost nothing about each other.[23]

As an adult, Buber would speak of the difference between living *nebeneinander* — next to one another (tolerantly, but without mutual understanding or genuine respect) — and *miteinander* — together *with* one another (a distinction he would eventually, and particularly, make in his writings on the Zionist-Palestinian conflict). He depicted miteinander as a demand — indeed, as an existential and religious commandment: to meet the other as a Thou, as a fellow human being in the deepest and most compelling sense.

When Buber left Lemberg to begin his university studies in Vienna, this vision, which would in time become the hallmark of his philosophy of dialogue, was still just an inchoate intuition. He was eager to embrace the city's cosmopolitan ethos, which promised to transcend the parochial boundaries that had prevailed in Lemberg, and he distanced himself from Judaism and religious practice. But during his 1898 summer vacation, which he spent at his father's country estate in eastern Galicia, Buber dashed off a note to Eliasberg, dramatically announcing that he had decided to change course and "agitate for Zionism."[24] As he explained, he had come across a recently published pamphlet by Mathias Acher, the pen name of Nathan Birnbaum. Acher's pamphlet, *Jüdische Moderne*, was a tightly argued, thirty-eight-page endorsement of Herzl's envisioned establishment of a Jewish state as a "modern" solution to the Jewish question.[25] Echoing Herzl, Acher argued that efforts to combat anti-Semitism through the courts were a "farce, and assimilation a phantom," and that the promise of a just society in the future was merely illusory. The Jewish Question, he held, would endure as long as the Jewish people do not have "a home, and national center" of their own. Such a solution would bring an end to, or at least greatly reduce, the friction between Jews and the respective host societies in which they reside. But what specifically inspired Buber to join the Zionist cause was undoubtedly Acher's argument that adherence to the ancient faith of Israel was not the only way to express solidarity with one's fellow Jews. Although Jewish belonging until that point had been sustained by communal religious practice alone, Zionism provided a revolutionary, secular alternative for maintaining a Jewish national consciousness and solidarity.

Inspired by Birnbaum's pamphlet, Buber soon returned to Leipzig to found, together with his cousin, a local Zionist Jewish Students Association, which elected Buber as its first officer. In this capacity, in March 1899, he attended a German Zionist conference in Cologne; from there, he would head to Zurich to continue his university studies (and meet his future wife). As a parting gift, Eliasberg gave Buber a copy of the recently published, posthumous volume by the Swiss historian Jacob Burckhardt, *Griechische Kulturgeschichte*.[26] While still in Cologne, Buber wrote Eliasberg that he had the volume before him and wondered, "When would we [Jews] have such a work with the title *Jüdische Kulturgeschichte?*"[27] This was no idle wish, nor was it meant merely as a desirable academic project; rather, it expressed the hope for the creation of a Jewish culture.

As Buber's Zionist vision evolved, it would in fact be guided by Burckhardt's conception of culture, embracing the totality of a people's spiritual life and self-understanding and constituted by the life of the intellect, art, and literature in addition to religion. The far-reaching significance of the Italian Renaissance, then, was the seismic cultural shift from the Middle Ages to the modern period, in which the individual emerges as a self-conscious creative agent (determining his own destiny and inner spiritual life) as well as an agent of cultural creation.

In Burckhardt's most renowned work, *The Civilization of the Renaissance in Italy* (1860)—which years later Buber would have translated into Hebrew—he famously depicts this process in terms that were surely resonant for a young man eager to find his place in modern culture, free of the claims of one's primordial affiliations.[28] Burckhardt argued that by removing the "veil" of corporate identities—"woven of faith, childlike prejudices and illusion"—the Italian Renaissance had initiated the liberation of the individual and thereby paved the way for passage into the modern world. The term "renaissance" thus came to connote a true "rebirth," a reawakening of the creative spirit of the individual that had been characteristic of classical antiquity, but was eclipsed during the Middle Ages.

Buber's understanding of renaissance as rebirth was filtered through the writings of Burckhardt's friend and colleague at the University of Basel, Friedrich Nietzsche.[29] In an article published in a Berlin Jewish student journal shortly after Nietzsche's death in August 1900, Buber highlighted a conception of rebirth that he would introduce into Zionist discourse. In the article, a quasi-eulogy entitled "A Word about Nietzsche and Life Values," he claims that Nietzsche's legacy could not be classified under any discipline or vocation.[30] Instead, he was the embodiment of a new vision of what it means to be a human being—an "emissary of life," a heroic individual who "created" himself and thus surpassed himself.[31]

For Buber, what made this teaching so powerful was that Nietzsche too suffered from the endemic sickness of the age. Hence, what he proclaimed was not his "own being but a longing for [true] being," glorifying "the will to power and the rebirth of the instinctual life, [which] seems to us [Jews] to be a crystallization of our own tragedy." The illness of the age was, Buber argued, even more acute among the Jews—hence, their urgent need to heed Nietzsche's healing message of a rebirth.

But the alignment of Nietzsche's emphatically individualistic notion of rebirth with that of a national community courted inherent tensions, if not outright contradictions. Buber initially sought to resolve this uneasy alliance through a romantic conception of peoplehood. Conscripting the late eighteenth-century category of a *Volksseele* (the soul of a people), he spoke of a "Jewish renaissance"—a term he introduced in an essay of 1901—that would give expression to the soul of the Jewish people, that is, to its "innermost essence" and distinctive "individuality."[32] Noting that "we live in a period of cultural germination" with an "artistic feeling that is awakened everywhere," he also argued that national groups are no longer motivated by a basic impulse for self-preservation or by a need to defend themselves against hostile attacks from outside. "These nations do not wish to exercise a desire for territorial possession and expansion, but want to live fully in accord with their individual character, [spurred by] a self-reflection of their national soul. They wish to make conscious the unconscious development of their national psyche. . . . Goethe's dream of a world literature takes on new forms: Only when each people speaks from its innermost essence is the collective treasure [of humanity] enhanced."[33]

Buber thus identified the desired dialectic between the creative rebirth of the individual and that of the collective—a dialectic that envisions the common life of humanity, "saturated with beauty and nurtured by the creative spirit of each and every individual and people."[34]

Invoking Burckhardt's monumental work on the Italian Renaissance, Buber went on to caution his fellow Zionists not to construe the call for a Jewish cultural renaissance as "a mere return to old traditions that are sentimentally rooted" in the Jewish people's folkways. "Such a return would in no way deserve the noble designation 'renaissance,' this crown of historical periods."[35] The renaissance to which Zionism refers is born of a "painful" understanding of *galut*, the torment of two thousand years of exile that has allowed the so-called custodians of tradition—the rabbis—to shackle the Jews "with the iron chains" to a "senseless tradition." Galut has also enslaved the Jews to the ethos of "an unproductive money economy and hollow-eyed homelessness, which destroys a harmonious will to power." Only by waging an unyielding "struggle against these powers can the Jewish people be reborn."[36]

This struggle echoed Buber's own anguished estrangement from the Judaism of his youth, which we can see in a suggestively autobiographical essay he published two months later: "Festival of Life: A Confession."[37] Addressing the traditional Jewish festivals as a personified "you," he confesses, "Once I turned from you, like a child from his mother, whom he believes he has outgrown, tired of the monotony and desiring adventures. You were like the poetry of a prayer whose words the child recites in formulaic fashion, casually, unaware of the meaning, and dreaming of play. So I left you."[38] But (continuing the Oedipal metaphor) he acknowledges that he cannot free himself from the maternal warmth of the festivals, and declares, "I love you, festivals of my people, *as a child loves his mother.*"[39] Re-embracing the "festivals" of the Jewish religious calendar is essential to the restoration of the "beauty and happiness" of the child's "kindred family." Resuming a first person voice, he explains, "I know my family" can regain a wholesome existence only by reaffirming its "peoplehood" (*Volkstum*). "For I know: A people, bereft of a homeland (*Heimat*), if it wishes to remain a people (*Volk*), must replace territorial unity (*heimatliche Einheit*) with a living bond of a shared and meaningful experience."[40]

The communal celebration of the traditional Jewish holidays would provide this experience, the concrete lived experience (*Erleben*) of belonging, a bond that "purely intellectual possessions" could never forge.[41] They are to be affirmed as "festivals of life" and not as "rigid monuments of a protective tradition," and certainly not "because God commanded them."[42] Instead, they are sanctioned and "commanded by the people," giving joyful expression to the life experiences (*Seelenleben*) of the Jewish people past and present, which cumulatively inform and shape its Volksseele.[43] Significantly, the festivals, as "old forms" that are continually "revived through new contents and values," intrinsically "anticipate rebirth."[44]

Continuing in an autobiographical vein, in 1902–1903 Buber published a cycle of three poems elaborating his affirmation of cultural rebirth. The poems are written in the voice of "Elischa ben Abuja, called Acher." (In the Talmud and subsequent rabbinic tradition, Acher represented a reprobate dissenter, a heretic. Early Zionists like Mathias Acher defiantly referred to themselves as descendants of Acher, rejecting rabbinic tradition in favor of a secular Jewish nationalism.) In these poems, Buber speaks of Acher finding his way back to Jewish practice, but not to a spiritually desiccated religious law. While having discarded the "chains" of rabbinic tradition, Acher has rediscovered the passionate joy of celebrating the ancient rituals of Judaism with his fellow Jews.

In the most developed of the three poems, "Two Dances" (*Zwei Tänze*), Buber depicts Acher and his disciples observing the beauty of the natural world.[45] The disciples bemoan that the Jewish people, despite experiencing the allure of nature's splendor, are assumed by non-Jews to be incorrigibly "ugly," incapable of "blossoming in passionate beauty." Acher responds by telling his disciples of two dances. One is by "Greeks, a young, exuberant people"—in which young Hellenic tanned men and lithe women dance together, "the melody of their limbs so peacefully sweet," in their response to nature's splendor. Mother Nature, in response, rejoices in "the beautiful, birdlike happiness of her children." But, Acher continues, "the other dance I saw—oh how long ago"—Buber's own experience clearly bleeds through Acher's voice at this point—"as a boy, but it seems that it is but today." Acher then recalls his childhood experience, when "young Jews danced" during the holiday of Simchat Torah, when the Torah scrolls would be removed from the Ark and each one held by a different person who would dance joyously with the scroll around the sanctuary. But young Acher "lay at the edge of the forest, dreaming of far-off lands / For, already then I hated the Law / Like ropes on the staves of a cage." Then suddenly he saw the procession in a new light. "They begin to dance, moving in a circle. . . . They are brothers bound by life and of like mind. . . . Eye meets eye / Soul meets soul: They love each other." They "rejoice *not* in the Law" but as "sons of the Storm," in fraternal ecstasy. "And in the fervor of their heart slumbers / The new world, a world that one day will be renewed." One of Acher's disciples then protests, "The dance is dead." No, replies Acher, "It lives in us. . . . It lives in our souls." He heralds the rebirth of Jewry— Jews now dancing to a new tune, one no longer determined by the rhythm of the Law but by the exuberant beat of their Volksseele.

In the effort to revitalize Jewish existence and rebirth, Buber assigned a pivotal role to the "Jewish woman." In a lecture entitled "The Zion of the Jewish Woman," which he delivered in Vienna before an audience of teenage Jewish girls, he held that "national renewal can in its innermost essence originate only with the Jewish woman."[46] Toward that end, she will once again have to "be a mother."[47] In the long years of Israel's exile, especially in the ghetto, he said, it was the Jewish woman who had created and maintained "a close family culture" to replace "the lost young green of the homeland."[48] In the face of the tribulations of exile and the ghetto, she had "encouraged the men to hold fast to their faith."[49] But with the emancipation of the Jews and their attendant *embourgeoisement*, the Jewish woman soon proved to be the weakest link. With a frenzied adoption of the narcissistic, egotistic, and materialistic values of modern society, he claimed, she had contributed to "the loss of the Jewish home, fidelity, and love as well."[50] Her children sought to sublimate their resulting "feeling of abandonment" into an ostentatious display of material well-being.[51] Betrayed by the Jewish woman and the withdrawal of the nurturing warmth she had provided the home, "the Jewish male" is at most only able to maintain a semblance of traditional observance with a "pedantic and empty passivity." Hence, he loses "more and more his high-minded zeal and lives primarily in his work."[52]

One cannot but hear autobiographical murmurs in this troubling, damning indictment of the modern Jewish female, and see Buber's vision of "the Zion of the Jewish woman" as a lingering longing for what he regarded as the fundamental missing piece of his childhood. Inspired by the Zionist project, the Jewish woman, Buber wistfully proclaimed, "above all, will again be a mother."[53] She "will once more turn the home and family life into what it was—a center of Jewish existence, a place of recovery, a source of ever-new strength. . . . In her children she will foster, through careful physical care, through the harmonious unfolding of their strength, the necessary personal courage that the Jew needs so badly. . . . She will stifle neurosis, the central illness of the modern Jew."[54] Above all, the Jewish woman will heal the psychic wounds of modernity by infusing once again into the substance of Jewish life the balm of love. For, indeed, "the Zion of the Jewish woman is: love."[55]

For Buber, then, Zionism was, first and foremost, a spiritual fulcrum by which to overcome the personal—indeed, existential—condition of the modern Jew, and not (as it was for Herzl) a political ideology.[56] Nonetheless, Herzl would appoint him in August 1901 to serve as editor-in-chief of *Die Welt*, the weekly publication of the World Zionist Organization whose principal mandate was to promote the political agenda of "establishing for the Jewish people a publicly and legally assured home in Palestine."[57] Herzl was clearly taken by Buber's charismatic personality and oratorical skills, which he had witnessed firsthand when Buber served as the chair of the so-called Agitation Committee of the Third Zionist Congress held in August 1899 in Basel, Switzerland. In an impassioned speech before the committee, the twenty-one-year-old Buber had argued that the movement should direct its "agitation" or propaganda not toward non-Jewish political opinion, but rather "inwardly," to one's fellow Jews.

To the rousing applause of the audience, he spoke of the pressing need to revitalize the spiritual and cultural life of the Jewish people. "We wish to be effective through life. We wish to create songbooks, literature, a youth library, because our youth is our life and our future." Although Herzl did not view the revitalization of Judaism as a secular culture as the most pressing issue facing the Jewish people, he apparently recognized that Buber had the rhetorical skill and poetic flair to speak to a younger generation. Moreover, Buber concluded his remarks with words that surely reassured Herzl that his young colleague ultimately shared his own political vision: "The time will come when, on our own soil, from our own homes, the flag of national freedom will fly in our land and will once more convey to our children the eternally new message [of the Jewish people]."[58]

The power that Buber's oratory exercised on a generation of youth in the thrall of neo-Romanticism is floridly described in a memoir by Buber's future wife. Having met and befriended Buber only a few months earlier at the University of Zurich, Paula accompanied him to Basel to attend the Third Zionist Congress. There, as he addressed the Agitation Committee, she recalled:

> I experienced a human voice speaking to me with wonderful force. At times it was as if a child were speaking shyly, hesitantly, tenderly, timidly, not sure it would meet with understanding. And now and then the delicate blush of an unsullied soul spread over this person's countenance. One moment it was as if my heart stood still, touched by sanctity. And at other moments it was as if he spoke with brazen tongues, as if all the bells in the world were clanging above me. This was no longer an individual human being; with primordial violence the tremendous longing, wishes, and will of a whole people poured over me like a raging torrent.[59]

Paula would not only consecrate her relationship with Buber by bearing him two children, but by also adopting his devotion to Herzl's movement as a self-declared "philo-Zionist" (and eventually converting to Judaism).

In negotiating with Herzl the conditions under which he would accept the invitation to edit *Die Welt*, Buber insisted on editorial independence (as well as higher fees for writers) so as to attract gifted, young Jews to write for the Zionist weekly. "As I read it," he explained to Herzl, "*Die Welt* is destined to become the organ and spearhead of the intellectual and cultural movement among Jewish youth. We have many talented young people struggling to make their mark. Most of them do not know where they belong. If we can bring them together, give them some directed support and guidance, before too long we will be able to surprise Europe with a literary manifesto. This would run parallel to our political growth."[60] Herzl warmly endorsed Buber's editorial vision. Although using the formal word for "you" (*Sie*), Herzl addressed his much younger colleague as "Dear Friend," and continued: "You have given me great pleasure by accepting my offer, and I shall certainly grant your wishes. . . . What you say about the literary and artistic direction you wish to give *Die Welt* meets with my fullest approval."[61]

Buber formally assumed the duties of editor of *Die Welt* in September 1901. But before then, Herzl requested that he write an editorial in anticipation of the convening of the Fifth Zionist Congress to take place in Basel during the last week of December 1901.[62] In his editorial, Buber called upon the readers of *Die Welt* to prepare joyously for the event with thoughtful debate. "Although we have experienced much suffering and dastardly deeds on the way, the silent song of our happiness rises to the dark heavens together with the flames of our bonfires."[63] (Curiously, but characteristic of Buber's encyclopedic reading in the widest range of literature both secular and religious, he is evoking here bonfires associated with the Christian celebration of Saint John's Eve, heralding the advent of Christmas.) To be sure, "the bonfires are lit on the mountaintops, [but] life itself is lived mostly in the valley," where the Jewish people dwell. To ensure that their deliberations will be truly the work of the people (*Volksarbeit*), the delegates to the Congress "should listen to the heartbeat of the people, to the secret voices that communicate to him the dark, subterranean will of the people."[64]

Buber elaborated on what he believed was the vox populi in the lead article of the very next issue of *Die Welt*. In his first statement as the editor of the central organ of the Zionist movement, Buber delineated the agenda of the approaching

Congress.⁶⁵ In addition to a continued consideration of "practical" organizational and political questions, he exultantly proclaimed, the Congress will finally give priority to the complex of issues related to the spiritual and intellectual development of the Jewish people. "Why and in which way," he rhetorically queries, are "the Jewish people in need of *geistige Hebung* [literally, spiritual uplifting]?" To be sure, since the eighteenth century the votaries of the Enlightenment—Jews and non-Jews alike—had advocated Jewry's spiritual renewal. But what they conceived as an intellectual and spiritual refinement of Jewry had been "excessively oriented to a European civilizational sensibility," and the Zionist leadership had "naively and unconsciously" accepted this conception of cultural advancement.⁶⁶ It was thus essential to revisit and critically assess the very notion of "geistige Hebung," to determine whether it was more than simply a process measured against European culture and letters, in which Jewish cultural inheritance and disposition play no part.

For Buber, the most important task of the Fifth Zionist Congress was to develop a comprehensive program to reintroduce contemporary Jews to the "Jewish spirit" (*jüdische Geist*) and to Judaism's own spiritual and cultural resources. Such re-education would be the basis of the renewal of Judaism as a creative *modern* culture. "All this greatness, all this power, all this beauty we wish to render intimately familiar for the [Jewish] people; [and thereby] foster the true use of their strength when they become conscious of it, . . . this we call the education of the people."⁶⁷ Buber urged the readers of *Die Welt* to participate in an open debate on the direction this program should take.

A lively debate on the pages of *Die Welt* did, indeed, ensue. As he promised Herzl, Buber solicited young writers from throughout the Diaspora, especially central and eastern

Europe, to contribute to this debate—"to speak, to inspire, to promote." As editor, Buber energetically promoted the vision of a "cultural Zionism" as articulated by the Russian Hebrew writer Ahad Ha'am (the pen name of Asher Ginsberg). In the third issue under his editorship, he published a German translation of Ahad Ha'am's 1894 Hebrew essay "Imitation and Assimilation." In this founding text of cultural Zionism, Ahad Ha'am distinguished between the "self-effacing" assimilation that threatens the very existence of the Jewish people, and "imitative" assimilation in which the best of Western humanistic values are creatively adapted to authentic Jewish values.[68] Much to Buber's delight, Herzl was exceedingly pleased with the first issues under his editorial stewardship. With the publication of his fourth issue, Herzl wrote him: "*Die Welt* is excellent. I have read both the previous and the current issue with pleasure and pride. The new generation has arrived."[69]

Yet after four months at the helm of the weekly, Buber suddenly resigned. The reasons for this break seem more interpersonal than ideological. Herzl, as noted, had unhesitatingly supported Buber's opening the pages of *Die Welt* to the younger generation of Jews as a way of ensuring a wide-ranging discussion of the cultural issues facing the Jewish people. Moreover, Herzl had endorsed a proposal that the Democratic Fraction—an alliance of "young Zionists" (none of whom was older than twenty-five) of which Buber was one of the leaders—had presented to the Fifth Zionist Congress 1902, a proposal that committed the movement to advancing the "cultural amelioration" of the Jewish people through a spiritually invigorating "national education."[70] As Buber himself acknowledged, Herzl did so with "an absolutely supportive and pleasant statement" and, indeed, promoted the proposal "with all his influence."[71] But in supporting the resolution set forth by Buber and his colleagues, Herzl had not only deliberately overlooked that the

Democratic Fraction not only represented the younger generation, but also questioned Herzl's leadership and the "bourgeois" values with which he was associated.

The very name by which Buber and the young Zionists called themselves gave voice to a generational antagonism. "Fraction" (*Fraction*) was initially meant as a pun in German mocking the custom of Herzl and the older members of the Zionist movement to attend the Zionist congresses in tuxedos (*Fracks* in German)—that is, as Buber, ironically noted, "Fractionisten gegen Frackzionisten."[72] After the Fifth Congress, the name "demokratische Fraction" stuck as the quasi-official name of the group. Despite whatever misgivings Herzl may have had about its irreverent partisans, his support of the Democratic Fraction was consistent with his desire to expand the constituency of the Zionist movement. Toward this end, he also encouraged religious Jews—that is, eastern European orthodox Jews—to join the movement, but in doing so, he unwittingly planted the seeds of an ultimately irresolvable conflict within Zionism. As the Lithuanian orthodox rabbi Yitzhak Reines, leader of the Mizrahi Religious Zionists, claimed at the debate on the aforementioned resolution of the Democratic Fraction: "The cultural question is a disaster for us. [The demand for a secular national] culture will destroy everything. Our audience is entirely Orthodox and will be lost [for the Zionist cause] by this demand for culture."[73] Being the diplomat that he was, Herzl sought to maintain a balance between the deeply opposing interests and sensibilities of the religious and cultural Zionists.

It was Max Nordau, vice president of the Fifth Congress and Herzl's closest ally, who would eventually play an important role in Buber's break with Herzl, and who had his own conflict with Buber. At the session of the congress in which the proposal to advance Jewish culture and education was being discussed, Nordau intervened and exclaimed, "Whatever can be said on this subject is empty rhetoric as long as we lack the basis of a thorough, well-rounded national culture, namely money."[74] What especially irked Buber and his colleagues was Nordau's accusation that the failure of the "young Zionists" to appreciate the financial constraints of the movement was typical of the "divisive, politically immature mentality of *galut* Jewry."[75]

At a plenary session of the congress devoted to "Jewish art," Buber began by giving voice to the umbrage the Democratic Fraction had taken at what its members regarded as Nordau's supercilious dismissal of their cultural aspirations:

> Honored Delegates, Today Dr. Max Nordau spoke to you on the question of the cultural amelioration of the Jewish people in a way that made a most painful impression on my friends and me. And may I point out that my friends and I represent a good portion of the young generation of Zionists. As Zionists, we have shown Max Nordau love and admiration. Precisely for that reason I must here point out that we have been hurt in our deepest sensibilities, to the core of our emotional connection with Zionism, by the way Nordau treated our concerns. Dr. Max Nordau declared that it is frivolous and fanciful to debate the issue of spiritual amelioration here. But he did not take into consideration that these issues concern nothing less than the wonderful budding of a new Jewish national culture.[76]

The stenographer's record of this address indicates that Buber's words evoked "rousing applause" from the delegates and the many guests in attendance. As he continued his more than hour-long address, he was frequently interrupted by applause. Indeed, this address marked Buber's emergence as a major voice in Zionist affairs; he would be no longer merely an eloquent spokesperson for his generation.

Turning to the question of Jewish art, he made a final swipe at Nordau by posing a rhetorical question that touched on the very nature of the Zionist mission:

> And finally I ask Dr. Nordau whether he believes that Zion-ism will affect only our destitute proletariat. Zionism is for all the people. And truly, we need spiritual amelioration espe-cially for those of our classes who are not completely desti-tute. We need to educate especially the propertied classes, spiritually and morally, before they will be a capable and re-spected resource for Palestine. (Applause.) And we wish to suggest to you here means of education that will improve large groups of our people, strengthen our movement, and lend new and valuable sources to our national cause. Jewish art is such a means![77]

That Jewish art was a vibrant reality was palpably illustrated by the exhibition of young Zionist artists, which had been or-ganized (in conjunction with the Congress) by the Galician-born art nouveau painter (and member of the Democratic Frac-tion) Ephraim Moses Lilien. With poetic enthusiasm, Buber spoke of the exhibition of visual arts as "a great educator."[78] In his view, it had inspired the regeneration of the Jewish people whose spiritual and aesthetic sensibilities had been blunted by the long years of galut:

> For thousands of years we [Jews] were a barren people. We shared the fate of our land. A fine, horrible desert sand blew over it and blew over us until our sources were buried and soil was covered with a heavy layer that killed all young buds. . . . We were robbed of that from which every people takes again and again joyous, fresh energy—the ability to behold a beautiful landscape and beautiful people. . . . All things . . . whose forms are forged through art's blessed hands, were something foreign to us and which we encountered with an incorrigible mistrust. . . . Wherever the yearning for beauty

raised itself with tender shy limbs, there it was suppressed with an invisible, merciless hand.[79]

Fortunately, Buber continued, Jewry's political emancipation and entry into Western civilization triggered a process in which (at first) a "blind adaptation" of modern values (that is, assimilation) was giving way to the awakening of a national consciousness that allowed for the rebirth of "Jewish art."[80]

Though the Jews at the time lacked the necessary conditions in which a genuine national art could prosper—namely, its own "soil from which it grows and a sky to strive for"—it was, he said, incumbent upon the Zionist movement to nurture the "artistic seeds" that had begun to sprout buds, as attested to by the exhibition. Pausing to interject a "personal note," Buber observed: "Of all the indescribable riches with which the modern Jewish renaissance movement showered us, nothing moved me so strongly, so magically, as the renaissance of Jewish art."[81] Concluding his talk, Buber outlined a series of projects to promote the Jewish renaissance and the "aesthetic education of the [Jewish] people"—such as "the newly established Jüdischer Verlag," the Jewish publishing house that would serve to foster both Jewish letters and the visual arts. Calling on the congress to support this particular project financially, he declared, "It will depend on your decision whether Jewish art, which has blossomed so wonderfully, so promising, in such a short time, will wilt in a corner like a misunderstood and neglected stepchild or whether the doors will be opened wide so that she may enter into her kingdom—the young, lovely, royal daughter—and sit on her throne, bestowing sunshine and rain on all who behold her face. Confidently, we put our affairs into your hands. (Lively, long-lasting applause and clapping.)"[82] The recorded proceedings also note that the presiding chair of the session—that is, Theodor Herzl—congratulated the speaker.[83]

Despite the warm response to his address, Buber's request

for a subvention in support of the Jüdischer Verlag was denied—yet, as he elatedly wrote Paula, he still felt it had been "a magnificent struggle in which our minority faction [of cultural Zionists] has won, although our special motions (including one for financial support of the publishing house) have lost. Now everyone is thinking and talking about us."[84] Herzl held that the movement lacked the fiscal resources to underwrite the publications of a Jüdischer Verlag, though he pledged his intellectual support of its other projects.[85]

But as the cultural Zionists resolved to pursue their program without the formal blessing of the Zionist movement, Herzl's feelings toward Buber perceptibly cooled.[86] Though the two men at first maintained a cordial, if strained, relationship, an out-and-out break in their collaboration was soon precipitated by Herzl's angry response to the fact that his former protégé had signed, along with many others, an open letter in the Hebrew press denouncing a piece by Nordau. The offending article, published in *Die Welt*, was Nordau's impassioned response to a trenchant critique by Ahad Ha'am (the leading advocate of cultural Zionism) of Herzl's utopian novel *Old-New Land*.[87] Ahad Ha'am had decried Herzl's Zionist vision of the future Jewish society to arise in Israel's ancient homeland as "aping Euro-Christian culture" and as utterly bereft of Jewish content, downplaying the rebirth of Hebrew and Jewish culture.[88]

After the publication of the open letter denouncing Nordau, Herzl's defender, Herzl (in a personal letter to Buber) withdrew his support for yet another project of Buber's, a journal he and his colleagues were about to launch called *Jüdischer Almanach*. "After the manner in which you attacked Dr. Nordau," Herzl explained, "I cannot, without gravely offending him, participate in any literary undertaking headed by you."[89] A heated exchange of letters ensued between Buber and Herzl, which soon lost sight of the original issue of Nordau's essay.

As their correspondence came to a polemical crescendo, Buber accused Herzl of forfeiting the opportunity to "rejuvenate the movement" and court young, creative talent. "You have preferred [instead] to support a dying generation with dying traditions and to surround yourself with mediocrities."[90] In his reply, Herzl assumed a paternalistic tone, reaffirming his goodwill toward Buber and his "friends" but concluding by expressing his "hope that your minds will be clear again and that you will recognize the grave errors you have committed, especially against Nordau, and actively repent them."[91] Buber's response was immediate and curt: "The final sentence of your letter both alienates and offends me. Of all the feelings we may have, repentance is the least likely, and we are prepared now and at any time to stand up for what we have said and done. It surprises me that in all these discussions you consistently make use of such an impermissible line as to doubt the clarity of your opponent's mind."[92]

The break was now final and irreparable.[93] In retrospect, it was perhaps inevitable, despite the desire of both (especially Herzl) to avoid it. Already during the deliberations of the Fifth Congress, tension between Herzl's political agenda and patriarchal leadership and Buber's Democratic Fraction had begun to surface.[94] Shortly after the congress, Buber recorded his simmering disaffection with Herzl, whom he had until then venerated, in a poem. Entitled "Der Jünger" (The disciple), the poem concludes with this stanza: "The master spoke: 'From much wandering / I took the golden might of the one truth: / If you can be your own, never be another's.' / And silently the boy walked into the night."[95] (The quoted words would have been widely recognized by Buber's generation to be from Paracelsus, the staunchly independent-minded Renaissance savant of the sixteenth century.)

For a while after his break with Herzl—a person whom, as he confessed in another poem, he had hoped to love—

Buber continued to work on various projects sponsored by the Democratic Fraction, especially within the framework of the Jüdischer Verlag, the publishing house that he had founded together with Chaim Weizmann and others just prior to the Fifth Zionist Congress.[96] Under the imprint of the Jüdischer Verlag, Buber published, among other works, a highly acclaimed book on Jewish artists in 1903.[97] But, as he wrote to Weizmann some six months after he had ended his relationship with Herzl, his priorities had slowly shifted, and now he wanted to devote his creative energies to his own literary work. Appealing to his friend to understand his decision, he explained: "I have convinced myself recently that I might well accomplish something in the realm of quiet, serious, concentrated literary work. I would have to give that up completely [were I to continue my activities on behalf of Zionism], and I feel that would be a sin against myself."[98] Gradually Buber withdrew from all Zionist affairs, and by 1905 he had ceased to be involved in the movement altogether.

Some twelve years later, Buber had occasion to reflect on his years as a young Zionist activist: "The first impetus toward my liberation [that is, from the adolescent ambivalence toward the Judaism of my youth] came from Zionism. I can here only intimate what it meant to me: the restoration of the connection, the renewed taking root in the community." But he eventually realized that "national loyalty alone does not change the Jew; he may remain as impoverished spiritually—if not quite as unsupported—with it as without. For some people, however, national loyalty is not sufficient unto itself, but a soaring upward. It is not a harbor, but a passage to the open sea. For such people it can lead to transformation, and so it happened to me."[99] Indeed, upon withdrawing from Zionist politics, Buber would himself set sail onto open seas, where he would soon gain recognition beyond Zionist circles.

# 3

On the Open Seas

All journeys have secret destinations
of which the traveler is unaware.
—Martin Buber

BUBER'S VOYAGE on the open seas had begun years earlier, at the very start of his university studies. Immediately upon unpacking his bags, the eighteen-year-old set out to explore the cultural and intellectual landscape of "this original home of mine, now foreign. . . . The city of my earliest childhood taught me daily, although still in unclear language, that I had to accept the world and let myself be accepted by it; it was indeed ready to be accepted."[1] In time, Buber would find that he needed to develop his own distinctive approach to the world awaiting his acceptance—an approach that would develop incrementally over the next decades, ultimately crystallizing in an engaged response to everyday reality and those within it, or what he would call "the life of dialogue."

As a young university student, with a singular exuberance primed by an eagerness to move beyond what he regarded as the parochial limitations of the intellectually and socially sheltered world of his youth in Lemberg, Buber delved into the competing intellectual movements, doctrines, and ideologies reflected in the vibrant cultural life of fin-de-siècle central Europe— from the poetry of Young Vienna to neo-Romanticism, from the anti-bourgeois ethic of the youth movement to utopian socialism, from mysticism and myth to depth psychology. He embraced a wide range of ideas and intellectual trends, especially in theater and the arts, that engaged his lively intellect—and drew him away from the university. As he wrote to Paula, he found academic scholarship "something stiff," a "drudgery."[2] Explaining to Paula, who had just given birth to their first child, why he found it impossible to write a doctoral dissertation that would open the path to a career as a university professor, he coined the term *Stundenmenschen* for individuals who spent hours upon hours pondering scholarly minutiae.[3] A year later, after the birth of their second child, he pleaded with her to understand why he continued to postpone writing his dissertation:

> Above all, it has become painfully evident to me that I must pull myself together with all my strength, and that I must in the next few months, or rather weeks, accomplish something. Otherwise I will lose the last remnant of my artistic initiative. . . . You know that I have no sprawling talent; I must keep a taut rein. . . . You must understand, dearest, that this is a matter of life and death. What is at stake is simply my art: if I let myself go, I will go to seed—that is definite. Then I can go on shaping myself as a university lecturer and as a respectable bourgeois individual in general. But it will be all over with the creation of something vital.[4]

With resolute determination, Buber thus joined his generation's resistance to what his revered Nietzsche derisively called *Bildungsphilister*—educated philistines—who dominated the universities and who propagated in his view a perversion of learning, draining it of the passionate cadences of life as it is lived and experienced.[5]

Buber thus saw himself as a member of the nonacademic literati, the class of educated individuals who lived on the margins of academia and whom the sociologist Karl Mannheim aptly called "free-floating intellectuals." Educated at the university, they continued to follow its scholarly debates and developments while maintaining a scornful distance from it. Years later Buber would reluctantly don the scholarly robes of a professor, yet proudly maintain that he remained an outsider to the university. As he explained to a friend, "I have never striven for an academic career."[6]

As defiant outsiders, Buber and his fellow literati allowed themselves to cross the boundaries of academic disciplines, boldly risking the accusation of being dilettantes. Looking down on standard scholarly forms of publication, they preferred the essay, a form of expression that allowed for what Richard Rorty describes as "the discovery of new, better, more interesting, more fruitful ways of speaking."[7] Essays allowed for rhetorical experimentation and innovation, and an eclectic weaving of themes, disciplines, and types of discourse. They also often dealt with genres of literature and thought that were not yet recognized or valued by the academy, including folklore, myth, and mysticism—expressions of human experience to which Buber would devote his initial writings and through which he would eventually gain his reputation beyond Jewish circles.

Despite his ambivalence toward the academy and its regnant modes of scholarship, Buber continued his university studies.

Actual tuition costs at central European universities were minimal, and as long as he studied, he enjoyed the financial support of his grandparents and father for all his other living expenses. His chief problem was how to manage with their stipend while supporting a wife and two children—of whose existence he had yet to inform them. In the winter semester of 1899–1900, he attended classes in Berlin and registered for courses with two professors who would have a seminal influence on him, shaping his philosophical horizons: Wilhelm Dilthey and Georg Simmel.

Dilthey, whom Buber would refer to until the very end of his life as "my teacher," is best known for establishing a firm epistemological and methodological distinction between the natural sciences and the humanities.[8] He described the natural sciences as dealing with empirical phenomena that are subject to the physical laws of cause and effect, and thus given to "explanation," while the humanities focus on the expressions of *Geist*, the life of the mind and spirit—inner experiences that are to be "understood," not explained. To understand why a child cries, one does not seek to explain the cause of a child's sobbing by analyzing the chemical composition of her tears or the physiological process of ocular tearing; rather one seeks to understand the inner "lived experience" (*Erlebnis*) that is prompting the emotional state of crying. Understanding (*Verstehen*) the lived experience of others, and the expressions that embody it, requires an imaginative entry into the other's experience (*Nacherleben*).

Understanding is thus an act of empathetic interpretation, but interpretation (through understanding) of that experience is not merely subjective; access to the inner experience of others is primarily through its expression in language, gestures, or artistic production. One understands the inner experience of others through these culturally recognized structures that give expression to that experience. The interpretive decoding of another's experience, then—such as the crying of one who is hurt, physically or psychologically—has the dialectical effect of acknowledging the subjective uniqueness of the experience of that person while also allowing it to be recognized, through familiar structures, as familiar—as an experience the interpreter can recognize as one they have had or can imagine having.[9]

In his twilight years, Buber would recall that Dilthey "was an especially important teacher; I am greatly indebted to him in particular with regard to historical understanding."[10] The premise of historical understanding is that others are not mere extensions of oneself; hence one gains understanding of others through approaching others as they approach us, that is, from the outside—interpreting their "objectified" expressions of life-experience (speech, writing, art)—through analogous personal experiences. We can discern here in Dilthey's approach to historical understanding the seeds of Buber's later philosophy of dialogue, whereby the Otherness of the Other—what he would call "the Thou"—is acknowledged and endowed with an autonomous cognitive and existential dignity. Of more immediate significance for Buber's intellectual development, he learned from Dilthey's "art of interpretation" how to read texts as the apprehension of the lived experience to which they give expression.[11]

Perhaps of equal significance for Buber's more immediate intellectual development was Dilthey's understanding of religion as not confined to institutional practices and theological doctrines. Dilthey sought to uncover the innermost nature of religious life, believing that religious consciousness is not merely an inner spiritual state; it posits a given view of reality. As he put it in a diary entry: "This means looking for religion not so much in its institutional practices and its theological doctrines as in the recesses of human experience" in order to recover the "religious-philosophical worldview that is buried under the ruins of our theology and philosophy."[12] Dilthey's related deep distaste for metaphysical speculation in either philosophy or religion also resonated with Buber.

In the last weeks of his life in the late summer and autumn of 1911, Dilthey began to write an essay on "The Problem of Religion," which was to serve as an introduction to a new edition of his biography of the Protestant theologian and father of modern hermeneutics, Friedrich Schleiermacher. In this never-completed essay, he summarized his view that human beings are fundamentally spiritual in nature. Religion, he argued, is not properly understood as speculations about "ultimate reality" or "God." Rather, it attests to the universality of religious feelings, expressed not only in prayer and ritual practices but also "in art, worldly activities, poetry, science, [and] philosophy"—feelings that are primed by fundamental intuitions about the underlying coherence and meaning of the world.[13] Mystical feelings and experiences and their mythic representations, then, are not to be interpreted as primarily reflecting esoteric communion with God. Such experiences, he emphasized, "defend the joy of life, justify the objectives of life in worldly activity and turn against the fear of the gods, against the fear of punishment in the afterlife as well as against ill-considered means of appeasing [the gods] through sacrifice, ceremonies, [and] sacraments."[14] This conception of religion and mysticism would inspire Buber's approach to the study of religion, and specifically of Hasidism. At the time of Dilthey's death on October 1, 1911, Buber and his wife happened to be on vacation not far from where Dilthey had been staying, and he immediately went to offer Dilthey's widow, Katharina, his condolences, as well as his help in the funeral preparations and subsequently in organizing her late husband's papers.[15] In a letter written two months after Dilthey's death, Katharina asked Buber to review the inventory of her late husband's papers to fill in any gaps he might find.[16] She also shared with him the uncompleted draft of "The Problem of Religion."

Buber's intellectual debt to Simmel was perhaps even greater than it was to Dilthey; indeed, he credited Simmel for teaching him "how to think."[17] Buber and Simmel developed a personal and professional relationship, which had not been the case between Buber and Dilthey. Indeed, Buber became one of Simmel's closest students and a member of his inner circle. He was even invited to participate in Simmel's weekly *Privatissimum*, a private seminar hosted by Simmel and his wife, Gertrud, at their home in Berlin's stately Westend. The seminar was restricted to no more than twelve participants, mostly postdoctoral students; in this regard, Buber (who had yet to earn a doctorate) was an exception. This select cadre in Simmel's seminar was occasionally joined by special guests such as the sociologist Max Weber and his wife, Marianne; the poet Rainer Maria Rilke; and the philosopher Edmund Husserl (who upon meeting Buber for the first time is reported to have exclaimed, "Buber?! I thought he was a legend").

Women were also prominent participants in these weekly seminars. Beginning in the late eighteenth century, women, who were otherwise excluded from intellectual life in central Europe, conducted salons in which they were equal partners with men in the life of the mind. It was only toward the end of the nineteenth century that they were, with the permission of the lecturer or professor, welcome to audit university classes — and not until the winter semester of 1908–1909 were women allowed to enroll in Prussian universities. Simmel was among the very first to encourage women to attend his lectures, and they did so in great numbers.[18] (In this respect, he was undoubtedly under the sway of his wife, Gertrud, an artist of some renown and powerful intellectual presence in her own right, who after her husband's death in 1918 would remain close to Buber.)[19] In evoking the unique, captivating spirit of the Simmels' seminar, Margarete Susman, the German-Jewish poet and critic, related that the "weekly *Jours* . . . were organized entirely in the spirit of the couple's culture. They were a sociological work in miniature, the product of a society that aimed to cultivate individuality in the extreme. Conversation took shape there such that no one could impose his idiosyncrasies, problems, or needs; it was a form that, liberated from all weightiness, floated in an atmosphere of spirituality, affection, and tact."[20] The participants would gather first in the living room for tea, then proceed to sit around a large dining table, often sharing in the preparation of a communal soup. The conversation that would follow focused on select philosophical topics as well as on issues in art history, which would, in time, become one of Buber's passionate interests.

Susman first met Buber at the seminar, his "delicate, slight" build creating the impression for her that he "was not a human being, but pure spirit."[21] Judah L. Magnes, an American rabbi who in 1900 attended one of Simmel's lectures as a visiting graduate student at the University of Berlin (and who years later would work closely with Buber to promote Arab-Jewish coexistence), also noted the aura of the young Buber. "After everyone had taken their seats, from a side-entrance in marched [Buber] leading a group of young men and women, who took seats in the first row apparently reserved for them." Baffled by the sight of this young man, sporting a black beard and walking with "slow but determined steps at the head of this group like a *Tzaddik* [with] his hasidim," Magnes turned to the student next to him, "a blond Aryan," and asked who it was. His neighbor replied, "This Jew has founded a new religious sect."[22]

Buber's seemingly privileged position within Simmel's coterie served to introduce him to some of Germany's intellectual elite—he would, for instance, maintain a friendly relationship with Max Weber for years to come. Above all, as a self-styled academic maverick, Simmel himself appealed to Buber's own intellectual inclinations. Both Simmel's intellectual style, which oscillated between scholarly disquisitions and essays (feuilletons) addressed to the educated lay public, and his interdisciplinary bent, which ranged from philosophy to art history and the fledgling discipline of sociology, placed him at the margins of the university—exactly where the young Buber found himself.[23]

It was particularly his interest in sociology that cast Simmel as an academic outsider. Since at the time sociology tended to focus on the social structure and cultural codes of modern urban society, it was widely viewed as giving undue attention to what many members of the academy viewed as the manifestations of bourgeois materialism and crass ambition. To its critics, sociology—also known in German as *Gesellschaftslehre* (that is, the theory of urban society)—represented "an illusionless affirmation of contemporary reality," even though it was often critical of many aspects of contemporary society. This opposition to sociology was compounded by the fact that urban "civilization"—*Zivilization* as opposed to *Kultur*— was popularly associated with Jews. Indicatively, Simmel also focused on such unconventional topics as coquetry, rumors, secrets, fashion, and the philosophy of money in order to unravel the dynamic of modern urban life, especially as it affected interpersonal relations. It was precisely this micro-sociological perspective, centered on the interactions between individuals within the modern context, that commanded Buber's fascination. In the fall of 1905, he approached the publishing house Rütten & Loenig of Frankfurt am Main with a proposal to have Simmel edit a series of monographs on the social psychology of life in the city, to be appropriately entitled *Die Gesellschaft* (Society). With the publisher's approval, Buber extended the invitation to Simmel, who graciously declined, but pledged to support the project "behind the scenes."[24] Buber would take it upon himself to edit the series.

His introduction to the series bears the unmistakable imprint of his esteemed teacher (as well as traces of Dilthey's hermeneutics of lived experience, *Erlebnis*):

> This collection of monographs, *Die Gesellschaft*, addresses itself to the problem of the inter-human (*das Zwischenmenschliche*). . . . When two or more individuals live with one another, they stand to one another in a relation of interaction, in a relation of reciprocal effect. Every relation of interaction between two or more individuals may be designated as an association or a society (*Gesellschaft*). . . . What one could comprehend in his own sphere of existence, without having to postulate the existence of another intentional individual, is simply the human or individual. The notion of *das Zwischenmenschliche*, on the other hand, assumes the existence of diverse, distinctly constituted intentional human beings, who live with and affect one another.[25]

In a statement that Buber made some sixty years later, the introduction takes on added significance. Asked to summarize his life's work, Buber, who was otherwise generally wary of categorical labels, reluctantly described his teachings as "die Ontologie des Zwischenmenschlichen" (the ontology of the inter-human).[26] It is particularly striking that he encapsulates his own work in this way, since the term *das Zwischenmenschliche* is a neologism that Buber himself had coined to capture the essence of Simmel's conception of society as the matrix of interactions between individuals.

Editing *Die Gesellschaft* propelled the twenty-eight-year-old Buber onto the center stage of European culture. From 1906 to 1912, he published forty volumes of *Die Gesellschaft*, each written by a prominent author; among them were the

Swedish feminist Ellen Key, who wrote on the women's movement; Eduard Bernstein, the founder of evolutionary socialism, who addressed the question of the political viability of
the mass worker's "strike"; the sociologist Ferdinand Tönnies,
who penned a volume on "customs"; and the Russian-German
writer Lou Andreas-Salomé, whose friendships with Nietzsche, Rilke, and Freud intrigued an entire continent, and who
contributed a volume on eroticism.

Simmel himself—surely in Buber's eyes the guiding spirit
of the series—provided a volume on religion in 1906. In it, he
analyzed the dialectical relationship between religion (an objective, social, and historical phenomenon) and religiosity, a
subjective "attitude of the soul" that not only informs institutional religion, but also can express itself through cultural
pursuits such as art and science. Most significantly for Buber's
own evolving thoughts on religion, Simmel (not surprisingly)
deemed religiosity a form of faith that is first and foremost
manifest in the relationship of trust between individuals, on
the basis of which the idea of God crystallizes as "the absolute
object of human faith." For Simmel, the idea of God (which
integrates the diverse, even opposing elements of experience
into an ultimate unity) is in the realm of religion.[27] In his early
efforts to identify the spiritual core of Judaism, independent of
its traditional normative structures, Buber would adopt Simmel's distinction between "religion" and "religiosity," echoes
of which would resonate in his later conception of the I-Thou
relationship as one of trust, sustained by the Eternal Thou.

In addition to Simmel, there was one other individual
whose participation in *Die Gesellschaft* was especially important
to Buber: Gustav Landauer. Shortly after he came to Berlin in
the autumn of 1899 to study with Dilthey and Simmel, Buber
met Landauer, who would soon become his intellectual and
political alter ego. A polymath who developed a unique blend
of mystical anthropology and ethical anarchism, Landauer first

met Buber in the Neue Gemeinschaft, an anarchist commune he cofounded in 1900 together with the brothers Heinrich and Julius Hart in the Berlin suburb of Schachtensee. Located in a twenty-nine-room villa (and former sanatorium), the commune quickly became a center for bohemian writers and artists.

Although they were active members of the Neue Gemeinschaft, neither Buber nor Landauer actually lived in the commune; they resided with their respective families elsewhere in Berlin. The two would become fast and lifelong friends. On the face of it, their friendship undoubtedly struck observers as improbable, and not only because Buber was barely five-feet, two inches tall, and Landauer was an imposing six-feet, five inches. Having formally withdrawn from the Jewish community at the age of twenty-two, Landauer was markedly indifferent to Judaism; indeed, in his writings he expressed a pronounced affinity with the Christian mystical tradition and with Buddhism. Further, his political loyalties were to anarchist socialism, a cause for which he was arrested several times and twice incarcerated. Also, while Buber enjoyed a measure of material security, Landauer was a bohemian intellectual who lived from hand to mouth.

Nonetheless, the two immediately bonded. Their friendship extended to their respective families. Landauer took a special liking to Buber's children, and would often stretch out on their beds, telling them bedtime stories; they were, however, far more fascinated by his immense torso with his legs dangling off the edge of the bed, "seemingly kilometers in the distance."[28] Buber and Paula, too, would frequently visit Landauer and his wife, Hedwig Lachmann, a poet and accomplished translator (from English, French, and Hungarian to German). Landauer met her at a poetry reading in 1899—more or less at the time he became friends with Buber—and moved in with her, even though he was married. Even before he had divorced his first wife, a seamstress, he and Hedwig had a daughter; four years later in 1906, Hedwig (now his wife) gave birth to their second daughter, Brigitte, who would become the mother of the award-winning Hollywood film director and Oscar laureate Mike Nichols. Landauer was wont to call Hedwig affectionately "my Jewess," for as the daughter of an orthodox *chazan* (cantor) and a passionate collector of traditional Jewish liturgical music, she introduced her husband to traditional Jewish culture, about which, despite his Jewish parentage, he knew virtually nothing. Her warm, unapologetic Judaism undoubtedly played a role in drawing him close to Buber.

Landauer, for his part, with his mystical conception of community, helped refine Buber's nascent interest in mysticism, and especially his own understanding of community. Instead of the divisive social structure of modern urban society (*Gesellschaft*), Landauer argued that a universal, unitive community (*Gemeinschaft*) of being—of human beings and things—should be affirmed and sought at the deepest level of consciousness: "The community we long for and need, we will find only if we sever ourselves from individuated existence; thus we will at last find, in the innermost core of our hidden being, the most ancient and most universal community: the human race and the cosmos."[29] He held that the cognitive and spiritual anguish of modern society is rooted in the tendency to view the world comprehended by our five senses, especially sight—including our fellow human beings—as a multiplicity of individuated objects, with each of us seeing ourselves as an isolated being. But paradoxically, by withdrawing into the deepest reaches of the self—what Landauer called "the innermost core of our being"—we can discover the essential spiritual unity of all beings, leading to the reestablishment of Gemeinschaft.

As Buber wrote with specific reference to Landauer, the mundane rhythms of everyday modern urban civilization that toss one into a web of "conflict and doubt" are wondrously interrupted by the mystical *Gemeinschaftsgefühl*—the deeply felt experience of the unity of the self with the world: "In quiet, lonely hours all our endeavors seem meaningless. There appears no bridge from our being to the great Thou [*dem grossen Du*]— the Thou we felt was reaching out to us through the infinite darkness. Then suddenly came this *Erlebnis*—and like a mysterious nuptial festival we are freed from all restraints and we find the ineffable meaning of life."[30] These sacred moments—with their embryonic intimations of the later Buber's eternal Thou (*ewiger Du*) sustaining I-Thou relations—endow all of life with new meaning and direction: "A few of us want to live the ideal. . . . According to the ideal, we will live [in the concrete reality of the everyday] the meaning of the universe (*Weltall*), the endless unity of becoming."[31]

Buber also endorsed Landauer's anarchism, expressing an antagonism to normative religious structures: "Only when the jubilant rhythm of life has conquered regulation, only when the eternally flowing, eternally self-transforming inner-law of life replaces dead convention—only then can one be considered free from the coercion of vacuities and untruth. Only then could humankind be said to have found truth. The Neue Gemeinschaft fervently seeks to pave the way to this truth."[32]

But Landauer himself soon came to see in the mystical affirmation of community an uncritical optimism, and would break with the Neue Gemeinschaft. In a volume published in 1903, *Skepsis und Mystik*, he presents a long critique of a monograph by Julius Hart. What troubles him is Hart's tendency to facilely dismiss all polarities—no matter how existentially painful or unjust the reality reflected in them—as illusions of the perceiving mind. Landauer sarcastically remarks: "The magical word with which Julius Hart dismisses all spiritual and physical pain is 'transformation.' . . . Should a lion devour a lamb, neither the lamb nor men have the right to complain about it: the life of the lamb had simply been transformed into the life of the lion. . . . Accordingly, when a capitalist exploits his workers, human flesh has simply been transformed into furniture.'"[33] For Landauer, genuine social transformation necessarily entailed political action, but the Neue Gemeinschaft never transcended the level of intellectual experiment. The closest it ever came to realizing community, one observer noted, was its monthly bacchanalian festivals that lasted into the early hours of the morning.[34]

More than two decades after the demise of this experiment in 1904, Buber wrote in his introduction to Landauer's post-humously published correspondence that the Neue Gemein-schaft had taught Landauer "how community does not [simply] rise."[35] It would take Buber himself considerably longer to learn this lesson.

# 4

*From Publicist to Author*

WITH THE DISSOLUTION of the Neue Gemeinschaft, Buber resolved finally to write a doctoral dissertation, apparently at Paula's insistence. At the time, she was living apart from Buber with their two children at the home of a friend in the Austrian Tyrol, while he was in Berlin engaged more with the city's intellectual life and Zionist affairs than with his university studies. To complete his doctorate, he returned to Vienna in order to prepare for his qualifying exams in his major, philosophy, as well as in his minor subject, art history; after a few months of intensive study, he successfully passed the exam in philosophy, but failed in art history. He was allowed to retake the art history exam, and barely managed to pass with the grade of *genügend* (satisfactory).[1]

With his exams behind him, he embarked on a dissertation under the supervision of Friedrich Jodl, a venerable professor of philosophy. His dissertation examined the problem of individuation in the writings of the German neo-Platonic philosopher Nicholas of Cusa and the German mystic Jakob Boehme, both of whom, he argued, anticipated the fundamental epistemological and existential problems of the modern age, individuation and isolation. All of forty typewritten pages, the dissertation was approved in July 1904. Upon completing it, Buber decided to write a second thesis—a so-called habilitation thesis, a monograph representing substantial and original research—which would qualify him for a teaching appointment at a German university. Setting his sights on a thesis not in philosophy but in art history, he resolved to conduct research in Florence, Italy, on the art of the Renaissance.

Eager to facilitate her grandson's path to a "respectable" career, his grandmother, who ran the financial side of her husband's various banking and commercial interests, agreed to underwrite the costs of his scholarly sojourn in the birthplace of the Renaissance. But once Martin, Paula, and their children had settled in Florence, his research agenda was soon richly complemented, if not utterly compromised, by a fascination with the cultural life and landscape of the city. On the eve of Christmas 1905, he dashed off a buoyant note to a friend, reporting:

> Florence suits me, as all of us, well; we have no contact with other people at all and hardly miss it, for one lives with this city, with its houses, with its monuments, with its former generations. . . . I am writing various things about Florence. I hope in this way slowly to accumulate a whole collection of essays, primarily, however, about little or utterly unnoticed things (destroyed frescoes, street tabernacles, gravestones, Gothic traces, street culture, lay religious orders, street songs, sayings, the old [Jewish] Ghetto, etc.), which could be later united into one volume, perhaps under the title, *The Hidden Florence, Winter Strolls*.[2]

Above all, Florence brought liberation from what Buber had increasingly experienced as the oppressive effects of Zionist politics. As he plaintively wrote during the conflict with Herzl and Nordau in a letter to his close friend Chaim Weizmann—who was to become the first president of the State of Israel—these politics had paralyzed him, draining him of all creative energy: "I often lie on the sofa in convulsions for a half a day at a time, can work neither on my dissertation nor on anything else. I have in fact had to put all work aside."[3] But in the aforementioned letter of Christmas eve, he described how Florence now made possible a

> separation from all that only seemed to be ours, only seemed to belong to our own life, but which had not nurtured and enhanced our understanding, which had not excited and satisfied us, which had not carried us through the world and calmed us. Only through a separation from all this can we be brought to ourselves. . . . How do I live? How one feels at the beginning of a good journey, a journey that one does not fully know [where it will take one], but one knows it is the right way. . . . How happy I am that I have been released from flawed spheres of activity; I feel that I am now once again free to work as I have not for years. . . . I am happier. . . . And also my connection with Judaism free from the whirl of party politics has deepened; should I once again occupy myself with [Jewish matters], it would be something purer and greater than the slogans to which I once shamefully subscribed.[4]

Buoyed by the distance from everything that he felt had compromised his spiritual and intellectual integrity, Buber experienced a burst of creativity. While doing research for his habilitation thesis, he was also determined to enhance his appreciation of the cultural life of Florence by mastering Italian. A passionate polyglot since his youth, he retained as a household tutor a young woman named Santina, who came from

Siena, where the purest Italian was said to be spoken. Santina, who would remain with the Buber family as a governess and cook for the next two decades, was encouraged to speak only Italian with Buber and his family. As a result, they each gained fluency in Italian (though she would never master German).

Reminiscent of his initial days as a student in Vienna, when he would frequent the Burgtheater in order to hear and learn how German was truly spoken, Buber attended many theater performances at Florence's historic Teatro della Pergola. Among the first plays he saw was *Monna Vanna* by the Belgian playwright Maurice Maeterlinck. The principal role in this dramatic portrayal of the new, emancipated woman was played by perhaps the most acclaimed actress of the time, Eleanora Duse. In an article published in a Berlin theater journal, Buber focused on the thespian skills of "Madame Duse," who through the inflections of her speech and gestures "gathers into herself what in everyday life remains fragmentary, troubled and broken. . . . Within this givenness of word and gestures [of the Italian street, marketplace, and courtyard]," Duse, he said, "gave expression to the personal. By the subtle intonations of voice and movement, she portrayed the paradoxical effect of individuation"—the emergence of the individual as free from the constraints of tradition yet, at the same time, torn "from the security of the familiar into the threat of the infinite."[5] Thus Duse poignantly articulated the existential problem of modernity, the opening of "the abyss . . . between person and person," when "all tradition fades away, and the individual is awakened who can only defend itself and contest [its fate] but no longer speak. The individual's word is no longer communication but a battle." With this observation, Buber broached what would be a paramount issue in his life's work.

We have no record of the subject of Buber's habilitation thesis, which was near completion when he decided to set it aside unfinished.[6] The decision was probably due to the sudden death in June 1905 at the age of forty-seven of his thesis adviser Alois Riegel, who together with Franz Wickhoff, his older colleague at the University of Vienna, had helped to establish art history as an academic discipline.[7] Buber's decision to postpone the completion of his habilitation thesis was perhaps also influenced by the looming deadline for submission of his first anthology of Hasidic lore, *Die Geschichten des Rabbi Nachman* (The tales of Rabbi Nachman), the contract for which he had signed with Rütten & Loening just before he left for Florence. (He had contracted with the same publisher to edit the first volumes of *Die Gesellschaft*.)[8] But he was undaunted by the tight schedule of these literary obligations; indeed, he found working on them exhilarating. As he wrote to a friend in the fall of 1906 on the eve of his return to Berlin: "I can now utter an earnest and joyful yes to my life."[9] Years later, he would look back on his time in Florence as marking his transition from "a publicist to an author."[10]

Putting aside his habilitation thesis meant that, in all likelihood, he would forgo the possibility of ever becoming a university teacher (his heart had never been fully devoted to that prospect); instead, he would become a freelance writer and editor. In addition to writing and editing for the eminent publishing house Rütten & Loening, he became one of its acquisitions editors, in which capacity he solicited and reviewed manuscripts for possible publication.[11] This salaried position allowed him to reside with his family in a six-room rented apartment with a garden in the affluent Berlin neighborhood of Zahlendorf.[12]

Buber's contract with Rütten & Loening marked the auspicious beginning of his life as an independent scholar and author. As acquisitions editor, he was assigned to launch an ambitious new program. In 1903, Wilhelm Oswalts, at the age of twenty-five, had assumed the directorship of the publishing house from his deceased father, and was determined to challenge what he regarded to be the provincialism of Germany's

Wilhelminian culture. With Buber's editorial assistance, he issued—in addition to the forty volumes of *Die Gesellschaft* edited by Buber—translations of world literature, such as a novel by Stefan Żeromski, Polish realist; a novel condemning militarism by the Danish author Aage von Kohl; Micha Joseph bin Gorion's *Gesammelte Sagen der Juden* (Collected sayings of the Jews); Lafcadio Hearn's sensitive evocation of "exotic" Japan, *Das Japanbuch;* Waldemar Bonsel's *Indienfahrt* (Indian journeys); the Dutch author Multatuli's scathing critique of colonial rule in the Dutch East Indies and the hypocrisy of the bourgeoisie; the novel *Manja* by the young Russian author Anastasia Werbitztaja, championing women's emancipation; and a book of Chinese ghost and love stories, edited by Buber himself. His two anthologies of Hasidic lore were an integral part of this program to render the scope of German culture more cosmopolitan.[13]

To enhance the appeal of his list of publications, Oswalt devoted a great deal of attention to their aesthetic detail. With the publisher's encouragement, Buber hired the famed architect and designer Peter Behrens—a pioneer in modern decorative and applied arts—to design the cover and decorative endpaper of *Die Gesellschaft;* the distinctive lettering of the volumes was designed by Hermann Kirchmayr of the Tiroler Kunstbund, a center of Jugendstil artists in Innsbruck, Austria. As a self-consciously modern aesthetic idiom, Jugendstil was fashionable among "the cultured and urbane middle class" of Wilhelminian Germany—that is, Rütten & Loening's target audience.[14]

Bringing Hasidism to this audience presented Buber with a considerable challenge. Emerging in eighteenth-century Ukraine and Poland, Hasidism, a popular movement of mystical piety, had come to represent—for German Jews and non-Jews alike—the quintessence of eastern European Jewry's cultural backwardness. Buber himself often found Hasidism's literary sources to be lacking in aesthetic grace, at least by Western standards. Yet the increasing prestige that mysticism and folk-lore enjoyed among the educated elite of central Europe provided Buber with a way to leverage Hasidism as an intellectually respectable expression of religious spirituality. We can see this strategy reflected in a letter he wrote to the Austrian poet Hugo von Hofmannsthal:

> If you have no objection, I shall shortly be sending you a book now being printed by [Rütten & Loening]. It contains a number of tales and legends of an eighteenth-century Jewish mystic, Rabbi Nachman of Bratzlav, which I have found and reworked. A number of the rabbi's sayings are quoted in the introduction, and one of them might particularly interest you: "As the hand held before the eye conceals the greatest mountain, so the little earthly life hides from the glance the enormous lights and mysteries of which the world is full, and he who can draw away from behind his eyes, as one draws away a hand, beholds the great shining of the inner worlds." *Isn't that a singularly simple metaphor for the thought common to Eckhart, the Upanishads, and Hasidism?*[15]

Echoing the hermeneutic approach of Gustav Landauer's "translation" of Meister Eckhart, Buber explained in a letter to Samuel Horodetsky, a scholar of Hasidism who wrote largely in Hebrew and Russian: "My aim is not to accumulate new facts, but simply to give a new interpretation of the interconnections, a new synthetic presentation of Jewish mysticism and its creations and to make these creations known to the European public in as *artistically pure a form* as possible."[16] Sharing Buber's reservations about the literary merits of the original texts of Rabbi Nachman's stories, the Russian Jewish historian Simon Dubnow wrote Buber from Saint Petersburg to congratulate him for expurgating the tales of their *anima vili*, their worthless, vile soul (apparently referring to what he regarded to be their primitive superstitious elements). Dubnow, however, delicately questioned whether Buber had embellished the stories: "In the rendering of 'The Rabbi and his Son,' I notice an addition which is not in my 1881 Warsaw edition of [Nachman's tales]. Perhaps you have [an] older edition or used a variant?"[17]

Although he would probably reject the charge of embellishment per se, Buber acknowledged that he retold rather than translated select legends and symbolic fairy tales by Rabbi Nachman and later the Baal Shem Tov. As he relates in an essay of 1918, "My Way to Hasidism," after he tried several times to render the Hasidic stories from the Hebrew directly into German:

> I noted that the purity [of the original text] did not allow itself to be preserved in translation, much less enhanced— I had to tell stories that I had taken into myself, as a true painter takes into himself the lines of the models and achieves the genuine images out of the memory formed of them. . . . And, therefore, although by far the largest part of [*The Tales of Rabbi Nachman* and *The Legend of the Baal-Shem*] is autonomous fiction composed from traditional motifs, I might honestly report of my experience of the [Hasidic] legend: I bore in me the blood and the spirit of those who created it, and out of my blood and spirit it has become new.[18]

Some five decades later, Buber would acknowledge that this approach had resulted in an undisciplined and overly free rendering in German of these Hasidic tales. "I was still at that time, to be sure, an immature man; the so-called *Zeitgeist* still had power over me."[19] Hence he had tendentiously adapted Hasidism to the dominant cultural discourse of the period. "I did not listen attentively enough to the crude and ungainly but living folk-tone which could be heard in this material."[20] What he did not acknowledge then was that his wife, Paula, had helped him to render the legends of the Baal Shem Tov into German. He would supply her with motifs he had translated, and she would give them a narrative fullness. He recalled their collaboration in a poem he inscribed in a copy of an anthology of Hasidic tales he published later, in 1948:

> Do you still know, how we in our young years
> Traveled together on the sea?
> Visions came, great and wonderful,
> We beheld them together, you and I.
> How image joined itself with images in our hearts!
> How a mutual animated describing
> Arose out of it and lived between you and me!

The inscription concluded, notably: "For something eternal listens to it and listens to us, / How we resound out of it, I and Thou."[21]

Buber's early representations of Hasidism were primed by a desire to counter the negative views of eastern European Jewry. His interest in the largely maligned religious world of eastern European Jewry as represented by Hasidism was ultimately animated by a resolute commitment to rehabilitate the image of the so-called *Ostjuden* — and thus to secure the dignity of Jewry in general. In a letter in December 1906, he expressly admitted that his anthologies of Hasidic mystical teachings had an apologetic motive. While he was still working on *The Legend of the Baal-Shem*, which would be published in 1908, he shared with a close friend his anguish upon learning of a recent pogrom in June 1906 in the Polish city of Bialystok, which had left close to ninety Jews dead and a similar number wounded: "I am now writing a story, which is my answer to Bialystok. It is called *Adonai* [the name of God used when addressed in prayer, hence, an evocation here of the spiritual world of the Jews]. . . . I am now in the midst of the first real work period of my life. You as my friend will understand me: I have a *new answer* to give everything. Only now have I found the form of my answer. . . .

I have grown slowly into my heaven—my life begins. I experience ineffable suffering and ineffable grace."[22]

Buber viewed the representation of Hasidic spirituality as a calling. Despite its medieval exterior and what he deemed to be the inevitable social and spiritual degradation that had overtaken the movement, he felt that Hasidism continued to embody the inner truth of Judaism, which "knows multiplicity" but "no division of essential being."[23]

Prior to hearing the call to highlight and proclaim the spiritual message of Hasidism, Buber's desire to rehabilitate the image of eastern European Jewry had focused on Yiddish. In 1902, he founded in Berlin, together with other Polish Jews (an identity he proudly claimed), the Jüdischer Verlag as the publishing house of the "Jewish renaissance." The first publication of the Jüdischer Verlag, which proved to be an immensely successful and dynamic venture, was the *Jüdischer Almanach 5663*, issued in the autumn of 1902. The handsomely produced hardbound volume of about two hundred pages included translations of Yiddish and Hebrew poems by Morris Rosenfeld, Hayim Nachman Bialik, Sholem Aleichem, Yehuda, Leib Peretz, Shimen Frug, Sholem Asch, and Avrom Reyzen, and was introduced by an urbane essay on Yiddish literature ("Über Jargon und Jargonliteratur"). Of the sixty illustrations, two-thirds had eastern European themes, the most famous being a reproduction of the *Polnischer Jude* by Hermann Struck, one of the leading artists of the time. This inaugural volume was followed in 1903 by *Jüdische Kuntsler*, a collection of essays on Jewish artists, edited by Buber. In his introduction, he wrote for the first time, albeit parenthetically, of Hasidism as a possible inspirational source for the Jewish Renaissance: "The silently flickering mystical energies [of Judaism], which have found expression in the glowing ardor of the Hasidim, nurture the creativity of the artists of our time."[24] He also wrote in praise of a distinctive Jewish musical tradition, which is "preserved in the synagogues of the [eastern European] Ghetto."[25]

In the following year, the Jüdischer Verlag published Buber's German translation of a Yiddish "workers' drama" by David Pinski.[26] In the foreword, he hails the Russian dramatist as an authentic voice of the eastern European "Jewish proletariat." In his plays and stories, Buber observed, Pinski seeks "to convey nothing but the grim reality [of the Jewish working masses] as he sees and hears it. But in conveying this reality—unadulterated and in all its harshness—he discloses the meaning of the oppressed, enslaved reality of eastern European Jewry. He discloses the prevalence of the most terrible misery." Buber also emphasized that Pinski's language is Yiddish—"the popular idiom (*Volkssprache*) of the Jewish masses"—which, though it had been falsely characterized as a "Jargon," a crude patois, in reality had developed from a dialect into a sophisticated, highly nuanced language. While it is "not as rich" as Hebrew, it is "more supple"; it "is not as abstract but it is warmer than Hebrew"; it might lack the spiritual pathos of Hebrew, but "it is full of incomparably gentle and rough, tender and graded intonations." In Yiddish, "the Jewish people itself becomes language."[27]

Buber's celebration of the culture of eastern European Jewry was an expression of his reaffirmation of his own Jewish identity, which he had consciously allowed to atrophy as he eagerly embraced a European education and culture. The "whirl of the age," as he later noted, had taken hold of him: "My spirit was in steady and multiple movement, determined by manifold influences, taking ever new shape but without a center. . . . Here I lived—in versatile fullness of spirit, but without Judaism and humanity."[28] Zionism had first facilitated his reconnection with the Jewish community. He had been "seized" by Herzl's plea for "Jewish solidarity." A few weeks after having formally joined the Zionist movement, he wrote Paula, who was pregnant with their first child, and related that he and his cousin Ahron Eliasberg had gone to a Berlin railroad station to greet a group of Russian Jewish refugees en route to America. He poignantly described to her the "forlornness" of the leaderless refugees who "were treated like animals by the [German immigrant] officials." Appalled he told Paula how deeply he identified with their desperation and humiliation.

But he soon came to feel that an affirmation of Jewish national solidarity was only a first, albeit necessary step toward the spiritual transformation of the assimilated, forlorn Jew. The appropriation of a Jewish national identity was not to be construed as the longed-for "harbor," but rather as a setting sail onto "the open sea" in quest of the sources that would inspire one's transformation as a Jew who is spiritually at home in Judaism. "Thus," he wrote, "it happened to me."[29] After "some blind groping," he realized that he would reach his destination by renewing his knowledge of Judaism—to know it, however, not simply as "the storing up of anthropological, historical, and sociological knowledge" but from within "its creative primal hours."[30] Thus began his voyage on the sea of Jewish tradition, with the intent of discovering those resources that would furnish him with a spiritual home within Judaism. "On this way," he reported, "I came to Hasidism."

Buber, to be sure, set sail with a map and compass in hand; he had a clear sense of what he was looking for. Consistent with his equation of spirituality with mysticism, he sought the "primal creative hours" of Judaism in its mystical traditions; one of the first publications of the Jüdischer Verlag was a 1904 German translation of an essay by Solomon Schechter, "Die Chassidim: Eine Studie über jüdische Mystik." Turning to Hasidism was surely not accidental; Buber drew on his childhood memories of visiting Hasidic communities with his father, which had left powerful, albeit ambivalent, impressions on him.

As part of his resolution to learn more about Hasidism,

Martin Buber solicited his grandfather's assistance. A renowned scholar of rabbinic texts, Salomon Buber had wide-ranging connections with eastern European scholars of Hasidism and Kabbalah, many of whom he supported by underwriting the cost of publishing their writings. In addition to providing his grandson with Hasidic publications not readily available in Berlin, he seems to have facilitated the support that Martin enjoyed (in preparing his anthologies) from such eminent scholars as Micha Joseph Berdichevsky, Simon Dubnow, and especially Shmuel Horodetzky, who had published studies of Hasidism in Hebrew, Russian, and Yiddish.[31] In the preface of the first edition of *The Tales of Rabbi Nachman*, Buber acknowledged the assistance he had received from each of these scholars. This edition, published a month before the passing of his grandfather in December 1906, also bore the dedication: "To my grandfather, Salomon Buber, the last of the great scholars of the old-style Haskalah [eastern European Jewish Enlightenment], I dedicate this work on Hasidism with respect and love."

The dedication reflects what one may surmise was a reconciliation. Martin's grandfather had not been particularly approving of his pursuit of a university education, and as someone who was wary of Jewry's turn to nationalism, his grandson's adoption of Zionism did not particularly please him.[32] But upon learning of Martin's intention to engage in a study of Hasidism, he wrote him a brief but ecstatic letter (in Yiddish): "My dear Martin, I have your good letter, which gave me special pleasure. I read it with tears of joy. May it also make for you a great name in the world. . . . This is the hope and wish of your loving grandfather."[33] He added that since he was gravely ill, "it should be *soon* so that I could experience [the public esteem it will bring you]. The time is short."[34] It was undoubtedly especially gratifying for Salomon, shortly before his death, to have the pleasure of seeing his grandson's book on Nachman of Bratzlav in print. (Upon the death of his grandfather, the dedication of the second edition of the volume was emended to read: "In memory of my grandfather.") Martin's grandfather's exuberant approval of his interest in Hasidism was in striking contrast to his father's letter to him on his thirtieth birthday, in which he pleaded with him, as we have seen, to "give up this Hasidic and Zohar stuff" and stop "[wasting] so much time and effort [on something] so utterly useless for yourself and the world."[35]

Unmoved by his father's admonition, Buber continued his writing on Hasidism, which was part of his wider interest in mysticism generally. As early as 1903, he was in discussions with the Leipzig publisher Eugen Diederichs regarding a proposal to edit an anthology of essays on European mystical traditions. The project eventually evolved into an anthology of mystical testimonies by "fervent individuals from various ages and peoples that I have been collecting over many years," as Buber wrote to Diederichs.[36] He further explained that the volume would be concerned "much more with the affirmation of life and a positive spirit than with asceticism and a flight from the world," reflecting "the communication of visionaries—individuals graced with dreams about their innermost life." Since the volume would "bring together entirely forgotten documents that are of utmost importance for the soul of humanity," he wrote, he was reluctant to entrust its publication to any publisher other than one as spiritually and aesthetically sensitive as Diederichs.[37] The volume, *Ecstatic Confessions*, was accepted and published by Eugen Diederichs Verlag in 1909. Presenting voices of mystical rapture from various Occidental and Oriental traditions, theistic and pagan, the volume was, as Buber had hoped, exquisitely produced. Enjoying numerous editions, the volume's enthusiastic reception enhanced the thirty-one-year-old Buber's stature as a significant voice in German intellectual life.

Despite the fame the volume would later bring him, at the time Buber considered it to have only "a thoroughly episodic" significance for him.[38] Nevertheless, he was eager to have the confessions seen in print, if for no other reason than that they represented years of research. In his introduction to *Ecstatic Confessions*, he thus expressed a muffled ambivalence about what he referred to in his correspondence with Diederichs as the life-affirming impulse of the mystic. Driven by a deeply felt need to voice the experience (Erlebnis) of the "primal unity of being," the mystic perforce enters through language the world of space and time, the world of multiplicity. This is the "monstrous contradiction" inherent in ecstatic confessions: The ecstatic seeks "to tow the timeless into the harbor of time," but befuddled by the manifest chaos of the world of space and time, takes recourse in the creation of myths of unity, in which the experience of unity "becomes plurality because it wants to gaze and be gazed at, . . . to love and be loved." Buber then concludes the introduction on a surprisingly skeptical note: "But is not the myth a phantasm? . . . We listen to our inmost selves—and do not know which sea we hear murmuring."[39]

Less than a year after the publication of *Ecstatic Confessions*, Buber's ambivalence came to a resolution with an emphatic denial of the fundamental presupposition that mystical experience embraces fragmented, individuated social existence. Attending the First German Conference of Sociologists organized by Max Weber in October 1910, Buber entered into a debate with Ernst Troeltsch in which he protested the Protestant philosopher of religion's reference to mysticism as a sociological category. Buber insisted that the mystic's experience is in fact asocial, and should properly be understood as "religious solipsism":

> Mysticism . . . is an absolute realization of [individual] religiosity, achieving both an apprehension of one's self and an "apperception of God." In the intense exaltation of the self the mystic establishes a relationship to the content of

his soul, which he perceives as God. . . . [Hence,] it seems
to me that mysticism negates community—mysticism does
not struggle with any organized community, nor does it set
itself up as an alternative community, as a sect would. Rather
mysticism negates community, precisely because for it there
is only one relation, the relation to God. The process noted
by Professor Troeltsch, the coming together of believers
. . . does not at all occur in mysticism. The [mystic] remains
thoroughly isolated in his belief, for nothing else matters to
him than to be alone with God.[40]

He also remarked parenthetically that "mysticism seems to me
rather different from religion, which is [indeed] a sociological
entity constituted by religiosity." This critical characterization
of ecstatic mysticism reflected an incipient shift in his understanding of religious life, which would also inform his later
"dialogical" representation of Hasidic spirituality. His interest in myth and mysticism would indeed ultimately prove episodic; he would decades later apologetically call it his "mystical
phase," which he had to pass through before he "could attain an
independent relation with being."[41]

The axis of Buber's quest for unity in the world of plurality
increasingly shifted from myth to religiosity, which is "manifest
in deed." The transition, however, was slow and incremental. In
his early writings on Hasidism, he was still in the thrall of myth
and the mythic articulation of the mystical experience. Thus,
in *The Legend of the Baal-Shem*, he exuberantly claimed, "The
Jews are a people that has never ceased to produce myth."[42]
Although the custodians of the religion of Israel had sought
since time immemorial to keep myth—and mysticism—at bay,
they never could quite suppress the mythopoetic imagination,
attuned as it is to "the fullness of existence" and the torments
of individuation. "It is strange and wonderful," he wrote, "to
observe how in this battle religion ever again wins the apparent victory, myth ever again wins the real one." Buber cited the

prophets as exemplary representatives of the Judaic voice of myth: "The prophets struggled through the word against the multiplicity of the people's impulses, but in their visions lives the ecstatic fantasy of the Jews, which makes them poets of myth without their knowing it."[43]

Buber's Hasidic anthologies were followed by collections of Chinese, Finnish, and Celtic myths and legends. The editing of the volume *Reden und Gleichnisse des Tschuang-Tse* (Sayings and parables of Zhuangzi) led to an intensive study of Chinese philosophy, particularly Daoism, of which the late fourth-century B.C.E. sage Zhuangzi was a seminal figure.[44] Although he worked with available English translations, Buber translated some of the tales himself with the help of a Chinese scholar then living in Berlin. (When Buber's children—nine-year-old Rafael and his eight-year-old sister Eva—were told by their mother that a Dr. Wang Jingtao was going to visit in order to work with their father, they scrambled to the window of the apartment facing the street, excitedly waiting for the arrival of their "Oriental" guest, hoping to catch a first glimpse of his ponytail; they were profoundly disappointed that he did not have one.)[45]

Long after his interest in myth had waned, Buber maintained what became a lifelong interest in Chinese philosophy. Both the volume on Zhuangzi and the volume of Chinese ghost and love stories he published a year later went through many printings.[46] In the 1920s, he was active in the China Gesellschaft, founded at the University of Frankfurt by the famed sinologist Richard Wilhelm, to which he delivered several lectures on Chinese philosophy; it was through membership in the society that he met the psychoanalyst Carl Gustav Jung, and deepened his friendship with the novelist Hermann Hesse and the poet (and his future son-in-law) Ludwig Strauss. When he later taught at the Hebrew University of Jerusalem, he assigned his students texts by the Daoist philosopher Laozi, which he translated into Hebrew with the help of a German-Jewish sinologist then living in Tel Aviv.

In the introductory chapter of the volume on Zhuangzi, Buber explained that the Dao (the path to true knowledge of the world) is actually not a matter of knowing, but of being—it is not static, but unfolds through endless change. Unity, first within oneself and then within the world, is sought within that change. Western epistemologies had led humanity astray; in Daoism, true knowledge is found not by thinking (whereby one stands over against the world as an independent observer, and seeks to penetrate its mystery through metaphysical or instrumental reason), but in action—or rather, non-action, a process of becoming. Through this active non-action, one becomes "part of the natural order" of the world, free of the distinction, division, and anguished separation in the Western quest for knowledge of reality, and of the inherently "violent" impulse to impose a conceptual or empirical unity on the natural order. But Buber would soon come to wonder whether the doctrine of non-action might be no more than a spiritual attunement to the world of becoming, not a true process of becoming itself, and inadequate to the task of concretely (and thus actively) fostering the unity within the diversity of the world as we experience it.

Soon after publishing the *Reden und Gleichnisse des Tschuang-Tse*, Buber embarked on the work of clarifying how the task of promoting the essential unity within a world of diversity might be realized. By the late spring of 1912, he was ready to share with friends the drafts of what would be his first full-length monograph, *Daniel. Gespräche von der Verwirklichung* (Daniel: Dialogues on realization). His most attentive reader was Gustav Landauer, with whom he shared numerous versions. Upon revising the manuscript in accordance with his friend's extensive stylistic and substantive emendations, he submitted the manuscript to Anton Kippenberg, director of Insel Verlag, which was then widely considered the premier literary publishing house in Germany. With palpable joy, he wrote Landauer in September 1912 to inform him that Kippenberg had accepted the volume for publication.[47] In a journal he kept while working on *Daniel*, he drafted an appreciative note: "For Landauer. Among my friends you are the only one for whom *Daniel* was always there. It is thus more than an expression of a feeling when I dedicate the first announcement of its birth to you."[48]

Among the working notes Buber made while writing *Daniel* is a short one possibly hinting at the programmatic thrust of the volume: "Conjoin the biographical with the dialogical."[49] One may reasonably surmise, then, that a variety of autobiographical moments inform the conversations (*Gespräche*) between Daniel and five different interlocutors. The first conversation is between Daniel and a woman (who is identified only as "Die Frau")—whose voice might very well be that of his wife, at least in part—and takes place while strolling in the mountains (something that Martin and Paula often did). The woman, Daniel's partner, is portrayed as a mother and companion. The maternal womb and life force of being, she stirs his passion, binding him to earthy reality, flush with multiple, "formless" possibilities, tensions, and feelings. But Daniel strives to give his life direction, which knows no multiplicity: "Direction is that primary tension of the human soul which impels it from time to time to choose this [way] and no other from the infinitude of possibilities and *to realize it in action*."[50] Daniel's direction is fired by passion, for "direction is only perfect when it is fulfilled with power, the power to live the whole . . . together [they] allow you to penetrate into [the] substance of [life-experience], that is into the unity itself."[51]

In response, the woman wonders whether the experience

of unity is in the end just the "ingenious spin" of intellectual constructs, rather than embedded in "the deep element [of life itself]: the mother's lap in which we save ourselves from the cruel laws of isolation. . . . Is not all ecstasy a merging into the Other?"[52] Daniel agrees, while reiterating his caveat that ecstasy bereft of direction inevitably ravishes and devours the soul. To avoid this tragic fate, ecstatic experience must take its clue from Orpheus, who descended into Hades—the realm tormented by both multiplicity and the isolation wrought by individuation—attuned to the music of his inner soul, and thereby experienced unity of all being in his own unity. Finally, Daniel and the woman grasp hands, at her suggestion, and he comments that the act of clasping their hands is not driven by compulsion—a pure erotic drive—"but the choice of the other; the direction of the holy spirit, the flowering of the cross of community."[53] (The reference to the "cross" as a metaphor for religious commitment is not unique here. Throughout his writings, Buber would employ Christian symbols, particularly those associated with Jesus, whom he regarded as a representative of primal Jewish religious sensibilities.)

There are other autobiographical resonances in the remaining four conversations, although few as obvious as this initial palpably romantic dialogue. One particularly poignant moment occurs in the fifth and final conversation, which takes place by the sea. Daniel's interlocutor, Lukas, tells of a thirty-year-old acquaintance who had drowned at sea, an experience that engendered in Lukas metaphysical reflections on the meaning of life in the face of inevitable death. Daniel responds by relating his own experience with death, a clear reference to Buber's own life: "Let me tell you an event out of my youth. I was seventeen years old when a man died whom I had loved." (Indeed, on a visit to his father's farm, as a boy of seventeen Martin witnessed his uncle Rafael, his father's brother, fall from a horse to his death. He would later name his first child after his beloved uncle.) With only oblique reference to the specifics of this terrible event, Daniel continues to tell Lukas:

> Death laid itself about my neck like a lasso. . . . Because of my isolation I could take no sleep and because of my disgust with living I could tolerate no nourishment. . . . My family, strengthened by friends and physicians, regarded me fussily and helplessly as a changeling. Only my father met me with a calm collected glance that was so strong that he reached my heart . . . [He] soon came to the special decision through which I was saved: he sent me all alone into a secluded mountain place. I believe that the great time that I lived through there [on the mountain] will return once more in the images of my dying hour.[54]

(The "secluded mountain place" to which Daniel's father sent him may allude to Martin's great-uncle's summer vacation home nestled in the bucolic Carpathian mountains.)[55] Daniel tells Lukas that wandering through mountain and dale, punctuated by woods and lakes, "facing the towering pride of the earth," he found himself "before the eternal wall" that marked his finitude—that demarcated life from death, yet joined the two realms just the same. Emerging from despair, he "saw nothing isolated any longer. . . . I saw everything as [a] cloudy image in which all separateness dissolved. Light and dark were entangled in each other."[56] Realizing that he was no longer a separate, isolated being, Daniel also tore down the wall within himself. "From life to death—from the living to the dead there flowed [a] deep union." He was now united with his beloved friend, despite the finality of death, "because I was united in myself."[57] Though presented as a mystical awakening, Daniel's decision to bear within himself the defining tensions of existence and the deep experience of unity anticipates the later existentialist turn in Buber's thought.

Daniel concludes his dialogue with Lukas, with which Buber brings the book to a close, by noting:

> We spoke of death, my friend Lukas; we have all the time spoken of nothing else. You wish to know the holy sea, the unity that bears life and death in right and left hand. You cannot know it otherwise than when you take upon yourself the tension of life and death and live through the life and death of the world as your life and your death.

The distinctive religiosity espoused by Buber in *Daniel* and its "dialogues on realization" are not specifically Jewish, although the title of the book had led some to believe otherwise. The book's stylistic affinities to Nietzsche's *Zarathustra* suggest that Buber named his book and its principal protagonist Daniel after the biblical contemporary of the Persian seer Zarathustra; otherwise, Buber's Daniel has nothing to do with the biblical prophet, and those who have assumed any other connection have clearly not read the book. (One amusing example of this misattribution is the scroll accompanying an honorary doctorate Buber would receive in 1958 from the Sorbonne. Signed by some of the most eminent dignitaries of the venerable French university, the scroll lauds among Buber's distinguished accomplishments his "great Jewish book" *Daniel* as expressing Israel's prophetic "voice for justice . . . and redemption.")[58]

Buber's *Daniel* is at most a prophetic counter-voice to Nietzsche's *Zarathustra*. Upon reviewing a draft of the first part of the volume, Landauer remarked in a letter to Buber that, with *Daniel*, "you are achieving what Nietzsche did not achieve in his *Zarathustra*."[59] Focusing his comparison solely on matters of style and rhetoric, he notes the tension in Nietzsche's dialogue (characteristic of German didactic writing more generally) between the speaking subject's unreserved speech and "the speech of the soul," and credits Buber with overcoming, in *Daniel*, this problematic narrative duality: "I find this greatness in this aspect of your book: the passion of the subject in the form of the language, which is shaped so that it is at once entirely the language of the speaker and entirely the speaking subject. In this work about unity in duality you have achieved *what the work is all about*." Like many of his generation, Buber had clearly been inspired by Nietzsche's effort to create a new poetic language, a language not so much grounded in conceptually coherent argumentation, but instead representing the act of thinking itself in its "rhythmic diversity" and "corporeality of expression."[60] Indeed, in *Daniel*, Buber allowed his thoughts to unfold dialectically and poetically, rather than analytically.

Landauer clearly viewed Buber's eschewal of abstract discourse in favor of an evocative, poetic voice to be more successful than Nietzsche's own effort to do so. In the lead article of a special issue of an avant-garde journal devoted to Buber, Landauer approvingly characterized Buber's thought as "feminine (*frauenhaft*)." With reference to *Daniel*, Landauer noted, Buber "awakens and advocates a specific feminine form of thought without which our exhausted and collapsed culture cannot be renewed and replenished. Only . . . when abstract thought is conjoined and submerged in the depths of feeling, will our thought engender deeds, will a true life emerge from our logical desert. Towards that objective women will help us."[61] As a philosopher attuned to the poetic cadences and emotional ground of life, Landauer proclaimed approvingly, Buber belongs to the spiritual family of the feminine.[62]

The Austrian poet Rainer Maria Rilke also waxed enthusiastically about *Daniel* in a letter to the publisher of Insel Verlag, who had sent him a complimentary copy of Buber's book.[63] Other readers of *Daniel* were critical; the twenty-year-old Gerhard (Gershom) Scholem wrote in a letter to friends in the Jewish youth movement a scathing critique of what he deemed to be Buber's tediousness and "mystical rhetoric": "The most unimaginable phantasy, the theoretical vacuous twaddle, the most irrelevant mysticism could have chosen no better residence as the living corpse of a man, who has stumbled over the [purported] importance of his experience. It is *very* tragic."[64] While this rant reflected his disaffection with Buber (a dynamic that would recur over the course of their decades-long relationship), like many of his generation of Jewish youth, Scholem had initially been inspired by the text of three lectures Buber had delivered in 1911 to Jewish university students in Prague—lectures that portrayed his experience-rooted mysticism as consistent with the deepest sensibilities of the Jewish people.

# 5

—◆•◆•◆—

## *Prague: Mystical Religiosity and Beyond*

SHORTLY AFTER APPROVING the final proofs for *Ecstatic Confessions*, Buber received a letter from Leo Herrmann, the newly elected chair of Bar Kochba, the Association of Jewish University Students in Prague—an organization identified with cultural Zionism and the vision of a Jewish renaissance.[1] In the letter, dated November 11, 1908, the eighteen-year-old law student extended an invitation to Buber to speak at a "festive evening" scheduled for the following January. Herrmann explained that the event, which would be open to the wider community, was intended "to remind the large assimilated public in Prague of our and their Judaism." The envisioned program was to include several speakers as well as the recitation of poems on Jewish themes.

Thus far, Herrmann was happy to report, he had secured the participation of the Viennese writer and critic Felix Salten, one of the most famous authors of the time (who is now best

known for his 1923 novel, *Bambi: A Life in the Woods*, the basis for
the Disney animated movie). Since Salten would speak about
the roots of Jewish "national and cultural assimilation," Herrmann hoped that Buber could counter "the negative side of our
cultural problems" with a positive vision, including a strategy
to reverse the lamentable process of "defection" that was particularly rampant among Jewish denizens of western European
urban centers. "How is the remnant of Jewishness, even that of
the west European Jew, to be transformed into something of his
own?" Herrmann underscored the enormity of the challenge
posed by this question, stating that in Prague "almost everyone
resists accepting a conscious Judaism." He concluded his appeal
to Buber with words clearly intended to flatter him: "You of all
persons, dear Herr Doktor, would be best equipped to undertake this task. Everyone knows that throughout the West these
days, in fact everywhere, we have no more sensitive interpreter
of the Jewish sensibility than yourself."

The thirty-year-old Buber accepted the invitation with
alacrity; it seems to have tapped into his growing desire to become actively engaged once again in the life of the Jewish community. It would also be an opportunity for him to develop a
new conception of Judaism and Jewish renewal. Having withdrawn from Zionist affairs, he had soon come to the realization
that his own advocacy of a Jewish renaissance was peppered
with slogans but lacked substance; by his own admission, he
"professed Judaism before having known it."[2] Having spent the
formative years of his youth in the home of his orthodox grandparents, he certainly knew the religious practices and foundational texts of traditional Judaism; he was now determined to
understand the "primal creative hours" that had given birth to
those practices and texts.

Buber saw his study of Hasidism as a gateway to knowledge of the underlying spiritual foundations of Judaism, upon
which any new expression of Jewish culture must rest.[3] The

knowledge that emerged from his immersion in the sources of Hasidism, which would gain conceptual crystallization in the lectures he was to give in Prague, constituted what he would later (in a 1929 essay) refer to as the second of three "stations" that would ultimately lead to his mature conception of Judaism. This, the second stage, was born of the realization that the desired renaissance of Judaism could not be simply willed into existence; it must be grounded in Jewry's primordial life experiences. "This stage," he later wrote, "is what was meant by religious renewal."[4]

Still, Buber surprised himself with his ready acceptance of Herrmann's invitation. He was generally reluctant to accept speaking engagements; in fact, until then he had only addressed Zionist audiences, on topics that he himself determined and that reflected his own intellectual agenda. Herrmann's letter, as he later recalled, "affected me in a special way. It was the nature of the invitation, not its ideational content or the thoughts it evoked, but rather [I was moved] by the gravitas of the request that was directed to a specific person—and I was that person." He understood Herrmann to be an emissary of a group of young university students who had addressed to him a specific (and, for them, an existentially urgent) question. "This fact simply demanded of me an answer. It aroused in me a sense of responsibility to respond."[5]

But at night, after having accepted Herrmann's invitation, Buber began to think about the substance of the lecture. "Sometime later these thoughts took on a concreteness, I imagined the faces of those whom I would address, their look, their voice. My late grandmother would often say that 'one never knows the face of the angel [God's emissary] who will appear before one.' The angel that first appeared before me was a human being. . . . Herrmann was the first angel that called upon me."[6] Responding to that call, he delivered three lectures between January 1909 and December 1910, which were published in 1911 under the title *Drei Reden über das Judentum* (Three addresses on Judaism). These lectures inspired a generation of central European Jewish youth. Though as we have seen he would soon become a sharp critic of Buber, Gershom Scholem—a member of that generation—testified to the impact that Buber's lectures had on him and his peers:

> We high school and university students searched for a way [to Judaism]. There was much fervor among us, a great awakening of spirit and eagerness to listen to the voices that reached us from the past and present. These voices were few; we did not know Hebrew, hence, primary sources were closed to us. The prospects of being nurtured by them seemed exceedingly remote. Who was to instruct us in the phenomenon called Judaism and its heritage? . . . Buber's first books on Hasidism and the *Drei Reden* found in us a powerful receptiveness. The voice speaking from his books was promising, demanding, fascinating, uncovering the hidden life beneath the frozen official forms [of Judaism], uncovering its hidden treasures. The power of his expression has always been tremendous, fascinating in its beauty and in its resonance. He demanded attachment to and identification with the heart of the people as he had then understood it, demanded of the youth that they become an additional link in the chain of the hidden life [of Judaism], that they become heirs to a sublime and hidden tradition of revolt and uprising.[7]

The *Three Addresses* marked Buber's debut as a public intellectual, a scholar participating in the wider cultural and political discourse. During his first appearance in Prague, delivering a lecture on "Judaism and the Jew," on Saturday evening, January 16, 1909, he was initially hesitant and faltering. Having arrived a bit early, he had met Herrmann and several other members of Bar Kochba at a local cafe for a relaxed, friendly conversation. But when the time came to address the large audience that had crowded into the ballroom of the Hotel Central, he became visibly anxious. He was scheduled to follow Salten, an experienced and polished public speaker. Indeed, Salten "gave a brilliant and forceful lecture" while Buber waited with Herrmann in a small chilly room underneath the stage. He confided in Herrmann that he feared that "he would not successfully make contact with the audience," and that after Salten's commanding performance, many would leave in the middle of his lecture. Herrmann suggested that he not consider the audience, "but only us, the inner circle of the Bar Kochba Association whom he met earlier that day." Accordingly, it was arranged that Buber would from time to time look up at the box in the balcony where Herrmann would be sitting. If the lecture was not going well, Herrmann would signal him, and Buber would quickly bring it to a close.[8]

Rather than standing to deliver the lecture as Salten had, Buber sat on a stool, wrapped in an overcoat someone had lent him because he felt cold. After ten minutes, he looked up questioningly to Herrmann's box, "but receiving no signal continued without once again looking for [it]." As he proceeded, he became considerably more relaxed and confident, expressing "his innermost thoughts with enthusiasm and depth. Although many in the audience certainly did not fathom fully what he said, we [the inner circle of the Bar Kochba] were intoxicated. He descended the stage and silently took a seat among us. No one dared thank him for his brilliant address. I simply grasped his hand warmly."[9]

The success of the lecture led to further invitations, with each address more inspiring than the preceding one. But it was the conversations with Buber before and after the lectures that most impressed Herrmann and the Bar Kochba leadership. After the first meeting with Buber, Herrmann recorded in his diary that "he made a powerful impression on us as a deep and critical thinker. He was in our eyes like a prophet of yore: convincing and honest. We were very much inspired by him. He spoke with great intensity about his conception of Judaism. He was the first authentic Zionist whom I got to meet up close. He was also the first to identify the Jewish problem with the problem of man. At the same time, he held there was no solution [for Jews] other than in the land of our fathers."[10] Franz Kafka, who was a peripheral member of Bar Kochba, also had a favorable impression of Buber, but only from his experience of him offstage. As he wrote to his fiancée, Felice Bauer, he found Buber's lectures "dreary; no matter what he says, something is missing." But when after one of the lectures Kafka had the opportunity to engage Buber in conversation, he reported to Felice, "I talked to Buber yesterday: as a person he is lively and simple and remarkable, and seems to have no connection with the tepid things he has written."[11]

Buber's first two lectures were not delivered from prepared texts, although he may have had outlines.[12] The third lecture, however, was read from a carefully crafted text. He first delivered it in Vienna on December 16, 1910, as a sort of dry run that he would fine-tune before heading to Prague two days later. Herrmann, who was by chance in Vienna, attended the lecture, "The Renewal of Judaism," and afterward had the opportunity to discuss it with three of Vienna's literary luminaries whom he had spotted in the audience—Richard Beer-Hofmann, Arthur Schnitzler, and Jakob Wassermann—whose very presence was an indication of Buber's rising reputation. Buber soon joined the four in the discussion. The next day, Herrmann again met with Buber, who asked him whether in light of the previous night's discussion there were passages that should be changed or clarified. In response, Herrmann suggested that he might consider bringing together points he made in the first two lectures, and present them in an integrated, coherent manner in the third. Buber eagerly heeded his advice, as Herrmann recorded in his diary: "I felt that the third address had grown out of the first two."[13]

It is also clear that all three of the addresses were originally and specifically tailored for the audience of acculturated Jews, especially youth who, as Scholem underscored, were eager to "revolt" and "rise up" against the bourgeois values of their parents' generation—values that Buber described in the third address as the instrumental aims that drive the whirl and bustle of modern society.[14] Buber's neo-Romantic rhetoric was shared by many of the Jewish youth of central Europe. He spoke of the Jews' *Volkscharakter*, the "innate dispositions" inscribed in their blood that have determined the Jewish people's formative values and understandings of the world, at least during the distinctively creative moments of Judaism.[15] Sadly though, he argued, the Jews of modernity, in their eager embrace of bourgeois ambitions and values, have betrayed the calling of their blood—but so had the Talmudic sages and their contemporary descendants, with their inflexible, spiritually vacuous approach to rabbinic ritual law.

With inflections suggestive of Nietzsche's *Zarathustra*, Buber attributed the "sterility" of the modern period to the "extinction of heroic, unconditional living," which does not bow to convention or even to what seem to be the intractable aspects of reality.[16] Modern determinism in particular, he felt, had undermined "confidence in the supra-human" and in the potential of an individual's will, decisions, and deeds to shape the "becoming" of the world.[17] The "power of the spirit" had been replaced by instrumental reason and "the might of sacrifice by bargaining skill."[18] The eclipse of the ethic of heroic, unconditioned decisions and deeds, he argued, is fundamentally inimical to Judaism as an ongoing "spiritual process."

The renewal of this process would require nothing less than a spiritual revolution. Buber gave the traditional Jewish term for repentance—*teshuvah*, which literally means "returning"—a Nietzschean twist: "a sudden and immense return (*Umkehr*: turning) and a transformation." Return here is an unmediated experience (*unmittlebares Erlebnis*) of one's essence in accord with "the essence of the world." The renewal of Judaism, as Buber put it in his second address, "Judaism and Mankind," is forged by "a striving for unity: for unity within the individual; for unity between mankind and every living thing; and for unity between God and the world."[19] It is the experience of the "primal power of unity" that will engender "not merely a rejuvenation or revival but a genuine and total renewal."[20]

Behind his neo-Romantic expression and the deliberately sermonic voice that Buber assumed in the *Drei Reden* (he was clearly intent on inspiring and edifying a community of young, deracinated Jews), there was a potent existential call to his audience subsumed under the metaphor of blood. As "the deepest, most potent stratum of our being," blood signifies that "which is implanted in us by the chain of fathers and mothers, by their nature and fate, and by their deeds and by their sufferings."[21] As used by Buber, though, "blood" here is ultimately meant to allude to the existential condition of the modern Jew, which perforce takes on for each individual Jew a personal dimension, and thus should be considered "the root of all Jewish questions, the question we must [each] discover within ourselves, clarify within ourselves, and decide within ourselves."[22] At its core, he felt, the question of what it meant to be Jewish was a deeply personal one. Indeed, as Buber's good friend, the writer and literary critic Moritz Heimann, observed, "Whatever a Jew, stranded on the most lonely, most inaccessible island, still considers to be the 'Jewish question,' that, and that alone, it is."[23] The challenge according to Heimann, as cited by Buber, is "to live as a Jew with all the contradictions, all the tragedy, and all the future promise of his blood."[24]

This was precisely the message that the organizers of the Bar Kochba lectures sought to promote. Significantly, after Buber's first address, he was followed by the Viennese actress Lea Rosen's recitation of Richard Beer-Hofmann's "Lullaby from Miriam," which had been composed in 1897 for his two-week-old daughter. In four lyrical stanzas, Beer-Hofmann addresses his infant child, pondering the meaning of the journey of life upon which she is about to travel—a journey fraught with uncertain fortunes and imponderable experiences that none of us can ever adequately communicate, even to those closest and dearest to us. The absolute loneliness that each person is destined to suffer sets up the tragic necessity for each generation to repeat the mistakes—and freshly bear the miseries—of the past. Yet, in the last stanza, Beer-Hofmann assures his infant daughter that she will find in the primordial bonds of "blood"—the fraternal support of her people, the Jewish people—the strength to withstand the trials and tribulations that await her:

> Are you sleeping, Miriam?—Miriam, my child,
> We are merely the banks [of a river].
> And deep in us rushes the blood of those who were;
> Rolling on to those who are to come,
> Blood of our fathers, flush in restlessness and pride.
> *In* us they *all* dwell. Who feels oneself alone?
> You are their life now, and their life is yours—
> Miriam, my life, my child—sleep soundly![25]

For Buber, the mere bonds of blood alone were not sufficient in and of themselves, nor was fidelity to the external religious forms of traditional Jewish practice, nor even an allegiance to a Jewish "national consciousness."[26] He now also found the Zionist project wanting. He supported Zionist settlement in the land of Israel and the vision of Zion as a spiritual center of a vibrant secular Jewish culture, but in looking to inspire the renewal of Judaism in the Diaspora, he questioned the ultimate significance of those two pillars of Zionism:

> [The Zionist project] could not guarantee a renewal of Judaism in the absolute meaning of the term; moreover, the cen-

ter of the Jewish people would become the center of Judaism as well only if it were created not for the sake of renewal but out of and through renewal. An intellectual center [in Palestine, such as envisioned by cultural Zionism] can promote scholarly work; it can even disseminate and propagate ideas, though it cannot create them. Indeed, it could perhaps even become a social model. But it cannot beget the only things from which I expect the Absolute to emerge— [spiritual] return and transformation, and a change in all elements of life.[27]

Indeed, Buber all but utterly dismissed the spiritual significance of the Zionist project by suggesting that the assimilated Jews of the Diaspora might actually be in a better position emotionally than the Zionist pioneers to realize the renewal of Judaism: "It seems to me that the great ambivalence, the boundless despair, the infinite longing and pathetic inner chaos of many of today's Jews provide more propitious ground for the radical shake-up that must precede such a total renewal than does the normal and confident existence of a settler in his own land."[28]

Hence, while seemingly remaining within the Zionist discourse, Buber reinterpreted one of its key concepts. The "galut Jew," the Diaspora Jew, was in the Zionist framework unavoidably scarred—psychologically, spiritually and politically—by Israel's two-thousand-year sojourn in exile (galut), banished from its ancient territorial patrimony. The resettlement of Jews in the land of Israel, as affirmed by classical Zionist doctrine, would—could—heal them of the multiple torments of galut (not just narrowly defined as physical exile, the end of which will not automatically cure those torments). A New Jew—unscathed by the galut—would arise. In his Bar Kochba addresses, Buber introduced a new term to counter the Galut-Jew: *Urjude*— a Jew whose very being as a Jew is grounded and nurtured by the primal "spiritual process" of Judaism. By an Urjude, Buber explained, "I mean the Jew who becomes conscious of the great powers of elemental Judaism (*Urjudentum*) within himself, and who decides for them, for their activation."[29] A Jew who is not attuned to the inner experience of Urjudentum is a Galut-Jew, whether he or she resides in Prague or on a kibbutz in Palestine. Conversely, an Urjude may plough a field at the shore of the Lake of Galilee or stroll across Prague's historic Charles Bridge.

Buber would remain an atypical Zionist throughout his life. He urged his Prague audience to embrace the cardinal Zionist imperative of solidarity with the suffering of the Jewish people. Paradoxically, by rendering the Jewish Question and the renewal of Judaism a *personal*, subjective calling, Buber sought to deepen the sense of responsibility to the "whole of Jewish existence":

> Then our feelings will no longer be the feelings of individuals; every individual among us will feel that he is the people, for he will feel the people within himself [its past as well as its present]. We shall become aware of . . . those people out there—the miserable, stooped people dragging their feet, peddling their wares from village to village, not knowing where tomorrow's livelihood will come from nor why they should go on living, and those dull, stupefied masses [of eastern European Jews], being loaded aboard ships, not knowing where or why—we shall perceive them, all of them not merely as our brothers and sisters; rather, made secure within himself, every one of us will feel: these people are part of myself. It is not together with them that I am suffering; I am suffering their tribulations. My soul is not by the side of my people; my soul *is* my people.[30]

The alignment of one's inner subjective and objective life as a Jew is what Buber celebrated in each of three addresses as the "striving for unity" that is the defining characteristic of Urjudentum. In philosophical terms, the desired unity would be the correlation of Erlebnis—one's affective, subjective experience—with *Erfahrung*, the objective realm of experience in which our social and political life takes place. This too would remain, albeit with a shift in conceptual terms, a paramount concern of Buber's later thought.

After publication of the three addresses, Buber maintained his relationship with Bar Kochba. He not only returned to Prague to give additional lectures, but also developed life-long friendships with several of the members of the association, among them Leo Herrmann, Hugo Bergmann (later Samuel Hugo Bergman), Max Brod, Hans Kohn, and Felix and Robert Weltsch, each of whom would regard himself as a disciple of Buber and assume a significant position both in the cultural life of German-speaking Jewry and, later, in Palestine.[31] The first expression of their adherence to Buber's vision of Jewish renewal was a volume of essays, *Vom Judentum*, published in 1913. Nominally edited by the Bar Kochba Association of Jewish University Students, its principal individual editor was Kohn, who in 1930 would publish an intellectual biography of then fifty-two-year-old Buber. Herrmann also played a role in organizing the volume; both he and Kohn actively consulted with Buber on the content and structure of this very well-received anthology of essays. In the preface to the volume, Kohn explained: "Since Martin Buber held his 'Three Addresses on Judaism' before our association—their influence on us is abundantly attested to in this volume—we have become ever cognizant that Zionism has deep roots in the spiritual struggle of Urjudentum against those who flow apathetically with the times. [Buber taught us that Zionism is] 'an ethical movement that relates seriously to both Judaism and humanity.'"[32]

The volume's affirmation of Jewry as a *Volksgemeinschaft*, Kohn insisted, had nothing to do with racial theories and other putatively scientific conceptions of ethnicity. "Zionism is of a different order altogether. It is not a form of knowledge, but life"—life embodied in "the rise of a new type of Jew."[33] Born of a realization that "life is a continuous struggle," this "New, Zionist Jew" struggles "against all that is old, inert, tired, and no longer capable of growth."[34] Zionism was thus presented as the struggle and voice of youth, though among its twenty-three contributors there were representatives of an older generation as well, such as Karl Wolfskehl, a poet affiliated with the Stefan George circle; the literary critic Margarete Susman, whom Buber befriended at Simmel's salon; and his close friend, the anarchist Gustav Landauer. The essays, particularly by the members of Bar Kochba, explored issues raised by Buber in his *Drei Reden* and subsequent lectures in Prague: Jewish religiosity, the Jew as bearer of distinctive Oriental sensibilities, Jesus and early Christianity as expressions of Urjudentum, and Judaism and humanity. Significantly, as an expression of the Bar Kochba Association's affirmation of aspects of traditional Jewish religiosity (as conceived by Buber), the volume concludes with passages from the Zohar, the foundational text of Kabbalah, selected by Micha Josef bin Gorion (the pen name of M. J. Berdyczewski) and translated by various members of the association.

For a planned second edition of the volume, Hans Kohn and his colleagues received (though ultimately rejected) an unsolicited essay that was severely critical of trends in both Jewish and Christian religious thought in which God was reduced to a conceptual projection of human experience. This essay, entitled (with an arresting oxymoron) "Atheistic Theology," was written by a twenty-eight-year-old scholar of German philosophy, Franz Rosenzweig.[35] Although Rosenzweig did not mention him by name, Buber was clearly one of the Jewish thinkers he had in mind as having removed the God of biblical faith from their conception of Judaism and spirituality, thereby failing to affirm the transcendent, autonomous God who initiates a relationship with human beings and the world through the act of revelation.

Any intention that Buber might have had to respond to Rosenzweig was deflected by more urgent concerns surrounding the mounting threat of war. In early June 1914, Buber joined a small group of eight prominent intellectuals from various countries on a three-day retreat to consider establishing a "supranational [spiritual] authority" to prevent what they perceived to be the impending conflagration facing Europe. At the suggestion of the eccentric mystical pacifist Erich Gutkind, the son of a wealthy Berlin Jewish industrialist, the retreat was convened at his parents' summer home on the shore of the tranquil waters of Jungfernsee, a lake just north of Potsdam, Germany. In addition to Buber and Gutkind, six others attended, including Gustav Landauer; Frederik van Eeden, a Dutch pacifist and psychiatrist whose utopian vision was the group's principal source of inspiration; Florens Christian Rang, a German Protestant theologian and Prussian civil servant; Dutch sinologist D. Henri Borel; Poul Bjerre, a Swedish psychoanalyst with strong ties to Freud; and the Expressionist poet and art critic Theodor Däubler.

The gathering came to be known as the Forte Circle, because its official founding as a transnational spiritual authority was to take place in August 1914 before a much larger group at Forte dei Marmi, Italy—an event that did not come to pass due to the outbreak of the war about which the "group of eight" had dark premonitions. The intense exchange at the preparatory meeting and its aftermath ultimately caused a decisive turn in Buber's intellectual trajectory, what Hans Kohn called Buber's "breakthrough" to the philosophy of dialogue.[36] Somewhat less emphatically, Buber himself recalled the conclave at Gutkind's summer home as a seminal moment in shaping his understanding of dialogue as a spontaneous "inter-human" encounter:

> Without our having agreed beforehand on any sort of modalities for our talk, all the presuppositions of genuine dia-

logue were fulfilled. From the first hour [interpersonal] immediacy reigned between all of us, some of whom had just gotten to know one another; everyone spoke with an unheard-of openness, and clearly not a single one of the participants was in the bondage of semblance. With respect to its stated purpose, the meeting must be regarded as a failure (though even now in my heart it is still not a certainty that it had to be a failure). . . . Nevertheless, in the time that followed, not one of the participants doubted that he shared in a triumph of the inter-human (*an einem Triumph des Zwischenmenschlichen*).[37]

Buber credited van Eeden with the atmosphere that encouraged the development of "genuine conversation," and nominated him to become chair of the Forte Circle, a position to which he was subsequently elected. In a letter to van Eeden, Buber affectionately noted:

You did not take an active part in any of the discussions, and yet you were present in each of them by virtue of the trusting kindness of the look with which you regarded each of us. You beheld us with your whole soul. You looked at each of the disputants not neutrally, no, but joyfully and full of love. You saw with loving clarity the transition from speaking *to* one another to meeting one another. . . . Most of all, you were there with your eyes, not as one who consciously observes but as one who looks on naturally. . . . You entered with your gaze into the happenings between us. Your gaze lived in the space of our conversations, when we fought with one another and met each other in mutual deliverance, we met at the same time in the life of your gaze. And that helped us.[38]

Van Eeden for his part noted in his diary his initial impression of Buber at the preparatory meeting of the Forte Circle: "The slender, fragile, subtle but strong Buber, with his straight look and soft eyes, weak and velvety, yet deep and sharp. A rabbi [*sic*], but without a narrow mind, a philosopher, but without aridity, a scholar but without self-conceit."[39]

In a 1929 essay in which Buber elaborated his concept of dialogue in a narrative voice, punctuated with occasional autobiographical anecdotes, he would recollect a fraught exchange with Florens Christian Rang when the Forte Circle had gathered to consider whom to invite to the larger meeting scheduled to take place in Italy in August 1914. Rang protested that an inordinate number of Jews had been nominated, which would lead to their "unseemly" disproportionate representation in the circle. Clearly piqued by what he construed to be an anti-Semitic stance, Buber recalled that the "obstinate Jew that I am, I protested against [Rang's] protest. I no longer know how I came to speak of Jesus and to say that we Jews know him from within, in the impulses and stirrings of our being, in a way that remains inaccessible to people submissive to him." Addressing the former clergyman directly, he repeated pointedly, "In a way that remains inaccessible to you." In response, Rang "stood up"—and immediately, so did Buber. "We looked into the heart of one's another eyes." And Rang declared, "It is gone"—and "before everyone we gave one another the kiss of brotherhood."[40]

The beginnings of Buber's lifelong dialogue with Christians can be traced back to this exchange with Rang. Decades later, Buber would write: "The discussion of the situation between Jews and Christians had been transformed into a bond between the Christian and the Jew."[41] The communication of thoughts can at best lay the ground of interfaith dialogue, a communion between individuals that transcends thought, even language.

The outbreak in August 1914 of the war, which would convulse Europe for four protracted years, dashed the hopes of the Forte Circle to launch that very month their envisioned transnational "spiritual authority" to prevent the catastrophe. That "Vesuvian hour," as Buber put it, marked the eruption of a febrile nationalism that would enrapture several members of the Forte Circle. As soon as Germany entered the fray, fifty-year-old Rang volunteered to fight in the Kaiser's army. From the front he cheerfully informed van Eeden: "My dear friend, I am conscripted—hurrah! And may I join in this struggle of the most noble and the most peace loving people against envy and vengefulness, which seeks to strangle [us]."[42] Less than a month later, he wrote a long letter to Buber justifying his donning "the uniform of war" as a supernal, messianic duty:

> The human being who has been thrust into the uniform of war conducts a dialogue with all the fibers of his will with the Other inside himself, with the Thou in which humanity gives ear to its own demands. . . . Something beyond contention, absolutely necessary, transcendent, is breaking through to the surface! Man is once again serving God in freedom. . . . My grievance with our time is that we cannot live with our souls. But now the dictum of old Heraclitus *polemis arche panton* [war is the beginning of things] is once more coming true, and the bleeding [bourgeois] hearts (always aiming at happiness, peacetime prosperity) have fallen on their faces, while in their place there emerges in the consciousness of nations the one thing that is universal: the spirit of sacrifice. What for? Who knows? But surely not for something that could be defined as an instrumental end, especially not, say, the end of regaining peace, prosperity, and the like. . . . The modern age of *faith* is dawning, in which people believe in what they are doing because they are doing what God wills, not what their own human welfare wills. I am not speaking of enthusiasm for war—which fortunately is not rampant in Germany—I am speaking of the fearsome inner resolve to give one's life for the unknown higher cause. Nation and fatherland are in this case mere covering labels . . . the real core is the Divine.[43]

Less than two weeks after receiving Rang's letter, Buber in a similar vein wrote to Hans Kohn, then serving in the Austrian army:

> Never has the concept of peoplehood (*Volk*) become such a reality to me as it has during these weeks [since the beginning of the war]. Among the Jews, too, the prevailing feeling is one of solemn exaltation. . . . I myself unfortunately have not the slightest prospect of being utilized, but I am trying to help in my own way. . . . [Echoing Rang's theological exaltation of the war, Buber adds:] To everyone who would like to save himself in these times, the words of the Gospel of John apply: "He who loves his life loses it" [12:25]. . . . If we Jews could really feel, feel through and through, what this means to us: that we no longer need our old motto, *Not by might, but by spirit* [Zechariah 4:6; cited in Hebrew], since power and spirit are going to become one. *Incipit vita nova* [A new life has begun; an allusion to Dante's *La Vita Nuova*].[44]

The sense of fraternity born of common struggle led to similar nationalistic enthusiasm among many German intellectuals, irrespective of their previous political commitments. Buber's teacher Georg Simmel, for instance, who detested Prussian militarism, nevertheless approvingly greeted the war as evoking a healthy, robust sense of community; even the most indifferent German, he proclaimed, now "bears the whole in himself, he feels himself responsible for the whole."[45] What distinguished Buber's particular position was his tendency to view the war from the perspective of his Erlebnis-mysticism. The war, he held—or rather the Erlebnis quickened by the war, shared by both those on the battlefield and the civilian population alike— ushered in an "eon of realization" of unity and an overcoming of the divisive individualism of modern society.

In the wake of the German invasion of France and Belgium, van Eeden wrote a letter to the members of the Forte Circle in which he condemned Germany's actions.[46] In response, Buber wrote a long letter to van Eeden in which he expressed agreement with his Dutch friend's remonstrations against the brutality of war and the crass myopia of realpolitik, but faulted van Eeden for his failure to distinguish between the horror of war and the metaphysical significance of the *Kriegserlebnis*, the spiritual experience engendered by the war. Objecting to van Eeden's characterization of the enthusiastic support for the war by all the populations engaged in the conflict as "mass psychosis," Buber argues that at least from what he had observed in Germany "there is no sign of hysteria. . . . What prevails everywhere is a calm, clear resolution and readiness to sacrifice. At the bottom of all hearts may be found [an] unconditional faith in an absolute value, to die for which will mean the fulfillment of life." Although still inchoate, this "elemental emotion," when it attains its "true direction," will having nothing to do with "patriotism or nationalism or the like."[47] It was, Buber explained to his Dutch friend, to be understood as an awakening of *kinesis*, what in his book of 1913, *Daniel*, he referred to as a "nameless spark . . . through which the deed from being the experience of an individual becomes an occurrence given to all."[48]

Kinesis, an Aristotelian term for the transition from the potential to the actual, denotes for Buber the power actuating the longed-for realization of unity, albeit without a specific direction.[49] "We long for kinesis, and suddenly with the war we witness its glorious arousal; it has been our solitary wish until now, lying dormant in us, and we were unable to awaken it."[50] The awakening of kinesis is the "magic power" of the war.[51] Hence, despite "the horrors and bitter anguish of this war," it constitutes a moment of grace, a "terrible grace, the grace of a new birth."[52]

To be sure, kinesis has yet to find its true "direction" and indeed "kinesis without direction is blind" (though "direction without kinesis is lame").[53] But Buber seeks to reassure van

Eeden that once aroused, kinesis "will grow more and more conscious of its direction and doing so create its own world."[54] As he wrote in an essay "Direction Shall Come," published a few weeks after his letter to van Eeden, "we believe that the [surge of kinesis] will swell over the war and become the power of a new age of realization."[55]

Buber thus appeals to van Eeden to acknowledge the dialectical importance of the war, as horrific as it is, in unleashing kinesis—a powerful stirring of moribund souls. The Age of Kinesis inaugurated by the war is to be likened to the work of a ploughshare and the violent upheaval of encrusted soil; the sowing comes only afterward. To maximize its effectiveness, the ploughshare must be unencumbered by the ethical will. It is precisely in order to achieve its initial task that kinesis is unfettered by rational, ethically determined, unifying direction. Its significance is not to be sought in its content, but in its compelling force to unconditional action.

Nevertheless, for Buber, allegiance to a fatherland (constituting a direction of sorts) did, in fact, have the emotive power to inspire unconditioned action and to free the individual from the bourgeois ethos of self-serving instrumental aims, and so is not irrelevant to kinesis. But the evaluation of the metaphysical significance of the spiritual experience of war should not be confused with the troubling nature of the realities of war and nationalism.

Patriotism, then, should not be summarily rejected. Kinesis is aroused in the Dutch and in the Swiss when each fights for his respective fatherland—provided that each ultimately "means God when they say fatherland."[56] For Buber, it does not matter that it is patriotism that drives the members of contending armies to fight—and thus kill—one another. Though God is One, God is realized through diverse, even conflicting kinetic experiences that inspire unconditional, self-sacrificial action. In an age that seems to have been abandoned by God, the period of the war is instead one of "the Unconditioned's revelation."[57] Accordingly, as Buber sought to explain to van Eeden that: "the experience of these times confirms me in my fundamental view that our connection with the Absolute is not in our knowledge but in our actions. We do not experience the Absolute in what we learn but in what we create. The Absolute is not manifest in us as a What but as a How, not as something to be thought but as something to be lived." Even in mortal conflict, it is thus the common experience of the Absolute that ultimately establishes the universal bonds of humanity. The Kriegserlebnis bonds individuals, whatever their national affiliation and loyalties, in a "transcendental" unity, a unity eminently more real than the lesser unity engendered by patriotism.

> Therefore, it is not those who harbor the same intentions who are transcendentally close and related to one another, but those who carry out their intentions—no matter how disparate—in the same way; not those who profess the same beliefs, but those who translate what they believe into deeds with the same intensity, integrity, directness, etc. . . . And what is true of individuals is true of peoples.[58]

Kinesis, or that which endows individuals with the requisite power and the intensity of action needed to break the shackles of a life conditioned by convention, tradition, and instrumental rationality, is then the true source of community—the path to this "transcendental" community arising through one's local community, connected with feelings toward fatherland and nation. However Buber may have wished to avoid this conclusion, his position amounted to a metaphysical endorsement of German nationalism and, in effect, the war.

Although Buber had yet to articulate his "metaphysics of war" in print, he apparently shared his views with Gutkind, who, in turn, related them in a conversation to Landauer. Following that conversation, a greatly agitated Gutkind telephoned

Buber and reported that Landauer had accused both him and Buber of "aestheticism"—of viewing the world through the lens of quasi-aesthetic categories, unconscionably beautifying an ugly reality. Immediately after receiving Gutkind's call, Buber dashed off a letter, dated October 18, 1914, to Landauer, in which he urged him not to accept Gutkind's report of his views at face value:

> Gutkind probably misunderstood me. Eeden is the one person I felt I had to answer by letter, and on the other hand there are many things I cannot write to him that I can to you. I'll be glad to talk with you as soon as possible, although I'd rather not do so in a café, preferably in your home or ours. Gutkind reports that you charge me—as you do him—with aestheticism. Can you really misunderstand me so much and confound me with others? I cannot believe it.[59]

In his letter, Buber also makes parenthetical reference to some action of his thirteen-year-old daughter Eva that had offended Landauer and his wife, and expresses the hope that the incident would not affect their friendship either, concluding: "In general, I would consider any estrangement among us adults a calamity. I mean, our relationship is so solidly founded that none of this can shake it, and hope you think likewise."

They appear to have made amends, but concerns about epistolary communication and disagreement persisted, regarding their larger Forte Circle. A month later, Landauer and Buber cosigned a letter dated "end of November 1914" to the members of the Forte Circle, calling for its original eight members to convene by the end of the year. The meeting, they wrote, was urgent because in the "epistolary exchanges" between members of the circle, some troubling differences had surfaced. Since these differences might in part have been due to a "semantic" confusion that had been only compounded by written correspondence, "the advantage of personal encounters over discussion through letters need not be spelled out." Hence "we are duty bound to hold another meeting of the original group"—and despite the ongoing war engulfing Europe as they had feared, as soon as possible. "In this time of bitter testing, we have to determine by direct contact whether we are the right people for one another and are equal to our first task: in spite of and because of the divergences in our character and thinking, to let our mutual interaction take its course with the fullest respect and faith." Only when this is clarified, he said, would they be in the position to "evolve as a community that would be of some significance for the future of the world."[60]

The proposed meeting did not come to pass, and both Landauer and Buber soon announced that they no longer regarded themselves as members of the Forte Circle. In a letter to van Eeden in September 1915, Buber explained the reasons for his resignation in terms that clearly suggested he was now fully in accord with Landauer, whom he noted was "the only one of us who had clearly seen the snarl we were getting into before things had gone too far":

> I no longer belong to [the Forte Circle]—not since I saw it as a phantom. In the rapture of those three days [we spent at the summer home of Gutkind], it seemed to be alive . . . and I thought that in it might lie the primal cell of that legitimate [spiritual] authority, which I consider more necessary than anything else. I recognized my self-deception when it turned out that the circle was not—as it ought to have been—superior to events but was dominated by them; that it did not stand outside the tremendous tangle of the nations from which those events stemmed but was involved in it and deeply caught up in it. . . . May the ghost of the circle, which I was once very close to loving, remain far from me![61]

Concerns about the implications of one's support or critique of the war in its particulars also hit home. The same day that he mailed the letter to van Eeden, Buber wrote to Paula, reassuring her that a critique by Bjerre of Rang's theological glorification of the war as "Lutheran" was not meant to impugn German culture or the Germans. Bjerre is "solely against Rang's ideology of war. . . . So calm down, my dearest." In the same letter he informed his wife that "I no longer belong to the [Forte] circle, and neither does Landauer."[62] Two days later, he again wrote to Paula, reiterating that although he had some reservations about Bjerre's critique of Rang's theology, it "has nothing to do with German culture and Germans." She should rest assured that his own abiding fidelity to German culture and Germany is, in fact, reflected in his decision not to "collaborate with people like van Eeden who distort the great problem of the moment and transform the just slogan 'against the entanglement of the nations' into an incitement against Germany. . . . So I cannot work with Eeden as long as he goes on parroting English slogans." He further explains to his wife, "In general, at present, I do not care for international meetings at all and expect nothing from them. But it is important to me to gather together those people *inside Germany* who are seeking a way out of the entanglement into an atmosphere of freedom and truth, and who are striving to build a new Germany that will know how to go about using its strength for just ends." Accordingly, "I now find myself joining with people like Landauer."[63]

Buber and Landauer indeed appear to have been fully reconciled and their friendship firmly secured. They cooperated on various projects, and their families continued to visit one another regularly. But returning to Berlin after one such visit to Paula and Martin in their new home in Heppenheim, a bucolic town located some thirty-three miles south of Frankfurt am Main, Landauer read some of Buber's recently published essays addressed to the Jewish community and saw, much to his chagrin, that the *Kriegsbuber* (the War-Buber), as he now bitingly called him, was still very much alive and kicking. In a long letter from May 1916, he informed Buber that certain passages in these writings "are very painful to me, most repugnant and border on incomprehensibility."[64] He specifically referred to Buber's recently published essay "The Spirit of the Orient and Judaism," in which Buber refers to Germany's "world historical mission" in the war to bridge the Occident and the Orient and thereby to rescue the Oriental Spirit (of which Judaism is a quintessential representative) endangered by the aggressive forces of the West.[65] "Object as you will," Landauer exclaims, "I call this a species of aestheticism and formalism, and I say you have no right—in your own best interests—to publicly take a stand on political events of the day, which is called the World War; you have *no right to try and tuck these tangled events into your philosophical scheme;* what results is inadequate and outrageous."[66]

Significantly, Landauer prefaced his criticism of the Kriegsbuber by noting that the time they had spent together in Heppenheim confirmed their "fellowship" (Gemeinschaft), a "fellowship that existed before the war and will outlast it." Due to that bond of fellowship, as Landauer had conceded to his wife, Hedwig, a year earlier, he had chosen to overlook his friend's tendency to "extravagant and uncritical expression"; an individual of acute "poetic sensitivity," Buber "allows for no analysis whatsoever and becomes particularly incensed when one speaks of mass-suggestion." He was to be forgiven, for "he thoroughly appreciates my position towards the war."[67] But when Landauer read Buber's more recent writings on the metaphysical significance of the war for Jewry, he could no longer dismiss Buber's words as mere poetic hyperbole, and thus as inconsequential.

Buber's paean to the New Jew to which the war had given birth made Landauer's "blood boil." The readiness with which tens of thousands of young Jews joined the ranks of the various armies in the conflict, Buber proclaimed, heralded the emergence of a new, heroic Jew. This Jew "does not suffer passively, but fights; he does not forever ponder, but decides"—he is a Jew who acts on his convictions![68] The fact that Jewish soldiers were wearing the uniforms of opposing armies, and thus were obliged to kill one another, was, to be sure, tragic, but in the ultimate scheme of things, of little significance. For although "Jewish soldiers are fighting one another, they nevertheless fight for their Jewishness."[69]

The paradox, Buber told an audience of Zionists in Berlin at a Chanukah celebration in December 1914, is apparent. Why, he asked the festive gathering, does the Jewish religious tradition focus its celebration on the rededication of the Temple in Jerusalem, rather than on the military victory of the Maccabean warriors? Because, in accordance with Judaism's religious genius, the tradition rightly understands that "all external events are but symbols of inner, hidden cosmic events; external liberation is but a symbol of . . . the inner liberation of the suffering and struggling world from the power of evil. The locus where this liberation is directly manifest is in the soul."[70] In the Maccabean revolt, the Jewish warriors overcame *malkhut yavan ha-resha'ah*, the evil dominion of Hellenistic Greece, the symbol of the world's fundamental evil, which the Hasidic master Nachman of Bratzlav identifies with egotistic desire. This desire enslaves contemporary bourgeois civilization to instrumental ends, which by their very nature destroy the fabric of human solidarity.[71] The vanquishing of malkhut yavan was thus in the deepest sense an act of self-purification—symbolized by the rededication of the Jerusalem Temple.

Now in the World War, he said, the Jewish warrior is again seeking victory over malkhut yavan—this time battling his inner enslavement to false, idolatrous values and ambition. The latter-day Maccabean is passing through a liberating *Gemeinschaftserlebnis*—a deep inner experience of Gemeinschaft that purges him of egotistic desire. "A feeling of Gemeinschaft has been set aglow in him, he feels something burning in himself before which all instrumental aims collapse."[72] Even though he fights for a European nation-state, like Judah Maccabee before him, the Jewish soldier of 1914—irrespective of which flag he follows into battle—"has overcome his inner duality, and has become a unified [person]."[73] Once again, the Jew is capable of serving the world.

This Gemeinschaftserlebnis, Buber believed, is of special significance for the Western Jew, whose deepest problem is not that he is assimilated, but rather that he is atomized and fragmented—the dictates of modern civilization have torn him from the source of wholeness, his primordial community, and his heart is no longer guided by "the heartbeat of a living community."[74] This atomized Jew, having experienced community (fostered in war), will in time hearken to the "call of the deep community of his [own] blood."[75] To be sure, in wartime Jews find themselves subject to the urgings of a community not of their own; they will emerge from the war with a deeply felt need to sustain and deepen their experience of fraternal bonding, and "return" to the primordial community of their fellow Jews.

Buber reiterated this thesis in the editorial introducing the inaugural issue of *Der Jude*, a monthly publication he founded in April 1916—in the midst of the World War—and edited until 1924. In that editorial, entitled "Die Losung" (The watchword), he quoted extensively from his Berlin Chanukah address of December 1914, and added: "What I said at the time has since been confirmed. . . . By virtue of the Jewish Erlebnis of this war, erstwhile assimilated Jews now feel responsible for the destiny of their own community (*Gemeinschaft*). A new Jewry has taken shape."[76]

It was this proclamation that Landauer found especially problematic. In his letter denouncing the Kriegsbuber, he angrily tells Buber that he must assume that he is included in Buber's "description of the psychological state of the Jews who cherish the passionate longing to participate in Europe's fateful hour on the battlefield and to share in the suffering."[77] Landauer sarcastically dismissed this "childish simplification" by suggesting that it is highly unlikely that the hundreds of thousands of Jews and non-Jews, whose supposed readiness to die in battle Buber celebrates, desire anything besides surviving the war and returning to their families and the tedium of everyday life:

> I feel myself personally disavowed. But I also feel that you are disavowing the thousands and tens of thousands of poor devils who are not at all conscious of a mission but are indeed submitting to compulsion out of a paramount duty (namely, to live), because by so doing they can hope they will be more likely to come out alive. . . . Is there not an ordinary person in this psychology of yours? The Jews left out of Buber's equation, the average Jews, feel that this madness is none of their affair and that they would be shot if they did not submit; they feel that what counts in this war is to survive in order to go on peddling or carrying whatever trade theirs may be, and to go on living with wife and children.[78]

Landauer comments with bitter sarcasm that Buber should be humble enough to acknowledge that among the vast multitude of combatants currently engaged in deadly battle, "there were, say, twenty to thirty-seven who did not go off to war out of an overwhelming sense of duty." Moreover, Landauer noted, the emotions and modes of acting that Buber applauds—"virility, manliness, sacrificial courage, devotion"—are not intrinsic or unique to the experience of war. "No living human being senses and needs such a detour." He similarly found it utterly scandalous that Buber saw in the carnage of war, destruction, and death "the spirit of community," cavalierly imposing on it a conceptual construct drawn entirely from his wishful imagination. Though this imposition grew out of Buber's "desire to see greatness . . . desire alone is not sufficient to make greatness out of a confused vulgarity." The true sense of Gemeinschaft that humankind seeks is distant and distinct from everything associated with war, and requires no dialectic of the kind presented by Buber in his fanciful defense of the metaphysics of war. Landauer's long and acerbic letter concludes with a refusal to cooperate with Buber's newly founded journal *Der Jude*—that is, as long as the journal and its editor continued explicitly or implicitly to support the war. "A journal that publishes . . . what the Hapsburgs and the Hohenzollerns, and the interests allied with them want to hear, but does not publish contrary views, cannot be my journal."[79]

Buber was clearly taken aback by Landauer's trenchant criticism and the tone of his rebuke. The initial blow was surely not mollified by the reassurance with which Landauer had prefaced his excoriation, that the fellowship they had forged prior to the war would endure beyond it. Shortly after Buber received the letter, the two men met over several days at Landauer's home, from July 11 to July 14, 1916. Whatever transpired, it is evident that their time together occasioned a radical transformation in Buber's thinking—marked by a fundamental break with his Erlebnis-mysticism. This transformation paved the way for his philosophy of dialogue, which would be formally inaugurated by the publication of *I and Thou* in 1923. In his writings published after the summer of 1916, we notice three new distinctive elements: an explicit opposition to the war and chauvinistic nationalism; a reevaluation of the function and meaning of Erlebnis; and most significantly, a shifting of the axis of Gemeinschaft from individual consciousness to interpersonal relations.

In September 1916, Buber addressed an open letter to his "Prague friends": "You who are in danger, you in captivity, you in the trenches (*Gräben*) and you in graves (*Gräbern*)." For a moment, Buber tells his friends (referring to the members of the Bar Kochba then in uniform) that he was possessed by a vision that they and he were together once again. In this vision, Buber and his friends, strolling along the streets and visiting the taverns of "immortal" Prague, were engaged in amiable and edifying conversation. Surely, in this moment when "those holy hours of great togetherness" are reborn, Buber relates to his Prague friends, one word comes forth "out of our memory, from out of the memory of the world-spirit: Sabbath."[80] But, alas, it is not Sabbath. Why not? Buber's answer is allegorical.

The Golem of Prague, the human-shaped mass of clay said to have been created by the wondrous sixteenth-century Rabbi Judah Loew, was reportedly brought to life by placing under its tongue a piece of paper upon which was inscribed God's secret Name. But as the Sabbath arrived, Rabbi Loew would remove the sacred piece of paper from under the Golem's tongue so that it could join in the Sabbath rest. Should the paper not be removed, however, the Golem would go berserk and threaten the Sabbath peace. And so it happened that one Friday evening, with the start of the Sabbath, Rabbi Loew somehow forgot to remove the sacred paper from under the Golem's tongue. As a result of his unfortunate oversight, the Sabbath was detained both in heaven and on earth. Buber cryptically concluded: "Friends, it is not yet Sabbath. We must first remove the holy name from under the Golem's tongue."[81] The crazed automaton to which he alludes, of course, is the war, brought to life by human folly and animated with a misguided and fatal attribution of its sacredness.

# 6

*Heir to Landauer's Legacy*

A CHASTENED BUBER radically revised his views—about the still-raging war that was ravaging Europe, but also about political nationalism. In a letter of February 4, 1917, requesting revisions to an article submitted to *Der Jude*, Buber, the journal's editor, urged the author, Moritz Goldstein, to reconsider his claim that though nationalism is a mistaken path to community, patriotic loyalty to the state engenders positive, genuine, and enduring communal bonds. Clearly annoyed by what he found to be a specious argument, Buber chides him, "Yes, I too have 'overcome nationalism,' but certainly not in favor of the idea of the state." In response to Goldstein's myopic celebration of patriotism per se, born of a disaffection with the experience of war, Buber responds that it is not consistent with his experience. "What I and some of the best among my friends in the field and at the home-front have experienced" is that both a nation and a state are at best relative ideals, legitimate only to the extent that they foster the birth of a new humanity. These "cursory words," he concludes, should suffice "to indicate . . . that there exists a different experience of these years, a different lesson derived from them, a different 'conquest of nationalism' inspired by them," and, moreover, "a different conception, generated by [this experience], of our task as Jews"—a task he identifies with Zionism.[1]

Exactly a year later, in a letter of February 4, 1918, Buber assured the novelist and playwright Stefan Zweig that Zionism did not aspire to establish yet another political state. Zweig, the author of a recently published pacifist play, *Jeremiah*, had asked Buber whether, in the wake of the sobering lessons of the war, Zionism was still beholden to "the dangerous dream of a Jewish state with cannons, flags, [and] military decorations."[2] Zweig viewed *Jeremiah*—published in the midst of the war, and soon to have its premier performance in neutral Switzerland— as a "hymn to the Jewish people," who, suffering eternal defeat, had transformed their fate. That fate would the source of a new Jerusalem: a life beyond political nationhood, embodying the vision of transnational human solidarity, and a "permanent rebellion" against the very notion of a nation-state and its pernicious claims. As a Jew, he explained to Buber, he had "resolved to love the painful idea of the Diaspora, to cherish the Jewish fate more than Jewish well-being." What will remain of the Jews spiritually, he asked Buber, if they deny their destiny to dwell among the nations of the world as a people that has transcended the folly of nationalism? The establishment of a Jewish state in Palestine, Zweig held, would be a betrayal of the people's prophetic vocation and thus a "tragic disappointment."

In response to Zweig's impassioned affirmation of the Diaspora, Buber registered his own distrust of nationalism and the nation-state and clarified the nature of his abiding Zionist commitment. Acknowledging the troubling ambiguities of

Zionist aspirations, he tells Zweig that they must be embraced as a creative challenge if Judaism is to cease being an ethereal, disembodied entity, devoid of concrete expression:

> I do not know anything of a "Jewish state with cannons, flags, and military decorations," not even as a dream. What will become [of the Zionist project] depends on those who create it. And precisely for that reason individuals like me, who are of a human and humane disposition, must take a resolute part *here*, where human beings are once again granted the opportunity of building a community (*Gemeinschaft*). . . . I for my part prefer to participate in the extraordinary venture of something new, in which I do not see much "well-being" but quite a good deal of great sacrifices. I prefer this, rather than to go on enduring the Diaspora, which for all its beautiful and painful fertility, passes on the nourishing substance of that [purely spiritual] movement piece by piece to inner decay. I even would prefer a tragic disappointment to a not-at-all tragic but continual and hopeless degeneration.[3]

Yet only a day before sending his letter to Zweig, Buber had confided in a letter to Hugo Bergmann, a member of the Bar Kochba circle who would become one of his closest lifelong friends, that he too harbored the fear that Zionism might very well degenerate into unalloyed political nationalism:

> We must not deceive ourselves that most of today's leading Zionists (and probably also most of those who are led) are thoroughly unrestrained nationalists (following the European example), imperialists, even unconscious mercantilists and worshipers of [material] success. They speak about rebirth and mean enterprise. If we do not succeed to construct an authoritative counterforce, the soul of the movement will be corrupted, possibly forever.[4]

Manifestly alarmed by "the misguided spirit" that he feared had overtaken Zionism, Buber wrote to Bergmann, "I am at any rate determined to throw myself into the struggle [against this lamentable development] with everything I have."[5]

Buber's fears had been especially aroused by the publication in November 1917 of the Balfour Declaration, which aligned the Zionist project with British colonialism. With bitter sarcasm, he warned that Britain would introduce into Palestine *Fußball-geist*, the spirit of soccer, and worse, "the demon of mercantilism." Buber's opposition to the Balfour Declaration placed him at odds with most Zionists, even those who like him gave priority to cultural renewal. In this regard, the Hebrew novelist Shai Agnon recounted an exchange between Buber and Ahad Ha'am, the *spiritus rector* of cultural Zionism. Sometime after Lord Balfour issued his letter proclaiming Great Britain's commitment to the "establishment in Palestine of a national home for the Jewish people," Agnon, then living in Germany, invited Buber, Ahad Ha'am, and the Hebrew poet Chaim Nachman Bialik to his home in a suburb of Frankfurt am Main. Sitting on the balcony of Agnon's apartment overlooking a garden of pine trees, they discussed (presumably in Yiddish, their common language) the most pressing issues facing the Jewish nation.

The conversation eventually touched upon the Balfour Declaration, at which point Ahad Ha'am argued that, should the Zionist movement fail to seize the opportunity presented by the declaration to establish a Jewish homeland in Palestine, it would be a grievous error—indeed, it would be the forfeiture of the last opportunity to bring about the nation's "redemption." Visibly taken aback, Buber protested that he envisioned the people's redemption to come about in a fundamentally different manner. With a gentle smile at what he undoubtedly regarded as Buber's incorrigible romanticism, Ahad Ha'am, the rationalist, bowed his head in silence.[6] Agnon, too, saw Buber's position as endearingly idealistic, as well as anachronistic. Buber, he would write decades later, was "among the remaining few who still upheld a belief, inherited from the cosmopolitan spirit of the Enlightenment, that in the first instance, we are to regard ourselves as citizens of the world dedicated to *tikkun olam* [repair of the world]. . . . He nurtured this view with a cherubic innocence, a purity of heart, but at times with extreme naiveté."[7] What Ahad Ha'am and Agnon regarded as naiveté, however, Buber held to be a "greater realism," viewing the prevailing political pragmatism of the Zionist movement as short-sighted. Although his voice would be increasingly marginalized, in the initial years of the British Mandate of Palestine he continued to argue that the diversity of Zionist ideological discourse, especially with regard to the movement's ultimate political objective, merited resisting the pull toward political nationalism and realpolitik.

In the decades before the establishment of the State of Israel, the *Endziel*, the ultimate goal of Zionism, was indeed officially left undefined, if only to avoid antagonizing the British Mandatory government and the Arabs of Palestine.[8] Placing in brackets the Endziel of Zionism had the effect of encouraging open debate on the objectives of the movement. Rejecting the goal of Jewish political sovereignty in Palestine, Buber was reluctant to define the Jews as a "nation," preferring to call them a "people" (Volk). The significance of this semantic distinction is highlighted in an exchange he had during the summer of 1916 with Hermann Cohen, the doyen of German neo-Kantian philosophers. Cohen, who was prominently associated with liberal Judaism, assailed Zionism for undermining the integration of Jewry into German culture and civil society, and believed that Zionism betrayed the religious vocation of Jewry, which should instead be to act as "suffering servants," dispersed among the nations, heralding the future messianic era of universal fraternity, justice, and peace. The Jews, he argued, are not a nation, but merely a "nationality"—hence the necessary loss of its ancient statehood—since a nation is a political entity, which requires a state for its full expression, whereas a "nationality" is a "fact of nature," an ethnic group. (A nation-state may contain many nationalities; Cohen believed that in Germany, the Jews should be integrated into the German nation-state as members of one of its diverse nationalities, much like the Saxons, Bavarians, and Prussians.)

In response, Buber accused Cohen of terminological (and thus conceptual) obfuscation, arguing that the Jews are neither a nation nor a nationality, but rather a people (Volk):

> The Jewish people are not a fact of nature but a historical reality that can be compared to no other; not a concept but a towering [reality], living and dying before my and your eyes; not a means for the transmission of religion, but the bearer of this religion and with it all the Jewish ideologies, all [expressions of] the Jewish ethos, all [forms of Jewish] social life—a people debased as it has been [in the Diaspora] to dust.[9]

For Buber, the Jews as a people are characterized by their spiritual vocation, defined not solely by the Law of Moses but also by an ongoing quest to exemplify (rather than merely point to, as for Cohen) the ideal human community, and as such to be a "light unto the nations." Accordingly, Zionism does not, as Cohen contended, betray Judaism's "messianic ideal," for the realization of that ideal does not require "the dispersion, debasement, and homelessness" of the Jews. "The Jewish people must persevere in the midst of today's human order—not as a fixed, brittle fact of nature appended to an ever more diluted confessional religion, but as a people pursuing its ideal . . . *for the sake of the human order.*" Although for Buber, as for Cohen, a struggle for a "homeland" is by definition a national struggle, he saw Zionism as sui generis, because "the struggle for a Jewish communal existence in Palestine [is] a supranational one (*übernationales*)." That is, "we do not want Palestine for the Jews, we want it for humankind, for we want it for the *realization* of

Judaism."[10] Still, Buber would surely have been hard-pressed to elaborate what would in practice distinguish a "Jewish communal existence" (*jüdisches Gemeinwesen*) from a national "homeland" (*Heimstätte*) in Palestine. As we shall see, this ill-defined distinction would mostly function as a way of trying to steer the Zionist project away from unbridled political nationalism.

Before his exchange with Cohen went to press, Buber sent Landauer a copy of his statement, requesting comments. Landauer gave a qualified approval to Buber's attribution of universal significance to Zionism: "What you say about . . . the task of *a* people [the Jewish people] for humanity," he writes, "is of such a nature that I ought to say: for me too." Yet, he continues, the task of collective self-actualization, of benefit to the entire world, is incumbent on each people. He notes that he had in fact recently signed a proclamation calling upon the Germans to dedicate themselves to serving all of humanity. He did so, he tells Buber, "as a German who feels responsible for what other Germans do to themselves and other peoples." His allegiance to the German people, he assures Buber, "coexists with my Judaism without the slightest conflict." He noted that he had previously elaborated this position, writing of the "intimate unity" of his dual identity as a Jew and German, which he would not deny by distinguishing "one element of this relationship within myself as primary, and the other, as secondary. I have never felt the need to simplify myself or to create an artificial unity by way of denial; I accept my complexity and hope to be an even more multifarious unity than I am now aware of." He pointedly expressed his dismay that, in contrast, in Buber's rebuttal of Cohen's affirmation of a German-Jewish identity, he spoke "*wholly* as a Jew."[11]

Buber conceded that he regarded his dual identity as a German and a Jew differently than Landauer did, but insisted that his position was not the same as that of the "official Jewish nationalists. I do not reject dualism as they do; rather I acknowledge it like you, but unlike you I feel it to be a dynamic and tragic problem, a spiritual *agon* [struggle], which like any agon, can become creative."[12] By framing settlement of the Land of Israel as a propitious context in which to pursue this struggle, he held, Zionism challenges the Jews to live with their dual identity at its deepest and spiritually most authentic level—that is, both as Jews and as citizens of the world, beholden to the prophetic voice of universal fraternity. Thus, in an essay written a few weeks after the Russian Revolution of March 1917, he called on his fellow Jews to celebrate the liberation of the masses of Russia from Tsarist tyranny. "We do not separate our human and Jewish feelings, human and Jewish responses from one another. We celebrate the freedom of human beings, the freedom of peoples, whoever they may be. . . . We believe that the emancipation of the Jews and that of humanity go hand in hand, for we believe that humanity's soul is beginning to come of age. Our Zionism has its roots in this belief."[13]

Buber's political vision developed and shifted during his tenure as the editor of *Der Jude* beginning in the spring of 1916. Over a decade earlier, in the fall of 1903, Buber (together with Chaim Weizmann) had proposed the founding of a journal to be called *Der Jude* (The Jew), but the pair failed to marshal the necessary financial support for the project. The envisioned monthly, as Buber stated in the original prospectus, would address a younger generation of Jews "for whom Judaism is not something that is bygone and closed, not something banned to rigid formulas, but is the living spirit of the people in all its depth and breadth in all its variety, in all its forms and articulations."[14] With the outbreak of World War I, the idea of the journal was broached once again by the Jewish National Committee, which had been cofounded by Buber in October 1915. As Germany's troops pushed into Tsarist Russia, the committee sought to mobilize German public opinion in support of a comprehensive program to improve the lives of eastern European Jewry. Toward this end, the committee, which enjoyed the support of the World Zionist Organization, allocated funds to establish a journal and asked Buber to serve as its editor. Buber agreed—on the condition that the journal not be formally affiliated with the Zionist movement. This, he hoped, would let him include Zionists and non-Zionists (as well as non-Jews) as both writers and readers of a literary and political monthly of the highest quality.

Buber devoted himself fully to organizing and editing *Der Jude*, putting on the back burner all of his own major projects. For the next seven years, he did not take a vacation, often working from 8:00 a.m. to midnight. Moreover, he did not receive a salary (his financial support came from his father and dividends from properties bequeathed to him by his grandparents), though he did eventually receive a very modest monthly stipend to help defray incidental expenses.[15] He successfully recruited many leading minds of his day to contribute to the journal, assuring them that doing so would draw serious attention to what he regarded as the exigent political and cultural issues facing contemporary Jewry.

Buber did not limit his pursuit of contributors to established authors. Similar to when he had edited Herzl's *Die Welt* some fifteen years earlier, he sought to engage the voices of the younger generation, even those like Gershom Scholem who were critical of his views and literary style. Rafael Buber recalled the then nineteen-year-old Scholem paying an unannounced early morning visit to his father. Hearing the young man shouting at his father, Rafael ran to his father's study and waited outside, ready to pounce on the impudent intruder, but Scholem said his piece and quickly left. With his fists still clenched, the sixteen-year-old Rafael asked his father, "How did you let that rascal shout at you?" Buber softly replied, "My son, some day that young man will attain intellectual renown."[16]

Shortly after Scholem's outburst, Buber invited him to

contribute a critique of the Zionist youth movement to *Der Jude*.[17] At Scholem's behest, Buber also solicited an article from Scholem's friend Walter Benjamin, even though Buber had been deeply offended by a particularly vitriolic letter Benjamin had written to him, castigating the jingoism in *Der Jude*'s inaugural issue.[18] (What had actually troubled Buber, who since the publication of that first issue of the journal had recanted his own position toward the war, was Benjamin's thinly veiled but damning critique of Buber's expository voice: "To me, . . . every action that originates from the . . . heaping up of word upon word seems frightful . . . I continue to think that by striving for crystalline clarity and eliminating the unutterable in language, we will arrive at an acceptable and logical form for achieving effectiveness in language.")[19] Benjamin ultimately declined Buber's invitation to contribute to his journal. He was more successful, however, in soliciting an article from Franz Kafka. At first the little-known, diffident writer from Prague hesitated, explaining to Buber that he was "far too burdened and insecure to think of speaking up in such a company [of established authors], even in the most minor way."[20] But Buber persisted, and Kafka finally yielded. Learning that two of his short stories had been accepted for publication, Kafka humbly wrote: "So I will be published in *Der Jude* after all, and always thought that impossible."[21]

The numerous essays that Buber himself authored in the journal signal a shift in his conception of the axis of community (Gemeinschaft), away from subjective experience (Erlebnis) and toward interpersonal relations. He no longer conceived of Jewish renewal as principally an aesthetic-spiritual process. "Cultural work," he declared in an essay of March 1917, "is a misleading term," for "the word 'culture' is too great and too limited for what we want. What we want is not 'culture,' but life. *What we want is Jewish life.*" In a radical reversal of his previous teachings, Buber now contended that "what we want cannot be attained by spirit and creativity; it certainly does not come from 'culture.'" The renewal of Judaism cannot be realized through individual experience, he believed, but only in "living with, helping and serving one another."[22]

Buber's vision of community as the basis of Jewish renewal would henceforth be distinctively utopian, requiring nothing less than a radical transformation of the structure of human relations. His emerging ethical socialism bore the unmistakable imprint of Landauer, to whom he became particularly close after their reconciliation. While previously Buber had been primarily drawn to Landauer's writings on mysticism and literature, in a 1904 article with a palpably autobiographical echo he summarized Landauer's teachings as "self-liberation": "We must break all bonds in order to find ourselves. The prohibitions of laws ᵒnd traditions are nothing but impoverished, miserable words for one who deprives oneself of happiness."[23] In an earlier time, as the editor of *Die Gesellschaft*, Buber had little practical interest in Landauer's anarcho-socialism, even though he had commissioned Landauer to write a volume on revolution. But in the wake of Landauer's trenchant critique of his glorification of the war experience as engendering community, his friend's utopian socialism would now decisively inform Buber's vision of Jewish renewal.

Landauer was most pleased with this turn in Buber's thought. Upon reading Buber's polemical exchange with Hermann Cohen, in which his friend explained that the goal of Zionism was not the founding of a state but true human community, Landauer wrote Buber: "With what heartfelt joy, I once again read your Cohen booklet. Also in the notes there are much of those elements that bind us."[24] For Landauer, true socialism could not be realized only through institutional change, either of the power structures of the state or of the economic order: it required as well a fundamental spiritual regeneration of the individual and of the moral quality of interpersonal relations. Genuine social change would proceed from the individual, in a personal decision to awaken the love that slumbers within one's self and within others. Yet we should not be satisfied with the creation of an inner, personal socialism; we must call upon our "ethical will" and work toward a socialist society in the here and now.

Revolution, for Landauer, should take place to whatever degree possible under prevailing conditions, through the construction of alternative communitarian modes of social and economic conduct, including the nascent kibbutz movement in Palestine. His socialism was an endless historical process in which each generation would work to realize social and economic justice as much as possible—paradoxically inspired by the ideal that can never be fully realized. His seminal lecture "Aufruf zum Sozialismus" (Call to socialism) greatly informed what Buber would later call "Hebrew humanism" and, indeed, his philosophy of dialogue. At the funeral of Landauer's daughter Charlotte (who passed away in 1927 at the age of thirty-three), Buber would take the opportunity to summarize her father's political legacy in consonance with his own developing approach: the "new community of humankind for which we hope cannot coalesce out of [isolated] individuals . . . but rather there must exist cells, small communal cells out of which alone the great human community can be built."[25]

But the bond between Buber and Landauer, forged through their occasionally fraught dialogue on political and ethical issues, was not only ideological; it was primarily grounded in an existential bond of an enduring and earnest friendship. Indeed, Buber was one of Landauer's few genuine friends. As the theater critic Julius Bab noted, despite Landauer's prominence as a writer, translator, editor, and political activist, he "had very few friends in the true sense of this difficult word and also no lasting comrades. The demon in Landauer that sacrificed all the forces of his inner life to a passionate goal also sacrificed friendships and comradeships in great number. . . . Thus this prophet of genuine, deeply felt community was in his personal life almost a solitary man."[26] His friendship with Buber was a rare exception.

When the two first met at the Hart brothers' Neue Gemeinschaft in 1900, they were each at a critical juncture in their lives. The twenty-two-year-old Buber was trying to find a footing outside of Jewish circles, to define himself in ways beyond the claims of traditional Jewish law and loyalties. Landauer's Nietzsche-inflected anarchism—with its unique blend of individual self-determination, mystical epistemology, and communitarian socialism—exercised a powerful pull on the young Buber. Landauer, for his part, was at the time in the midst of an intense extramarital affair with Hedwig Lachmann, whom he would eventually marry, and whose warm, unambiguous Jewish identity prompted him to clarify his own ties to Judaism, toward which he had been, until then, utterly indifferent. Buber, the Polish Jew, offered Landauer personal knowledge of Judaism as a way of life and, as refracted through his writings on the Jewish Renaissance, a culturally and spiritually engaging worldview. It was Buber's early writings on Hasidism in particular that inspired Landauer to affirm with manifest pride his Jewish spiritual patrimony. In a review of Buber's *The Legend of the Baal-Shem*, he wrote that "Judaism is not an external accident [of birth], but a lasting inner quality, and identification with it unites a number of individuals within a community," observing obliquely about their then-embryonic friendship that, "in this way, a common ground is established between the person writing this article and the author of the book" under review.[27] Ultimately, Landauer and Buber were bonded by the ineffable element of personal compatibility, which evolved over the years into a relationship of mutual trust.

Their friendship took on an added significance for the "lonely revolutionary"—as Bab aptly called Landauer—

following Lachmann's sudden death after a bout of pneumonia in February 1918. Unable to reconcile himself to his beloved Hedwig's untimely passing, Landauer fell into a period of extended bereavement. Perhaps in an effort to extricate his friend from prolonged mourning, Buber sought to engage him in various projects. His efforts were not successful, and Landauer apologized to Buber, explaining that he hoped his inability to participate "doesn't affect our harmony and community, which has grown much deeper in the course of these years and which, as far as the future goes, has much to do with my desire and willingness to preserve life and strength."[28]

Other than preparing an anthology of his late wife's poetry, Landauer had little resolve to do anything else.[29] In a letter of August 1918 to the dramaturge Hans Franck, he apologized for not writing. "I am not a whole person, and I don't know whether I will ever be again. If you knew how much my work is affected thereby—wanting to work but not able—you would understand how difficult and nigh-impossible it is for me to take on something that would be but a diversion and not genuine work."[30] A month before declining Franck's request for his collaboration on a project for the municipal theater of Düsseldorf, Landauer received a visit from Buber, who stayed with his bereaved friend for three to four days.[31] In October of that year, Landauer, in turn, visited Buber and his wife in their home in Heppenheim.[32]

Less than a month later, in November 1918, the Jewish journalist and theater critic Kurt Eisner led a socialist revolution to overthrow the monarchy of Bavaria, proclaiming Bavaria a free state and republic and serving as its provisional premier. Landauer was apparently drawn out of his prolonged mourning by the promise of Eisner's government to effect a "spiritual revolution," believing that "Marionettes [would] turn into human beings; rusty philistines [would] become capable of emotion; every fixed thing, even convictions and denials, [would] begin to totter; the intellect, usually concentrated on one's own well-being, [would turn] into reasonable thinking . . . for the common weal; everything [would be open] to the good; the unbelievable, the miracle [would become] feasible; the reality otherwise hidden in our souls, in our religious beliefs, in dream and in love, in the dance of the limbs and in sparkling glances, is pressing to become reality." Eisner, who had met Landauer a few years earlier through their mutual involvement in the pacifist organization Bund Neues Vaterland, wrote Landauer on November 14, beseeching him to join in the Bavarian revolution "as soon as your health allows." Alluding to Landauer's reputation as an inspiring orator, Eisner continued, "What I would like from you is to contribute to the transformation of souls by means of [public] speaking."[33] Despite a lingering flu on top of his ongoing depression, Landauer eagerly accepted Eisner's invitation. On the day after he received Eisner's letter, he wrote Buber, informing him that he would accept Eisner's invitation. "You ought to come too; there is plenty of work. I'll write you as soon as I know of anything definite of concern to you."[34] Less than a week later, he again wrote Buber, requesting that he send Landauer his "ideas on adult education, organization of publications, etc.," and added, "or better still come with them to Munich soon."[35]

Buber would join Landauer in Munich only three months later. The delay was apparently due to his efforts to organize a conference of German socialist Zionists, to take place in Munich in February 1919, in solidarity with the revolution and Eisner's government. The conference had to be cancelled because of the increasing instability of the situation in the Bavarian capital. Nonetheless Buber went alone to Munich in mid-February, where with Landauer he attended a session of the parliament of the Bavarian republic and participated in the parliamentary debate on "political terror." Although Landauer had proposed the topic, as Buber recalled, "he himself hardly joined in the debate; he appeared dispirited and nearly exhausted—a year before his wife had succumbed to a fatal illness, and now he re-lived her death in his heart." The discussion was largely between Buber and a leader of the Spartacus League (the predecessor of the German Communist Party): "I declined to do what many apparently had expected of me—to talk of the moral problem," he proudly noted, "but I set forth what I thought about the relation between end and means. I documented my view from contemporary historical experience." The Spartacus representative responded with documentation of his own to justify political terror. He noted that the head of the Cheka, the secret police established by Lenin in December 1917 to secure the revolution against enemies of the Bolshevik regime, "could sign a hundred death sentences a day, but with an entirely clean soul"—to which Buber retorted, "This is, in fact, worst of all. . . . This 'clean' soul you do not allow any splashes of blood to fall on!" Buber's Spartacus opponent said nothing, but simply looked at him with "unperturbed superiority." Landauer who sat next to Buber, "laid his hand" on Buber's, and "his whole arm trembled."[36]

On February 21, a despondent Buber left Landauer and Munich. Upon reaching his home in Heppenheim that evening, he learned that earlier that day Eisner had been assassinated, shot in the back by a right-wing nationalist. His fear that the revolution would be met with violence—a fear that he shared with Landauer—had been suddenly and tragically realized. In a letter he wrote the following morning to the poet Ludwig Strauss, he reflected on the "profoundly stirring week" he had spent "in constant association with the revolutionary leaders, a week whose grimly natural conclusion was the news of Eisner's assassination." As he explained to his future son in-law—Strauss would marry Buber's daughter Eva in 1925—during that turbulent week "the deepest human problems of the revolution were discussed with utmost candor . . . I threw out questions and

offered replies; and there occurred nocturnal hours of apocalyptic gravity." Sadly, all but a few of his interlocutors were
prepared to acknowledge the tragedy that he believed awaited
them and the revolution. "Face to face with them I sometimes
felt like a Cassandra."[37]

For Buber, the tragedy of the revolution, in which Jews
played a prominent role, was captured in Eisner's fate: "To be
with him was to peer into the tormented passions of his divined
Jewish soul: nemesis shone from his glittering surface; he was a
marked man. Landauer, by dint of the greatest spiritual effort,
was keeping his faith in him, and protected him—a shield-
bearer terribly moving in his selflessness. The whole thing is
an unspeakable Jewish tragedy." In this lament, he parenthetically remarked that for "Landauer himself, who witnessed the
assassination of Eisner and who refused to take the opportunities to escape that were offered him, it was more the road
into the future that could come only through self-sacrifice."[38]
This passing comment may have expressed a premonition that
Eisner's fate also awaited Landauer—as indeed, it did.

At the state funeral for Eisner, Landauer delivered a eulogy
that theater critic Julius Bab described as "burning with indignation and love."[39] Perhaps to honor the legacy of his martyred
comrade, he stayed in Munich despite the violent turn in the
revolution. On April 7—Landauer's forty-ninth birthday—a
parliamentary opposition to the government that had replaced
Eisner's declared the Bavarian Council Republic. Landauer was
appointed "the People's Delegate for Education," but within
a week the Council Republic was overthrown by the commu-
nists, whose regime was also short-lived. At the end of April,
counterrevolutionary troops entered Munich to suppress the
revolution. They did so with unbridled vengeance, killing over a
thousand "revolutionaries." On May 1, Landauer was captured;
on the following day—less than three months after Eisner's assassination—he was savagely bludgeoned to death as a crowd

gathered, cheering and chanting: "Bump him off, that dog, that Jew, that rogue."[40]

Buber was deeply shaken by the tragic death of his friend; he viewed Landauer as a martyred idealist, a gentle anarchist who had sacrificed his life in a doomed effort to herald an era of politics without violence. Buber would devote himself to honoring the memory and vision of Landauer—a man he would unabashedly eulogize as a "crucified" prophet:

> Gustav Landauer had lived as a prophet of the coming human community and fell as its blood-witness. . . . In a church at Brescia [Italy] I saw a mural whose entire surface was covered with crucified individuals. The field of crosses stretched until the horizon, hanging from each, men of varied physiques and faces. Then it struck me that this was the true image of Jesus Christ. On one of the crosses I saw Gustav Landauer hanging.[41]

Poignantly, Buber would later recall in the twilight of his years, "I experienced [Landauer's] death as my own."[42]

A year before his brutal assassination, shortly after his wife's unanticipated death, Landauer had written a last will and testament (including instructions for handling his intellectual legacy) in which he expressed fear that his own end would come soon. Addressed to his cousin, Siegfried Landauer, the document read: "Dear Siegfried! I never believed that I would outlive my wife. Since I have now experienced what one only in such circumstances realizes[ h]ow quickly one can die, I would like, as far as it is possible, in the case of my death to express my wishes for my daughters."[43]

After delineating how his modest material and financial resources should be distributed, Landauer stipulated that "in all matters pertaining to my publishing contracts, I request the help of my friend Dr. Martin Buber." He further requested that Buber administer his and his late wife's literary estate, and that "all their unpublished writings should be given to him" to arrange for their publication. Indeed, "in all literary matters Buber's voice takes precedence." Upon collecting Landauer's correspondence, the will stated, Buber should have it published, but not include anything that might "hurt anyone living and their heirs."[44] Buber would faithfully fulfill his role as executor of Landauer's literary estate. With fastidious care, he edited several volumes of Landauer's writings and two volumes of his correspondence.[45] Buber also published several stirring essays about Landauer's work and introduced Landauer's ideas to the postwar generation, especially to Zionist youth whom he hoped would be inspired by Landauer's conception of communitarian socialism.[46]

Landauer, as noted earlier, had a formative influence on Buber's own thinking, especially regarding the salience of interpersonal relations in shaping spiritual and communal life. In 1918, a year before the Bavarian revolution and Landauer's assassination, Buber gave a lecture in Vienna in May, Berlin in October, and Munich in December on "Judaism and Authentic Community" (alternatively entitled "The Principle of Community in Judaism"). In 1919 he published this lecture as a short book, under the title *The Holy Way: A Word to the Jew and to the Nations*, with the dedication "In Memory of My Friend Gustav Landauer."[47] The subtitle of this book alludes to Fichte's famous *Addresses to the German Nation* of 1808, in which he called upon the German nation to regard itself as an instrument fulfilling universal ideals, and to view patriotism as the path toward realizing the ultimate, cosmopolitan goals of humanity. Buber's call for Jewry to embark on the "Holy Way"—which would be free of Fichte's contemptuous views of lesser nations (especially, it should be noted, the Jews)—reverberated with Landauer's anarchist, communitarian teachings in which the realization of socialism is an ongoing process centered on interhuman relations in the here and now.

Buber declared that "the world of true Judaism" is the work of being "God's 'partner in the work of creation,' to finish the work begun on the sixth day . . . in the all-embracing and all-determining sphere of community."[48] Israel was thus to be a "holy people" by demonstrating to the world that "the realization of the Divine on earth is fulfilled not within man but between man and man, and that, though this does indeed have its beginning in the life of individual man, it is consummated only in the life of true community."[49] The neglect of the divinely appointed vocation of Israel was, he believed, what marked the tragedy of modern Jewry, not what is conventionally called "assimilation." For Buber, the fact that Jews had allowed "another people's landscape, language and culture [to permeate] our soul and life" was not, in the end, what had drained Judaism of its vitality and spiritual significance, for

> even if our own landscape, our own language, our own culture were given back to us, we could not regain the innermost Judaism to which we have become unfaithful. Not because many of us have renounced the norms of Jewish tradition and the system of rules imposed by this tradition; those of us who kept these norms and rules inviolate in their yea and nay have not preserved [the] innermost Judaism any more than those who renounced them. . . . All that is customarily referred to as assimilation is harmlessly superficial compared to what I have in mind: the assimilation to the Occidental dualism that sanctions the splitting of man's being into two realms, each existing in its own right and independent of the other—the truth of spirit and the reality of life. . . . All renunciation of the treasures of national culture or religious life is trifling compared to the fateful renunciation of the most precious heritage of classical Judaism: the disposition toward realization [of unity of spirit and life].[50]

Although Buber would eventually drop the term "realization" (*Verwirklichung*), the underlying idea would remain cen-

tral to his later philosophy of dialogue: the disposition to realization "means that true human life is conceived to be a life
lived in the presence of God." God's presence is realized—
"encountered" will be the term Buber would later prefer—
in the realm of the "Between": the Divine "attains its earthly
fullness only where . . . individual beings open themselves to
one another, disclose themselves to one another and help one
another; where immediacy is established between one human
being and another; where the sublime stronghold of the individual is unbolted, and man breaks free to meet another man.
Where this takes place, where the Eternal rises in the Between,
what is a seemingly empty space is [in fact the] true space for
realization of community, and true community is that relationship in which the Divine comes to its realization between man
and man."[51] Accordingly, "the innermost Judaism" is marked by
a resolve "to create the true community on earth."[52]

Buber concluded this call to reaffirm that "Holy Way" with
a swipe at the "dogmatizers of nationalism"—his fellow Zionists—who were gathered under the banner of "Let us be like all
the nations, O House of Israel." He accused them of hypocriti-
cal denunciation of the assimilationists of the Diaspora, claiming that "you who would readily approve of idol-worship in our
homeland if only the idols bear Jewish names" actually subscribed to the most egregious form of assimilation: "You are
assimilated to the dominant dogma of the century, the 'unholy
dogma of the sovereignty of nations,' which assumes that one's
nation is 'answerable only to itself.'"[53] Buber was quick to add
that his fulminations against nationalism were not to be construed as denying that the existence of nations is "a fundamental reality in the life of mankind," one that "can no longer be
eradicated from man's consciousness, nor should it be. But this
recognition must, and will, be augmented by another: that no
people on earth is sovereign; only the Spirit is."[54] And should
the Zionist project aspire to establish in Palestine just another

state "devoid of spiritual substance," it will find itself "in the war of all against all," inexorably bound to be "crushed in the machinery of its own intrigues."[55]

In voicing these concerns, Buber was well aware that he was swimming against the current, and that his jeremiad against political nationalism would be dismissed as hopelessly detached from the brutal realities faced by the Jewish people. In a letter to one of his friends from the Prague circle, he lamented that "there are but very few Zionists who share or even understand the pain that [the movement's] 'external' [political] success causes me."[56] His ongoing anguish would lead him not only to be deeply ambivalent toward the Zionist project, but also to question his own fundamental intellectual and spiritual commitments.

Upon returning in June 1920 from a conference in Prague of Hapoel Hatzair, a non-Marxist socialist Zionist movement whose name means "the young worker," Buber shared these doubts with a conference organizer. With disarming candor, he revealed: "Truth be told, my dear friend, I can no longer make sense out of Hapoel Hatzair, or Zionism, or even Judaism, and, least of all, 'myself,' that is, of all I have hitherto spoken and written."[57] These festering existential doubts had already prompted him to begin work more than a year earlier on a manuscript that would lay "the general foundations of a philosophical (communal and religio-philosophical) system to which I intend to devote the next several years." Since engaging in the writing of this manuscript—which after four years would appear under the title *Ich und Du* (I and Thou)—he had experienced "a strange dejection, a feeling of standing between two worlds, the sense of having reached a frontier that grows ever stronger within me."[58]

Martin Buber as a student in Vienna (1896–1897). Martin
Buber Archive, The National Library of Israel, Jerusalem.
Courtesy of the Martin Buber Literary Estate.

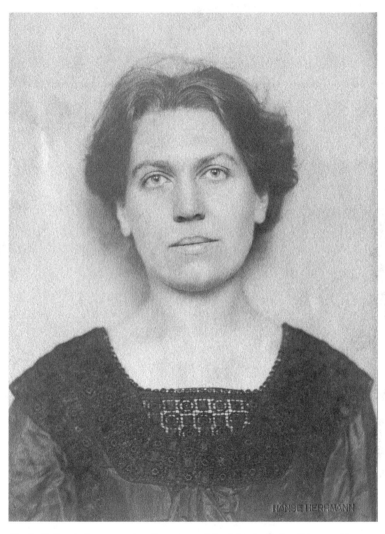

Paula Buber in her twenties. Courtesy of the Martin Buber Literary Estate.

Martin Buber in the company of Martin Heidegger (*second from right*), 1957. Courtesy of the Martin Buber Literary Estate.

Martin Buber, when he was about eighty years old, with
his grandchildren and great-grandchildren in Jerusalem.
Courtesy of the Martin Buber Literary Estate.

Martin Buber in 1949. Courtesy of the Martin Buber Literary Estate.

*Left to right:* Ernst Simon, Hugo Bergmann, and Martin Buber at Buber's Jerusalem home, 1963. Courtesy of the Martin Buber Literary Estate.

Students of Hebrew University celebrating Buber's eighty-fifth
birthday. Courtesy of the Martin Buber Literary Estate.

Buber at age eighty-five. Photographer: David Rubinger.
Courtesy of the Martin Buber Literary Estate.

# 7

◆·◆·◆

## *A Reverential* Apikoros:
## *Friendship with Rosenzweig*

> Yes, I can calmly say: The fact that you
> belong in such a manner to Franz and he
> to you, makes my present life possible,
> just as it joins in sustaining Franz.
> —Franz Rosenzweig's mother to Buber

AT THE threshold of his fifth decade, Buber found himself torn between his abiding (if conflicted) fidelity to the Zionist project of Jewish cultural and spiritual renewal and an ongoing reevaluation of the fundamental presuppositions of his core religious and political commitments. He was fully aware—and thus worried—that the process of clarification might very well challenge those commitments. As he faced these uncertain horizons, he would greatly benefit from a new friendship with Franz Rosenzweig, eight years his junior.

The two first met when Rosenzweig paid Buber a brief visit

at his Berlin residence in 1914, in order to share a draft of a pamphlet he was soon to publish, *Zeit ists* (It is time), which called for a radical reconstruction of Jewish education in Germany.[1] A few months earlier, Rosenzweig had reversed his decision to convert to Christianity, and as an initial step toward affirming his ancestral faith had come to Berlin to study at the Hochschule für Wissenschaft des Judentums. Buber was clearly so impressed by Rosenzweig's earnest efforts to acquire a systematic knowledge of Judaism that he invited him to contribute an article to the second edition of *Vom Judentum*—the article, titled with the bold oxymoron "Atheistic Theology," was rejected, presumably because it was perceived to be a veiled critique of Buber's neo-Romantic conception of Judaism. It would eventually be published posthumously.[2]

Rosenzweig reached out to Buber again in a letter at the end of August 1919.[3] Reminding Buber of their earlier meeting, Rosenzweig informed him about *Der Stern der Erlösung* (The star of redemption), a book that he had written in the trenches during the World War. Though in many respects it was a ponderously philosophical book, Rosenzweig regarded it as a "Jewish book" and to ensure that it would be received as such, he requested Buber's assistance in placing it with a publishing house that focused on issues of interest to the Jewish community—while acknowledging that "the whole manner and direction of my work is remote from yours." He offered to send Buber a copy of the manuscript with the hope that he would "objectively see a necessity for having the view I am advancing appear before the public as a Jewish view; not whether you yourself approve of this view."[4] *The Star of Redemption* would be published in 1921 by the Jewish publishing house Kauffmann of Frankfurt am Main (although it is unclear if that was due to any intervention by Buber).

Shortly after the publication of *The Star*, Rosenzweig, with the assistance of Ernst Simon, prepared a volume of essays to commemorate the fiftieth birthday of Frankfurt's beloved communal rabbi, Nehemiah Anton Nobel. Simon wrote Buber to solicit a contribution to the volume; although Buber had at best a superficial acquaintance with Rabbi Nobel, Rosenzweig hoped that Buber's name would enhance the prestige of the volume.[5] Buber consented, and contributed a translation of three Hasidic tales. Before sending the volume to press, Rosenzweig sent to each of the contributors the wording of a dedication to the volume, to which he had affixed all of their names. Introducing an essay written by Nobel upon his first appointment as a rabbi, the dedication read, "With these words written twenty-five years ago you have formulated the views of all of us about the essence of the rabbinical calling."[6]

Upon receiving the dedication to sign (along with a copy of Nobel's essay), Buber sent a telegram to Rosenzweig indicating that he would not add his signature to the dedication, for he could not endorse the contents of the essay. Taken aback, Rosenzweig and Simon reread the essay, and to their embarrassment, realized that neither of them (nor most of the other contributors to the volume) could lend their support to Nobel's youthful affirmation of "conservative Judaism," a version of German orthodox observance to which neither of them subscribed.[7] Rosenzweig immediately wired Buber a revised dedication.[8] Upon receiving it, Buber, then in Munich, telegraphed his approval with a brief "*einverstanden*" (agreed). Recalling Buber's gracious collaboration in the Festschrift for Rabbi Nobel, Rosenzweig later mused that "it was magnificently emblematic of what is great about Buber, whom everyone regards as a king of the spirit, but who is in truth a genuine king, even 'in his underwear'"—an allusion to Hegel's maxim that no one is a king in the presence of his valet.[9]

Rosenzweig's exchange with Buber inspired him to renew their personal acquaintance. A week after the festivities in honor of Rabbi Nobel, Rosenzweig arranged to visit Buber in

Heppenheim am Bergstrasse, a bucolic, medieval town some thirty miles south of Frankfurt, where Buber and his family had lived since 1916. Rosenzweig and his wife arrived on the afternoon of Sunday, December 4, 1920, for what was to be a casual social visit. To Rosenzweig's utter delight, "in the course of the conversation, while we were having coffee," he suddenly realized that Buber "was no longer the mystical subjectivist that people worship," and that he was "becoming a solid and reasonable man." Furthermore, he was "utterly astonished and impressed by the extreme honesty with which [Buber] spoke." The conversation turned to the sources of Buber's work on Hasidism. Buber mentioned in passing that he would like some time to study the original Hasidic texts with a few people, whereupon Rosenzweig said he would gladly put together such a group to come to Heppenheim from time to time for that purpose. ("Only on the way home," he later reflected, "did it occur to me that it would be cheaper to transport the prophet than twenty of his disciples.")[10] Thus began Buber's relationship with Rosenzweig's Freies Jüdisches Lehrhaus, the school of Jewish adult education that Rosenzweig had founded in Frankfurt in August 1920.

Upon returning to Frankfurt, Rosenzweig quickly sent an invitation to Buber to deliver a lecture at the Lehrhaus, and Buber accepted with what was for him uncharacteristic alacrity. "To my own amazement (for having to say no is gradually becoming a habit with me), I have from the first moment had an affirmative feeling about your proposal for a lecture. I owe that chiefly to your visit, which left me with the sense of a lasting relationship."[11] Instead of a single lecture, Buber expressed a desire to give a series of lectures to be entitled "Religion as Presence." To complement these lectures, he further proposed a seminar, a "discussion of select religious texts," among which would be some Hasidic sources. Rosenzweig warmly endorsed Buber's proposal, although he had reservations about the title.

He felt that "religion" in its institutional and philosophical expression often got in the way of a genuine encounter with God. But he also acknowledged that precisely because it avoids any implication of responding to the divine, "religion" would sound less threatening to the public. Hence, Rosenzweig conceded, "it will be best to call [the lectures] 'Religion as Presence,' even if afterward it turns out in truth to deal with 'God's Presence.'" The lectures on "Religion as Presence," eight in all, would attest to Buber's turn from a Romantic Erlebnis-mysticism to a philosophy of dialogue that affirms the transcendent Otherness of God. The stenographer's transcriptions of the lectures would, as Buber told Rosenzweig, serve as "the prolegomenon to the work" he had been engaged in for the past several years. The lectures were, in effect, a draft of *Ich und Du* (I and Thou).

Ten days after Buber delivered the first lecture before an audience of about 150 people, Rosenzweig informed him that Rabbi Nobel had died suddenly the previous morning, just weeks after the festive celebration of his fiftieth birthday. Marking his letter in italicized letters as "*Urgent*," he confessed to Buber that he felt compelled to share with him the "terrible blow" that he had experienced with the death of his spiritual mentor and Talmud teacher:

> Part of the basis of my life has been snatched from underfoot. We never know our future, but we can nevertheless see before us the beginning of the road that leads into the future. At least we call them fortunate who can see this beginning of the road before them. And until yesterday morning, I would call myself so.[12]

It may not have been merely fortuitous, he wrote to Buber, that in "the last hour of his good fortune" before his grievous loss, the two of them had begun to forge bonds of friendship. Rosenzweig abruptly concluded his letter by beseeching Buber: "Stay with us, stay in this world for me!"[13]

Although less than two months had passed and only a few letters had been exchanged since Rosenzweig and his wife had visited the Bubers, both men sensed that they were being drawn to one another by a compelling intellectual and spiritual affinity. In response to a letter from Rosenzweig inquiring why he had not replied to his previous missives, Buber apologized for his silence by explaining that he found epistolary communication to be an inadequate form of conducting their "dialogue" (Gespräch).[14] Already in the second half-hour of their visit in Heppenheim, he wrote, his interaction with Rosenzweig had taken on for him a nigh-messianic quality of mutual trust. To be sure, Buber acknowledged, one could discuss matters in letters, "but I seem unable to do so. You must know that I am always surprised when I have written an authentic letter; for weeks at a time, I often succeed only in 'attending' to my correspondence, twenty, thirty items in a usual day, none without an attempt at summoning to mind the real presence of the addressee, but also none with a real giving of the self." With disarming candor, he confessed that Rosenzweig was one of the very few individuals, particularly in "this decade" (that is, presumably, since Landauer's assassination) who has been able to "draw me out of the cave."[15]

Rosenzweig seems to have gladly taken on the task of drawing Buber out of his inner isolation. He was also determined to teach him to "speak properly" and be an effective teacher.[16] When during his visit to Heppenheim, Buber had parenthetically mentioned his desire to read Hasidic texts with a few people, Rosenzweig first suggested that Buber do so then and there with him and his wife. Buber then "disappeared among his bookshelves, returned with two or three texts, and we started reading." He proved to be a rather clumsy teacher. At the Lehrhaus under Rosenzweig's tutelage, Buber would slowly hone his pedagogical skills. His initial steps as a teacher were faltering and uncertain, particularly in leading seminars. Ernst Simon —

who would in time become one of Buber's closest associates—
wrote a scathing critique of the manner in which he conducted
a seminar on Hasidism.[17]

In a long, detailed letter to Buber, Simon candidly expressed the "deeply depressing impact" the seminar had upon
him and "everything that troubled me about you as the leader
of the seminar." He faulted Buber for thoughtlessly inviting the participants to "speak their minds" so as to allow for
mutual "advising and helping." The result was "a partly hys-
terical, somewhat shameless barrage of questions" that appalled
not only Simon but also many others. "From the expression on
your face—rarely a flicker of irony, mostly a kindly smile—it
was apparent that you did not feel the full force of what was
going on out there." Simon attributed Buber's inability to
conduct an orderly and constructive seminar to his failure to
take into account his audience: "You thought you were standing 'naked before God' [when you were only] standing before
Fräulein H.—a terrible sight! Everyone who loves you had to
cry inwardly. And you were not even aware of it." In essence,
Simon concluded, Buber's pedagogic failure was due his "pi-
etistic idealism," which naïvely and thus tragically was leading
him to believe that "every person is a Thou to an I."

Taken aback by Simon's rebuke, Buber turned to Rosenzweig, and reported that "Simon was upset by what he regarded
as the shameless questions of the last lesson and my connivance
thereto."[18] Rosenzweig too was interested in improving Buber's
teaching, but he reassured Buber that he was on the right track:

> [Simon] first showed me [his letter]. Of course, he is "right."
> As right as somebody who does not believe in the transforma-
> tion of merchants into worshippers through the *minyan* [the
> quorum required by Jewish law for communal prayer]—the
> transformation of sensation-seekers into people in [genuine]
> need, though not demonstrable. Nevertheless, one must be-

lieve in the possibility, and Ernst Simon will also believe in it one day, once he gets over the hangover from his [dreamy faith] in the power of form to save a person. Then he too will remember the healing power of freedom, which he is wont to regard merely as a poisonous flower (which it surely is *also*).[19]

In contrast to Simon's more conventional conception of the role of the teacher and its formal tasks, Rosenzweig supported here a less structured, dialogical mode of teaching, which he encouraged Buber to develop.

Rosenzweig composed this letter in early January 1923, by which time he had already lost his ability to write legibly due to a progressive paralysis, diagnosed less than a year earlier as amyotrophic lateral sclerosis (ALS, now popularly known as Lou Gehrig's disease). At that time, he was still able to dictate letters and essays, albeit with great difficulty. But by the spring of 1923 he was unable to speak at all. Ultimately by means of a specially constructed typewriter, he somehow maintained his correspondence and literary activity, even as his disease progressed. Although the medical prognosis was that he had only a year to live, Rosenzweig endured for another six years, graced by a fruitful collaboration and a deepening friendship with Buber.

The first expression of their collaboration was Rosenzweig's active role in commenting on Buber's lectures "Religion as Presence," which he attended as much as his failing body would allow. Upon reviewing the transcription of the lectures, he would offer critical comments to Buber either orally (when it was still possible) or in writing (with assistance from his wife). Similarly, he read and offered critical comments on the printer's proofs of *I and Thou*. Buber would gratefully respond to Rosenzweig's critiques and duly attend to the clarifications and revisions his friend suggested. ("I want to thank you from the bottom of my heart for your thorough, magnificent criticism.")²⁰ Their exchange was also interspersed with reflections on the nature of "religion"—again, a term Rosenzweig vehemently rejected as constricting and distorting the genuine life of faith. "Religion? . . . I . . . shudder at the word whenever I hear it." Cautioning Buber not to privilege I-Thou relations at the expense of the world of It (that is, God's created order), he mused, "What is to become of I and Thou if they will have to swallow up the entire world and the Creator as well?"²¹

Rosenzweig and Buber shared a conviction that since the Enlightenment, the life of religious faith (which had previously governed all aspects of human life) had been lamentably constricted—confined to one of the disparate, competing spheres of activity and value that characterized modern society. Consigned to the domain of individual choice, religious faith had become a subjective option. Max Weber famously noted that one either had an "ear" for religion or didn't. (Weber frankly admitted that he did not, despite his interest in the sociology of religion.) At the very outset of his lectures, Buber roundly rejected Weber's view. Religious faith, he argued, is "not a gift among other gifts that one has or does not have. One is not religious in the same way as one is artistic or even in the same way as one is moral."²² Limiting religious faith to personal inclination, to "moments of the soul," Buber decried, is tantamount to its "annihilation" and the "suicide of the spirit."²³ Rather, he argued, religious faith is attuned to the true ground of life, which one does not need "some spiritual talent" to "unlock."²⁴ Religious faith is responsive to "the mandate of a being, the mandate of *the* being" we usually call God, whom Buber calls in his Lehrhaus lectures "the Absolute Presence," and in *I and Thou*, "the Eternal Thou."²⁵

As Buber described it in the lectures (and later in *I and Thou*), religious faith has its foundation in "the bond of being, a bond with being." Without this bond, all religious concepts and practices are vacuous, or at most a mere creation of the human spirit, a "species of art." "The bond of being" is not properly called "faith," but is established by virtue of a relationship (*Beziehung*) to God. Derived from the verb to pull (*ziehen*), Beziehung denotes the dynamic quality of a mutual relationship between two autonomous subjects, an "I" (*Ich*) and a "Thou" (*Du*). (The familiar second-person German pronoun, *Du*, is conventionally restricted to addressing close friends, relatives, and children—yet one also addresses God as *Du*, which since the King James Bible translation had been represented as "Thou.") Buber viewed the *Ich-Du* relationship between two individuals as "bonding in and with being," as the quintessential religious act, with God's Presence (*Gegenwart*) refracted through the Presence of a *Gegenüber*, another person whom one faces.

The etymology of Buber's terms is significant: Gegenwart (literally waiting over-against one) denotes meeting someone or something as a Presence as a subject that is waiting before one to be acknowledged and responded to as a Thou. In contrast, *Gegenstand* (something, an It, standing over-against one) denotes viewing that someone or something as an object to be used or placed within a matrix of other objects. A Gegenwart transcends the particular context of time and space; viewed in this way, another human being—as well as the flora and fauna of the natural order, and the works of art that embody the creative spirit of one's fellow human beings—are all grounded in Divine presence. Buber, as well as Rosenzweig (who described God as Presence, eternally present), would render *ehyeh asher ehyeh*, God's reply to Moses's request to reveal God's name (Exodus 3:14), as "I shall be present as I shall be present."

I-Thou and I-It are thus two fundamental and dichotomous modes of relating to the world. One may relate to the world, including one's fellow human beings, as objects, as an It (even if one says *Du* to him or her), or one may meet the Other as a Presence, as one who awaits to be related to as a Thou. One bearing oneself in the I-Thou mode meets the Other at a moment of grace, when one is addressed by the Presence of the Other; one needs to prepare oneself and nurture a ready state of openness and an existential commitment to meet the Other as a Thou, and to be alert to the address of and by the Other as a Thou. This is "the basic meaning of revelation": a calling, "the sending forth of the human being . . . to humanity, into the world, into the We." The entering-into-relation with the eternal Presence does not take place in "solitude but by our also stepping into the world, putting the meaning [of God's call]" into the concrete reality of the world by actualizing it.[26]

Rosenzweig voices a similar understanding of the commanding voice of revelation. In a passage in *The Star of Redemption*, which Buber underlined in his own copy of the volume, we read: "Love thy neighbor. That is, as Jew and Christian assure us, the embodiment of all commandments. With this commandment, the soul is declared of age, departs the paternal home of divine love, and sets forth in the world."[27] In an essay that Buber and Rosenzweig would later coauthor, they presented the this-worldly call of revelation as the homiletic core of biblical religiosity: "In the Torah no distinction is made between the 'social' and 'religious': the religious element marks the direction, the social determines the course."[28] In one of his earliest letters to Rosenzweig, Buber held that this teaching was epitomized by a dictum of the first-century Roman scholar Pliny the Elder: *Deus est mortali invare mortalem*, which Buber explains to Rosenzweig is to be properly understood as "God exists for man [to the extent] that he serves [his fellow] man."[29]

Buber shared Rosenzweig's fear that "religion" per se often deflects one from God, and from heeding the call to what in his writings on Hasidism he celebrated as the "hallowing of the everyday." In an essay he wrote shortly after the publication of *I and Thou*, he observed: "It is far more comfortable to have to do with religion than to have to do with God, who sends one out of home and fatherland into restless wandering. In addition religion has all kinds of aesthetic refreshments to offer its cultivated adherents. . . . For this reason at all times the awake spirits have been vigilant and have warned of the diverting force hidden in religion."[30]

God is thus not an object of Erlebnis, an experience of one's "detached subjectivity" cut off from "the totality of the actual world," as Buber put it in a 1923 essay, clarifying—and, in effect, revising—central concepts of his early writings on Judaism as a "religious reality."[31] In that essay, published a few months after *I and Thou,* he underscored that any experience "is of concern to me only insofar as it is an event or, in other words, insofar as it pertains to the real God." An "eventless experiencing" of God is "a cosmic perversion." Buber follows this indictment with a mea culpa: "If I have at any time contributed" to this perversion, "I now feel duty-bound to point out all the more emphatically" that the religious does not begin in one's inner life, but is constituted by a mode of being in the world whereby one enters into relation with the presence of the Other and ultimately with the Presence of God. In the I-Thou relationship, one does not experience, but meets, the Other.[32]

Judaism, then, exists to give witness to this religious reality—a reality, however, that is "not the prerogative of particular religions."[33] Divine revelation is not the privileged knowledge of any religion; it "does not flash from the cloud, but . . . whispers to us in the course of every ordinary day, and is alive quite near us, quite close; the *shekhinah* [the Divine Presence] dwells among us [Jews] sharing our exile . . . and our suffering heals and is hallowed through the immanence of the Word [revealed in the whispers of the everyday]. This is the history of Israel, as it is the history of the human person; and it may well be the history of the world."[34]

The elaboration of this thesis—that true life is realized in the I-Thou encounter—was henceforth Buber's life's project.

In his lectures on "Religion as Presence," Buber assumed a conversational voice, often pausing to appeal to the audience to reflect on this thesis by examining their own lives: "I ask you to grasp this as concretely as you are able, each of you from his own life, from what he himself knows in an unmediated way of the I-Thou relation."[35] In *I and Thou*, he similarly seeks to prompt his readers to introspective reflection, but not by direct appeal. Rather he adopts poetic pathos to evoke an "aha!" effect and the acknowledgment of what he regards to be a common human experience. *I and Thou* is full of aphoristic formulations and evocative figures of speech, and has an almost musical cadence. Indeed, the work is configured in a quasi-musical form of three parts, akin to the movements of a sonata, each with a distinctive internal rhythm, punctuated with thematic motifs. It is written in sixty-two short sections that grow along the way with an ever fuller conceptual resonance. *I and Thou* has thus been characterized as a philosophical poem.

Buber's use of poetic rhetoric is consistent with his rejection of traditional forms of philosophical discourse. He regarded the function of philosophical thinking to be that of *deixis*, pointing, rather than *apodeixis*, demonstration. Accordingly, he viewed cognition to be recognition, and knowledge as acknowledgment. He thus conceded that he had no "teaching" to offer in a conceptually rigorous sense: "I only point to something . . . in reality that had not or had too little been seen. I take him who listens to me by the hand and lead him to the window. I open the window and point to what is outside. I have no teaching, but carry on a conversation."[36] (It was precisely the poetic voice in which this conversation was conducted that the celebrated Argentinian poet Jorges Luis Borges found so compelling about Buber's writings. Recalling a bon mot of Ralph Waldo Emerson that "arguments convince nobody," he remarked: "When something is merely said or—better still—

hinted at, there is a kind of hospitality in our imagination. We are ready to accept it. I remember reading . . . the works of Martin Buber—I thought of them as being wonderful poems. Then, when I went to Buenos Aires, I read a book by a friend of mine, and found in its pages, much to my astonishment, that Martin Buber was a philosopher and that all his philosophy lay in the books I read as poetry. Perhaps I accepted these books because they came to me through poetry, through suggestion, through the music of poetry, and not as arguments.")[37]

Rosenzweig shared Buber's reservations about traditional philosophical discourse, proposing an alternative he called "New Thinking," in which

> the method of speech replaces the method of thinking main-tained by all earlier philosophies. Thinking is timeless and wants to be timeless. . . . Speech is bound to time and nour-ished by time, and it neither can nor wishes to abandon this element. It does not know in advance just where it will end. It takes its clue from others. In fact, it lives by virtue of an-other's life. "Speaking" means speaking to someone. . . . And this someone is always quite a definite someone, and has not merely ears, "like all the world," but also a mouth.[38]

Also similarly to Buber, he encourages his readers to confirm the validity of this observation in their own everyday experi-ence, a commonsense experience that he refers to as a "healthy human understanding": "This holds true for everyday matters, and everyone grants it. Everyone knows it."[39]

But it was not only their shared convictions about philo-sophical and religious discourse that drew Buber and Rosen-zweig together in a friendship whose compelling power sur-prised them both. At its core, their friendship was sealed in some intangible existential affinity of the kind that Rosen-zweig anticipated in a diary entry he wrote as a twenty-year-old emerging from the turmoil of adolescence: "The older one gets, the more difficult one finds it to make friends, because one's own store [of experiences] is so great that while there be individual items in common, these items seem too small a fraction of the whole to form the basis of a common fortune." And yet "for the same reason, as one gets older it becomes easier to make acquaintances and cultivate them, since out of a large store it is easier to find suitable articles of exchange."[40]

A shadow was soon cast over the "common fortune" that had shaped Buber and Rosenzweig's acquaintance into a deep friendship: Rosenzweig's debilitating and ultimately fatal illness. Bracing himself for imminent death, Rosenzweig reflected on his blossoming friendship with Buber:

> Yes, he might have marked an important epoch in my life; the day after Nobel's death I wrote him to this effect. Now it has turned out not to be an epoch, since epochs require long perspectives, an epoch can only be such when we feel that it is still the penultimate one. Death no longer marks an epoch. . . . But [nonetheless, my friendship with Buber] is marvelous for me, and a great blessing.[41]

Entombed in an increasingly paralyzed body, Rosenzweig was confined to his small attic apartment in Frankfurt, where Buber would visit him on a regular basis. He somehow fought on for five years past his doctor's prognosis, resisting despair and thoughts of suicide (as he confided to his mother) by affirming "simply an elementary desire and infinite ability to enjoy" the measure of life that his deteriorating body allowed. Buber explained his friend's indomitable affirmation of life and unabated intellectual passion as animated by a faith sustained by an incorrigible wit: "[For] the fulfillment of such dedication in the midst of and despite all repulsiveness and loathsomeness of actual circumstances, humor is required. His whole being accepts life as a whole, but to accept life in the steady course of its daily detail, moment by moment, a life of utmost pain and physical helplessness, is an achievement which only a combination of faith and humor can bring about."[42]

At Rosenzweig's request, Buber took a more active role in the Lehrhaus. No longer able to conduct the affairs of the thriving center of adult Jewish learning (by January 1923 more than 1,100 students were enrolled), Rosenzweig, in the late summer of 1922, appointed the Egyptologist Rudolf Hallo as director. Informing Buber of the appointment, Rosenzweig urged him to take Hallo—who like Rosenzweig had considered baptism—under his wing: "[He] is a friend ten years younger than myself. I would like to commend him to you. . . . For you are now more than I . . . the person he needs for giving him certainty about his Judaism. Today he does not know that. But I know it. He does not need *homecomers* like me, because he is one himself; he needs the 'reverential' *apikoros*—none other."[43]

As an *apikoros* (in Yiddish, a "heretic"), Buber knew Judaism from within, having acquired it in his youth—as the Talmudic Aramaic has it, *girsa d'yankuta*, "imbibed it with his mother's milk." Although he had long stepped beyond it with the eye of an ambivalent skeptic, Buber represented for Rosenzweig a "reverential" commitment to its spiritual renewal, if not to its rabbinically prescribed ritual and liturgical practices. Moreover, as Rosenzweig explained to a member of the board of the Lehrhaus who questioned Buber's faculty appointment, it was a commitment informed by a compelling intellectual and spiritual integrity, and "a commanding erudition—without a trace of pretentiousness."[44]

These remarks in praise of Buber's erudition and integrity were written two weeks after Rosenzweig had asked him to consider accepting an appointment at the University of Frankfurt as a lecturer in Jewish religion and ethics.[45] The position, in the Department of Theology, had originally been offered to Rabbi Nehemiah Nobel, but he died before the appointment was official; it was then proposed that the lectureship be offered to Rosenzweig. Though he was like Buber "entirely free of silly academicism (*Universitätsfimmel*)," Rosenzweig was initially inclined to accept the position in order to prevent the danger of it being offered to some rabbi who would turn the department that "will surely emerge from it" into yet another institution for training rabbis. But by the time the appointment was actually granted to Rosenzweig, he was too ill to accept it. He thus urged Buber to consider assuming the lectureship "both for the sake of theology, which must be detheologized, and for the sake of the university which must be universalized."[46]

As an "indubitable apikoros," he continued, Buber's presence on the faculty would ensure that its theological discourse would not be confined to parochial or doctrinal apologetics, but would serve to elucidate the universal truths disclosed by the faith experience and foster the universal scope mandated by the mission of the university. This task, Rosenzweig told Buber, could be realized only by someone "who is wholly free of any deference for the existing university" and who will bring to the position "the kind of personal reputation" that will forbid the university's administration from interfering with him.[47]

Before consenting, Buber set several conditions, chief among them that he would, indeed, be free of any intervention, and that neither the university's department of theology nor the Jewish community would have any right "to supervise, to question, or make any suggestions." And should even Rosenzweig reserve the prerogative to intervene, Buber urged him to "consider how different is the situation of a repentant Jew, a *returner* [to Jewish tradition], from that of—as you so trenchantly put it—a 'certified *apikoros*." What Buber sought by this stipulation was to avoid a possible conflict that Buber's rejection of rabbinic tradition might come to be seen negatively by his friend, who was, for all of their deep philosophical similarities, moving toward traditional Jewish ritual practice.[48] His conditions met, Buber began teaching in the summer of 1924, bringing the approach of comparative religion (*Religionwissen-schaft*) to the study of Judaism.

The difference between Rosenzweig's perspective as a "homecomer" and Buber's as an "apikoros," did, in fact, soon surface in an impassioned critique by Rosenzweig of Buber's unbending rejection of "the Law"—the ritual and liturgical commandments (*mitzvot*) of rabbinic tradition—as a viable basis of Jewish spiritual renewal. The critique was occasioned by Rosenzweig's reading of a recently published anthology of Buber's addresses on Judaism.[49] In particular, it was the last of the volume's eight lectures, "*Herut* [Freedom]: On Youth and Religion," that provoked his ire.

Originally delivered in Vienna at a conference of Zionist youth in May 1918, the lecture had attested to Buber's fundamental reevaluation of his own understanding of a Jewish renaissance. Until then, he had focused on the renewal of a "primal Jewish religiosity" as exemplified by Hasidism. A growing critique of that vision for a renewed Jewish spirituality had prompted the founding in 1915 of *Die Blau-Weisse Brille*, a satirical newsletter addressed to Berlin's Zionist youth, edited by the eighteen-year-old Gerhard (Gershom) Scholem (who already, at his young age, was becoming disillusioned with Buber) and Eric Brauer. The first page of the inaugural issue of this mimeographed review featured a caricature of Buber, accompanied by handwritten text suggesting that Buber was responsible for fostering the intellectual shallowness of a "youth movement without Judaism." In a diary entry following a lecture by one of Buber's disciples, the teenage Scholem exclaimed: "What one would dare nowhere else: to speak before an assembly as one speaks about Hasidism without a study of the sources. And those congregated there stood in aesthetic ecstasy and whispered so to speak ah, ah, religiosity. . . . These people, who have absolutely no conception of Judaism, in unheard of shamelessness pass the time ruminating about Jewish 'religiosity,' citing passage after passage from Buber's *The Legend of the Baal-Shem.*"[50]

Attentive to such murmurings, Buber himself eventually acknowledged the inadequacy of grounding Jewish renewal in an ill-defined religiosity alone. In his address in Vienna, *"Herut: On Youth and Religion,"* he shared two dialogues between a youth leader and a young boy, who asks "What is Jewish life?" Dedicated to his son, Rafael, the dialogues may have reflected actual conversations that Buber had with his teenage son. In the first dialogue, conducted on a meandering stroll, the youth leader argues that, while a young Christian can have an unself-conscious, organic bond to the German people—"he is like a tree with strong roots and its fruit falls into his hands, which he can enjoy with utmost joy"—his Jewish peer, despite an ardent attachment to German culture and desire to live as a German, could never have such an organic bond to the German people. In the second dialogue, the leader asks: How is a young German Jew to develop an organic bond to the Jewish people? The young Jew replies that he has done so through the study of Hebrew (which Buber's son in fact devotedly studied with Agnon) and Jewish history. The youth leader responds with approval, but also notes that a knowledge of Hebrew and Jewish history can sustain a genuine and compelling Jewish life only if one experiences oneself as "entrusted" with the life and destiny of the people.[51]

This mandate, as Buber underscores in *"Herut,"* extends beyond mere "declaration of solidarity with one's people." As indicated by the lecture's subtitle—"On Youth and Religion"—the mandate with which Jewish youth are entrusted entails a bonding with "the religiously creative life" of the Jewish people, its "sacred work, expressed in literature and history, the scroll of words and deeds whose letters tell the chronicle of this people's relation to its God." Only on the basis of this foundation could

Jewish youth build a solid "inner religious life." Moreover, bonded in this way to their people's sacred life and work, they could also resist the "phantom of community"—nationalism—to which European youth at large had surrendered in the cataclysmic World War that had just come to an end.[52]

Buber, however, cautioned Jewish youth "dissatisfied with their experience of Jewish nationalism" not to embrace, as an alternative, "traditional Jewish teaching and law" with the hope of becoming "an organic part of the people": they should "grasp the old, with [their] hearts and minds," but be wary of losing "[their] hearts and minds to it." Affirming the Law—and all the mitzvot (commandments) of traditional Jewish religious practice—as a gesture of national loyalty or as a quest for community, would be, he argued, a veritable "profanation of the Torah" (a sacrilege compounded when understanding the Torah as Law). Rather, Torah is correctly understood as teaching (*Lehre*), the divine instruction that is continually revealed in the ongoing flux of life. Accordingly, Buber implored his audience to "show that nothing is incapable of becoming a receptacle of revelation" or ongoing divine instruction, and that the primal creative forces of Judaism are engendered by the human response to that instruction—not Jewish law, but Jewish teaching.[53] It was this dichotomous formulation of the task facing contemporary Jews that prompted Rosenzweig to compose an open letter of rebuke to his friend. In response to *"Herut,"* Rosenzweig polemically entitled his letter, "The Builders."

Both titles—*"Herut"* and "The Builders"—are derived from rabbinic literature, and connote contrasting approaches to the Law. The title of Buber's lecture is taken from the Ethics of the Fathers (6:2): "'God's writing engraved on the tablets' (Exodus 32:16)—read not *harut* (engraved) but *herut* (freedom)." Buber reads this midrash as sanctioning his nonlegal understanding of the Torah: "Rather than commandment, 'God's writing on the tablets [of the Torah] constitutes freedom.'" But tragically, the original, pristine tablets of the Torah were broken, and throughout the generations, Jews had to "persistently strive to restore the blurred outlines of divine freedom on the second tablets." Jewish renewal thus required reviving a never-ending, loosely held approach to spirituality and interpretation, free of doctrinal orthodoxy. To immerse oneself in this process, one must first acquire a "reverent and unbiased knowledge" of Judaism in all of its varied literary forms and expressions, in order to have access to the "primal forces" informing the spiritual biography of the Jewish people.[54]

Rosenzweig introduced his open letter to Buber "concerning the law" with another midrashic quote: "'And all thy children shall be taught of the Lord, and great shall be the peace of thy children!' (Isaiah 54:13). Do not read '*banayikh*,' your children, but '*bonayikh*,' your builders."[55] Regarding this dictum, which is part of a passage often recited to mark the communal study of rabbinic texts, Rosenzweig notes that the constructive "growth of the Law is entrusted . . . to our loving care." (Here he was understandably questioning why Buber didn't advocate gaining a "reverent and unbiased knowledge" of Jewish law itself.) As heirs of the covenant that God made with our forebears, Rosenzweig writes, we have the responsibility to bear the mantle of the Law and "to become builders."[56]

In contrast to the contemplative act of reading a body of literature, the cognitive significance of the mitzvot can be learned only from within the process of performing them. Also, it is only in their observance that the mitzvot can possibly be known not merely as laws (*Gesetze*) but also as divine commandments (*Gebote*), addressed directly and personally to the individual in the here and now; the commanding voice of God can be heard only from within the lived experience of observing the mitzvot. Rosenzweig concludes his critique of what he regarded as

Buber's facile dismissal of the Law as the revealed Word of God with a cri de coeur: "I could not believe that you, who have shown us again the one path to the Torah" and its "teaching"—as documented in its literature—"should be unable to see what moves us as well today along the other path," the Law.[57]

Buber arranged for "The Builders" to be published in his journal *Der Jude*, but refrained from responding publicly, confining his response to personal correspondence.[58] In urging Rosenzweig to allow him to publish "The Builders," which despite its nature as an "open letter" Rosenzweig sent directly to Buber to read first, Buber wrote:

> If I am able to write an answer [to "The Builders"], it will contain nothing in disagreement with its details. I agree to what follows from the letter's premises, but not to those premises themselves. It is my faith that prevents me from doing this. You know, my friend, that I do not use this word lightly, and yet here it is quite appropriate. I do not believe that *revelation* is ever a formulation of law (*Gesetzgebung*). It is only through man in his self-contradiction that revelation becomes legislation. . . . I cannot admit the law transformed by man into the realm of my will, if I am to hold myself ready as well for the unmediated word of God directed to a specific hour of life. It is part of my being that I cannot accept both together.[59]

The inadmissibility of identifying the Law with the word of God, he affirmed, was central to his very sense of being—a position, as he reiterated in subsequent letters, that he could not imagine would ever change. Significantly, he assured Rosenzweig that this position was not driven by a typical liberal estrangement from traditional Jewish piety, for in his youth, he had passionately adhered to orthodox religious practice. On the eve of the Day of Atonement in 1922, he confessed to Rosenzweig that:

there is something serious that I must tell you: that in my innermost heart . . . I strongly feel the mood of *erev*—the sense that today is the eve of Yom Kippur. This feeling probably comes (were I to reflect on its genesis) from my having experienced this day between my thirteenth and fourteenth year—at fourteen I stopped putting on my *tefillin*—with an intensity I had not felt since. And do you think I was a "child" then? Less so than now, perhaps, in a crucial sense; in those days I took space and time seriously, and did not just dismiss them from mind, as I do now. [Hence, I did not hold back then as I do now.] And then, when the night came—sleepless—my body, which was beginning to fast, was very real to me as a sacrificial animal. Exactly like that. I was acutely aware, that night and the following morning, and the day with all its hours, that not a moment should be allowed to slip past. No, not from the start [was I exposed to "liberal" influences in my religious education].[60]

Recalling that as a child he would often accompany his grandfather to pray at a small Hasidic *Klaus* (prayer room), he underscored that "all this does belong to the past; it is [present]. And yet I feel the way I do and am conscious of my frailty but no longer of a lack. May your heart understand me!"[61] He was, as Rosenzweig himself had noted, an apikoros, but a profoundly reverential one.

The abiding presence of Buber's traditional upbringing and youthful piety did not only engender an enduring reverence for the tradition. Despite his claim that "nothing is . . . missing anymore," his inability to affirm the traditional ritual and liturgical practices of Judaism, he confessed to Rosenzweig, had also left a gnawing void. "No other 'Yes' can replace the missing affirmation. This missing 'Yes' is not quietly absent: its absence is noted with terror." Nonetheless, he would remain resolute in his conviction that revelation is not legislation: "I hope I would be prepared to die for this postulate if I were to face a Jewish universal church that had inquisitorial powers."[62]

This was Buber's last communication with Rosenzweig concerning "the Law," at least in writing. Apparently sensing that even these disarmingly forthright reflections appeased his friend, Buber seems to have continued to ponder the gap between them. Some fifteen years later—a decade after Rosenzweig's death—Buber would once again return to the question of religious observance as governed by the Law, but now in the form of an allegory.

In his novel *Gog and Magog*, published initially in Hebrew in 1940, Buber chronicles the debate between two Hasidic rabbis over how to respond to the messianic hopes that accompanied Napoleon's invasion of Russia and its promise of Jewry's liberation from Tsarist oppression.[63] One school, led by the Seer of Lublin, advocated theurgic practices to "force the end"; the other school, heeding the teachings of the Holy Jew of Pzysha, rejected the apocalyptic strategy of the Seer and taught that one could prepare oneself for redemption only through inner purification. The Holy Jew—with whom Buber expressly identifies in the novel's epilogue—has a friend, whom he calls Yeshaja (Isaiah)—alluding to the biblical prophet whose "suffering servant" was the subject of Rosenzweig's own theological reflections in the last days before his death on December 10, 1929.[64]

Yeshaja and the Holy Jew had both been disciples of the Seer, and despite their age difference, were friends. On the eve of his departure from Lublin, Yeshaja reprimanded his friend for not adhering to set hours for communal prayer. The Holy Jew insisted that "as in [his] boyhood, he would wait to pray until enthusiasm" overcame him.[65] But Yeshaja protested that one's liturgical obligations are not a matter of subjective disposition:

We do not pray according to the inspiration of the individual heart. We join an ordering of the word of prayer which generations of our fathers organically *built*. We subordinate ourselves to and within this ordering and not as this *I* or *you (Du)*, but as part of that congregation in the act of prayer with which you and I are integrated. What your single heart bids you to tell your Creator, you can utter in the utter solitariness of your waking at the dawn or your lonely walks. But the order of prayer has its place and appointed times, which you should respect.

The Holy Jew with a palpable sadness cried, "Do you, too, address that reproach to me, Yeshaja? . . . When I stand alone before the Lord, I stand there, not as a single soul before its Master, but as the community of Israel before its God."[66]

Yeshaja does not deny the sincerity of his friend's testimony, but nonetheless faults him for shirking his responsibility as a leader. "When you gain disciples—and I know that they will be many and great—[but their actions perforce will betray you. For] this particular meaning of yours is not communicable nor can it be handed down."[67]

The Holy Jew has the last word, but one that is hardly defiant. "It may be that it will come about as you say, Yeshaja . . . [but] God marches to His victory by the path of our defeats."[68] By this, he seems to mean that, even as we falter along the way, our relationship to God is vindicated and actualized in the very process of seeking an authentic relationship with the Divine. With a melancholic resignation to the irreconcilability of their respective positions, the friends "parted with their friendship unimpaired, but their mood was one of unconquerable melancholy."[69]

Despite Buber and Rosenzweig's very public disagreement and unbridgeable theological divide, the pair's friendship endured, and would continue to deepen. At the beginning of May

1925, Buber received a letter from a young Catholic publisher from Berlin, Lambert Schneider, in which he wrote of "the pressing need" for a German translation of the Hebrew Bible from a Jewish religious perspective. Intrigued by the proposal, Buber invited the twenty-five-year-old publisher to visit him to clarify what he had in mind. Gratefully accepting the invitation, Schneider promptly boarded a train in Berlin for the six-hour journey to Heppenheim. Buber cordially greeted him and ushered him into his study. With his "brown, kind eyes" gently focused on him, Schneider recalled, Buber "listened to me attentively, so attentively and openly as no one had listened to me for a very long time."[70]

> Then he took from a shelf Luther's translation of the Bible, opened it to a passage, read it aloud to me and translated the same passage freely from the Hebrew text to show me that my view had its justification. But at the same time he made clear to me what inconceivable work, what responsibility lay in such an undertaking—all this without grandiloquence—and let me know that he did not believe he could accept such a task which would claim his time for years. All this was put forward so simply and plainly that I made no attempt at all to press him further and stood up to take my leave.[71]

But sensing Schneider's disappointment, Buber stood up from his desk and in a soft, consoling voice indicated that his reservations should not be construed as a definitive refusal. Rather, "he wished to talk the matter over with his friend Franz Rosenzweig . . . because such a request from a young man who was a Christian seemed to him a sign that he could not dismiss without further ado." Buber promised to give Schneider a response soon.[72]

The next day, Buber visited Rosenzweig and presented Schneider's proposal to publish a Jewish translation of the Bible. He told his friend he was inclined to accept, but only if Rosenzweig would take on the daunting—and long-term—project with him:

> I had a feeling that my suggestion at once pleased and disturbed him. Later I came to understand his reaction. Though he no longer expected death within the next few weeks or months, as he had done during the first stage of his illness, he had given up measuring his life in long periods. He was being offered, and therefore considered equal to, participation in a project which, as he recognized much sooner than I, would involve several years of intensive work. It meant adopting a different calculus of the future.[73]

Rosenzweig's response was surprisingly unhesitant: "Let's try it." Which chapter? Buber asked, to which Rosenzweig immediately replied, the first.

Thus began their monumental translation, or what they preferred to call a *Verdeutschung* (Germanification) of the Hebrew Bible. To capture the semantic texture of the Hebrew, they plumbed the often arcane registers of German, and when necessary, created neologisms. Their overarching premise was that the Hebrew Scripture is at root a record of the dialogue between God and Israel; hence, it was crucial to convey in German the "spokenness" (*Gesprochenheit*) of the original text. The task they set for themselves was, accordingly, both linguistic and theological. In consideration of Rosenzweig's physical limitations, Buber would prepare drafts, which he would mail to Rosenzweig and then discuss with him by letter. "Whatever remained controversial we discussed during my Wednesday visits; I lectured every Wednesday at the University of Frankfurt, and spent the rest of the day at the Rosenzweigs' home."[74] In notes accompanying the draft translations he sent to Rosenzweig, Buber would include excerpts from scholarly literature and classical Jewish commentaries to support his suggested rendition of more difficult passages.[75] "And

yet a single word often became the subject of weeks of correspondence."

Within five months, they had completed the Verdeutschung of Genesis. To celebrate the occasion, Rosenzweig composed a poem, which he sent to Buber in a letter at the end of
September 1925:

> Dear Friend,
> I have learned that every beginning is an end.
> Free of the burden of writing, I wrote [the closing
> words of *The Star of Redemption*] "Into Life"—
> After scarcely two years
> The hand ready for work grew lame,
> The tongue for speech already stood still,
> So only writing [*Schrift*, which also means Scripture] was left
>     to me.
> But this end became a beginning for me:
> What I wrote
> Has not—thanks to you (*dir*), beloved friend—
> Remained mere writing.
> We have written the Word of the Beginning,
> The initial act that pledges the meaning of the end.
> And thus the [translation of the] Holy Writ (*Schrift*) began.[76]

Upon receiving the poem, in which Rosenzweig unchar-
acteristically addressed him with the informal second-person
pronoun *dir*, Buber replied by addressing Rosenzweig with the
informal pronoun *Du*, adding that he hoped that it "would not
be difficult for you to get used to addressing as *Du* someone who
is nearly nine years older."[77] Whereupon Rosenzweig replied:

> It is not difficult for me at all; in thoughts I have used the
> familiar *Du* in addressing you all too often for that. The dis-
> tance between us is not so much caused by the difference in
> our age, for you at age twenty were already a public figure,
> while I was still dancing to Rumpelstiltskin's jingle when I

was thirty. Rather, it is due to a feeling in me to which I have hitherto been able to give expression through the customary [more formal] form of address [*Sie*] in my letters. I am almost sorry that this would not be in good taste now; but it will remain as my secret undertone, like the tacit *Du* [has been] until now.[78]

That is, though he would now address Buber as *Du*, signaling the intimate bond of mutual trust that sealed their friendship, he would continue to say *Sie* in his heart, signifying his unyielding respect for his venerable friend.

While working with Rosenzweig on the Bible translation, Buber conceived of a very special gesture in celebration of their friendship. Leading up to Rosenzweig's fortieth birthday on December 25, 1926, he distributed to forty-six of Rosenzweig's relatives, associates, and friends — Jews and non-Jews — portfolio-sized (twelve- by fifteen-inch) high-quality paper, with instructions to write whatever each deemed appropriate: congratulatory messages, personal reminiscences, essays, poems, even drawings. Buber requested that contributions be handwritten, to underscore the personal nature of the birthday gift. Everyone Buber invited — Jews and non-Jews alike — participated. Among the contributors were the Hebrew novelist S. Y. Agnon — who opened his contribution with a short story in Hebrew — and Gershom Scholem, who shared with Rosenzweig reflections on the ambiguous fortunes of Hebrew as the spoken language of the fledgling Zionist community in the Holy Land. Buber himself contributed a translation of Psalm 40, a psalm of thanksgiving and lament that contains the line, as rendered by standard Jewish translations, "I delight to do Thy will, O my God; yea, Thy law is in my inmost parts" (40:8). Buber, however, renders the Hebrew *toratkha* (your Torah) not as "Thy law" but "Thy instruction" (*Weisung*).[79]

The gift was presented to Rosenzweig on his birthday.

Placed on a low, wide lectern, the large portfolio pages were arranged in a way that allowed him, seated and strapped to his chair, to read at ease, with someone turning the pages as needed. A few days later he wrote Buber: "I have been through a great deal of the portfolio. It's bursting with spirit. It is a strange thing to see your own biography unfolding right before your eyes. The number four [presumably referring to his forties], which you are just about to leave behind, is after all a serious number. Three still shows traces of the baby: one still has *carte blanche* for occasional blunders. When one reaches the four—at least that's the way I feel about it now—one is finally and hopelessly grown up."[80]

Rosenzweig would in turn edit (together with Buber's son-in-law, the poet Ludwig Strauss) a *Festsgabe* (festive gift) to mark Buber's fiftieth birthday. Entitled *Aus unbekannten Schriften* (From unknown writings), the volume included contributions by fifty-five renowned scholars, of whom just more than half were Jews; the others were mostly religious Catholics and Protestants, as well as a few "baptized Jews." Each author presented excerpts of "unknown" literature, with a brief commentary, on themes that reflected Buber's polymathic interests—from the Upanishads to the Greek philosophers and poets; from Talmudic sages and medieval mystics to an early Renaissance alchemist; from German poets Goethe and Hölderin to Buber's contemporaries—Georg Simmel, Franz Kafka, Florens Christian Rang, and A. D. Gordon. The penultimate essay of the volume was a homily on Genesis 37:24—"The pit was empty, there was no water in it"—by Buber's grandfather, the midrash scholar Salomon Buber. Rosenzweig himself closed the Festgabe with a fragment from Buber's unpublished doctoral dissertation on German mystical philosophers and the problem of individuation.

As Rosenzweig had intended, the sheer number of participants in the volume gave expression to the esteem with which the fifty-year-old Buber was held among scholars, representing the diverse disciplines that had engaged his lively intellect. It was precisely by having the contributors to the volume focus on "unknown" literature that Rosenzweig highlighted the source of Buber's uniquely acclaimed position within German letters. His choice of focus for the Festgabe may have been inspired by the Protestant literary historian Wilhelm Michel, who, in a volume published two years earlier on Buber's contribution to German thought and letters, had applauded Buber for introducing into the German literary canon previously unknown and forgotten literature: "One of [Buber's] messages has reached each one of us at one time or other. To some he is important as a chronicler and interpreter of Hasidic piety. For others he has revealed the translucent world of Tchuang-Tse. He was among the first contemporaries to hear once again the ecstatic, enthusiastic voices of medieval Germany."[81]

Rosenzweig passed away less than two years after the publication of *From Unknown Writings*. At his request, no eulogies were delivered at the funeral, which took place on Thursday, December 12, 1929. It was also his wish that Buber read Psalm 73, which contains the verse that Rosenzweig had selected for his gravestone: "I am continually with thee."

# 8

---

## *The Tragic Grace of Everyday Reality*

BUBER'S FRIENDSHIP with Rosenzweig marked the crystallization of what he referred to as the third and ultimate station in the maturation of his understanding of Judaism.[1] The first had been inspired by the vision of the cultural rebirth of the Jewish people, though he soon concluded that culture is "but the by-product of a life process" and cannot be simply "willed into existence." "Culture develops like an individual's personality"; it evolves naturally from the "primal ground of one's life." The "primal ground of the life of the Jewish people must, then, be first aroused anew. This is what we [mean] by religious renewal." This he came to identify as his second station, one shaped by his increasing belief that the desired spiritual renewal should be distinguished from the normative structures of institutional religion. Rather it should seek to re-tap the primordial spiritual sensibility that had given birth to Jewish

religiosity, which, alas, had been overwhelmed and suffocated
by rabbinic Judaism. Hence, Buber concluded that "only when
religion strives to overcome itself," and no longer advocates the
"kingdom of religion" but affirms "God and his kingdom," will
Israel's foundational religiosity regain its hold on the life of the
Jewish people. What the spiritual renewal of Jewry—indeed, of
all humanity—requires is neither "culture" nor "religion" (nor
even religiosity), but a firm grounding in "the whole of reality,
inclusive of man and God in the world, the encounter with God
in the world, the redemption of the world *through* man." [2]

It is in the reality of "the lived everyday," therefore, that
genuine spiritual renewal is to be realized. According to Buber's
friend the Protestant historian of literature Wilhelm Michel,
this insight—the core idea of the third and ultimate station
of Buber's evolving conception of Judaism—was his seminal
contribution to German thought. In a small volume in 1925,
*Martin Buber: Sein Gang in die Wirklichkeit* (Martin Buber: His
way into reality), Michel hailed him as "the pioneer of the way
to the eternal other side of mysticism, namely, to new, capacious facets of reality." [3] Buber's "way into reality," Michel argued, had rescued German thought from the cul-de-sac of an
idealized quest for pure inwardness.

Buber chiefly credited this development in his thinking to
his beloved life partner, Paula, whom he regarded as his most
unyielding critic and a bastion of intellectual and emotional
integrity; the poem he wrote for her on his fiftieth birthday
(see Chapter 1) attests to his gratitude to Paula as his truest *Ge-
sprächspartner*, his ever-present dialogical companion.

Paula's unbending integrity and insight not only made her
Buber's most trusted critic and intellectual collaborator, but as
the realist of the two, she also early on had a more sober view
of the threat posed by the rise of National Socialism than did
her husband (who initially deemed it a passing setback for German democracy). While he clung to the belief that the devotees

of the German humanistic tradition would rally their fellow citizens to resist the allure of Hitler's diabolical nationalism, Paula keenly observed how easily decent and upright Germans were sucked into the vortex of Hitler's shrewdly choreographed madness. In her diary, she recorded her observations of her respectable, bourgeois neighbors in the small west German town of Heppenheim, in which she and her family had lived since 1916, on the basis of which she would write (upon the Bubers' immigration to Palestine in March 1938) a 650-page novel. The name she would give the novel, *Muckensturm*—doubtless an allusion to *Der Stürmer*, the vehemently anti-Semitic Nazi weekly—literally means an "assault of mosquitoes." Its subtitle is no less significant: "A Year in the Life of a Small Town." It was, as Buber later insisted, not an indictment of Heppenheim per se, but rather of the average German. The novel included individuals of courage who reached out to Jews and offered support.

Paula, of course, was not able to publish the novel in Hitler's Germany. In fact, starting in 1935 she was expressly prohibited from publishing any of her writings in Germany, for that was when she was officially expelled from the German Chamber of Writers, whose imprimatur was necessary before an author could send anything to press. The reason for her expulsion was provided in a letter addressed to her by the president of the Nazi writers' guild:

> By virtue of your marriage to Martin Buber, who is of the Jewish religion, you are considered Jewish. Moreover, according to your own declaration, although you are a full-blooded Aryan, you were converted on March 26, 1934, to Judaism by the rabbinate of the Berlin community. Clearly you feel yourself to belong more to the Jewish race than the Aryan. On these grounds, I cannot grant you the requisite permission to participate in the cultural life of the Third Reich.[4]

The conversion to which this letter refers was Paula's second formal adoption of Judaism. Prior to marrying Martin in April 1907, she had converted in January of that year, apparently under the auspices of a liberal rabbi. The second conversion was through the orthodox rabbinate of Berlin, and was likely a defiant gesture to dispel any ambiguity about her solidarity with the beleaguered Jewish people.

In September 1941, Buber would write from Jerusalem to Thomas Mann, who lived at the time in Pacific Palisades, California, to request his assistance in finding a U.S. publisher for Paula's novel.[5] Although impressed by Buber's detailed description of his wife's novel and tempted by the opportunity to read the manuscript, Mann replied that unfortunately it was highly unlikely an American publisher would undertake the translation of such a lengthy volume.[6] It was only after World War II that *Muckensturm* would be published, in Switzerland—as with all of Paula's previous novels and short stories, under the male pseudonym Georg Munk.[7]

For his part, Buber's initial assessment of the prospects of National Socialism and Hitler's regime did not last long. With the boycott of Jewish-owned businesses beginning on April 1, 1933, just two months after Hitler was appointed chancellor of Germany on January 31, troops of the Sturmabteilung (SA), the so-called "Brown Shirts" of the paramilitary wing of the Nazi Party, marched menacingly through Heppenheim, demonstratively stopping in front of the Bubers' home. A week later, the Reichstag passed a "Law for the Restoration of the Professional Civil Service," barring non-Aryans from serving in governmental institutions. Anticipating the dismissal of Jews from teaching positions, in October 1933 Buber resigned his professorship at the University of Frankfurt.

Buber was not naïve about the depths of German anti-Semitic sentiments, even among intellectuals. He was acutely aware of the paradox of the Enlightenment, which, while promoting Jewish emancipation, had also engendered what the philosopher Ernst Bloch called "metaphysical anti-Semitism," characterized by a repudiation of Judaism as alien to Christian and European spiritual and ethical sensibilities.[8] The trappings of learned discourse gave the contempt of Judaism and thus Jews a veneer of respectability. And in the throes of assimilation, western Jews had become estranged from their ancestral religion, so they themselves often perceived Judaism through the distorted and hostile lens of the educated European.

With the contemptuous context of metaphysical anti-Semitism in mind, Buber would devote himself to retrieving for the educated Jew—and non-Jew—of the West the spiritual core of Judaism. Long before the rise of Nazism, his writings on Judaism were subtly encoded with responses to prevailing defamations of Jews and Judaism. Among the notes he made in preparing the "Three Addresses" he delivered to the Bar Kochba student association in Prague, there are several folio sheets with citations in three parallel columns from the writings of Werner Sombart, Otto Weininger, and Houston Stewart Chamberlain, each asserting that Jewry is utterly bereft of any competence for mysticism and religious mystery, and noting the Jews' putative lack of a genuine understanding of German culture.[9] The fact that Weininger was himself a Jew only underscored the tragedy of Jewish deracination.

In his Prague addresses, as in his early writings on Hasidism, Buber implicitly appealed to the cosmopolitan humanistic values of the German educated classes. Anyone who recognized the essential human truths in the teachings of the Zen masters, or the legends of the pre-Christian Celts and Finns, might also come to see Jewish mystical tradition as a fount of universal wisdom. Such recognition, he had hoped, would lead to a sense of shared humanity with the Jews. But the chauvinistic nationalism unleashed by World War I—and the consequent intensification of metaphysical as well as vulgar anti-Semitism—

forced Buber to reassess his strategy of rehabilitating the image of Judaism and the Jew in the forum of educated European opinion.

Along with Rosenzweig, Buber had concluded that apologetics, inherently tendentious as they are, lacked the dialogical dimension of frank, open encounter taking into account the theological and existential differences that separate Jew and Christian. As Rosenzweig put it in a 1924 letter to Buber, "Today we are entering or rather are already in a new era of persecutions. There is nothing to be done about that, neither by us nor by the well-intentioned Christians."[10] "Even if apologetic thinking," Rosenzweig held, could overcome the constraints of its original polemical motive, it could not move past the barrier imposed by abstract theoretical categories to point to the lived reality to which it referred. "If one wants to understand a spirit," he wrote, "one cannot abstract it from its adhering body."[11]

In consultation with Rosenzweig, Buber organized a series of theological encounters between Jews and Christians at the Freies Jüdisches Lehrhaus in Frankfurt. Both men were wary of these dialogues simply dissipating into the platitudinous drivel of liberal understanding. But though authentic exchange cannot be contrived or forced, the conditions for open, spontaneous, and meaningful interfaith dialogue can be organized. The first step in maximizing the likelihood of frank theological dialogue was to solicit the participation of Christians and Jews who were up to the challenge. The second step was novel: Jews would present before Christians their understanding of Christianity, and Christians in the presence of Jews would reveal their conception of Judaism. Buber and Rosenzweig hoped that this format would encourage the charitable, open-minded attitude conducive to a dialogical appreciation of the spiritual and existential reality of the other faith community.

The planned interfaith colloquium, however, eventually

took place not at the Lehrhaus—which, while sponsoring a substantial number of lectures and courses by Jews on Christianity, rarely succeeded in soliciting Christians speakers on Judaism—but instead in the pages of Buber's *Der Jude*.[12] In a series of four Lehrhaus lectures on Christianity, Buber outlined the thematic parameters that he and Rosenzweig believed would foster genuine religious exchange. "One should speak about Jewish and Christian faith, rather than speaking about Judaism and Christianity"—not about doctrine or abstract theological concepts, but the way of faith as experienced by Jews and Christians.

A special issue of *Der Jude* in 1924 was devoted to "Judentum und Christentum." Of the twelve participating authors, five were Christians. Two other themed issues, "Judentum und Deutschtum" and "Antisemitismus und Volkstum," also contained articles by both Jews and Christians that touched on relations between the two faith communities. But with few exceptions, the Christian authors failed to sympathetically transcend the theological divide; in the pages of *Der Jude*, these Christian theologians and scholars repeated the negative images of Judaism that since the Enlightenment had often appeared in the work of German philosophers and theologians. They continued to hold tenaciously to the prevailing view of postbiblical Judaism as a religion beholden to a deficient conception of God, legalism, and dry ritual—in a word, what was derisively called Pharisaism. They also frequently contended that Judaism, as a fundamentally this-worldly faith, was bent on fostering secular activism, noting the propensity of Jews for leftist politics. Buber was clearly perturbed and disappointed, not only by the tone of most of the Christian contributors to *Der Jude*, but especially by their failure to transcend a polemical mode of discourse inflamed by metaphysical anti-Semitism: "I have once again . . . noted that there is a boundary beyond which the possibility of [dialogical] encounter ceases and only the reporting of factual information remains. I cannot fight against an opponent who is thoroughly opposed to me, nor can I fight against an opponent who stands on a different plane than I."[13]

The reluctance of German Christians to engage Jews and Judaism on their own terms was immeasurably deepened by a radical shift in post–World War I German-Protestant thought, from an emphasis on the Christian's ethical responsibility for the social realm to a reaffirmation of the New Testament promise of individual salvation through Christ—a promise that highlighted humanity's fallen state and its utter dependence on God's grace and deliverance. The efficacy of the moral deed and the meaningfulness of history, accordingly, were increasingly called into question. The emerging religious mood suggested that human action was of little meaning; one's only hope was divine salvation. This radical departure from the this-worldly optimism of liberal theology led to a growing interest in Marcion of Sinope, who had been long held by Christianity to be a heretic. Marcion elaborated the Pauline distinction between law and grace with a far-reaching gnostic (and ultimately anti-Semitic) twist: the God of the Hebrew Scriptures—the God of Creation—is not identical with the true God, who is essentially alien to this fallen world, and whose promise of redemption from the torments of life in this world is granted in the person of Jesus, the Christ. The God of the Old Testament, then, is the God of law and earthly justice; the God of the New Testament is the God of love and salvation. In his own time, Marcion had urged the Christian church to dissociate itself from the God of the Jews and creation, and to affirm the Father of Jesus, the God of truth and hope.

While Buber saw that antipathy to "the Jewish Bible" inevitably fostered the hatred of Jews, he was also deeply concerned with the fate of the biblical text itself and the core existential meaning to be derived from it. When he and Rosenzweig set out to translate the Hebrew Scriptures, they understood their task as rescuing not only the God of Creation, but also the Hebrew Bible itself. As Rosenzweig wrote to Buber: "The situation for which the neo-Marcionites have striven to achieve on the theoretical plane has in practice already been attained. When the Christian today speaks of the Bible, he means only the New Testament, perhaps together with the psalms, which he then tends to believe do not belong to the Old Testament. Thus, in our new translation of the Hebrew Bible we are becoming missionaries."[14] In accepting this "mission," Buber noted: "Although I am a radical opponent of all missionary work, I allowed myself to accept the mission, for it appertains to neither Judaism per se nor Christianity per se, but rather to the primal truth they share, on whose rehabilitation the future of both depends."[15]

For Buber, the neo-Marcion attempt to discredit the Old Testament and the God of Creation strikes at the very core of Western civilization and its humanistic foundations—namely, the presupposition that history and morality are ontologically and existentially meaningful. The abrogation of this premise, abetted by the neo-gnostic disdain for the mundane order celebrated by the Hebrew Scripture as Creation, breaks open the floodgates of cynicism and nihilism. Buber maintained that Western humanism was ultimately rooted not in Greek *Sophia* but in the biblical concept of Creation, and thus the struggle against neo-Marcionism—which Buber and Rosenzweig regarded as the most pernicious form of metaphysical anti-Semitism—was much more than a question of securing the dignity and honor of Judaism (though the two were not unrelated). Biblical humanism, as Buber explained in October 1934 to an audience of German Jews in the throes of the initial Nazi assault on their humanity, affirms that "the world is creation, not a reflection, not semblance, not play. The world is not something that must be overcome. It is a created reality"—the realization of which requires human partnership in God's work.[16]

Buber and Rosenzweig's translation of the Hebrew Bible, then, was not simply another translation, but their attempt to capture in German the unique cadences, inflections, and texture of the Hebrew, and thus revive for both and Jew and Gentile the power of the Word spoken by God to Israel. Through this "colometric" translation (the rendering of the "cola" or the speech units of the original Hebrew), they hoped, the abiding dialogical voice and thus the Presence of God—and God's ever-renewed relationship with the world of creation—would be palpably evident. For both of them, the God who speaks in the Hebrew Scriptures is not merely the God of Israel: He is the God of Creation, and thus the shared destiny of all who inhabit the world. In rejecting Marcion's original exhortation to jettison the Old Testament, Buber and Rosenzweig noted, Christianity in effect had long acknowledged that the concept of Creation was essential to the universality of the promise of salvation.

In affirming the God of Creation, the two were not utterly alone in Weimar Germany, as witnessed by an ecumenical journal with which they were both associated. Founded in 1926 at Buber's initiative, it was indicatively called *Die Kreatur* (The creature), and edited by a very deliberately chosen trio: a Jew (Buber), a Protestant, and a Catholic. Initially conceived of by the Protestant theologian Florens Christian Rang, the journal was originally to be called "Greetings from the Lands of Exile," to reflect the view that the monotheistic faiths are locked in doctrinal and devotional exile from one another, an exile from which they will be liberated only at the end of time when all the contradictions that blight earthly existence will be overcome; until then, they can only greet one another in a dialogical spirit. "What is permissible," as noted in *Die Kreatur*'s inaugural foreword, "and at this point in history mandatory, is dialogue . . . the opening or emerging of one's self out of the severity and clarity of one's self-enclosedness, a conversation on matters of common concern for created being."

Buber's acquaintance with Rang dated back to the Forte Circle of 1914 and its quixotic and stillborn effort to prevent the conflagration that became World War I. Rang, a former Protestant minister, had become aligned with right-wing German nationalism when the war broke out, but in the aftermath of the carnage, underwent a religious crisis that brought him to reject nationalism and embrace a messianic critique of politics. Numerous intellectuals were drawn to and praised his religious writings and especially his critical philosophy of politics; Walter Benjamin hailed Rang as "the most profound critic of German culture since Nietzsche," and Buber himself regarded Rang "as one of the noblest Germans of our time."[17] Like Benjamin, Buber was a close friend of Rang; indeed, Rang was among the very few of Buber's correspondents whom Buber addressed with the familiar pronoun *Du*.

In a letter of March 1924, Rang declined an invitation from Buber to participate in the special issue of *Der Jude* on "Judaism and Christianity," responding that at that juncture in Jewish-Christian relations, though conversations and relationships were important, genuine interfaith dialogue was untenable because most Christians knew so little about the lived reality of Jewish spirituality and teachings that sharing their opinions would serve no one.[18] By contrast, Rang held that what was possible, indeed urgent, at this historical juncture was a forum for Jews and Christians to affirm what they have in common as God's *creatures*. Upon Rang's death at the age of sixty just a few months later, Buber took it upon himself to realize Rang's vision of a post-theological ecumenical journal. In the course of his discussion with the young Catholic publisher Lambert Schneider about the proposed new translation of the Hebrew Bible, Buber broached the idea, and a month later, Schneider wrote Buber that he was eager to publish the proposed quarterly, with the first issue to appear the coming autumn.[19]

In consultation with Rosenzweig, Buber chose the title for the journal, *Die Kreatur*, which in German connotes all living created beings. Buber immediately moved to identify a Catholic and a Protestant as coeditors, successfully recruiting Josef Wittig, a recently defrocked priest, and Viktor von Weizsäcker, a Protestant physician and a close friend of Rosenzweig. As von Weizsäcker wryly observed, "the Catholic was no proper Catholic, the Protestant no proper Protestant, and the Jew no proper Jew"—for each editor was critical of the institutional expressions of their respective faith communities.[20] True to Rang's vision, *Die Kreatur* would eschew confessional theology, and the journal's Jewish and Christian authors (Catholic, Protestant, and Russian Orthodox) would "go together without merging, working together without living together," and affirm that "there is a unity of prayer without a unification of those who pray."[21] Religious differences would neither be ignored nor highlighted. Rather, as Buber—the journal's principal editor—expressed it, *Die Kreatur* would give voice to the existential bond that ultimately unites individuals of religious faith, irrespective of theological and creedal commitments: "A time of genuine religious conversations is beginning, not those so-called fictitious conversations where none regard and address his partner in reality, but genuine dialogues, speech from conviction to conviction, but also from one open-hearted person to another open-hearted person. Only then will genuine common life appear; not of an identical content of faith that is alleged to be found in all religions, but of the same situation, of anguish, and of expectation."[22]

*Die Kreatur*—published as an elegantly printed quarterly from 1926 to 1929—provided a forum for some thirty-six authors of diverse backgrounds, such as the syncretistic Russian Jewish religious thinker Lev Shestov; the Russian philosopher Nikolai Berdyaev, who spawned a weave of Marxism and orthodox Christianity; Ernst Michel, a representative of the left-wing Catholic "Awakening" movement; Jewish authors associated with Rosenzweig's Lehrhaus, and Rosenzweig himself; Christian thinkers, such as Eugen Rosenstock-Huessy, who shared Rosenzweig's and Buber's quest for a "New Thinking"; advocates of educational reform and psychoanalysis; and Rang himself (in posthumously published essays). Significantly, Buber did not solicit articles for *Die Kreatur*, but relied solely on submissions by authors who shared and were inspired by the journal's vision. Indicative of the enthusiasm engendered by that vision was a letter to Buber by Walter Benjamin, who had submitted an unsolicited essay on "Moscow," in which he hoped "to give voice" to the city's "creaturely aspect" (*das Kreaturliche*).[23] With the publication of his article in *Die Kreatur*, Benjamin wrote Buber: "I need not tell you how happy I am to be represented in [the journal] next to [an article by] Rang. . . . I should like to assure you expressly once again that I am ready to contribute to *Die Kreatur* in the future."[24]

Unfortunately, *Die Kreatur* and its distinguished cadre of authors could not stem the tide of neo-Marcionism, which Buber believed played a role in paving the way for National Socialism's virulent anti-Semitism. In a laconic lament, he noted that with Hitler's seizure of power, Marcion's gnostic denigration of the world of creation "was put into action; not however by spiritual means but by means of violence and terror."[25]

In the course of his theological encounters with Christians, Buber would experience the limitations of genuine dialogue, even with liberal Christians who resisted the seductive pull of neo-Marcionism. On January 14, 1933, two weeks before Hitler's appointment as chancellor of Germany, the Jüdisches Lehrhaus of Stuttgart sponsored a public dialogue on "Church, State, People, and Jewry" between the liberal Protestant theologian Karl Ludwig Schmidt and Buber.[26] Under the inspired leadership of Leopold Marx, who regarded himself a disciple of Buber, the Stuttgart Lehrhaus, since its founding in 1925, had been active in promoting interfaith understanding. The theme and guidelines of the Buber-Schmidt encounter were carefully considered. Buber asked that his Christian partner in the dialogue bracket his theological preconceptions and allow Judaism to speak for itself. This position was already implicit in Buber's objection to Schmidt's suggestion that the title of the program make reference to the "Synagogue" as the theological counterpart to the "Church." "Synagogue" is a term, Buber insisted, that is not at all in accord with the Jewish people's self-understanding. The Jews experience themselves as a living reality and faith, not as just a theological abstraction or an ecclesiastical religion bound by creedal doctrines and liturgical practices as implied by the term "synagogue." For Buber, the acknowledgment of the Jewish people as a living historical— and, hence, spiritually dynamic—entity was a crucial element in the struggle against theological prejudice and metaphysical anti-Semitism. To underscore the experienced reality of the Jews, he preferred the term "Israel." Schmidt was ultimately willing to compromise only with the term *Judentum*, which in German denotes both Judaism and Jewry.[27]

With regard to the structure of the dialogue, the director of the Stuttgart Lehrhaus instructed the speakers to treat the assigned themes in a "manner strictly substantive and to the point, neither polemically nor apologetically." This formulation was probably a guarded understatement of the sponsor's anxious desperation to foster a new type of interfaith encounter in a Germany darkened by the gathering clouds of a political apocalypse. As Buber later recalled, the debate was taking place in an "atmosphere of impending crisis." It was thus deemed crucial to identify a Christian who would engage Buber in a cordial and conciliatory dialogue.[28]

On the face of it, Schmidt seemed to fit the bill. A professor of the New Testament at the University of Bonn, he was sympathetic to Buber, having written warm reviews of his writings on Hasidism and messianism. Theologically, he was a liberal and forward-looking; the journal he had edited since 1922, *Theologische Blätter*, was widely considered the most distinguished organ of contemporary liberal Christianity. And the very fact that at a fateful hour in German history he dared to accept an invitation to address a Jewish audience testified to his liberal credentials and his civil courage. (Later, in 1935, due to his vociferous opposition to the Nazification of the church, he would be forced to forfeit his professorship and leave Germany.)

Schmidt's opening remarks initially demonstrated an effort to meet the expectations of his Jewish hosts.[29] He cited Buber on the need for partners in dialogue to speak on the "same plane"; he expressed a desire "to live together with you as Jews—as we must, as we wish—for you are our brothers in the whole world so also in our German fatherland." But it soon became clear that Schmidt's liberal affirmations were marred by his deep ambivalence toward the Jews, both theologically and socially. While condemning political and racial anti-Semitism as "wild and confused," he sternly reminded his audience that "Jews and Christians live in the same state not merely as separate religious confessions, but also as ethnically and racially apart." At this point he turned to Buber and (echoing many of the contributors to the *Der Jude* issue on Judaism and Christianity) asked, "How can one explain that the Jews, whose conservative sense we praise, have played and continue to play such a great role in revolutions?" Further, he absolved Christian theology of any responsibility for the framing of "the Jewish question," and even argued that "it would be an ostrich policy to deny the racial-biological and racial-hygienic problems which arise with the existence of the Jews among other peoples."

Theologically, he affirmed that Judaism should be taken seriously by Christians, not just with respectful tolerance, but also with an earnest regard for its religious claims. Problematic for his Jewish audience, however, was his insistence that Christians for their part should honor the Jews as God's people to whom Christ was initially sent. And he proclaimed that Jews must understand that the Christian whose faith is grounded in Scripture and the experience of Jesus Christ has no choice but to proclaim the Gospel to the Jews. Turning to his hosts at the Lehrhaus and specifically to Buber, Schmidt begged them to understand his intent was not polemical, but simply scriptural:

> Jesus of Nazareth had struggled against his contemporary Jewish Church in the name of the true Church [and] included heathens in this Church because he did not find in Israel such faith. . . . All this, we Christians if we truly stand within the Church, must let be said. The living Church of Jesus Christ cannot relinquish its claim: *Extra ecclesiam nulla salus* [there is no salvation outside the Church] is not only Roman Catholic dictum but a general Christian and Evangelical principle.

Schmidt went still further to argue that, with respect to their present anguish, the Jews must realize that the Gospel of Jesus Christ is their true succor, not Zionism, which not only was devoid of practical feasibility, but also — by advocating a political solution to *die Judenfrage* — erroneously treats the Jews as a natural nation and secularizes Jewish history, and thus disfigures and perverts the nature of Jewish destiny, which constitutes a divine scandal. The true Israel, he argued, cannot base its existence on blood, but solely on the call of God. Also, Zionism in his view was actually exacerbating anti-Semitism: "The modern world reacts to Zionism — which is national or even racist — in a correspondingly racist manner," he claimed — although he conceded that "it must not be forgotten that racial anti-Semitism in the modern world is pre-Zionist." At this critical moment in Jewry's anguished history, he believed, it was especially important to remind Jews that "Jesus, the Messiah, rejected by his people, prophesied the destruction of Jerusalem. It has been destroyed so that it will never again come under Jewish rule. Until the present day, the Jewish diaspora has no center." The Church, "Israel after the spirit," is Jewry's ultimate center and eternal refuge. With these words, Schmidt concluded his opening statement.

Buber was now invited to take the podium. In listening to Schmidt, he apparently realized something about the very premises of interreligious dialogue that required urgent clarification, and parted from his prepared text. (In his previous writings on the subject, this understanding had been an inchoate insight, but it seems here to have gained sudden clarity.) As in medieval disputations, Schmidt had tenaciously focused on the Christological question: the reality of the Christ event, versus Israel, and the attendant questions of the divine punishment of Israel and its destiny in exile. Israel was thus challenged to explain its obdurate stubborn rejection of Jesus Christ. But the very act of setting one's claim to revealed truth—which by definition is absolute and exclusive—against that of another revealed truth was inherently problematic; the opposing faith claims are by definition antagonistic and irreconcilable. Any theological encounter that pursues a confrontation on that level, no matter how cordially and respectfully conducted, can only produce discord and tension that "cannot be resolved . . . by human speech, by human willingness to come to terms, no matter how comradely." What is needed, Buber argued in his reply to Schmidt, is a totally new approach to interfaith encounter, which, while respecting the integrity and authenticity of the respective faith experiences of revealed truth, at the same time avoids futilely pitting irreconcilable truth claims

against each other. To go beyond this impasse, Buber proposed
to Schmidt:

> We can attempt something very difficult for the person with
> religious ties . . . we can acknowledge, as a mystery, what
> someone else confesses as *his* faith-reality, contrary to our
> own existence, contrary to our knowledge of our own being.
> We are not capable of judging its meaning, because we do not
> know it from within as we know *ourselves* from within.

In responding to Buber's appeal for theological humility and the
withholding of judgment of other faith commitments, Schmidt
insisted that it was in fact unreasonable to expect Christians to
compromise the truths they experience through the person of
Christ. "From the very beginning of Christianity, a sharp conflict [with Judaism] has existed. . . . We Christians must never
tire of keeping this one conflict alive." With this defiant assertion of Christian supersessionism, Schmidt turned the podium
back over to Buber.

Buber was clearly flabbergasted that a highly respected liberal Christian had proved to be an incorrigible supersession-
ist, bent on maintaining the church's theological antagonism
toward the Jews—an antagonism that he could not put aside
even temporarily for the purpose of dialogue on other grounds.
Rebuffed in his plea for a radically new approach to Jewish-
Christian encounter, Buber decided to forgo his prepared text.
As recorded by the stenographer, Buber's concluding words,
uttered with a palpable passion, took on the quality of a hymn,
a testimony of faith. Referring to the imposing twelfth-century
cathedral of Worms in whose shadow is an equally ancient Jewish cemetery, he mused, "I live a short distance from the city of
Worms," and when visiting,

> I always go first to the cathedral. It is a visible harmony of
> members, a whole in which no part deviates from perfection.
> . . . Then I go the Jewish cemetery. It consists of cracked and

crooked stones without shape or direction . . . there's not a jot of form; there are only the stones and the ashes beneath the stones. The ashes are there, no matter how thinly they are scattered. The corporeality of human beings, who have become ashes, is there. It is there. It is there for me . . . as corporeality deep in my own memories, far into the depths of history, as far back as Sinai.

I have stood there, united with the ashes, and through them the patriarchs. That is a remembrance of the divine-human encounter that is granted to all Jews. From this the perfection of the Christian house of God cannot separate me; nothing can separate me from the sacred history of Israel.

I have stood there and have experienced everything myself; all this death has confronted me: all the ashes, all the desolation, all the wordless misery is mine. But the covenant has not been withdrawn from me. I lie on the ground, prostrate like these stones. But it has not been withdrawn from me.

The cathedral is as it is. The cemetery is as it is. But nothing has been withdrawn from us [Jews].

Israel may be rejected by fellow human beings, humiliated and defamed. Compared to the magnificent power of the Church, Israel may indeed be humbled and destitute. But, Buber passionately asserted, its relationship with God remains firm.

Jewry's spiritual fortitude would soon be dramatically tested. Upon being granted "temporary" plenary powers by the Reichstag on March 24, 1933, Hitler ordered a boycott of Jewish-owned commercial establishments. Within days of the boycott of April 1, 1933, the National Socialist government passed a series of laws in quick succession that incrementally deprived Jews of civil rights. Buber viewed this initial assault on the dignity of German Jewry as a trial testing the spiritual and moral resilience of both Jew and (non-Jewish) German.

"The Jewish person today," he wrote in early April, "is inwardly the most exposed person in our world. [As for the Germans,] the tensions of the ages have selected [the Jew]. . . . They want to know whether human beings can still withstand [these tensions] and they test themselves on the Jews. . . . They want to learn through the Jews' destiny what a human being truly is."[30]

For Buber, "the hour and its judgment" was undoubtedly brought home to him by the experience of his two granddaughters, whose parents—Rafael Buber and Margarete Thüring (later Buber-Neumann)—had separated in 1925.[31] Since 1927, the girls had been placed by court order in the care of their grandparents Martin and Paula. Judith, the youngest granddaughter, later recalled that as a nine-year-old in school, her relationships with her fellow students suddenly changed with the rise of the Nazis to power. The four Jews in her class were assaulted during recess in the school courtyard. Literally adding insult to injury, she was barred from joining a school trip. Her eleven-year-old sister, Barbara, was no longer addressed by her name, but simply "you there" (*die da*).[32] Judith and Barbara also witnessed the parade of SA paramilitary troops menacingly stopping in front of their grandparents' home in Heppenheim, and later Paula being brought to the local police station for interrogation. In an article published in May 1933, Buber observed that:

> Children experience what happens and keep silent, but in the night they groan in their dreams, awaken, and stare into the darkness: The world has become unreliable. A child had a friend: the friend was taken for granted as the sunlight. Now the friend suddenly looks at him strangely, the corners of his mouth mock him: Surely you didn't imagine that I really cared about you?
>
> A child had a teacher, a certain one among all others. He knew that this person existed, so everything was alright. Now the teacher no longer has a voice when he speaks to

him. In the courtyard the space that leads to him is no longer open. . . . What has happened? A child knows many things, but he still doesn't know how it all fits together. . . . The child is fearful, but he can tell no one of his anxiety, not even his mother. That is not something that can be told about. He cannot ask anyone either. No one really knows why everything is the way it is.[33]

With the trauma in mind that his granddaughters experienced as the dark clouds of Nazi rule had begun to envelop Germany, Buber entitled this article simply, "Die Kinder" (The children).[34] Extrapolating from the child's experience of being suddenly branded an undesirable outsider, Buber concluded the article by adumbrating a strategy for "spiritual resistance" to the Nazi program of defaming the Jews and systematically removing them from the body politic of Germany and its cultural and social life:

> For its spirit to grow, a child needs what is constant, what is dependable. There must be something there that does not fail. The home is not enough; the world must be part of it. What has happened to this world? The familiar smile has turned into a scowl. I know nothing else but this: to make something unshakable visible in the child's world. Something that cannot fail because it is creating something constant and dependable that is not subject to the vicissitudes of current history. . . . Something that is ours; something that cannot be snatched away from us.[35]

This "something," Buber cautioned, cannot be construed as "replacing one nationalistic image of man with another nationalistic image," for Jews are "a different edition of the genus 'nation.'" Israel is sui generis: "Having been reduced and abandoned [over the centuries], we have remained impervious to categorization. I do not say this with self-assured pride; I say it with fear and trembling. This fate belongs historically to Israel—this fate of being thus entangled in the fate of the peoples [of the world] and thus discharged from it: being thrown out of it and remaining part of it in this way."[36]

In this hour of distress, Israel is confronted with the challenge to renew "the original covenant through which it came into being"—not as a badge of pride, or "one of the emblems on the pennants of the earth"; the covenant is "not a thing to be boasted about." Affirmation of the covenant does not simply— or necessarily—entail adherence to a given body of religious practices. "It is more than form and substance." One must, of course, teach one's children "Jewish substance," and encourage them "to form their lives in a Jewish way—but that is not enough. You must begin with yourselves. It needs to be realized in our personal, interpersonal, communal reality." Buber concludes this essay with an impassioned plea that poignantly echoes his own motherless youth: "It is up to us to make the world reliable again for the children. It depends on us where we can say to them and ourselves: 'Don't worry. Mother is here.'"[37]

To provide that "unshakable support," Buber here envisioned not a Jewish state but Jewish learning, and drew upon a concept of popular education (*Volkserziehung*) developed in Germany in the aftermath of World War I, focusing on extramural education for adults. Buber, along with colleagues in the German movement of adult education, turned to the teachings of the Danish pastor and educator Nicolai Frederik Severin Grundtvig, the father of adult education. With particular concern for the adult population of rural Denmark, Grundtvig had founded "Folk Schools" devoted to promoting "learning for life." Learning, Grundtvig held, should be a spiritual process that enhances community, not one that merely equips us with individual expertise and vocational qualifications. His educational vision had gained a powerful resonance decades earlier when he urged his fellow compatriots not to bemoan their defeat in the war of 1864 with Prussia, but rather to confront the crisis as an occasion for spiritual renewal; what was lost without would be regained from within. This message again found a receptive audience in Weimar Germany as its population emerged from the ignominy of the Treaty of Versailles after World War I.

Buber felt that adult education as envisioned by the Danish pastor would similarly prepare German Jewry to confront the assault on their dignity and self-esteem, nurturing their inner, spiritual resources in order to brave the collapse of the world in which they had felt secure—or hoped they would be. He viewed adult education as an essential tool for the survival of what might be ahead: "If one wishes to [simply] bring one's personality through the crisis intact, then it is bound to crumble, for then the crisis would have what it wants—an object that is brittle enough to be cracked by it."[38] The retrieval through education of the foundational spiritual resources of Judaism, he believed, would serve as the desired "something," that would be, in his words, worthy of eternal trust.

Buber associated Grundtvig's legacy with Rosenzweig's conception of Jewish learning, and regarded his late friend's pamphlet of 1917 *Zeit ists* (It is time) as a providing a programmatic springboard for the envisioned spiritual resistance.[39] In November 1933, upon reopening the Freies Jüdisches Lehrhaus (which had effectively closed its doors with Rosenzweig's death in December 1929), Buber cited Rosenzweig's speech at the original inauguration of the Lehrhaus in 1920: "The need demands deeds. It is not enough simply to sow the seeds, which perhaps will yield in the distant future their fruit. Today the need is urgent. And today the means of help must be found."[40] Buber observed that "only today thirteen years later, because of the situation in which we find ourselves have [Rosenzweig's] words revealed their full significance. Only today do we truly know from the very foundations of life that need and its demand for action."[41]

In conjunction with renewing the activities of the Lehrhaus, Buber put forth various proposals to advance a comprehensive program of adult education to the Reichsvertretung der
deutschen Juden (Reich representation of German Jews), which
was created in September 1933 to represent German Jewry at
large before the National Socialist government and to organize
Jewish cultural life (within the limits that the regime imposed
on the Jews). After intense negotiations with the Reichsvertretung president (Rabbi Leo Baeck) and executive director (Otto
Hirsch), Buber's proposal for the establishment of a Center for
Jewish Adult Education (Mittelstelle für Jüdische Erwachsenenbildung) was approved. Charged with directing the Mittelstelle, Buber explained its objective in a circular composed in
June 1934:

> The concept of "Jewish adult education" might have been
> understood even a short time ago to mean "elements of edu-
> cation" or "cultural values" that were to be passed on to
> those growing up and to the grown-up—for instance, giving
> an idea of "higher education" to those who were not privi-
> leged to obtain it, or to initiate those not familiar with Jew-
> ish subjects into some general knowledge of this community.
> When we gave this name to our newly founded experiment
> we obviously meant something else. The issue is no longer
> equipment with knowledge, but mobilization for existence.
> Persons, Jewish persons, are to be formed, persons who will
> not only "hold out" but will uphold some substance in life;
> who will have not only morale (*Haltung*), but moral strength
> (*Halt*), and so will be able to pass on moral strength to others;
> persons who live in such a way that the spark will not die. . . .
> What we seek to do through the educating of individuals is
> the building of a community that will stand firm, that will
> prevail, that will preserve the spark.[42]

To nurture that spark, he set out to train a cadre of teachers
and youth leaders. Drawing particularly on young adults who

had been prohibited from attending German educational institutions, Buber organized "Lernzeiten" (periods of learning),
retreats held for a few days in rural areas throughout Germany.
These retreats, which were usually kicked off with lectures by
Buber and the core staff of the Mittelstelle on various themes in
Jewish cultural history, were devoted to the reading of texts —
principally biblical, which for many was their first encounter
with the Hebrew Scriptures. Buber often led these seminars
himself, in which he sought to teach the "art of reading slowly"
(*die Kunst langsam zu lessen*) and with particular attention to the
biblical word in the context of its spokenness (*Gesprochenheit*).
This attention "endows it with a concrete [existential] embodiment. The commanding word of the Bible is not a [written]
sentence, but an address" — a personal address.[43]

Accordingly, Buber emphasized that "in discussing a text
from Jewish literature, such as the Bible, I acknowledge that
no interpretation, including my own, coincides with the original meaning and that my interpretation is conditioned by my
being."[44]

> If I attend as faithfully as I can to what it contains of word
> and texture, of sound and rhythmic structure, of evident and
> hidden connections, my interpretation would not have been
> made in vain, for I find something, have found something.
> And if I show what I have found, I guide one who lets oneself
> be guided to the actuality of the text. I place the one whom
> I teach before the effective powers of the texts, the effect of
> which I have experienced.[45]

No one reading is, therefore, authoritative. Nonetheless, the
fostering of diversity was not merely a question of tolerance but
rather, in Buber's words, "making present the roots of community and its branches" and creating "solidarity, living mutual
support and living mutual action." He viewed this as a model
of community, not merely an "amalgamation of like-minded

[people]" but rather a collective that "masters *otherness* in a lived unity."[46]

This educational vision of a "great community" embracing multiple opinions and positions was in consonance with the founding objective of the Reichsvertretung as an umbrella organization of German Jewry, representing Zionists and liberals, orthodox and reform Jews alike. During the five years he was at the helm of the Mittelstelle, Buber specifically addressed his fellow Zionists only once, in an unpublished lecture in December 1934 before the Zionist Association of Frankfurt about "the pedagogical problem of Zionism." At the outset of the lecture, he acknowledged what had been for him a deeply personal issue over the many years of his membership in the movement, and conceded that he was unable to deal with it in a purely objective manner: "I would be doing myself a disservice if I would do so." As such, "it is a problem that does not lend itself to an absolute solution"; one can at most clarify the problem.[47]

What was the problem? The premise of pedagogy, Buber argued, must be distinguished from that of politics and sociology. Whereas the principles guiding politics and sociology are inherently "hegemonic" and corporate, pedagogy is both "concealed" and directed to the education of individuals: the proper role of the educator is thus fundamentally different from that of a political thinker or sociologist. Within the context of Zionism, however, education was all too often merely a handmaiden of politics and sociological analysis. Buber identified this as the pedagogic problem of Zionism: While Zionism has the task of transforming the Jewish people and healing it from the spiritual and psychological torments wrought by exile, "education always applies to individuals. It cannot be otherwise; education takes place between one person and another."[48]

Buber put forth here a distinction between "small" and

"great" Zionism. Small Zionism deems it sufficient merely to transplant the Jewish people to their ancestral homeland, and thereby, with the grace of political and social sovereignty, redirect their destiny to happier pastures. The advocates of a "great Zionism," however, want something more: a Jewish commonwealth that will promote the construction of a "'genuine human community' (*Gemeinschaft*)," in accordance with the people of Israel's founding biblical mandate. This vision, of what Buber called elsewhere "biblical humanism," sets the true normative horizon of Zionism, dissolving the divide between the profane and the sacred, the public and private.[49] He rejected the claim of many of his fellow Zionists that, while this goal was a worthy one, such community could only be realized after—and could wait for—"the firm establishment of Jewish settlement in Palestine." Here, the "sociological principle rules." By setting their immediate objective sights only on Jewish settlement, these well-meaning Zionists perforce were confusing propaganda with education.

The "nationalization" of the Jew as a Hebrew-speaking pioneer (*chalutz*) may be necessary for the settlement project, "but this is hardly enough," said Buber. Nor is it enough to "live together politically" and to inculcate a "national consciousness":

> As I have already said, the work of the educator is inherently problematic, bordering on the tragic. The educator must ever again experience resistance, self-centeredness, and an unwillingness to change. The educator will recurrently experience moments in which he gives up and despairs. Nonetheless, I have a strong heartfelt feeling that these unsuccessful individuals, the educators, will from time to time be heard. In the world in which we live today, it certainly does not seem that the pedagogical principle could prevail. It seems that it would forever be defeated, that it will be politicized.
>
> But it only seems so. For the pedagogical principle en-

dures beneath the surface in the dark, inner, secret precincts of being. For thirty-three years and more, we the representatives and defenders of the pedagogical principle have criticized what took place [within the Zionist movement]. But our critical posture is one of hope.[50]

"It is a hopeful critique," he continued, for as severe as the critique may be, it pointed to what was still possible.

In his addresses to the wider German-Jewish public, Buber amplified these autobiographical reflections and his critique of Zionism—and indeed, all ideologies that he perceived as bifurcating the public and the personal. In a lecture at the Lehrhaus in February 1935, he insisted that the pedagogical principle bears on the entire reality of one's life, and thus is antithetical to ideological education, for in promoting the adoption of political positions, ideologies tend to neglect the personal and interpersonal demands of everyday life. Buber distinguished between the "fictitious conviction" (*Fiktivgesinnung*) of an ideology, and a "real conviction" (*Realgesinnung*), which attunes one to taking responsibility for the concrete realities of life. "My group cannot deprive me of this responsibility, nor should it."[51] This individual responsibility for the concrete, everyday reality in which one finds oneself yielded a central concept in Buber's thought, *Bewährung*—the "proving of the self" that "exists only in the factual moment. Biblical humanism," he wrote, "cannot raise the individual above the problems of the moment; it seeks instead to train one to stand fast in them, to prove oneself in them."[52]

Buber would travel throughout Germany teaching his fellow Jews and delivering lectures that included his barely disguised criticism of the Nazi regime. While, according to Ernst Simon, who worked closely with Buber to establish the Mittelstelle and to lead the spiritual resistance to National Socialism, the Nazi authorities had initially "seemed hardly to interest themselves" in Buber's activities, they gradually became more vigilant.[53] The turning point was an address Buber delivered at the Berlin Philharmonic in the winter of 1935. Before an audience of two thousand that filled the imposing concert hall on Bernburger Straße in the Kreuzberg district of Berlin — a hall that would be destroyed by British bombers on January 30, 1944, the anniversary of Hitler becoming chancellor — he spoke of "The Power of the Spirit." The life of the spirit, Buber observed, was under assault, due to a distorted concept of the spirit that had ruled Western civilization since the ascendancy of Pauline Christianity, which had severed the spirit from the totality of being, "which comprises and integrates all one's capacities, powers, qualities, and urges." The neo-pagan liberation of the elemental forces of life — hunger, sex, and the will to power — from a Pauline, indeed, gnostic conception of the life of the spirit, he observed, had inexorably led to a nihilistic glorification of these forces.[54]

In contrast to both the Pauline suppression of corporeality and its neo-pagan glorification, he argued, the Judaic conception of the spirit is informed by an affirmation of the world — in its totality — as created. Accordingly, "the world is not something that is to be overcome. It is a created reality, but created to be hallowed"; consequently the elemental forces of life, of reality, are neither to be suppressed nor glorified, but sanctified and transformed by the spirit. "In the reality system of Judaism," which Buber said designates as reality the "basic unity of social, family, and personal life," the world is to be rendered holy. To highlight the political intent and implications of his lecture — his critique of the nihilistic glorification of power, and of course his attention to what Judaism has to offer the world — Buber concluded with an allegory that was not included in the printed version of the lecture.[55] The enduring power of the spirit, he notes, is to be illustrated by the defeat of the Assyrian army that laid siege to Jerusalem. As reported by the prophet

Isaiah: "Woe to Assyria, the rod of My anger and the staff in whose hand is My indignation. I will send him against an ungodly nation . . ." (Isaiah 10:5).

Unbeknownst to Buber, scattered among the mostly Jewish audience was a large contingent of the Gestapo upon whom the allegorical allusion of Buber's concluding remarks was not lost. On February 21, 1935, Buber received orders from the Gestapo forbidding him to lecture at both public and closed forums of the Jewish community. On March 5, 1935, the ban was extended to all teaching activity. On July 30, 1935, he was notified that he was permitted to resume teaching, but not to give public lectures.[56] The restrictions on his educational activity did allow Buber to engage more fully in scholarship, particularly on the Hebrew Bible, and to develop further his conception of theopolitics as first articulated in his 1932 volume, *Königtum Gottes* (Kingship of God).[57] In this book, which Buber conceived as a critique of the ultra-conservative jurist Carl Schmitt and his notion of political theology as sanctioning the ascription of divine power to a human sovereign, Buber argued that the Hebrew Bible instructs that only God exercises absolute authority, which cannot be transferred to any human being or political institution. Buber advanced this thesis only one year before Hitler assumed dictatorial powers.

What had been merely a vague premonition soon became a frightening reality, a development that Buber ascribed in large measure to the pervasive neo-gnostic contempt of his generation for the concrete realities of everyday existence—a contempt that he believed fostered both a nihilistic political ethos and, alternatively, a studied detachment from the world. For Buber, the latter posture was represented by Søren Kierkegaard, whose writings had increasingly captured the imagination of German intellectuals in the post–World War I period. In a 1936 philosophical essay, Buber questioned the Danish philosopher's concept of the "Single One," who detaches from the crowd in order to secure existential and religious integrity.[58] To seek God's love by fleeing the crowd, Buber argued, is in effect to abandon one's fellow creatures. As challenging as the life of the crowd may be, that crowd is comprised of our fellow human beings who are the foundation of the divinely created order. Hence, contrary to Kierkegaard's quasi-Marcion premise, "God and man are not rivals."[59] Indeed, "creation is not a hurdle on the road to God, it is the road itself. We are created along with one another and directed to a life with one another. Creatures are placed in my way so that I, their fellow creature, by means of them and with them find the way to God. A God reached by their exclusion would not be the God of all lives in whom all life is fulfilled."[60] Buber summarized this credo with a quotation from his wife, Paula, that he placed on the book's title page: "Verantwortung ist der Nabelstrang zur Schöpfung"—responsibility is the umbilical cord of creation.

Although the Nazi authorities forbade the distribution among the general public of books authored by Jews—even in fields like botany and entomology—Buber hoped that his message would somehow be heard beyond the tyrannically imposed confines of a Jewish readership. This hope was fortified by his overarching sense of responsibility to his fellow human beings, Jews and non-Jews alike: "Nothing must dissuade us from standing by [non-Jewish] members of the German nation in unbroken personal integrity, without reservation and free of animosity, wherever we encounter them, in such a way that we are able to see and recognize one another. Even today, especially today, even though it has been made cruelly difficult for us, human openness is a dire need."[61]

Openness to non-Jews, he felt, was integral to spiritual resistance to the Nazi program to deprive the Jews of their humanity. Buber himself made a concerted effort to maintain relationships with Germans who refused to heed Hitler's call to yield their own humanity. Throughout the dark years of the

Third Reich, he conducted an active correspondence with, among others, the novelist Hermann Hesse; Protestant theologians Ernst Lohmeyer, Albert Schweitzer, and Karl Barth; Catholic theologian Ernst Michel; the psychoanalyst Hans Trüb; and the philosopher Rudolf Pannwitz. (Significantly, each of Buber's "Aryan" correspondents by then no longer resided in Germany.)

The National Socialist authorities also prohibited the publication of Jewish-authored books by "Aryan" publishing houses. Among the approximately thirty privately and publicly owned Jewish publishing houses in Germany in this period, the most active and dynamic was the Schocken Verlag, in which Buber was to play a seminal role as an adviser and author. In 1933, Buber and his wife attended a social evening in the Berlin home of Lambert Schneider, who had been recently recruited to serve as managing editor of the Schocken Verlag. Buber and Schneider had had a close working relationship ever since the Catholic publisher had contracted with Buber and Rosenzweig to translate the Hebrew Scriptures, a project he brought with him to his new position. In the course of the evening, the conversation turned to the fate of Jewish authors and publishers under National Socialism. As reported by Schneider, Buber mused, "We have to learn how to live in the catacombs. What is required of writers like us is to write so subtly that those in power won't immediately detect our resistance and grab us by the scruff."[62]

The challenge was to publish works advancing the revitalization of Jewish culture without provoking the ire of the Nazi authorities. The strategy adopted by the Schocken Verlag was to publish anthologies of literature representing traditional Jewish culture and thought. These ostensibly apolitical volumes were selected in a way that they, in effect, served as a new body of midrash; the themes of the works chosen were intended to mirror the contemporary concerns of the beleaguered German

Jewish community. Toward the end of 1933, six months after the Nazi burning of a Jewish book in April 1933, the Schocken Verlag inaugurated a series of relatively short volumes presenting representative texts of classical Jewish and modern Jewish cultures. At a rate of two volumes per month, these "Schocken Bücherei" sold between five and ten thousand copies each. By the time the publishing house was closed in 1938 by Nazi decree, eighty-three titles had been released. Tellingly, the first volume was entitled *Tröstung Israels* (The consolation of Israel), and presented Buber's translation of Isaiah 40–55. These "songs of the suffering servant" are read by traditional Jews as referring to the Jewish people. Echoing this theme, Buber presented in another volume a translation of twenty-three psalms. Giving it the title *Out of the Depths I Cry to Thee* (a line from Psalm 130), he explained in the preface that this selection of psalms represented the biography of Israel.

Upon receiving notice that the Gestapo had extended its ban to all of his teaching activities, Buber planned a visit to Palestine. Less than a month later, he and Paula arrived by ship in Haifa on April 1, 1935, where they were greeted by their son in-law, Ludwig Strauss, who in January of that year had settled in Jerusalem; his wife, Eva (Martin and Paula's daughter), and their two young sons would join him in May. From the detailed letters about their time in Palestine that Paula wrote to her fourteen-year-old granddaughter Barbara, the first of which is dated April 5, it is evident that she and Martin were enthusiastic about what they experienced.[63] As their ship, the *Roma*, docked in Haifa, it was joined by two other vessels. There were some four thousand passengers in all—among them many athletes who had come to participate in the Second Maccabiah, the Jewish Olympics, which was to be held in Tel Aviv from April 2 to April 10. Among the 1,300 athletes from twenty-six countries was a delegation of 134 German Jews, who at the last moment received permission from the Nazi authorities to travel to Palestine. Paula described with amusement the chaotic, four-hour scrabble of looking for one's suitcases among the voluminous heap of baggage.

Toward evening, they began "a splendid journey under a star-filled sky" to Jerusalem. Perhaps just to appeal to her granddaughter's fantasy, Paula told her that they rode on camels and donkey-pulled carts as they ascended the Judean hills to Jerusalem. They arrived at midnight at the home of their hosts. "Aunt Eva will be living very close to here in a district of new streets, new houses. Everywhere there is the hustle of building. . . . Already on the first morning, we went to the bazaar in the Old City. . . . [It is] just like in a Thousand and One Nights. I go there every day. Everything is behind the city walls; the high, vaulted streets are bustling with old Arab, Jewish, Armenian, and other pedestrians. . . . I believe no other place on the earth is like Jerusalem. I could spend the entire day wandering through the city." Paula then let Barbara know that her father, Rafael—who had the previous year emigrated to Palestine with his second wife, Ruth—would be visiting them in Jerusalem. A member of a kibbutz in the Jezreel valley, Rafael had gained a reputation as a highly skilled worker (he had studied agronomy and farming machinery in Germany in preparation for his emigration to Palestine), and had been duly praised by the Zionist officials in Jerusalem whom Paula and Martin met. "You can well imagine how proud this makes us. He has found here the place for which he was destined." In the same letter, she reports of her visit with Martin to the Ben Shemen Youth Village, founded by Buber's disciple Siegfried Lehmann in 1927.

Paula concluded her letter with an exuberant evocation of the "truly paradisical landscape"—the waft of fragrant orange groves, the majesty of the olive trees, "some dating back to the Roman period." "Liebes Bärbchen," Paula added, "you should not suffice with this report, but prepare yourself for next year." The thrust of this letter and the ones that followed suggest that Paula was preparing her granddaughters — Barbara and her younger sister, Judith — for their prospective emigration to Palestine along with Paula and Martin, their guardians. Indeed, in a subsequent letter, Paula assures Barbara that she will enjoy life in Jerusalem.

The letters also attest to Paula's and Martin's attempt to acquaint themselves with the Arab population of Jerusalem. A Hebrew University professor of philosophy and former member of the Bar Kochba circle of Prague, Hugo Bergmann, arranged for Arab acquaintances, a sheikh and his son who spoke reasonable English, to take them to places that "European tourists on their own would never see." Their Palestinian hosts also took them to a Muslim wedding. The colorful ceremony and joyous festivities brought tears to Paula's eyes. A Muslim teacher, also a friend of Professor Bergmann, arranged for Paula and Martin to sit on the stage reserved for the Arab dignitaries of Jerusalem and witness the Festival of Nabi Musa (the Prophet Moses) — a festival that entailed a procession, led by sword dancers under green banners of the Prophet Muhammed, from Jerusalem to the Tomb of Moses near Jericho. What Paula did not tell her fourteen-year-old granddaughter was how troubled she and Martin were by the deteriorating relations between the Jews and Arabs.

Less than two weeks after they arrived in Palestine, Paula and Martin would have to cut their visit short. On April 13, Paula informed Barbara that her great-grandfather, Carl Buber, was deathly ill. On April 23, Paula and Martin boarded a ship to Athens, whence they were to board a train to visit Martin's father in Lemberg. But it was too late; he had died on April 18. Upon learning of the death of Buber's father, at the age of eighty-seven, Rabbi Leo Baeck, the president of the Reichsvertretung, wrote him a letter of condolence, dated May 21, 1935: "I sincerely sympathize with you in your mourning of your father. The fluid line between past and present becomes a more definite dividing line when one loses one's father—only then, and even if he passes away at an age when the son is already looking at grandchildren." To these moving words, Rabbi Baeck added that Otto Hirsch, the executive director of the Reichsvertretung, told him about "the concerns you brought back from Palestine."[64]

These concerns deepened in the spring of 1936 with the outbreak of the Arab Revolt against British colonial rule in Palestine, sparked by the Mandatory government's seeming encouragement of Jewish immigration. The Arab population perceived this as British collusion with the Zionist leadership to create a Jewish majority in Palestine and strengthen the Zionist claim to exclusive sovereignty in the country. The October 1935 discovery in the port of Jaffa of a large arms shipment destined for Jewish paramilitary forces served to exacerbate these fears. The uprising began in mid-April 1936 with an attack on a convoy of Jewish vehicles, followed the next day by Jewish revengeful assaults on Arabs, unleashing a cycle of violence. The ensuing Arab general strike lasted until October 1936, but not before the death of hundreds of Jews and thousands of Arabs, as well as numerous British casualties.

In June 1936, Buber wrote to Hans Trüb, a Swiss psychoanalyst and close friend since the mid-1920s, that he and Paula were "very dejected by the course of events in Palestine. Events of which I have for long warned and foretold, which makes the matter that much more distressing. I have in the past days collected my warnings in a small volume, in order to arouse anew the conscience [of my fellow Zionists]."[65] The volume Buber referred to is *Zion als Ziel und als Aufgabe. Gedanken aus drei Jahreszehnten* (Zion as goal and task: Thoughts of three decades).[66] In the preface to this slim anthology of eighty-seven pages, Buber seeks to remind his readers that Zion is both a geographical and spiritual goal. Hence, "one can arrive at Zion only through Zion"—a paradox, he argues, that needs no explanation to a "healthy human understanding," but eludes those who are in thrall of the dubious political logic that currently rules the world. Following the "howl of wolves," he wrote, leads one only to the company of wolves.

The selection of writings in this volume, ranging from 1900 to 1932, is arranged thematically rather than chronologically. The first is a text, "Three Stations," referred to at the beginning of this chapter. It traced the trajectory of Buber's Zionism as a movement of spiritual renewal, from its earliest conception of a cultural renaissance to his ultimate realization that genuine religious and spiritual renewal must be grounded in the lived everyday reality of individuals and community. (As he put it in a lecture to the Frankfurt Lehrhaus in 1934, "Israel is renewed not only by what they say but by the totality of their existence.")[67] The concluding text of the anthology is the address on nationalism that Buber delivered at the Zionist Congress of 1921. In this address, he warned of the political perils of aligning the quest for a national home with the imperialistic interests of the newly established British Mandate, especially in the face of the resolute and understandable opposition of the Arab population of Palestine. To secure the moral and spiritual integrity of Zionism, he cautioned the movement to be wary of assuming the posture of a self-righteous, egocentric nationalism. Such a "hypertrophic" nationalism would undermine the very cure—the restoration of national dignity and spiritual renewal—that Zionism sought to offer the ailing Jewish people. Moreover, a myopic preoccupation with the problems of one's own nation invariably narrows one's moral consciousness, obscuring the humanity of other peoples, especially of one's enemies. The exaltation of a self-enclosed, parochial nationalism as morally self-sufficient distorts the original purpose of Zionism: to heal the afflictions of the Jewish people and thereby enable it to serve "the Sovereign of the world, who is the Sovereign of my rival, and my enemy's Sovereign, as well as mine."[68]

Despite his misgivings about the direction that the Zionist project had taken, Buber sought to reassure his colleagues in Jerusalem that "in no case shall I give up on Palestine."[69] For their part, his "friends in Palestine," as Gershom Scholem wrote Buber, "are convinced that—in this country and in the education of the young generation in Jerusalem—even more decisive things are at stake than in [Germany]. You must be here if you do not wish to forgo having an influence on the country."[70] In a later letter, he emphasized: "Your voice is bound to carry weight."[71] Writing Buber on the occasion of his sixtieth birthday, David Werner Senator, a member of the Executive of the Jewish Agency in Jerusalem, added to his greetings an appeal for Buber to hasten his emigration to Palestine: "You do not know and perhaps cannot estimate how eagerly some people here are awaiting you. For there are people here who believe that a person of your cohesive ability can bring together and thereby activate energies that exist today in invisible and inert form, and thus cannot be manifest and effective. We find ourselves in a tragic situation of realizing our aims in a transformed world that is no longer ours. Perhaps your wisdom and goodness can help us to find a way out of this confusion, which has made a person like me, for example, profoundly pessimistic. Come very soon!"[72]

Buber himself doubted that he could meet these expectations. To be sure, he had found a receptive audience in Nazi Germany, especially among Jewish youth. From her exile in Paris in 1935, the twenty-nine-year-old Hannah Arendt wrote an article in French attesting to Buber's impact on her generation of German Jews:

> When almost two years ago, the German Jewish community, in its entirety, had to respond to the isolation imposed by the laws of exception, and the material and moral ruin of its collective existence, all Jews, whether they liked it or not, had

to become aware of themselves *as Jews*. At that decisive moment, anyone who knew the situation intimately was bound to feel anxious about the most difficult question: will one succeed in giving this new ghetto, imposed by the outside, a spiritual content? Will one succeed not just in organizing these Jews superficially, but also linking them together by a *Judaic* bond, and making them real Jews once again?. . . Is there a leader who is more than a propagandist for Zionism, more than an eminent expert on Jewish problems, more than an excellent Judaic scholar and historian, and more than a living representative of Jewish culture—in short, someone who is all these things and more? In that sense, in our day, *Martin Buber* is German Jewry's incontestable Guide. . . . He was able to win over the youth because he didn't bury himself or Judaism under a great past, but knew how to rediscover the living roots of this past to build an even greater future.[73]

Arendt and others may have felt certain about Buber's significance, but Buber himself was not so sure. When at the end of March 1938, Buber finally emigrated to Palestine to assume a professorship at Hebrew University, he did so with a "heavy heart," uncertain whether at the age of sixty he could acquire in Hebrew the rhetorical and pedagogical skills to be an effective guide in the linguistic and political culture of his new home.[74]

# 9

---

## *Professor and Political Activist*

ON SATURDAY, March 19, 1938, Martin and Paula Buber and their two granddaughters boarded in Naples the Italian passenger ship the S.S. *Esperia* for the six-day voyage to Haifa. As they landed on March 24, Buber was filled with anxiety about his inaugural lecture at the Hebrew University, which he was scheduled to deliver just five weeks later, on April 25. It would be his first public lecture in Hebrew, which, as a modern spoken and literary language, he had yet to master—and given his age, he assumed he never would. He expressed this fear in a letter to Ernst Simon, noting that he had engaged an editor versed in modern Hebrew to polish the texts he had prepared:

> I would draft my lectures in German and then prepare a Hebrew version, whereupon [my editor] puts them into good Hebrew. But as I was working, I began to have doubts. When I compared my Hebrew version with [the editor's corrections], I became increasingly convinced that I shall *never* be

able to write like [him]—in fact, there is an unbridgeable gap
between my crude mode of expression (to say nothing of its
faultiness) and [the editor's] cultivated one. . . . Should I ever
get to the point where I write and speak a halfway decent
Hebrew, it will of necessity be a *relatively* untalmudic [i.e.,
unlearned] one.[1]

Having achieved with great effort the status of a respected *German* writer—as he underscored to one of his disciples in Palestine—he felt strongly that "it would be unnatural to me to go
over there [to Palestine] as a German writer, [and thus] without a profession tied to the [Hebrew-speaking] people living
there." "Don't you understand this?" he had written pleadingly
to a friend eighteen months before his emigration.[2]

But Buber's disciple and future colleague at the Hebrew
University Hugo Bergmann was concerned that if Buber failed
to "influence the future shape of our people," it would be precisely because he still fancied himself a German writer.[3] On
the shaping of the future of the Jewish people, unfolding in
Palestine, "we—your circle," Bergmann wrote, have had little
impact on "the Jewish reality" of the country. Your voice, he
appealed to Buber, is urgently needed in Palestine, but in Hebrew: "You should begin by definitively renouncing the German language, and by expressing what you have to say to the
Jewish people in the plain form of a simple Hebrew. As it is, the
richness of your German has often led you astray, if I may say
so, and enormously impeded your effectiveness, especially in
these hard times." Accordingly, Bergmann reassures the sixty-year-old Buber that his "real work still lies ahead"—in Palestine
and in Hebrew.[4]

Buber accepted the challenge. Before his emigration, he
studied modern spoken Hebrew with Abraham Joshua Heschel,
who at the time was on the staff of the Frankfurt Lehrhaus; later
in Jerusalem, he took lessons in spoken, colloquial Hebrew with

the Hebraist Fritz Raphael Aronstein, who also worked with him on preparing his initial lectures at the Hebrew University. Buber's appointment to a professorship at the Hebrew University was finalized only after negotiations that lasted more than a decade. Starting in 1927, two years after the Hebrew University had first opened its doors, Judah Magnes, the founding chancellor of the university, had advocated the establishment of an Institute of Religious Studies under Buber's direction. In the face of faculty opposition to the proposal, Buber acknowledged that his "ideas and methods diverge considerably from those customary in the present-day study of religion."[5] Still eager to bring him to the university, in 1929 Magnes then explored the possibility of appointing him to serve as "academic head (president for life)" of the university. Deeply moved by Magnes's determination to bring him to Jerusalem, Buber sought the blessings of both Rosenzweig and Paula.

To Rosenzweig, Buber expressed his fear that leaving for Jerusalem would hinder the progress of their translation of the Bible. His friend's response was magnanimous: "As you yourself sense, anything but a Yes is out of the question—considering the cause ('for the sake of Zion' [Isaiah 62:11]) but also for your biography"—though he urged Buber to request extended annual leaves to return to Germany to work on the translation.[6] Paula's response was no less gracious: "Even if I truly could not have consciously desired what has emerged, it yet felt as if all doors were being opened. . . . [I]t is possible to shake things up, and behind it lies the unredeemed land and all things still undone."[7] For his part, Buber had told Paula that without her approval he "would rather be a vagabond with [her] than the academic head of this planet."[8]

In the end, Magnes again failed to get the approval of the faculty senate for the appointment. But he was unyielding, and solicited the support of two preeminent professors, Gershom Scholem and Hugo Bergmann. Their proposals (for example, to appoint Buber to a chair in Hebrew Bible or in Jewish Studies) were repeatedly rebuffed. But finally, their efforts bore fruit—or so it seemed. On February 14, 1934, the faculty convened and, with a very significant majority, approved Buber's appointment to a full professorship in "religious studies," conditional on the approval of the board of trustees—which at its annual meeting in August 1934 rejected the recommendation of the faculty. Needless to say, Buber felt dejected after this outcome, especially after having agreed to what Magnes had assured him was a fait accompli.[9] At the board's next meeting in September 1935, Magnes proposed that Buber's appointment to the faculty be considered independent of the proposed chair in "religious studies," which key members of the board held to be a questionable academic discipline. "Surprisingly," Buber reported to Paula, "at the end [of a heated debate] the personal appointment was accepted unanimously."[10] The field assigned to Buber's chair was designated as the "Philosophy of Society," which would draw upon "principles and methods" of general sociology.[11]

The appointment to a chair in sociology was not entirely arbitrary. Buber's highly acclaimed series of monographs, *Die Gesellschaft*, had served to establish the cultural, if not academic, prestige of the field, though his intellectual vistas reached far beyond sociology. In an anguished letter to Bergmann, then recently elected rector of the Hebrew University, he noted that only while setting out to complete several projects

> in the history and philosophy of religion, did I fully realize what a sacrifice I was making by changing to a discipline that has always been very important to me but is not, in the last analysis, "mine." A real sacrifice, because the celebration of independent viewpoints and methods (without which I could not undertake it), as well as work on the linguistic aspect [Hebrew], will keep me so busy for a long time that I

shall not be able to do any additional scholarly work in other areas—and also because I am no longer young.[12]

In expressing his anxiety about what awaited him in Jerusalem, Buber also revealed a barely contained bitterness, even a sense of betrayal: "Yet I have the feeling that, with two or three exceptions, no one there [in Jerusalem] knows how hard my decision [to accept the professorship in sociology] has been. All my life such feelings did not disturb me; for the first time I now feel that my heart is burdened."[13]

Filled with apprehension that his life in Jerusalem would be buffeted by "mismeetings," Buber joined the faculty of the Hebrew University with a lingering ambivalence. His misgivings about his level of Hebrew and the discipline to which his chair had been assigned were compounded by the fact that he did not consider himself a *Universitätsmensch*, an academic at heart. He had taught at the University of Frankfurt since 1924, but his acceptance of that appointment had been "bound up with my relationship with Franz Rosenzweig . . . it was in the nature of a sacrifice, and hence my dismissal [by the Nazi authorities] was like a solution."[14] He had long found the university alien to his intellectual and spiritual temperament: "I have never striven for an academic career. In 1918/19, I declined a full professorship which an intrepid institution [the University of Giessen] offered an *outsider*"—wrote Buber, pointedly using the English term in this German letter. His former research assistant at the University of Frankfurt, Nahum N. Glatzer, recalled that "aside from [Professor of Theology] Paul Tillich, Buber had no particular relationship to his colleagues."[15] He had allowed himself to be courted by Magnes for an appointment at the university "simply due to the feeling," as he confessed, that "I am being offered a position in Palestine."[16] But if "the entire university scheme proves unfeasible," I would have "to think of something else. In no case shall I give up Palestine."[17] He regarded the professorship as an "experiment" to "ascertain whether I am able to be of use to the cause of the country, *our cause.*"[18]

Buber had another concern, about the overall course of the university. As one of the forefathers of the Hebrew University—he coauthored in 1902 a program for a "Jewish university" to be ideally established in Palestine—he had opposed the founding in Jerusalem of "a university in the European sense."[19] Instead, he envisioned "a true people's academy of higher learning, a *Volkshochschule,*" which would "infuse a new spirit and lead to the building of a new life."[20] Robert Weltsch, a member of the Prague circle of Buber's disciples, urged Buber—who was, aside from the ailing Ahad Ha'am, the most respected representative of cultural Zionism—to attend a crucial June 1924 meeting in London of the board of trustees of the nascent Hebrew University. He hoped that Buber could help "Dr. Magnes, the confidant of the great [American] philanthropists," mobilize the support of the American members of the board to endorse his vision of the university, fearing that the meeting would be dominated by two factions: one advocating a faculty of natural science as the crown of the university, the other focusing on a faculty of Jewish Studies to promote academic Jewish learning in the discredited mold of the nineteenth-century *Wissenschaft des Judentums.*[21] Either camp's success would prevent the university from emerging as a "vital center for Jewish spiritual and intellectual life"; it would instead become "a typical Diaspora institution" (here Weltsch used the Yiddish-German hybrid term *Golusinstitution*). Buber was in the end unable to attend the meeting, but Magnes, who shared Buber's vision of the university as a fulcrum for the cultural and spiritual renewal of Judaism, returned from London to Jerusalem as the university's founding chancellor. He triumphantly wrote to Ahad Ha'am announcing the establishment of the university's first academic department, the Institute for Jewish Studies: "I think we can grasp and put into it all our aspirations for strengthening and expanding our concept of Judaism."[22]

Toward this objective, Magnes was most eager to bring Buber to Jerusalem as an ally. Although he ultimately would not join the faculty of the Hebrew University until the spring of 1938, Buber was associated with virtually all of Magnes's most significant cultural and political activities starting in the late 1920s. They forged a fast friendship despite a certain intellectual asymmetry. Magnes candidly admitted that he found it difficult to work his way through Buber's writings. With respect to *Daniel*, for instance, he wrote: "I have read it to the end and—understood nothing."[23] What brought them together, according to Magnes, was their shared sense of a calling to work for "the renewal and deepening of religion," and the common recognition that Judaism would play its proper role in this momentous process once it had been replanted in the soil of Jerusalem, inspired by its sacred geography and memories.[24]

Deeply troubled by the tensions in Arab-Jewish relations that had become acutely manifest in late 1928, Magnes resolved to found a religious association to counter the looming conflict, and sought the support of several Jerusalem intellectuals. Two of Buber's most fervid disciples, Hugo Bergmann and Hans Kohn, indicated their enthusiastic interest in the project, and at the behest of Magnes, Kohn sent Buber the five-page program that Magnes had drafted in English for the proposed association. In his reply of January 1929, Buber (writing in German) suggested this reformulation of the program's preamble:

> [The members of the association] are united in the conviction that faith, not any particular faith but the believing sensibility or attitude (*die gläubige Gesinnung*), is the genuine ground of life. By the believing attitude they mean that man strives to obtain an immediate relation to the truth of existence (*Sein*) not merely through intellect or feeling, but

through his entire being (*Wesen*). Such a sensibility cannot be constituted by the inwardness of one's soul: it must manifest itself in the entire fullness of personal and communal life, in which the individual participates.[25]

Buber's formulation was consistent with the principles of religious socialism, which had gained traction especially in the 1920s in Germany and Switzerland (and which for Buber was very much aligned with his conception of the foundational spirit of Judaism that he alternately called Hebrew or biblical humanism).

Together with such formidable Protestant theologians as Leonard Ragaz and Paul Tillich, Buber was one of the leaders of this small but intellectually influential movement. They contended that the anguish and disunion of modern society, as was brutally evident in the world war that had ravaged Europe, was fundamentally due to a radical polarization of the sacred and the secular, the ethical and the political. The modern ethos confined the quest for the sacred to confessional and liturgical communities (churches and synagogues), relinquishing all religious claims on the "secular," everyday world. But that division between the holy and the profane, they held, was both artificial and profoundly misguided. Though public and political activity were domains that in modern, bourgeois culture had been abandoned to instrumental reason, often resulting in ethically dubious judgments, all of creation is potentially sacred: The sacralization of all existence would require that faith in God the Creator be marshaled to shape all aspects of life. Religious socialism, along with the social gospel from which Magnes drew inspiration (originally a product of American Christian sensibilities), gained expression in the founding of a religious society in Jerusalem in 1939, Ha-'Ol (The yoke), founded by Magnes and Buber. Its ideology of the circle is expressed in this programmatic statement:

> We are united in the feeling of responsibility toward society
> in general, and the life of Israel [the Jewish people] in its land
> and in the Dispersion in particular. This sense of responsi-
> bility stems from a faith in eternal values whose source is
> God. We believe in a life of faith, which carries a commit-
> ment to social action and practical political work, and we re-
> ject any attempt to separate the dominions, which are one in
> theory and practice.[26]

The first two sentences of this statement reflect Magnes's Jewish version of the American social gospel; the last sentences
seem to bear the imprint of Buber's religious socialism.

Despite the activism pledged in these statements, the public activity of Ha-'Ol was limited to the publication of a brochure in English containing two open letters to Mahatma
Gandhi—one by Magnes, the other by Buber (which I shall
explore later in this chapter). They urged Gandhi to acknowledge the plight of the Jews in Nazi Europe and grant his blessings to Zionism as a movement of national liberation, assuring him that the renewal of Jewish patrimony in the land of
Israel need not be at the expense of the native Arab population and appealing to him (unsuccessfully) to lend his global
prestige to the project of gaining the Arabs' understanding of
the humanitarian and spiritual goals of Zionism. Otherwise,
Ha-'Ol was short-lived, its theological concerns likely super-
seded by the exigent political issues facing the Jewish community in Palestine (the Yishuv), as the intensification of Hitler's
assault on German and European Jewry heightened the resolve
of the Zionist leadership to seek Jewish sovereignty in Palestine regardless of Arab and British opposition. Virtually all the
members of Ha-'Ol participated in the League for Jewish-Arab
Rapprochement and Cooperation, founded in 1939, which opposed the policy of the Yishuv's leadership to pursue Zionist
priorities while ignoring Arabs' needs and political rights. In
August 1942, an independent political association affiliated with

the League, the Ichud (Unity), was founded at the initiative of Buber and Magnes. While its official platform promoting a binational state was formulated in strictly political terms, both Buber and Magnes clearly viewed its activities from a religious perspective.

In a disarmingly forthright and unabashedly sentimental open letter addressed to Magnes on the occasion of his seventieth birthday (July 5, 1947), Buber declared that the Ichud, especially as embodied in the person of Magnes, "has been a great gift to me."[27] After some bitter disappointments, Buber confessed, he had for years never truly believed that truth and politics, especially party politics, could be reconciled. But Magnes and the Ichud, Buber continues, "have made it possible for me to work politically once more within the context and in the name of a political group without sacrificing truth." As he explained to Magnes:

> I am not concerned with the purity and salvation of my soul; if ever it should be the case—which in the nature of things is impossible—that I had to choose between the saving of my soul and the salvation of my people, I know I would not hesitate. It is a question of not violating the truth, since I have come to know that truth is "the seal of God" [Babylonian Talmud, *Shabbat*, 55a], while we are the wax in which this seal seeks to be stamped. The older I grow, the clearer this becomes.[28]

He added, significantly, "I feel that in this we are brothers."

The fraternal bond between Buber and Magnes also reflected their shared positions as outsiders within the political culture of the Yishuv, which in the pre-state period was dominated by ideologically determined allegiances. In this regard, as Scholem observed, Magnes cut an uncommon but endearing figure within the cultural and political landscape of the Yishuv. He was not a revolutionary but nevertheless was a "radical"—

though in some basic sense he was also a conservative, appealing to his fellow Zionists to carry on fundamental Jewish values with utmost seriousness within the life of the community. Citing the voice of Israel's biblical prophets, Magnes spoke of goodness, justice, and compassion, without, as Scholem put it, "evoking laughter."[29] In his fearless, unbending, single-minded commitment to moral truth, these were not just uplifting words but commandments shaping the ethical and spiritual quality of life. He was an exemplar of Buber's biblical humanism, animated as he was by an ethical responsibility to the political and social order in which one finds oneself. In a private letter to Magnes, also on the occasion of his seventieth birthday, Buber expressed his gratitude to Magnes for exemplifying this political ethos:

> These days we feel nearer than ever to you, and to what you represent. In the near future, I believe, the existence of individuals like you, persons of truth and responsibility, will become even more important. . . . It is a joy to know that you are in this world; it is a consolation to be aware of the fact that one is fighting with you a common battle. May you enjoy the latent blessings of this quality of yours which has become so rare; the courage of *civil disobedience*.[30]

Although Buber wrote this letter in German, he cited "civil disobedience" in English—a term he expressly associated with Henry David Thoreau.[31] Thoreau was the bold dissenter of nineteenth-century New England who had, since Buber's youth, represented for him the best of the American ethos. Civil disobedience—"obedience to a law superior to that which is being disobeyed here and now," expressed an individual's ethical and existential integrity.[32] As Buber wrote on the centenary of Thoreau's death: "The question of [civil disobedience] is not just about one of the numerous individual cases in the struggle between a truth powerless to act and a power that has become the enemy of truth. It is really a question of the absolutely concrete demonstration of the point at which this struggle at any moment becomes a man's duty as man (*zur Pflicht des Menschen als Mensch*)."[33]

Buber drew inspiration from Magnes's resolve to translate the ethic of civil disobedience into a Jewish context: the struggle to create in Zion a truly just society and to rescue the Zionist project from the clutches of a "narrow nationalism." But Buber was beholden to Magnes not only as an inspiring exemplar of biblical humanism. His friendship with Magnes also fostered his own courage to be an "outsider"—here, in a positive sense—and to express his discontent with Zionist policies by embracing what Michel Foucault would decades later identify as the ethical practice of *parrhesia*, or fearless speech in the public square. He would assume this role also at the Hebrew University. In his inaugural lecture, he signaled that he understood his professorial appointment as transcending the institutional limits of scholarly research. Delivered in Hebrew before the faculty and students gathered in the university's largest auditorium, the lecture, in effect, indicates the cognitive and ethical compass by which Buber would navigate his life as a self-conscious outsider in the Yishuv, and later in the State of Israel.

In this ceremonial address, entitled "The Demand of the Spirit and Historical Reality," Buber expounds on the conceptual and methodological parameters of sociology.[34] Though a uniquely modern discipline, its "calling" may be understood as analogous to the role of the biblical prophets as social critics, that is, sociology is as much an ethical and spiritual endeavor as a purely academic discipline. Buber traces the very origins of modern sociology to the intersection of scientific inquiry and ethical-spiritual concerns, back to Henri de Saint Simon, the French social critic who sought to conscript "scientific knowledge of social conditions" in order to overcome "the inner contradictions of the age." His student, Auguste Comte, in turn argued that social change required "new spiritual attitudes" (*rénovation mentale*), and Buber articulates the central thesis of his lecture by referring to Comte: "I consider all discussions about institutions a pure farce so long as the *spiritual* reorganization of society is not realized or at least strongly furthered."[35]

From its very beginnings, Buber underscores, sociology was born of a desire "to know in order to change."[36] But the early sociologists were also fully cognizant that "man must change himself in the same measure as the institutions are changed in order that these changes may have their expected effect"—for "if the new house that man hopes to erect is not to become his burial chamber, the essence of living together must undergo a change at the same time as the organization of living."[37] The sociologist thus has a role that goes beyond mere scientific analysis: the sociologist "must also *educate* sociologically; he must *educate* men in living together."[38]

Buber acknowledges that the duty to educate stands in conflict with sociology's status as a supposedly value-free discipline. In addition, as a prescriptive science, sociology is subject to another inherent conflict, a seemingly contradictory mode of gathering and interpreting data. (Here one hears echoes of Buber's beloved teacher, Wilhelm Dilthey.) On one hand, sociological knowledge can be attained only through one's participation in the lived experiences of the society one studies. The sociologist cannot be a "stranger to its structures," for "without genuine social binding there is no genuine social experience and without genuine social experience there is no genuine thinking."[39] Hence, "no one becomes a sociological thinker if his dream and his passion have never mingled with the dream and passion of [the] human community" he studies.[40] On the other hand, in order for a sociologist's interpretation and analysis to be of sufficient quality that they merit and gain the epistemological dignity of "knowledge," the sociologist must maintain a critical distance. "On the basis of the knowledge thus won, the sociological thinker may [then] value and decide, censure and demand, when the urgent question approaches, without violating the law of his science." Sociological knowledge authorizes the sociologist to judge the actions of that society in a given historical reality, and even to "censure and demand," but as "a partner, not as a spokesperson."[41]

Similar to the biblical prophets, for Buber "the social thinker who understands his office must continually pose the question: How can the spirit influence the transformation of social reality?"[42] The comparison of the sociologist with the prophet allows Buber to highlight a fundamental, indispensable responsibility that goes with gaining sociological knowledge: "Being a prophet means being powerless, powerlessly confronting the powerful and reminding them of their responsibility. . . . To stand powerless before the power he calls to account is part of the prophet's destiny." In elaborating the nature of the prophetic calling, Buber also draws upon Gustav Landauer's anti-Platonic conception of political truth and action, whereby the prophet "sets no universally valid image of perfection, no *pan-topia* or utopia, before men," but directs his action (on behalf of truth) to a specific *topos*, a particular context demarcated by historically and socially specific conditions.[43]

With a thinly veiled autobiographical reference—surely understood as such by most of his audience—Buber further comments that the prophet, existentially bound to a given topos, has "no choice between his fatherland and another land that 'suits him' better"; it is to this topos, "to this place, to this people," to which he must deliver his message, even though it will be "misunderstood, misjudged, misinterpreted, misused" and will in all likelihood only "strengthen and 'harden' the people still further in their untruth. But its sting will rankle within them for all time."[44] The sociologist, of course, is not in fact a prophet; "he does not have a [divinely inspired] mes-sage, [but] he has a teaching," a teaching directed toward the transformation of social reality. In this respect, social think-ing brings with it a "prophetic task of criticism and demand"— a position, no doubt, that helped Buber to make his peace with his appointment in the field of sociology.[45]

In March 1939, a year after assuming his professorship and a few months before the outbreak of World War II, Buber was invited by the Friends of the Hebrew University in Poland to give a series of lectures. On March 12, Buber (accompanied by Paula) boarded a direct flight from Lydda, Palestine, to War-saw. His visit was warmly anticipated by the Warsaw Jewish press, which noted: "Within the next few days one of the most outstanding spiritual leaders of contemporary Jewry, Profes-sor of Sociology at the Hebrew University in Jerusalem Martin Buber, is expected to arrive in Warsaw. . . . This lecture [to be delivered in Polish] by such a famous speaker will undoubtedly awaken great interest within the Jewish community."[46] A War-saw Jewish daily carried a lead article, written by the celebrated historian of Polish Jewry Meir Balaban (who would meet his death in the Warsaw ghetto), with the banner headline: "Wel-come Professor Martin Buber: Scholar and Teacher." Balaban elaborated with exacting detail Buber's Polish-Jewish upbring-ing, his writings on Hasidism, and in light of "the horrific po-grom carried out against the [German-]Jewish community in November [1938] . . . the total collapse of his hopes of contrib-uting to a Jewish revival in the ancient Jewish lands [of Ger-many]."[47]

Over twenty-one days, Buber would give twenty-two lec-tures in more than a dozen Polish cities—among them Warsaw, Kraków, Lodz, and the city of his youth, Lvov. Despite the en-thusiasm with which Polish Jewry greeted Buber, his lectures were utterly ignored by the non-Jewish Polish public, with one noteworthy exception. The Catholic journalist Jerzy Turowicz, who would become the editor of an influential liberal weekly in postwar Kraków, recalled attending one of Buber's lectures:

> I found an announcement . . . in the Jewish *Nowy Dziennik*. I went to his lecture. Not without difficulty I managed to find the wretched building housing a large community center in Kazimierz [the Jewish quarter of Kraków]. The hall was packed to the brim with an enthusiastic audience, amounting to several hundred people; I must have been the only non-Jew among them. The sixty-year-old Martin Buber, sporting a long white beard, spoke in beautiful Polish about the spiritual state of the world and the threat of war. His words had a certain prophetic tone. Deeply moved, while leaving the hall, I bumped into a journalist I know, a Jew, who exclaimed in surprise on seeing me: "What are you doing here?" "What do you mean, what am I doing here?"—I replied—"I have come to hear Martin Buber's lecture." "I can see that"—he replied—"but how did you know about Martin Buber?"[48]

Buber seems not to have been particularly troubled by the lack of interest in his lectures—given in "beautiful Polish"—on the part of the general Polish public, certainly not in light of what he experienced during his three-week trip. Reporting about his visit to a friend, he noted that "most distressing of all was the war psychosis, and in the German border regions particularly, where I lectured on several occasions. I had visual instruction of the extent of Jewish poverty and the elemental hatred of the Jews—that is, not incited from above [as in Hitler's Germany]—which I have never before experienced, and as a result both of us [Paula and I] have returned home rather ill."[49]

Buber returned in early April to Jerusalem—via Czernowitz, Romania, where he also gave a lecture (presumably in German) on behalf of the Hebrew University—by then physically exhausted by the heavy schedule of lectures and travel. But what truly weighed on him were the undeniable intimations that Polish Jewry was facing an imminent disaster. He realized that the lecture on "Education and the People" that he had prepared and repeatedly delivered, with his discussion of contemporary trends in public education, had hardly addressed Polish Jewry's most immediate concerns.[50] His despair about the future of Polish (and German) Jewry—at the time, of course, he had no inkling that Auschwitz was on the horizon—seems to have strengthened his resolve to engage himself in the rescue of the Zionist project.

As Buber had indicated in his inaugural lecture at the Hebrew University, he was reconciled to being an outsider in Zion, and was prepared to bear the scorn and tribulations of an outspoken dissenter. What he did not anticipate were the financial difficulties that he and his family would face upon their emigration to Palestine. Their economic troubles had already begun in Germany. In order to emigrate, the Nazi authorities required an exit tax (*Reichsfluchtsteuer*) of 25 percent of one's estimated net worth. In Buber's case, the emigration authorities levied a tax of 27,000 Reichsmark, which would be the equivalent today of $583,000.[51] He might have been able to pay that sum had he not lost access to the estate his father had bequeathed him in Poland in early 1938, when the Warsaw government had imposed severe restrictions on the transfer of funds abroad. The Nazi officials nonetheless included his Polish assets in their assessment of Buber's wealth. Unable to pay the tax, he was granted only a permit to work abroad for nine months, on the condition that he leave behind the bulk of his financial assets, including his home intact with its belongings. But Paula surreptitiously arranged for acquaintances in Frankfurt who had received emigration permits to include in their shipments to Palestine some of Buber's fifteen thousand books, as well as furniture and personal items.[52] To meet the stipulations of the work permit, three thousand books and some furnishings were left in Buber's Heppenheim home, enough to leave the impression that he would soon be returning to Germany, though

Buber and his family, of course, left Germany with no intention of coming back. During the Kristallnacht pogroms of November 9, 1938, their home in Heppenheim was plundered and a large part of the library left behind was destroyed.

A year before the family's emigration, Buber had gone to Palestine to arrange living quarters large enough to accommodate his library and a family of four. He managed to lease a very spacious apartment in the upscale West Jerusalem neighborhood of Talbiya. Built in the early 1930s by a Christian Arab Yusef Said (the grandfather of the scholar of comparative literature Edward Said), the palatial building had three separate units. The upper-level apartment was rented to the consul general of the Kingdom of Yugoslavia; the Bubers would live in the ground floor apartment; and the basement apartment would house Buber's library. At the time he signed the lease, Buber still had access to his father's estate in Poland, and was presumably in a position to pay the rent commanded by such a prestigious address. In early 1944, Said's daughter-in-law, now the owner of the building, returned to Jerusalem from Cairo with her five children and sought through the court to break the lease with Buber and reclaim the apartment for her family's use. The Jerusalem magistrate ruled in her favor, forcing Buber to find an alternative housing. Fortunately, he found a spacious apartment in the predominantly Arab Jerusalem neighborhood of Abu-Tor.

With the loss of access to his inheritance, the financial strain that the rental of these expensive residences placed on Buber was exacerbated by the need not only to support his wife and two teenage granddaughters, but also to assist his daughter Eva and son-in-law, the poet Ludwig Strauss, and their two children, who upon their emigration to Palestine found it extremely difficult to make ends meet. Paula's well-being seems to have caused him particular concern. In addition to the challenge of learning Hebrew at the age of sixty (which she never would), she had to contend with the feeling that many in her husband's social and intellectual circles, despite their declared liberal and progressive views, regarded her as a *goya* (a gentile), irrespective of her conversion.[53] Buber sought to ease her quality of life by providing her with at least a semblance of the privileged standard of living that she had enjoyed in Germany.

Buber's financial woes worried some of his closest friends. On March 12, 1943, Werner D. Senator wrote about their concerns to Hans Kohn, who since 1934 had been teaching at various universities in the United States. Although Senator and Kohn were native German speakers, the Mandatory government's censor required Senator to write in English. After beginning with an appeal to "your friendship for Martin Buber and you[r] great appreciation of his work," he outlined the problem:

> Buber has a great library of some 15,000 volumes, mainly on *Religionswissenschaft* and related subjects (philosophy, art, etc.). It was this library which, to a certain extent, forced him to take a large flat, the rent of which is out of proportion to the salary he receives from the University (somewhat less than 50 [Palestinian pounds] per month).[54] Then there is Mrs. Buber whom I suppose you know and who still is a kind of "*Schlossherrin*" [lady of the castle] with the wonderful old furniture they brought over from Germany, in their rooms with high ceilings in a very romantic Arab house in Dar Abu Tor with a beautiful view over the Old City, the Kidron Valley and the mountains of Moab.[55]

In addition, he explained, Buber was the sole source of support for his two granddaughters (Rafael's daughters) and was helping to support his daughter Eva's family as well because of her husband's minimal income as a poet and teacher; his considerable estate in Poland had to be "regarded as lost" for all practical purposes; and there had been a "terrible rise in the cost of living." All of these factors meant that the family could not make ends meet. "Thus, he is forced to do all kinds of work, writing an article here and there, and trying to get an order for a book so as to be able to pay the installments of his debts and to keep the household going."

Senator continued with a proposal, which he said had Buber's endorsement: a group of philanthropic friends of the university would make a gift of the library to the university after Buber's death. They would, in essence, first buy it from Buber on an installment plan, each of them giving him a particular sum each year for five to ten years. This would allow him to "work freely, without the pressure of having to earn his or rather his family's daily bread. And I am convinced," Senator continued,

> that that would be all to the good not only as far as Buber is concerned, but also for all of us here in Palestine and for the spirit of Judaism in general. I think that Buber can still give us much and he himself feels strongly that he has much energy left and that he still has important things to say. Indeed, after my last conversation with him I felt deeply ashamed that this man who has given so much to some of us, I think to many, in our youth, should be left in such a state.

He concluded with some logistical thoughts, and a request to hear Kohn's opinion about his proposal.

Upon receipt of this letter, Kohn sent it on to the banker Max Warburg, who along with his late brother Ludwig Warburg was among the leading philanthropic supporters of the Hebrew University. His reply to Kohn, dated April 9, 1943, sheds light on the political background of Buber's professorial appointment as well as the sensitivities of an American (and former German) philanthropist:

> Dear Professor Kohn,
>     I received your letter of April 8th, with the enclosed

letter from Dr. Senator. I have great sympathy for Martin
Buber, although I think he lost a good deal of his importance
the moment he could not continue to work in German and
form his ideas in German, as he is more German than he
himself knows. In fact it was not easy to find a position for
him and his professorship at the University was more or less
created through my efforts. There were many jealousies and
they did not know what to do with him, but I am happy that
it has worked out well.

I think it is a very good idea to make the University
a gift of his Library, but I do not think we ought even to
try to find the money here [in the United States]. [Salman]
Schocken could very easily make such a present, or [Fritz
Willy] Polack and others in Palestine. People now make a lot
of money in Palestine—they are more or less *Kriegsgewinner*
[war profiteers]. I do not blame them, it is the nature of the
situation today, but these Palestine people ought to emanci-
pate themselves for certain ways and not always come here
[to America]. Not necessary to explain to you how difficult
it is to give money to the right and to the left, even to those
who otherwise would commit suicide.

I hope you understand why I do not follow your suggestion, which is very sympathetic to me and I would have liked
to say yes. . . .

Yours, Max Warburg

P.S.: I am returning Dr. Senator's letter to you.[56]

Without Warburg's support, Senator's suggestion to Kohn
never came to pass. Significantly, Buber had also written to
Kohn years earlier with a request to connect him with U.S.
publishers who might be interested in English translations of
his books. He told Kohn that because it was no longer possible to publish in German, he was contemplating translating
"in collaboration with Palestinian friends some new works of
mine into English."[57] The prospective publication of his writings in America, he told Kohn, was particularly important be-

cause of his changed financial situation and his children's and grandchildren's needs. He described six monographs on which he was working, then underscored the urgency of the request: "To be able to perform this big piece of work besides my university courses, I must free myself of all petty cares of the near future. . . . What I must therefore strive to find is an institution, which will grant me for some time an adequate allowance, in return for which I will deliver now my finished manuscripts and in a space [of time] to be agreed upon the other books mentioned."[58]

Kohn was also unable to offer Buber the assistance he requested, and Buber's financial situation would not substantially improve until after World War II, when many of his books were translated into English and sold in the United States. The only book of his to appear in English before the end of World War II was a translation of *I and Thou* by a minister in the Church of Scotland, Ronald Gregor Smith. Published in Edinburgh in 1937, the translation received little attention—thus earning minimal royalties for Buber—until it was reissued by an American publisher in 1958. For the duration of the war, Buber publications were virtually all in Hebrew, with occasional pieces appearing in the German language press in exile. Determined to find a voice in the public discourse of the Yishuv, he frequently published articles in the daily press, mainly op-eds and feuilletons.

On the first anniversary of Kristallnacht, Buber published a long analysis of Nazi anti-Semitism in the Tel Aviv daily *Haaretz*. Entitled "They and We," it typified the thrust and tone of his political and sociological writings, and offered insights beyond the descriptive analysis of his scholarly judgment. Distinguishing traditional, premodern religious hatred of the Jews from modern anti-Semitism, he argued that modern anti-Semitism should be understood in the context of Jews' general lack of participation in the basic means of production, such as through agriculture and mining. The Jews' participation in the modern economy, he wrote, "usually does not begin with the foundation of the house but rather with the second floor," a structural imbalance that prepares "the soil for a new anti-Semitism," which will erupt "when an economic crisis gives occasion for it." "The Jews," he wrote, "who stand out in the upper stories, actually or apparently unaffected by all this, become even more conspicuous than before, and in the hearts of those who were affected the impression is transformed into deep bitterness which can be compared to explosives." All that is needed to ignite their fury is an incendiary spark, in the form of "political catchwords" devised by the guardians of the state in order to deflect the frustration of the masses.[59] "Those who threw the spark into the powder keg," he assured his readers, "will not escape judgment."

Turning to the task of rebuilding Jewish collective life in Palestine, he wrote: "We are not fulfilling our duty by mourning and complaining. We must learn from what has happened and transform what we have learned into action." "We are finally building for ourselves a real house of our own, and in such a manner as one builds a house that is to last for long time, that is to say, on solid and strong foundations." Before rushing to its upper floors as the Jews had done in the Diaspora, they must continue the work of the *chalutzim*, the vanguard of pioneers dedicated to redeeming Zion and themselves through the "conquest of labor." Further, he argued pointedly, "the land cannot be built upon injustice. . . . Whenever any state banishes from the area of its protection and responsibility one of its minorities, one which is the most conspicuous, and annihilates it slowly or quickly, as Germany has done with its Jews, without the minority having transgressed against it—in so doing such a state shakes the foundations of its own existence." The Zionist project, he said, could not and must not be sustained by a "national egotism" like that reigning in Germany. The "building for ourselves a real house of our own," he argued, had until then concerned only the economic and political tasks at hand, and had sadly neglected to attend sufficiently to the ethical quality of its communal and interpersonal life, especially with respect to the Arabs of Palestine.[60]

In a similar vein, Buber's first course of lectures at the Hebrew University, titled "What Is Man?," can be viewed, among other things, as a meditation on the version of the Zionist project reflected in the popular folksong of the chalutzim, "*Anu banu artza, livnot u'lhibanot ba*—we have come to the land [of Israel] to build and be rebuilt by it."[61] Buber had earlier understood in an inchoate fashion that the process of returning to the land of the forefathers to rebuild it and, in the process, to reconstruct the Jewish people would entail overcoming and correcting the distortions of Jewish life in galut. In his early lectures—as in the "Three Addresses" to the Bar Kochba Circle of Prague—Buber had depicted a process of returning to a primal, pristine Judaism. As his thinking had matured, however, he hoped to avoid the romantic overtones of this vision by focusing on the reconstruction of community and interpersonal relationships that were characteristic of his "third station."

The university lectures addressed humanity's two opposing responses to the problem of existential solitude: modern individualism and modern collectivism. Individualism accepts one's destiny as an isolated "monad . . . not bound to others"; one's sense of homelessness in the world is to be affirmed as a "universal *amor fati*"—a love, or at least acceptance, of one's fate.[62] In contrast, collectivism provides one with a sense of home, but an illusory one, for it does not truly join person to person. "The tender surface of personal life which longs for contact with other life is progressively deadened or desensitized [by the collective]. Man's isolation is not overcome here, but overpowered and numbed."[63] But there is a third way to overcome cosmic and social isolation: to "meet" others as fellow human beings, to know them in all their "otherness as one's self [and] from there break through to the other," and then to build a common home in the world, a genuine community.[64]

Through its construction of new forms of communal life, Buber felt, Zionism exemplified the promise of this third way. But he was troubled by what he perceived to be the tendency of Zionist cooperative settlements, particularly the kibbutzim, to adopt ideological collectivism. In conjunction with his university lectures on communitarian socialism, in 1942 he began writing the book *Paths in Utopia*, which would be published in Hebrew in 1946, in English in 1949, and in German in 1950. In the book he addressed "the work of *our* socialist settlement in the land [of Israel] . . . I know no other blessing for [this book] than that it move the reader to acknowledge the fateful importance of our experiment [in utopian socialism] for us and the world." This experiment was, he argued, devoted—in the words of Landauer (to whose memory the volume is dedicated)—to the "renewal of society through a renewal of its cell tissue," a messianic and utopian ideal that the kibbutzim are meant to serve, and a pursuit that was inherently experimental rather than ideological, for there is no fast blueprint to the perfect communal order.[65]

Utopian messianism was, of course, for Buber, in line with the vision of Israel's prophets, who placed on every individual the responsibility for determining which deeds are necessary—within a particular historical context—to prepare the path to redemption, the hallmark of which is social and political justice. In this respect, Buber noted, prophetic messianism differs radically from the apocalyptic eschatology to which Marxists adhere, whereby "the redemptive process in all its details, its every hour and course, has been fixed from the very beginning and forever; and for whose realization human beings are but its tools."[66] Regrettably, Buber bemoaned, many kibbutzim subscribed precisely to that Marxist eschatology—including, to his great chagrin, the Werkleute, a German-Jewish youth movement that had often sought his counsel and claimed to be inspired by his teachings. For Buber, if the kibbutzim were to constitute utopian experimentation toward the realization of genuine community, it was not ideological solidarity that was needed, but a communal framework that facilitated openness to one another, a mutual readiness to be there for one another.[67] Buber thus called upon the kibbutzim to uncover what he believed was the original nondoctrinaire, utopian impulse behind all of them. Through a concerted (re)connection with that ethos, the kibbutzim might continue to be celebrated as an "experiment that has not failed."[68]

The distinction between prophetic realism and apocalyptic delusions was a consistent and insistent theme of Buber's biblical and political writings, especially in his two books that came out in Hebrew during World War II. In 1942, he published *Torat Ha-Nevi'im* (The teaching of the prophets). His preface to the volume—which is not included in the English and German editions that appeared in 1949 and 1950, respectively (under the titles *The Prophetic Faith* and *Der Glaube der Propheten*)—describes the prophets' faith as manifest in deeds. "The content of faith—God's essence and characteristic—is not what distinguishes" it, but rather the deeds that demonstrate their relationship with God and, accordingly, their relationship to humanity. "The mission of Israel is to prepare humanity for the rule of God," and this messianic goal is one to be reached incrementally, via various "historical junctions" over time, fluid and distinct from each other—each demanding political judgment appropriate to the specific era.[69] The future is thus "not something already fixed in the present hour; it is dependent upon the real decision, [that is to say], a positive and complete decision of the community. . . . I emphasize the word 'community,' for even where [the prophet] mentions individuals, the main purpose is the realization [of the prophetic injunction] in the whole of public life."[70]

Buber refers to this contextual and communal approach as "the theopolitical hour"—"a special kind of politics, which is concerned to establish a certain people in a certain historical situation under divine sovereignty, so that this people is to be brought nearer the fulfillment of its task, to become the beginning of the Kingdom of God."[71] In his monograph of 1932, *Königtum Gottes*, Buber had already developed at length the theme of theopolitics—the affirmation of the "absolute kingship of God"—as a radical critique of any protofascist political theology that claimed divine sanction for and sanctification of any given nation's quest for political power and sovereignty.[72] The urgency of his critique was underscored when Buber sent to a colleague in Amsterdam the revised (and abridged) version of an article on "The Faith of Israel" that focused on "the theopolitical hour," to be translated into Dutch; he "received it back from the post office as undeliverable: Holland had in the meantime been occupied by Hitler's armies."[73]

In the shadow of the Third Reich, Buber's nervousness about the sanctification of political sovereignty, whether founded on theology or merely unbridled national egoism, became particularly acute. The interlacing of the German experience and Buber's Zionist anxieties came to the fore in a "half-dream" he had on the day after the German invasion of Poland on September 1, 1939, which unleashed World War II with its "signs both on the one side and on the other of a false messianism." In the liminal space of Buber's half-dream, "a demon with the wings of a bat and the traits of a Judaized Goebbels" appeared to him—the Nazi minister of propaganda here merging with an imaginary foreboding Jewish counterpart, a "false messenger" of redemption.[74] He drew on this figure in creating, in a historical novel he was writing, the character of a Hasidic rabbi who is an apocalyptic enthusiast. Evoking the prophet Ezekiel's premonitions of an apocalyptic battle against forces of evil ("Son of man, set your face against Gog, of the land of Magog"), the novel was entitled *Gog and Magog*. First appearing in seven installments beginning in October 1941, in the Sabbath supplement of the Tel Aviv newspaper of the Labor Federation, *Dvar*, it was published as a book in 1943. Although the setting of the novel is an early nineteenth-century debate among Hasidic rabbis about whether Napoleon's invasion of Russia should be greeted as initiating the "the war of Gog and Magog," it should be read as a political allegory bearing on contemporary Zionist affairs.

The novel had a long and difficult gestation of some twenty years. In a letter to Rosenzweig from January 1923, Buber begged to postpone a promised visit. "I'm not in the right mood. The *Gog* is crowding in on me, but not so much in the 'artistic' sense. Rather, I am becoming aware of how much 'evil' is essential to the coming of the kingdom [of God]." A month later, he tells Rosenzweig "the *Gog* is not yet at all presentable.[75] Once it is, it will go straight to you. . . . [It] will only be a short story—a regular pamphlet—and aside from my wife, who's had to live through it, only you will know that it had not always been short." He reminds Rosenzweig that *Gog* was conceived as an introduction to the projected second volume of *I and Thou*, which would deal with the transition from magic to prayer as embodying the change to an I-Thou relation between man and God. In yet another letter to Rosenzweig, he confessed that he found none of the other volumes on Hasidic literature on which he was then working as "draining" as *Gog*. "In the book itself I have reached a stratum that I knew nothing or almost nothing about; that now demands serious work. . . . The work I must do is a far cry from what I imagined these past seven years."[76] The sequel to *I and Thou* was never completed, and *Gog* had to wait twenty years—and by then it was not a short pamphlet, but a Hebrew volume of 182 pages.

The novel (which, as noted in Chapter 7, was also a way of working out Buber's unfinished exchange with Rosenzweig on "the Law") is an imaginatively constructed narration of an actual theological debate about proper messianic action between two Hasidic rabbis, Jacob Yitzhak of Lublin, the "Seer," and his former disciple, popularly known as the "Holy Jew." Beholden to an apocalyptic view of Napoleon as a divinely appointed agent of redemption, the Seer urged his followers to engage in magical, theurgic practices in order to ensure Napoleon's defeat of the tsar and his oppressive regime. Objecting to his teacher's views, the Holy Jew adhered to the teaching of the biblical prophets that each person "can work on the world's redemption but none can effect it."[77] Further, he poignantly pleaded with the Seer regarding the source of "evil":

> "Rabbi," he said in an almost failing voice, "what is the nature of this Gog? He can exist in the outer world only because he exists within us." He pointed to his own breast. "The darkness out of which he [Gog] was hewn needed to be taken from nowhere else than from our own slothful or malicious hearts. It is our betrayal of God that has made Gog to grow so great."[78]

In a later comment on this passage, which he cited as the "central theme" of *Gog and Magog*, Buber would note: "To fully understand this passage the reader must recall the time at which the novel was written."[79]

In the epilogue to the German edition in 1948, Buber acknowledged that *Gog and Magog* had personal—indeed, autobiographical—significance. "When, in my youth," he reminisces, "I came in contact with my earliest Hasidic publication I accepted it in the spirit of Hasidic enthusiasm. I am a Polish

Jew." Although in his grandfather's home a more "enlightened" form of traditional Jewish observance was practiced, "in the most impressionable period of my boyhood a Hasidic atmosphere had a deep influence on me." There may have been, he candidly notes without elaboration, "other less discernable factors" drawing him to Hasidism as an adult. "What I am certain of is that had I lived in that period when one still contended with the living Word of God and not with its caricatures, I too, like many others, would have left my parental home and become a hasid." While he could not accept a "blind traditionalism," he also came to reject a "blind contesting" of the tradition of the kind that he had done as a young adult. To be sure, he said, his "entire spiritual existence" was in some sense indebted to Hasidism, and even though he did not conduct his life according to its normative teachings, "the foundations of my life are there, and my impulses are akin to its." Indeed, he wrote, as Rabbi Menachem Mendel of Kotzk, a disciple of the Holy Jew, taught, "The Torah warns us 'not to make an idol even of the command of God.' What can I add to these words?"[80]

This coda to Buber's autobiographical review of his relationship to Hasidism is no mere rhetorical gesture; it points not only to the fundamental theological principle informing what has been characterized as his religious anarchism, but also to the intensity of his connection to the traditional world of Jewish faith, texts, and teachings (and in particular, to Hasidism) even as he rejected normative Jewish practice—that is, to the complexity of his relationship to traditional Judaism. In a memoir by Buber's research assistant Moritz (Moshe) Spitzer, during the early 1930s in Heppenheim, we have a window onto the existential ground of his defiantly nonnormative Jewish theological commitments. On the eve of Yom Kippur, the Day of Atonement, Spitzer was visited by a young Jewish man of twenty, who asked if he might accompany Spitzer to the synagogue. When they arrived at the synagogue tucked in one of

Heppenheim's lush vineyards, they learned that due to a lack of the quorum (*minyan*) required for public prayer, it would not be possible to conduct the Yom Kippur evening service. The next morning, therefore, they went to a neighboring town that had a relatively large Jewish community and hence would surely have a minyan. At the conclusion of the service, an elderly congregant approached Spitzer and his young companion, and invited these "strangers" to come to his home and break the fast together with him and his family. At the end of the very modest meal of potato porridge and herring, the host, a pious man of clearly very limited means, asked where his guests were from. Spitzer told him he was from nearby Heppenheim, and upon the host's query, could not hide the fact he knew the famous scholar Martin Buber. With palpable sadness, the elderly host replied: "Rumor has it that Buber does not even observe Yom Kippur."[81]

Upon his return to Heppenheim, Spitzer told Buber how deeply his reputed irreverence had hurt the elderly Jew. Buber was visibly taken aback, as if he was a "child chided by his teacher," and protested: "Believe me it is more difficult for me not to observe Yom Kippur than it would be to observe it. And don't blame my wife. She wanted to keep a kosher home, but I refused. Were I in Lvov or any other community in which I could enter the synagogue as *one of the people* and participate in the prayer, I would. But to enter a synagogue where I would be one of the pillars of the congregation, I could not." Spitzer reported this exchange without comment, but added as an explanation: On the first day of Passover 1933, a week after the Nazi sponsored "Jewish boycott," Buber went to the Heppenheim synagogue, wearing a large *tallit* (prayer shawl) to join in the prayer and give a sermon, encouraging his fellow Jews to stand firm in the face of the nefarious designs of Hitler.[82]

Buber was, indeed, an anomalous Jew. As a Zionist, he was unbending in his solidarity with the torments and needs of the "natural Jew"—Jews buffeted by the daily, often brutal realities of the historical situation in which they found themselves. Yet he was equally unyielding in his objection to the Zionist quest for political sovereignty. As a religious thinker, he sought to revive what he deemed the primal spiritual sensibilities of biblical Judaism that had been suppressed by the normative strictures of the rabbis. Midrash, as he learned from his grandfather (to whose memory he dedicated *The Teaching of the Prophets*) exemplifies the dialectical tension between religion and religiosity, between rabbinic law (*halachah*) and the spiritual sensibilities that ideally nurture Judaism as a community of faith. Buber understood Hasidism as born of an impulse to renew this dialectic, which under the weight of overbearing rabbinic rule had been largely suppressed. As recorded in the movement's tales and anecdotes, the Baal Shem Tov and his disciples taught that God's presence is not restricted to the synagogue and the acts of worship prescribed by halachah, but may be encountered in the space of everyday life, allowing for spontaneous, individual expressions of divine service. Buber's anthologies of Hasidic lore had been intended to point to the challenge to serve God in the marketplace—that is, in the realms of human activity that modernity had rendered "secular."

Buber addressed this message to the Yishuv in a 1945 volume of Hebrew essays on Hasidism, *Be-Pardes ha-Hasidut* (In the orchard of Hasidism), and in a 1947 anthology, *Or ha-Ganuz* (The hidden light). The origins of this comprehensive gathering of Hasidic lore reach back more than two decades, to an ill-fated project Buber had undertaken with the writer S. Y. Agnon. In July 1922, the two men signed a contract with the Hebrew poet Chaim Nahman Bialik, who represented the Hebrew publishing company Moriah-Dvir, to edit an anthology in Hebrew of "four or more volumes, comprising the finest of the stories of the Hasidim and the basic elements of their doctrines." The anthology was to be called *Sefer haHasidut* (The book of Hasidism). The project, also known as *Corpus Hasidicum*, was initiated by Agnon, who had come to prize Buber's knowledge of Hasidic lore. While reminiscing about their first meeting in Buber's home in Berlin in 1913, when Agnon returned from Palestine after living there for five years, he noted that their conversation quickly touched on their shared interest in Hasidism:

> I told him a [Hasidic] story. After I finished, Buber took out a notebook, looked in it and then picked up an unbound book and showed me the story in print. The same thing happened with most of the stories I told him. I had a little more luck with the teachings I recounted, since many of them were not so familiar to him, or else he knew them in different versions. Buber would transcribe every story he found in those Hasidic collections, including each different version. All this was new to me, both because of Buber's systematic method and because I had never seen so many collections of Hasidic stories assembled by a single person. Until that day I did not know that there were so many published collections of Hasidic stories. I knew the stories from hearing them; only the doctrines had I learned from books.[83]

Agnon would soon become a frequent presence in the Buber home. Buber's son Rafael recalled that his father and Agnon would usually start their meetings with a glass of schnapps and continue with an animated discussion in Yiddish. Agnon would also send Buber an endless stream of postcards with Hasidic tales and anecdotes that he suddenly recalled or had recently heard. Thus, when the idea of the multivolume Hebrew anthology of Hasidic stories crystallized, it was natural that Agnon would think of collaborating with Buber. They worked diligently on the project for two years, but then catastrophe struck: in June 1924, a fire broke out in Agnon's home in Bad Homburg, a suburb of Frankfurt am Main. The fire consumed all of his belongings, including the nearly completed first volume of the *Corpus Hasidicum.*

Buber informed Rosenzweig of the calamity, and regretfully told him that Agnon "is giving up the plan 'for years,' and that probably means forever. I cannot try to persuade him otherwise, for I feel the blow too strongly myself; and I cannot think of collaboration with anyone else—there is no one. So it is simply erased." Rosenzweig was aghast at Agnon and Buber's resignation to their misfortune. "From day to day I become less able to accept the fact that the 'Corpus' is not to be done. . . . The more I think about it, the more definitely I see that we cannot let it be 'simply erased.' . . . [After all], Frederick the Great rewrote the *History of the Seven Years' War,* which his valet had used for kindling; and Carlyle's *French Revolution* was also a second draft—the complete first draft was burned while in the possession of [John Stuart] Mill. No, death alone erases, not fire."[84]

Prodded by Rosenzweig, Agnon and Buber intermittently tried to start afresh on the *Corpus,* but due to various factors— including geographic separation (Agnon returned to Palestine in 1924) and new, more pressing projects—they eventually had to abandon it. Their friendship, however, remained intact, and deepened with their reunion in Jerusalem in the spring of 1938. Indeed, Agnon was probably Buber's closest, most intimate friend in the years that followed; notably, he was the only one who ever succeeded in persuading Buber to attend Yom Kippur services with him. Buber also continued to consult Agnon about Hasidism. Before sending the Hebrew text of *Gog and Magog* to press, he asked Agnon to review the manuscript: "I am burdening you unwillingly," Buber contritely acknowledged, "with this chore. But there is no one else in the country who could help me."[85] Agnon duly suggested revisions and subsequently reread and edited the revised text. Buber's later publication of

*Or ha-Ganuz* apparently inspired Agnon to consider editing a Hasidic anthology of his own, but aside from a series of short collections of Hasidic lore published in various journals—one of which he dedicated to "Martin Buber, may God preserve him and give him life"—nothing else came to fruition.[86] It was only after his death that Agnon's anthology, *Sippurei haBesht* (Stories of the Baal Shem Tov), was published.[87] In their introduction, the editors of the posthumous volume noted that approximately 75 percent of the stories included in the book were based on material that Buber had sent to Agnon, though they underscored that Agnon had adapted the stories that Buber sent.[88] In stark contrast to the reception of Buber's similarly conceived anthologies, Agnon's free rendering of Hasidic lore did not arouse criticism. After all, he was, as Buber himself had admiringly noted, a "true storyteller."[89]

Buber, by contrast, made no claim to being a storyteller. Rather he saw himself as a teacher who, through tales and aphorisms that he selected from Hasidic literature—and from which he winnowed what he regarded to be their unessential elements—pointed the way for his readers. His criteria for selection were questioned by scholars, foremost among them the undisputed doyen of Jewish mysticism, Gershom Scholem. But it was Buber's volumes on Hasidism in the 1940s, especially those addressed (in Hebrew) to his fellow Zionists, that aroused the most contentious controversy. His interest in Hasidism occupied a place in the spiritual landscape of the Yishuv that his contemporaries found difficult to appreciate; for many Buber was neither fish nor fowl, neither secular nor observant.

Nor did he offer a clear formulation of his unique brand of religious anarchism. "No way can be pointed to in this desert night," he wrote; all that one can do is "to help men of today to stand fast, with their soul in readiness, until the dawn breaks and a path becomes visible where none suspected it."[90] Moreover, his Judaism with its nonnormative religious sensibility seemed to some to place him in the company of Saint Paul—which perhaps explains why he so consistently sought to distinguish his theology from that of Jesus's apostle. In *Two Types of Faith*, he argued that Pauline faith was inflected with gnostic conceptions of salvation, radically departing from biblical faith with its affirmation of the created order and a this-worldly vision of redemption—a faith that the pre-Pauline Gospels portrayed Jesus as upholding. Buber thus not only regarded Jesus as a representative Jew, but also affectionately embraced him as his "great brother."

Such views struck many of his contemporaries as compromising his loyalty to Judaism and the Jewish people, further exacerbating his position as an outsider. The extent of this perception was recounted in a letter to Buber by a distraught disciple, who in 1951 traveled throughout the infant State of Israel, enthusiastically evoking the teachings of his beloved teacher. To his profound chagrin, mentions of Buber were met with almost identical hostile responses:

> Whether on the street or in a café, among the intellectuals of Jerusalem or Tel Aviv, in Tiberias or Safed, in a kibbutz . . . nowhere did I hear a kind word about Martin Buber, and that surprised me greatly. I tried everything to find out why people were so unsympathetic and even unfriendly, and although I received answers like, "He married a *goy*." "He lived in the Arab quarter among *goyim*." "He belongs to an organization that concerns itself with Arab problems," I was not able to get to the bottom of the matter. Then I had a conversation with you; you were very friendly, and everything would have been wonderful, but. . . . When I faced you across the desk, the picture behind you with the cross or *tzailim* [Yiddish for idols or graven images], as the Ukrainian Jews say, cut into every fiber of my body and soul, and since then I had no peace. . . . I sincerely hope you will answer my questions as to why there is a cross in your room when we

all know what the *goyim* have done to us in the name of the cross.[91]

In his reply, Buber explained that the offending painting was an engraving by the eighteenth-century Italian artist Giovanni Battista Piranesi of three churches in the Roman ghetto, which had been converted into pagan temples. "The cross on the churches is part of the historical and symbolic reality. . . . But I hold no resentment against the *goyim*. I seek to tell you and the world the truth about Judaism and Christianity, as I did in my last book [*Two Types of Faith*]." And citing Leviticus 19: 17—"Do set your friend right"—he concludes the letter by declaring, "and I try to do precisely that, only I do not *hate* them [the gentiles], despite everything that, as you say, they inflicted on us."[92]

"Do set your friend right" is Buber's rendering of the commandment of rebuke from Leviticus. It may be understood as the principle guiding his critique of Zionist politics—a critique of the loyal opposition. His loyalty to the Zionist project had at its root an existential bond with the Jewish people and Jewish spirituality (if not Jewish "religion"), and, as such, was not limited to expressions of national solidarity. Rather, as he expressed it in a letter to his wife, Paula, on the occasion of the birth of their first grandson, Martin Emmanuel, on March 23, 1926, the Jews are bonded by a primordial covenant. Distressed to learn that his daughter Eva's husband, Ludwig Strauss, was inclined to forgo the ritual circumcision of their infant son, he urged Paula to speak to Ludwig: "In the course of my life I have learned that in the Diaspora (*das Exil*) we must not abandon this primordial certification of an affiliation, no matter what our personal feelings about it may be—simply because it is the only one available to us here and because through it we let the 'covenant,' which in the Diaspora lacks the community as the bearer, continue on a personal plane."[93] Though at a specific historical juncture, such as in an era of heightened anti-Semitism, the bond among these covenanted people might elicit an especially strong bond of national solidarity, Jewish affiliation, he believed, is fundamentally spiritual and, especially in exile, demands personal decision and action.

Beyond the rite of circumcision (and perhaps that of bar mitzvah), for Buber the spiritual consciousness and sensibility that constitutes Jewish affiliation were not to be expressed through the ritual and liturgical practices of rabbinic tradition.[94] In his earliest writings, he had spoken of Jewry as a "community of blood," in which Jews (even if utterly acculturated and assimilated) somehow share distinctive Jewish sensibilities. But his conception of the life of faith evolved into his biblical humanism, embodied in and mediated primarily through religious texts, principally the Hebrew Bible and Hasidic lore, properly studied and interpreted from the stance of dialogical existentialism. Consistent across the development of his adult conception of Judaism was a rejection of the normativity of religious practice as prescribed by rabbinic tradition and of most of the specific practices, though he retained select cultural forms and expressions of that tradition. Friday evening meals marking the beginning of the Sabbath were usually followed by Buber reading to his children (and later grandchildren) Hasidic tales, passages from the Bible, and occasionally even stories in Yiddish (especially those of Sholem Aleichem). He would often complement these readings with texts of a more universal nature, such as Kant's *Eternal Peace*.[95] He arranged tutors in Hebrew for them, and encouraged them to join Zionist youth movements with a progressive orientation. What Buber sought to instill in his children and grandchildren was a sense of responsibility to the Jewish people that should not diminish their commitment to the larger family of humankind.

To be sure, a dual loyalty to one's people and to humanity

could not be realized in slogans and pious litanies, but would be tested in the crucible of everyday experience. The Zionist settlement in Palestine provided a dramatic setting of such a test: how could one satisfy the objectives of the Zionist project while honoring the political and human rights of the Arabs of Palestine? Buber's most existentially probing response to this question was his open letter to Gandhi in February 1939 (paired with one by Judah Magnes), prompted by Gandhi's article in his prestigious Indian weekly, *Harijan*, in November 1938, just days after Kristallnacht. In it, Gandhi counseled the persecuted Jews of Germany to remain where they were, and to pursue *satyagraha* (in Sanskrit, soul-force, literally "holding on truth"): a determined but nonviolent resistance to evil, even until death. Satyagraha was, Gandhi claimed, not only noble, but the only tenable option available. Zionism was not an acceptable response to their situation. His sympathy for the Jews, he held, "could not blind me to the requirements of justice." "Palestine," he categorically declared, "belongs to the Arabs"—hence, it is "wrong and inhuman to impose the Jews on the Arabs," for the objectives of Zionism could not be reconciled with the rights of the indigenous Arab population of Palestine.[96]

Buber was clearly troubled by this position of the Mahatma, whom he had long revered as an unimpeachable moral authority. As he noted in his open letter, he found it exceedingly difficult to even formulate his response:

> I have been very slow in writing this letter to you, Mahatma. I made repeated pauses—sometimes days elapsed between short paragraphs—in order to test my knowledge and way of thinking. Day and night I took myself to task, searching whether I had not in any one point overstepped the measure of self-preservation allotted and even prescribed by God to a human community, and whether I had not fallen into the grievous error of collective egoism.[97]

With the words "the measure of self-preservation allotted
. . . by God to a human community," Buber pointed to the
"line of demarcation," a principle that would serve for him as
the ethical compass (and ethical limits) of his Zionism. The
"line of demarcation" represented the acceptable outer limits
of promoting the needs of one's community, while minimizing
the harm that attending to those needs might afflict on others —
a line that demands utter care not to overstep it. In articulating
this way of thinking, Buber in effect acknowledged that Zionist settlement did perforce infringe on the rights of the Arabs
of Palestine. With carefully chosen words, he beseeched the
Hindu sage to appreciate the ethical dilemma faced by Zionists who shared the Mahatma's vigilant attention to "the requirements of justice." He questioned whether justice could
really be served by calling on the Jews, as Gandhi had, to realize
God's commandment to be a chosen people by choosing non-
violence instead of Zionism, thereby vindicating their divinely
appointed place on earth. To Gandhi's suggestion that the Jews
could "add to their many contributions [to the world] the sur-
passing contribution of non-violent action," Buber in effect replied: Is it just to sacrifice the natural Jew on the altar of the
supernatural Jew?[98]

> But you, the man of goodwill, do you not know that you
> must see him whom you address, in his place and circum-
> stance, in the throes of his destiny[?] Jews are being perse-
> cuted, robbed, maltreated, tortured, murdered. . . . Now, do
> you know or do you not know, Mahatma, what a concen-
> tration camp is like and what goes on there? Do you know
> of the torments in the concentration camp, of its methods
> of slow and quick slaughter?[99] And do you think perhaps
> that a Jew in Germany could pronounce in public one single
> sentence of a speech such as yours without being knocked
> down?. . . An effective stand in the form of nonviolence
> may be taken against unfeeling human beings in the hope of

gradually bringing them to their senses; but a diabolic universal steamroller cannot thus be withstood. . . . The Jew [the natural Jew] needs a motherland, just like the oppressed Hindus of South Africa sought the comforting security of "the great Mother India." . . . [A]pparently you are entirely unaware of the fundamental differences existing between nations having such a mother (it need not necessarily be such a great mother, it may be a tiny motherkin, but yet a mother, a mother's bosom and mother's heart) and a nation that is orphaned or to whom one says, in speaking of his country, "This is no more your mother!"[100]

Jewry, Buber tells Gandhi, needs the primordial warmth and reassuring security, the nurturing bosom and heart of a mother, in order to fulfill its divine calling. (One cannot fail to note Buber's recurrent evocation of the quest for a lost mother.)

Buber acknowledged that there were too few in the orphaned people of Israel "who feel themselves entrusted with the mission of fulfilling the command of justice delivered to Israel of the Bible," for "Jewry today is in the throes of a serious crisis in the matter of faith." That crisis is not resolved in and of itself by the mere act of settling in Palestine. "But at the same time we realize that here [in Palestine] alone can it be resolved." Zionism, he explained, is based on the premise that "no solution [is] to be found in the life of isolated individuals. . . . The true solution can only issue from the life of a community that begins to carry out the will of God, often without being aware of doing so, [even] without believing that God exists and this is his will."[101] Hence, he said, "we cannot renounce the Jewish claim [to Palestine]; something even higher than the life of our people is bound up with the Land, namely, the work that is their divine mission."[102] He acknowledged, however, that this mission does not absolve the Jews of the "duty to understand and honor the claim that is opposed to ours and to endeavor to reconcile both claims."

Buber then introduced "a personal note," explaining that he belonged to small group of individuals, who, "from the time when Britain conquered Palestine, have not ceased to strive for the achievement of genuine peace between Jew and Arab." The reference is to Brit Shalom (The covenant of peace), an association founded in Jerusalem in 1925 that advocated the establishment in Palestine of a binational state in which Jews and Arabs, as two culturally autonomous communities, would share political sovereignty on the basis of absolute equality, irrespective of demographic considerations. What is crucial, as Buber explained to Gandhi, is the resolve "to find some form of agreement" to reconcile the Jewish and Arab claims to Palestine, "for we love this land and we believe in its future, and, seeing that such love and such faith are surely present on the other side as well, a union in the common service of the Land must be within the range of the possible. Where there is faith and love, a solution may be found even to what appears to be a tragic contradiction."[103]

Buber's ultimately unsuccessful appeal to Gandhi to understand the Zionist cause reflected the tensions and ambiguities of his Zionism, in which he sought to integrate the need to draw attention to the increasingly exigent political needs of the natural Jew and the unremitting calling of the supernatural Jew. In the 1940s, the plight of the natural Jew became ever more pressing, and paramount. The Zionist leadership went into emergency mode, impelled by the impending catastrophe facing European Jewry. In May 1942, an urgent meeting of the World Zionist Organization took place at the Biltmore Hotel in New York City, convened at the initiative of David Ben-Gurion, head of the executive of the Jewish Agency in Palestine. The delegates called on Great Britain to immediately repeal the White Paper of 1939, which had placed severe restrictions on Jewish immigration to Mandatory Palestine, and to establish Palestine as "a Jewish Commonwealth." Until that point, the ideological rationale behind the perennial Zionist demand that the Mandatory government allow unlimited Jewish immigration had been to hasten the creation of a Jewish majority in Palestine; now the supreme moral task of rescuing European Jewry was at stake.

Dissent regarding the demand for unfettered, mass Jewish immigration was no longer a matter of legitimate political disagreement; it was now construed as betrayal of the Jewish people. Buber, prepared to be cast as a traitor, profusely objected to what would be called "the Biltmore Program." He defiantly held that in the projected Jewish Commonwealth of Palestine, the Arabs would not only be deprived of "collective political equality," but, like the biblical Gibeonites, would also be subordinated to the economically stronger Jewish community.[104] Even more distressing to Buber was Ben-Gurion's readiness to postpone the goal of establishing a Jewish homeland in the whole of Palestine in order to seek the immediate partition of the country into separate Jewish and Arab states (which Ben-Gurion judged to be politically more feasible). Partition, Buber warned, would inexorably lead to unprecedented and interminable strife with the Arabs.

Buber was hardly indifferent to the plight of European Jewry. He was a member of the executive committee of Al-domi—meaning "do not keep silent!" (Psalms 83:1)—"a small, spontaneous protest movement" of mostly Jerusalem intellectuals founded at the end of 1942 to urge the Yishuv and the free world to make the rescue of European Jewry their utmost priority.[105] Giving voice to Al-domi's concerns, Buber published in Hebrew a particularly passionate plea addressed to the leadership of the Yishuv. "Never before have I been so aware of how dubious all our spiritual existence is—in spite of all our efforts at renewal—as in these days when the masses of our people have been abandoned to the violence of its worst enemies." Though one did not know "as yet the actual extent of the catastrophe" that had befallen European Jewry, "there is no doubt that it is far greater than any other in our history." The Yishuv, he felt, had resisted not only reckoning with the enormity of the horror, but also genuinely identifying with their European brethren: "It is certainly not appropriate for us just to carry on our lives; it is appropriate for us to weave whatever happens into the fabric of our lives—not in order to emit the customary roar of revenge in which the tension is relieved, but rather in order to be effective, to cooperate where it is possible to do something." He also indicted the Yishuv leadership for first withholding from the public a fuller knowledge of the catastrophe—"I do not understand that, and it cannot be understood"—keeping silent when it first learned in greater detail of the cruel fate of European Jewry, then harnessing for the service of particular political ends the eventual heartfelt expressions of solidarity. "There are parties which need the seething spirit of the nation in order to boil their brew."[106] They—the Yishuv leadership—had no compunction about exploiting "our catastrophe" to advance their political agenda:

> If you ask me at this hour what we ought to do, I have no answer other than this cruelly sober one: to save as many Jews as is at all possible; to bring them here or take them to other places; to save them by fully realistic consideration of all the means at our disposal. . . . Nothing of the spirit of partisanship, of politicizing, must be allowed to be part of this operation, nothing aside from the lives of the nameless ones who are to be saved.[107]

Those "who are anxious to rescue what can still be rescued," he insisted, must resist those who "want to make us . . . subservient to a [political] party with the [mere] watchword of rescue." This was an oblique criticism of Ben-Gurion, who viewed the rescue of the remnant of European Jewry as a unique opportunity to further the specific political objective of creating a Jewish majority in Palestine.[108]

In a speech before the Histadrut, the General Federation of Labor in Palestine, Ben-Gurion ridiculed a distinction that Buber often made between the goal of "as many Jews as possible" and "a majority of Jews" in Palestine as meaningless babble. To Buber's mind, the rejection of his semantic point betrayed a deliberate attempt to conflate ethical and political issues—that is, the exigent moral task of rescuing as many Jews as possible and the declared political goal of creating a Jewish majority in the country—in order to justify the demand for Jewish sovereignty in the country. By confounding the two issues, Buber argued, Ben-Gurion was mendaciously seeking to lend his political agenda an indisputable ethical authority, though the political objective of a Jewish majority in Palestine was hardly ethically unambiguous. Even politically, Buber believed, Ben-Gurion's policy was not necessarily the wisest strategy for securing the Zionist project and the future of Jewry in Palestine. For Buber, then, both morally and politically, the program of a binational state was eminently sounder—not an infallible formula, but a direction that could prompt thinking beyond the conceptual boxes of "majority" and "minority," political configurations that would inevitably lead to violent conflict between the Jews and Arabs. Most crucially, the vision of a binational state pointed to a horizon beyond the political quagmire of interminable mistrust and enmity between Jews and Arabs.[109]

An opportunity arose for Buber to elaborate this vision before an international forum, with the visit to Jerusalem of an Anglo-American Inquiry Committee in November 1946. The committee was charged with exploring alternatives to the British Mandate of Palestine, specifically to consider the pressing plight of the Jewish survivors of the Nazi "Final Solution" and the political feasibility of their immigration to Palestine, and its members sought "to hear the views of competent witnesses and to consult representative Arabs and Jews on the problem of Palestine." The official Zionist leadership forbade anyone in the Yishuv from appearing independently before the committee. Eager to present its program for a binational state, the Ichud decided to ignore the leadership's ban, and deputized three of its members, one of whom was Buber, to appear before the committee. He opened his testimony with a detailed review of the spiritual roots of Zionism, summarizing a series of lectures he had given the previous year in Hebrew, in which he sought to remind his fellow Zionists of the religious and ethical vocation that they had taken upon themselves by naming their movement after a place, Zion—a holy place and the focus of a divine mission.[110] It is thus "out of an inner necessity" that Zionism as "a movement of [spiritual] regeneration chose for its aim the reunion with the soil of Palestine," creating three "irreducible demands": the unhampered acquisition of land in "sufficient measure" to facilitate that economic and spiritual reunion with Zion; "a permanent powerful influx of [Jewish] settlers"; and the "self-determination of the Jewish community" in Palestine.[111]

Unfortunately, Buber bemoaned, these demands were "not yet adequately understood by large parts of the world," undoubtedly because of the erroneous belief that their fulfillment would necessarily encroach upon the rights of the Arabs of Palestine. But the advocates of a binational solution to the problem of Palestine, Buber underscored, in fact agree that the Zionist project "must not be gained at the expense of another's independence. . . . It is, therefore, ethically and politically incumbent upon 'a regenerated Jewish people in Palestine' not only to aim at living peacefully 'next' to the Arabs of the land but also 'with' them. . . . Together they are to work to develop the country for the equal benefit of both communities. Within the framework of a shared Arab-Jewish stewardship of the country, Jewish cultural and social autonomy would not, as the greater part of the Jewish people think today, necessarily lead to the demand for a 'Jewish State' or a 'Jewish majority.' We need for this land as many Jews as it is possible economically to absorb, but not in order to establish a majority against a minority."[112]

In its report, published on April 20, 1946, the Anglo-American committee echoed Buber's testimony and, in effect, endorsed the concept of a binational state in Palestine:

> It is neither just nor practicable that Palestine should become either an Arab state, in which an Arab majority would control the destiny of a Jewish minority, or a Jewish State, in which a Jewish majority would control that of an Arab minority. . . . Palestine, then, must be established as a country in which the legitimate national aspirations of both Jews and Arabs can be reconciled without either side fearing the ascendancy of the other.[113]

Commenting on the findings of the committee, Buber observed that the conflict between Jews and Arabs of Palestine is frequently said to be a tragic one and their interests presumed to be irreconcilable.[114] It would surely be foolish, he acknowledged, to deny that the conflict between Jew and Arab is real, but to move from an undeniable clash of interests to a political policy narrowly bound to the interests of one's group over those of the other would only exacerbate and further politicize the conflict. Under the banner of a binational state, Buber said, the Ichud sought instead to ground it in the "domain of life" (the matrix of everyday life, rather than political confrontation)—which ultimately required that people learn to live together, compromise, and reconcile differences.

But the recommendation of the Anglo-American Committee was ultimately rejected by the British government, which in February 1947 requested that the United Nations relieve it of the Mandate. On November 29, the U.N. General Assembly voted to terminate the Mandate and to partition Palestine into two independent states, Jewish and Arab. The leadership of the Yishuv greeted the proposal with unified enthusiasm; disregarding the mounting pressure from Western powers, particularly the United States, on May 14, 1948, the Yishuv under the leadership of David Ben-Gurion proclaimed its independence, reconstituting itself as the government of the State of Israel. The U.N. vote had already immediately precipitated in Palestine a virtual civil war between the Jews and Arabs; now, as Buber and the Ichud had feared, the Proclamation of Independence greatly intensified the conflict, especially with the invasion of the fledgling state by five Arab armies from neighboring countries. Two weeks into Israel's "war of independence," Buber published an article bemoaning the myopia of the quest for Jewish political sovereignty at any cost: "It was evident that the meaning of that program was war—real war—with our neighbors, and also with the whole Arab nation: for what nation will allow itself to be demoted from the position of majority to that of a minority without a fight?" Even if somehow the infant state were to prevail and fend off its Arab foes, he said, it would be a pyrrhic victory, for it would amount to the defeat of the Zionist ideal of national rebirth, the meaning of which "is not simply the secure existence of the nation instead of its present vulnerability" but also a revival of its ethical mission.[115]

For Buber, the focus on the political "normalization" of the Jewish people was tantamount to "national assimilation." While the ancient Hebrews did not succeed in "becoming a normal nation," under Ben-Gurion's leadership, the Jews of today were, he said, "succeeding at it to a terrifying degree. This sort of 'Zionism' blasphemes the name Zion. It is nothing but one of the crude forms of nationalism, which acknowledges no master above the *apparent* (!) interest of the nation."[116]

Buber concluded this jeremiad with a personal lament:

"Fifty years ago when I joined the Zionist movement for the rebirth of Israel, my heart was whole. Today it is torn. The war being waged for a political structure might become a war of national survival at any moment. Thus against my will I participate in it with my own being, and my heart trembles like any other Israeli. I cannot, however, even be joyful in anticipating victory, for I fear that the significance of Jewish victory will be the downfall of Zionism."[117]

# 10

---

*Despite Everything*

BUBER'S EVICTION FROM his residence in Talbiya initially proved to be a happy turn of fortune, for the apartment he and Paula found in Abu-Tor, a picturesque largely Arab neighborhood, brought them great joy. From their apartment, situated just above the Valley of Hinnom, they had a marvelous view of the Old City, Mount Zion, and the golden Dome of the Rock. And whereas their residence in Talbiya had been the only structure in the immediate vicinity of the relatively new neighborhood and thus socially isolated, Abu-Tor was a vibrant, friendly area, and a model of good relations between Jews and Arabs. Paula was particularly pleased that the wife of their landlord, Jussuf Wahab Dajani, spoke fluent German. The convivial spirit that reigned in Abu-Tor also delighted Martin. One of his Jewish neighbors often and admiringly observed him "in his conversations with members of his family, with his Arab servant Jalil, with Jewish students and Arab neighbors, with notables, scholars, and clergy from many countries and of many creeds, and even—especially—with children. In observing his phenomenal gift of communicating, I cannot recall one instance when Buber would have withheld himself."[1] At his home in Abu-Tor, Buber would host several study circles: one on the Hebrew Bible, another dedicated to the poetry of Hölderin, and yet another on contemporary political issues.[2]

Alas, this congenial and intellectually engaging setting was shattered in November 1947 by the outbreak of hostilities between the Jews and Arabs of Palestine. As troops of the Arab Liberation Army marched on Jerusalem, threatening to occupy Abu-Tor, friends prevailed on Paula and Martin to flee to safer quarters in Jewish neighborhoods of Jerusalem—especially after thirteen bullets were shot through their previously tranquil apartment, piercing, among other things, a portrait of Buber by the renowned painter Emil Robert Weiss.[3] The Anglican archdeacon Graham Brown picked them up in his car bearing the flag of the church. They left behind virtually all their possessions, including Buber's vast library and their beloved nine cats.

The Jewish defense forces, the Haganah, subsequently set up a position in the Abu-Tor apartment, barricading themselves with some of Martin's books. Although the Haganah soon retreated, and a contingent of Iraqi volunteer troops occupied Abu-Tor, Buber's library and possessions otherwise remained untouched; his Palestinian landlord had placed them in a locked room for safekeeping. In the meantime, Paula and Martin had taken up residence at Pension Grete Asher in the Jerusalem neighborhood of Rehavia, where they soon, on February 8, 1948, celebrated Buber's seventieth birthday.

To mark the occasion, Magnes published in the Ichud's journal reminiscences of his and Buber's friendship, which extended back to when they were both students at the University of Berlin. Magnes left to others to discuss Buber's achievements, but for his own part wrote, "I cannot help but devote my words to the tragic events that have transpired during these days when you are entering the 'club' of the hoary septuagenarians," with Buber now "witnessing the failure of almost all the things that have been dear to you. In *Eretz Yisrael*, the house of Israel has turned into a nation like all nations [an allusion to 1 Samuel 8:5], and does not believe in the religious and ethical mission of the people of Israel. . . . You see how all your efforts to instill into the people a spirit of mutual understanding with its neighbors is coming to naught." Magnes then raised the cardinal question of Buber's life work: "You combine within yourself two spiritual qualities that, viewed superficially, are in conflict with each other: you are capable of seeing reality as it is, but also the spiritual reality as it is. Can these two realities be reconciled?" He concluded his birthday greetings by wishing for Buber the courage to continue, "despite everything, your struggle against the prevailing reality, as you always have, that you may be vouchsafed a long life until you are permitted to witness God's return to Zion and to compassion."[4]

Buber would, indeed, continue his struggle "despite everything." He had long resisted the despair that had gripped some of his contemporaries, who had withdrawn from the struggle for Arab-Jewish understanding, abandoning what they regarded as a hopelessly sinking ship. In 1929, one of Buber's closest disciples, Hans Kohn (a devoted Zionist since 1909), had left the Zionist movement to which he had devoted twenty years of his life, having concluded that the Zionist project would by its very nature lead to a ceaseless conflict with the Arabs—an unacceptable prospect. As he explained in a letter he wrote to a friend on November 21, 1929: "I am not concerned with Ishmael, only about Isaac, that is, our aims, our life, our actions. I am afraid we [Zionists] support actions for which we cannot vouch. And because of a false solidarity we shall sink deeper into quagmire. . . . Zionism is not Judaism."[5]

Kohn was especially close to Buber, and would soon complete an authoritative biography, first published in 1930: *Martin Buber: Sein Werk und seine Zeit*. In this still unsurpassed study, which traces Buber's intellectual development through the first three decades of the twentieth century, Kohn presented Buber's struggle to shape Zionist policy as the practical expression of his evolving philosophical and religious teachings. Kohn's letter suggested by implication that his critique of and break with Zionism was consonant with those teachings, and, indeed, that they demanded it. But Buber, although he appreciated Kohn's predicament, found his decision to abandon ship, as he wrote Paula, to suffer from a doctrinaire moral idealism; he felt that to withdraw from what one views as an ethically untenable political reality is the very opposite of his understanding of political responsibility.[6] Kohn and others who were similarly troubled by the moral ambiguities of the Zionist project, he felt, proved more committed to the purity of their moral ideals than to the task of redeeming the world. To take refuge above the fray in the purity of moral ideals is to betray one's vocation as an intellectual (in both German and Hebrew, the intellectual is referred to as a person or custodian of the spirit). "If work is to be done in public life, it must be accomplished not above the fray, but in it."[7] The real world, while invariably compromising the purity of our moral principles, provides the only possibility for their actualization.

Hence, "despite everything"—the profound grief that Zion would be "built in blood"—Buber continued the struggle for a "politics born of faith" under new circumstances with the establishment of the State of Israel in May 1948. His resolve is captured in an anecdote told by Schalom Ben-Chorin, who at the height of the siege of Jerusalem, with the city near starvation conditions, happened to meet Buber on a walk, and asked him why he didn't avail himself of the opportunity to flee to Tel Aviv, where conditions were hardly so dire. Buber matter-of-factly replied, "Even if they were to send an airplane to my doorstep, I would still not leave this Jerusalem in which what I wanted to avoid is happening."[8] With a "trembling heart," he exclaimed:

> I have accepted as mine the State of Israel, the form of the new Jewish community that has arisen from the war. I have nothing in common with those Jews who imagine that they may contest the factual shape that Jewish independence has taken. The command to serve the spirit is to be fulfilled by us in this state, by starting from it. But he who will truly serve the spirit must seek to make good all that was once missed: he must seek to free once again the blocked path to an understanding with the Arab peoples. . . . There can be no peace between Jews and Arabs that is merely a cessation of war; there can only be a peace of genuine cooperation. Today, under such manifoldly aggravated circumstances, the command of the spirit is still to prepare the way for the co-operation of peoples.[9]

Although history had declared a victory for the idea of a sovereign Jewish state, and the defeat of binationalism, the goal of fostering positive relations between Jew and Arab remained as urgent as ever; the strategy for its attainment would have to be adjusted to the new situation.

On a personal level, Buber and his family would also have to make their own considerable adjustments. They needed, first and foremost, to find permanent housing. After their precipitous flight from embattled Abu-Tor, they resided in Pension Asher for more than a year; Martin's library and their other possessions were still in their former Abu-Tor residence, placed in a sealed room and guarded vigilantly by the Dajani family, who also cared for Martin's and Paula's beloved cats. The books were later stuffed into hundreds of sacks, and over the course of six weeks clandestinely transported (with Buber's other possessions) across the battle lines to Jewish-controlled Jerusalem, and stored in various locations until Buber was able to arrange for permanent living quarters. That opportunity came with the Armistice of March 1949 and the cessation of hostilities, at which time a committee was formed and charged with administering dwellings in Jerusalem that had been abandoned by Arabs fleeing Jewish armed forces. The committee proceeded to assign these properties to Jewish refugees from parts of the city that had fallen to Arab troops.

Buber was assigned a rather large house on an upscale street again in Talbiya—its Arab owners had taken refuge in Turkey—on the condition that he would share it with another family. He immediately asked his granddaughter Barbara and her husband to join him and Paula. Although quite spacious, the home was not large enough to accommodate all of his more than fifteen thousand books, but he was able to rent two rooms in the home of a neighbor to house the overflow. Shortly after moving into her grandparents' home, in 1950, Barbara gave birth to Tamar; Gideon followed in 1952. The house on Hovevei Tzion Street was next door to a grocery store, whose proprietor was one Mr. Rosenzweig; when anyone asked for directions to Buber's house, they would be told, "Next to Rosenzweig."

Although relieved to have found a relatively spacious and comfortable home, Buber was uneasy about living in the former residence of an Arab family. With his encouragement, Barbara managed to contact the family in Turkey, and at its request sent them the belongings they had left behind. Rent was paid to the Custodian of Absentee Property (established by an emergency ordinance of December 1948), which was to keep the proceeds in escrow until the legal status of the property of Arab refugees was adjudicated. But in time, it became clear that the intent was to confiscate their property. Buber's response was to conduct a determined campaign to allow the refugees to return to their homes or receive proper compensation, which led to a clash with David Ben-Gurion, the first prime minister of the State of Israel. Buber would soon have the occasion to challenge Ben-Gurion directly about the moral and political imperative of the proper treatment of Arab refugees. Shortly after Ben-Gurion was installed in early March 1949 as the first elected prime minister of the State of Israel, he convened at his home in Tel Aviv a meeting with some twenty of the country's leading intellectuals—distinguished authors, poets, and academics—to confer about the moral and spiritual direction of the fledgling state. Buber, who was one of the first to address the meeting, questioned Ben-Gurion's assertion that the government per se had no direct role in shaping the moral character of the state, insisting instead that the government's policies concerning any issues with an ethical dimension could not but bear on the infant state's guiding ethos. He thus appealed to Ben-Gurion to consider the ethical implications of the government's policies toward the Arabs, and initiate a just and expeditious solution to the Arab refugee problem:

> I admit that when the government [makes a policy decision out of ethical considerations], it is apparently doing something unnecessary from the point of view of "raison d'être." However, it is just those "unnecessary" acts, acts with no apparent explanation, that serve the true good of the state, the true good of the nation and of all nations. For example, take the question of the Arab refugees. The possibility existed for the government, and perhaps it still does now, of doing a great moral act, which could bring about the moral awakening of the public, and its influence on the world would certainly not be bad.[10]

Buber was persistent in calling on both the State of Israel's political leadership and its general public to have the moral courage to confront "the bitter reality" of the country's policies toward the Arabs of Palestine: to examine the facts of "the robbery and plunder, anti-Arab discrimination, the destruction of their villages" — "as painful as this will be" — and "together [to] search for a way out, if such a way exists. 'Redemption' of an external kind," he continued, "can be paid for with the blood of our sons. Internal redemption can only be brought about by gazing directly at the brutal face of truth."[11]

Further, he insisted, ethicists and politicians should avoid demonizing one another. Those concerned with ethics too easily perceive politicians as "despot[s], drunk with power, who [know] no direction above [their] own will. Politicians, in turn, see [ethicists] as ideologues enslaved to high-flown talk, living in the clouds, and not on an earth full of contradictions." When confronted by seemingly unyielding practical realities, politicians often do have at heart "the true interest of [their] nation." But Buber called on them, and specifically on Ben-Gurion, to adhere to a "greater realism," or a "sense of proportion of what can and should be done at any given time," and thus a sober realization that "all true responsibility is two-fold: directed towards heaven and the earth."[12]

> Such dual responsibility is not to be unified by means of principles, but rather through an examination [of factual realities] and restraint [determined by ethical conscience] constantly renewed. Individuals, in that they are human, cannot be entirely without sin, and the same is true of a nation that is a nation. How then will individuals and nations act in accordance with their conscience? The main point is to examine oneself at all times to ascertain whether one's guilt is not greater than the amount necessary to carry on living. . . . This is not simply the commandment of pure morality. Great statesmanship, which is directed to the true interest of the coming generation [of one's nation], is a policy by virtue of which the nation does not heap upon itself an excessive degree of guilt. Clearly one does not administer such a policy by generalizations and pure principles. We must take upon

ourselves repeatedly and continuously the hardest task: responding to both demands at the same time, the demand of the moment [the given earthly reality] and the demand of [ethical] truth.[13]

In short, for the Zionist state, "the hardest task" involved the responsibility to be both attentive to the political and quotidian needs of "the natural Jew," and mindful of the spiritual and ethical imperatives of "the supernatural Jew."[14]

The other dual responsibility that Buber had noted, toward heaven and earth, carried with it the risk of a pull toward political theology—that is, theology in the service of politics—that he knew had to be resisted. Buber was particularly wary of political messianism: "We cannot prepare the messianic world; we can only be prepared for it. There is no legitimately messianic-intended politics."[15] No doubt in part because of his own sobering experience in the context of World War I, when he passionately embraced German nationalism as an elevated spiritual mission to secure the promise of genuine community, and then firmly rejected that expression of nationalism, he was acutely attentive to the destructive potential of messianic political fantasies. Indeed, his monograph on the *Kingship of God* and his novel *Gog and Magog* may both be traced back to his own struggle to overcome the emotional lure of messianic politics. He was therefore alarmed by Ben-Gurion's view of Zionism as the fulfillment of the prophets' messianic vision.

In his opening address at the "First World [Zionist] Ideological Conference," which he convened in Jerusalem in August 1957, Ben-Gurion told the gathering that Zionism had been inspired and sustained by three primordial (albeit secularized) components of Jewish identity: the people's attachment to its ancient homeland, the Hebrew language, and the messianic promise of redemption. At the height of his address, he affirmed his conviction that the restoration of Jewish life in the land of

Israel and the creation of a model society will herald universal redemption. Buber, who had been invited to the conference at the behest of Ben-Gurion, was aghast, and requested to speak:

> [Ben-Gurion] is one of the proponents of that kind of secularization which cultivated its "thought" and "visions" so diligently that it keeps people from hearing the voice of the living God. . . . This phenomenon has very old roots. Even some of the kings in [biblical] Israel are said to have gone so far as to employ false prophets whose prophesying was wholly a function of state policy.[16]

One cannot say whether Ben-Gurion believed that Buber was suggesting that he was a false prophet, but he seems to have very much wanted Buber's approval, and was manifestly disappointed and even hurt by this criticism. Nonetheless, he continued to hold Buber in esteem, as is evident in a letter he sent Buber in February 1963:

> On your eighty-fifth birthday I send you my sincere blessings, the good wishes of a friend, admirer, and opponent. Your profound and original philosophy, your fruitful devotion to the work of Israel's rebirth from your youth to the present time, your profound ideational and existential relationship to the vision that the prophets of Israel had of a national and universal redemption as well as the rule of justice, peace, and fraternity in the world, the complete congruence between your endeavors and the demand and the conduct of your life—for all this you deserve praise and glory in the history of our people and our time.[17]

He closed the letter, "With love and veneration."

In his acknowledgment of Ben-Gurion's birthday greetings, Buber noted that despite their political differences, "I could characterize my attitude toward you with words similar to those you were kind enough to use in writing to me"—then proceeded to ask Ben-Gurion if he might find it possible "within the framework of your authority, to secure a pardon for the ailing Aharon Cohen, and his release from prison. That would make me very happy."[18]

Cohen had been sentenced to prison in January 1962, convicted of espionage on behalf of the Soviet Union. He and Buber had been friends and colleagues since the early 1940s, when both had been members of the League for Arab-Jewish Rapprochement and Cooperation. Cohen was arrested in 1958, but his trial didn't begin until three-and-a-half years later. The ailing eighty-two-year-old Buber asked to testify on Cohen's behalf, and made the then-arduous journey to Haifa by public transportation. He commenced his testimony with an autobiographical note, mentioning that he had befriended Cohen in 1941 when he, Buber, had joined with the likes of Jehuda Magnes and Henrietta Szold the League for Arab-Jewish Rapprochement, of which at the time Cohen served as general secretary. "These people" (the members of the League) implicitly including himself, "were not the kind commonly called idealists, in other words, people who believe and do not perceive the reality around them. All those who founded the League saw very clearly the reality of the situation and out of the reality they saw came to the conclusion that there was only one way for the people of Israel to enjoy a great future in this country."[19]

Buber proclaimed Cohen's innocence in an autobiographical vein:

> Since my youth, I have been studying human beings; my entire philosophical thinking is based on a knowledge of their nature. Knowing human nature means knowing people, and this is the only way to learn something about humanity as a whole. I mention this in order to indicate that I have some experience in knowing people, and I was extremely impressed by Aharon Cohen, his sincerity, his intellectual and moral integrity.[20]

The presiding judges, however, gained another impression from the evidence presented by the state's prosecutor, and sentenced Cohen to five years in prison. Ben-Gurion likewise rejected Buber's appeal to pardon him, though when Buber's longtime friend Zalman Shazar became Israel's third president in May 1963, his very first act was to pardon Aharon Cohen, and he personally informed Buber of his decision.

When Buber was on the stand as a character witness for his friend and colleague, the presiding judge asked him to identify his profession. Buber replied, "philosophical anthropology"— an understanding of his calling that had crystallized while he was preparing his first lecture course at the Hebrew University. Working on the lectures, as he related to Ernst Simon, "took me to the fundamentals of an anthropological system (the I-Thou anthropology, as it were) that I have evaded for such a long time."[21] The lectures (later published with the appropriate title *What Is Man?*), in addition to articulating a vision of building genuine community (as we saw in Chapter 9) would thus seek to show, through "the [philosophical] unfolding of the question about the essence of man, that it is by beginning neither with the individual nor with the collectivity, but only with the reality of the mutual relation between man and man, that this essence can be grasped."[22] As an elaboration of his philosophy of dialogue, he addressed the question of what essentially constitutes the human person, from the perspective of his fundamental thesis that "the world is twofold for man in accordance with his twofold attitude," each attitude establishing a distinctive way of situating oneself and living in the world: I-It and I-Thou.[23]

The human person, Buber believed, achieves the fullness of being by experiencing both modes of existence. Through the I-It mode, one enters the objective world, conditioned by the laws of nature. Modern epistemology and science account for the complex physical, historical, and sociological factors that structure objective reality; the knowledge and insights these disciplines provide help us navigate through the labyrinthine It-world we often call "reality." But to attain the fullness of life, we must through I-Thou relationships relate to much of the world, chiefly our fellow human beings, not as It (an object) but as Thou, each an autonomous subject with a distinctive inner reality. The I-It and I-Thou modes represent two aspects of being. It is our "sublime melancholy" that we are always dwelling in both the realm of necessity (the I-It world) and that of freedom (the realm of I-Thou relations): "I may not try to escape from the paradox I have to live by relegating the irreconcilable propositions to two separate realms; neither may I seek the aid of some theological artifice to attain some conceptual reconciliation: I must take it upon myself to live both in one, and so lived, both are one."[24] This insight, which Buber characterized as having crystallized over the course of a series of encounters and mismeetings he had experienced over many years, was at the core of his philosophical anthropology.

A brief lecture "On the Situation of Philosophy," presented at the summer of 1948 International Congress of Philosophy in Amsterdam, provided the occasion for Buber to outline for the first time what would become his postwar "contribution to a philosophical anthropology." He decried the "prevailing functionalizing of the concept of truth" by assigning it to epistemology and pragmatic disciplines—in other words, the world of It. The loss of faith in metaphysical truth—which illuminates the existential and religious significance of life—"threatens to disintegrate the human spirit." It was thus urgent, he said, to propose a new understanding of "truth" that would take as its point of departure the philosophy of Martin Heidegger, who argued that we should proceed not from a view of truth as "the agreement of the representation with the object, but from truth as an inherent property of Being."[25] Alas, Buber argued, "the fruits of this insight slip from our hands if, as Heidegger did, we relate the 'unconceal-ment' [of truth] simply to man and his essence[,] as though Being sent man forth in order to attain adequate openness [to ontological truth] through him." This understanding of truth reflected a "hopelessly illusory" view of humanity as an utterly detached, unconditioned subject set apart from the rest of the world, unconditioned by social, political, and psycho-logical reality. In contrast to Heidegger, Buber argued, "the future competence of the philosophizing man depends upon his knowing the conditionality and the unconditionality of his thinking *in one* and in such encompassing to fulfill the personal devotion of the undivided knowing creature to the Being of existing being" (*das Sein des Seienden*).[26]

Buber's philosophical anthropology may be viewed, in fact, as an extended debate with Heidegger. Despite his awareness that Heidegger was an unrepentant Nazi, Buber would later avail himself of the opportunity to meet him. But in the years immediately following World War II, he was reluctant to set foot again in Germany. In early April 1947, he left for Europe to deliver lectures at universities in Belgium, Denmark, England, France, Holland, and Sweden, deliberately omitting Germany from his itinerary. In a reply to a letter he received in Sep-tember 1946 inviting him to lecture at the University of Bonn, Buber explained why he felt obliged to decline. Although the question he was asked to address—"what will now become of man?"—strongly engaged him, he no longer felt himself "com-missioned" to speak to Germans, for, as he put it in this under-statement (the scare quotes are original), "Something has hap-pened." He asked his correspondent not to misread this laconic explanation as a lack of interest in sharing his thoughts on this and related issues. "It is thoroughly desirable that what I have thought and put into words during the more than one hundred months since I left [Germany] should be available to Germans, [but] I can no longer speak to them collectively." It was otherwise with individuals, "as I am now speaking to you."[27] But to enter into a dialogue with the German people and culture as a whole was no longer possible for Buber.

In declining yet another invitation to visit postwar Germany, he was even more emphatic: "I cannot bring myself to take part in the activity of German public institutions; for this demands a degree of intimate connection of which I do not feel myself capable."[28] In a lecture he gave a few weeks after Kristallnacht, Buber had already mournfully proclaimed "the end of the German-Jewish symbiosis." The fruitful collaboration of "the German and Jewish spirit as I experienced it in the four decades I spent in Germany has been terminated through the intervention of the 'host nation' (or more accurately, of the 'host state')." If the collaboration of the German and Jewish spirit "is ever resumed again," he said, "it will of necessity reestablish the ties with those values which supported the symbiosis, and with those works which resulted from it. But the symbiosis itself is terminated and cannot return."[29]

Nevertheless, Buber was eager to resume his publications in German. In the seven years from when he left Germany until the end of World War II, he had written no fewer than seven books in German, four of which had been published in Hebrew translation. In the quest to find a German-language publisher, he had written to several friends in Switzerland with a request for assistance in interesting a Swiss publisher in his writings. Due to a shortage of paper in the aftermath of the war, the publishers he contacted were reluctant to undertake the publication of writings they were uncertain would find a significant readership. Buber had better luck with a German publisher. Lambert Schneider had in November 1945 reestablished his publishing house in Heidelberg, which he inaugurated with the monthly journal *Die Wandlung*—beginning its publication immediately after liberation from the twelve years of Nazi rule as a way of fostering the spiritual and moral renewal of Germany. Toward this end, Schneider was determined to reintroduce Buber's work to the German public, for he was convinced, as he told Buber, that "the readiness [to receive your word] is today perhaps greater than it was twenty years ago."[30]

They resolved to meet in Europe before Buber returned home to Jerusalem after a European lecture tour. After giving more than sixty lectures in six different countries, Buber and his wife went to Switzerland for a vacation. Since as a German citizen Schneider was barred at the time from entering Switzerland, and Buber was reluctant to set foot in Germany, an influential friend of Buber's arranged for them to rendezvous in a no-man's-land near Basel where the German, French, and Swiss borders converge. In the midst of a nasty snowstorm, Buber and Paula waited for Schneider in a narrow sentry's house. Schneider recalled their reunion after close to ten years as "moving and near wordless." Buber came to their rendezvous with the manuscript of *Das Problem des Menschen* (The problem of humanity), which Schneider would publish in 1948.[31] The publication of other titles by Schneider was soon to follow.

Likely sharing with Schneider the hope of renewing the German-Jewish symbiosis, along with other motivations, German intellectuals repeatedly invited Buber to Germany. One of the most persistent was Karl Heinrich Rengstorf, who since 1948 had been a professor of New Testament and Jewish history and literature at the University of Münster. On the basis of a warm prewar personal relationship with Buber, Rengstorf was the first well-known Protestant theologian to reach out to him. Addressing Buber as "my esteemed colleague," Rengstorf urged him to resume the translation of the Hebrew Scriptures. "I have the impression that Germany would very much welcome it, were you to complete your translation of the Hebrew Bible. Unfortunately, it is still but a torso."[32] In his reply, Buber candidly acknowledged that Rengstorf's appeal touched upon a sensitive issue, for it was due to Nazi persecution and the war that he had had to put the translation on hold. "I have not for-gotten the task, which had been ripped from my hands, but never will there be as a consequence inscribed in my heart's memory a 'perhaps.'"[33] He thus implied that he would eventu-ally return to the translation—failing to add that the commu-nity for whom he and Rosenzweig had principally undertaken the project no longer existed.

A few months later, Rengstorf informed Buber that two prominent leaders of prewar German Jewry, Rabbi Leo Baeck and Alfred Wiener, had agreed to come to Germany to partici-pate in a student conference on "The Church and Judaism." He therefore hoped that Buber would accept an invitation to take part in the next conference, which would be devoted to theo-logical reflections on "the establishment of the Jewish State in Palestine."[34] Notwithstanding that Baeck and Wiener, two prominent German Jews, had accepted Rengstorf's invitations, Buber remained firm in his refusal to follow suit.

Eventually, however, Buber accepted an invitation by Schneider to come to Heidelberg in December 1950 and speak to a small, select group of discussants. He told Rengstorf that under similar conditions he would be happy to come to Münster.

Although he carefully sought to maintain a low profile dur-ing his first postwar visit to Germany, an interview he impru-dently (and inadvertently) gave to a Munich newspaper threat-ened to cause a scandal back in Jerusalem. The *Neue Zeitung* of Munich reported Buber as relating in the interview: "The Arabs occupied his apartment [in Abu-Tor], but treated him with exemplary politeness, [and] guarded the 17,000 books of his library, which were later used by the Jews as a barricade during the battle for Jerusalem." When the text of the inter-view reached Jerusalem, his friend Hugo Bergmann remarked, "How could Buber be so dumb to speak in such a fatuous man-ner?" In a letter he dashed off to Buber, Bergmann told him that his "disciples and friends here [in Jerusalem] are deeply shocked by the publication of this interview."[35]

Buber wrote Bergmann that he and his friends were rightly disturbed by the "absurd" distortion of what was said, in what he believed was a private conversation and later published without his consent as an interview. In fact, upon the publication of the "interview," he wrote the newspaper with the request that it publish "A Postscript to a Conversation," in which he declared that "nothing that I said was for publication." Moreover, he pointed out, "it was not *the* Arabs but the Arab landlord who safeguarded my belongings in the house" and "upon their capture of the house, Jewish soldiers found it necessary to use of a small number of my books for a barricade."[36] With this near-scandal in mind, Buber requested that, in all his private talks with small, select groups, he "not be questioned about political matters, the religious situation in Israel, and the like."[37]

The small colloquia he would give in Germany were thus restricted to academic and theological topics, and the initial colloquium in Heidelberg set the tone of those that would follow. It was scheduled for the winter of 1950 in conjunction with the founding of the Heidelberg School for Adult Education, whose mission was to renew the spirit informing *Die Kreatur*, the "trans-confessional" journal that Buber had co-edited in the last years of the Weimar Republic (and that Lambert Schneider had published). A group of former contributors to the journal were invited to participate in the seminar with Buber at Schneider's home as a sort of reunion. Seated, Buber read slowly from a written text of a lecture on "Primal Distance and Relation," in which he articulated the premises of his philosophical anthropology. Alfred Weber, the younger brother of sociologist Max Weber, was palpably engaged, continuously interrupting Buber to offer comments, until at one point, Buber rose from his chair and walked over to Weber, where he placed his hand on his shoulder and gently said, "Herr

Weber, please wait until I have finished reading the lecture, and then we can discuss it."[38]

Buber returned to his chair and finished his lecture. Weber listened attentively, and was the first to hold forth in the question and answer period, addressing the theme at length and in great but incisive detail.[39] His interventions proved to be atypical, for Buber's lectures at the subsequent colloquia elsewhere in Germany, to his great disappointment, generally failed to inspire discussion. It would seem that he had never fully mastered the skills of pedagogy; as was often noted, his lectures tended to be too complex to follow easily. One recalls here Bergmann's amusing comment to Buber that he should not feel too concerned about lecturing in Hebrew, reassuring him that his elementary Hebrew would allow his audience finally to understand what he had to say.

Not surprisingly, though, Buber's transition to Hebrew did not seem to enhance his pedagogical effectiveness. His lectures at the Hebrew University attracted "fewer and fewer" students.[40] Yet the seminars in which he did not read his lecture, and merely conducted a conversation about a given text, were highly regarded.[41] He was also more engaging as a public speaker, especially in German, although his reception was mixed. His student in Frankfurt, Nahum Glatzer, observed that as an orator Buber would style his lectures in a way that gave the audience the feeling that they were participating in the formulation of his thoughts. Glatzer and his fellow students would joke to each other that before his public lectures, Buber would stand in the mirror and practice being spontaneous.[42] Indeed, while Buber enthralled many, others found his public lectures to be theatrical and affected. These foibles, however, if noted at all, were overlooked in postwar Germany, where as Buber himself noted he was celebrated as an "arch-Jew," a representative of the surviving remnant of European Jewry.

Buber was also, and undoubtedly just as significantly and

sincerely, hailed as embodying the humanistic ethos that repentant Germans were seeking to restore. In December 1951, he received a letter from Professor Bruno Snell, rector of the University of Hamburg, informing him that he had been awarded the second annual Goethe Prize, intended to support "the promotion of supranational thinking and humanitarian endeavors in the spirit of Goethe." Snell further underscored that "the University of Hamburg and the prize committee wish to honor your scholarly achievements and above all your exemplary cultural activities in the service of mutual understanding among peoples and the preservation and continuation of a great intellectual tradition."

In his 1938 essay "The End of the German-Jewish Symbiosis," Buber reaffirmed the humanistic values of that tradition which had supported the symbiosis, even though the symbiosis itself—through which Jews had played a seminal role in German intellectual life—had been brutally terminated with the advent of the Third Reich.[43] In an address at a Goethe Bicentennial Convocation that took place just after the World War in Aspen, Colorado, which was read on his behalf by Ernst Simon because he could not attend, Buber identified Goethe's envisioned "triumph of the purely human" as a "message, both exhorting and encouraging . . . to our time, although, or precisely because, it is [now] so evidently remote from humankind."[44] It was in the spirit of that message that Buber accepted the Goethe prize. "I should like to regard it," he said in his letter of acceptance, "as one of the signs, still rare at present, of a new humanitarianism arising from the anti-human chaos of our time." He felt that the prize marked an engagement with the ethical obligation of every nation to purge itself of the pernicious impulses that deprive others of their humanity. "Unlike the old kind, this new humanitarianism will be able to prove itself adequately not in the great vision of individuals, particularly scholars and philosophers, but only in the struggle of every nation with itself." In establishing the Goethe Prize, he believed, the University of Hamburg was manifestly dedicated to meeting the challenge of the new humanism. "Permit me, therefore, to welcome [the prize] the way one welcomes a symbol."[45]

Back in Israel, the prize "symbolized" for many a call to exonerate Germany for the extermination of six million Jews. The announcement of the prize came at a particularly sensitive juncture in Germany's relationship with the State of Israel. Just three months earlier, West German Chancellor Konrad Adenauer had proposed to pay restitution to the Jewish people and the State of Israel in order to facilitate the absorption of a half million survivors of the Holocaust. A fierce public debate ensued, with impassioned voices arguing that the acceptance of restitution would be tantamount to forgiving the Germans for their crimes. The award to Buber of the Goethe Prize was viewed similarly. Upon reading in the Tel Aviv daily *Haaretz* a particularly mean-spirited attack on Buber for not immediately declining the prize, Ernst Simon hastily consulted with three of Buber's closest Jerusalem friends: Gershom Scholem, Hugo Bergmann, and Bergmann's wife, Escha. They appointed Simon to write on their behalf to Buber, who was at the time in the United States, in order to bring to his attention the offending article, and ask him whether he planned to accept the prize.[46] Whatever his decision, Simon assured Buber, they would rally to his defense, although as he noted in a subsequent letter, "you have not made it any easier for us who share your struggle for a Jewish humanism."[47]

In his reply, Buber indicated that he would himself explain to the Israeli public why he had decided to accept the prize. In an article published on the first page of *Haaretz*, he explained that the prize presented him with a dilemma: Were he to reject it, he would undercut the commendable efforts of those Germans "fighting for humanism" and thereby play into the hands of their enemies, even to those guilty of mass murder. Despite the delicate situation in which the acceptance of the prize would place him, then, as a Jew and an Israeli citizen he felt it was his duty to acknowledge (and thus encourage) the German advocates of a rededication to the humanistic tradition associated with Goethe. He concluded the defense of his decision by announcing that he would donate the prize money to a project that served to further in Israel a "new, supra-national humanism"—namely, to *Ner* (Light), a journal promoting Arab-Jewish understanding.[48]

When he was notified that he had been awarded the Goethe Prize, Buber was in New York City en route to California, where he was going to teach for a few months. Hence, he informed Snell, he would not be able to attend the award ceremony. Snell pressed Buber by suggesting an alternative date. Buber then confessed to Snell that what actually prevented him from accepting the invitation to come to Hamburg for the ceremony was existential, not circumstantial. "Ever since the events of 1938 and those that followed," he apologetically explained, he feared he would not be able to stand before "a faceless German public," perhaps one of the most difficult burdens that "the history of the age has laid on me."[49]

The metaphor of the "faceless" other had emerged in Buber's earlier exchange of letters with Rengstorf, where it came to denote the blurring of the humanity of the other. "I share the anguish in your heart," the Evangelical theologian wrote Buber, "as you behold your former compatriots (*Landsleute*): there are people who no longer have a face"—indeed, there are Germans who have lost their humanity. "And yet, and for this very reason, I venture to repeat my invitation [to address us in Münster]. I venture it because I am struggling with all my heart and all my strength to help people here to regain their faces. I do so all the more because I know that the loss of a face is bound up with what has been done to you and yours. But this is why people here can regain their faces or find new ones only if they encounter you again [as a Jew and fellow human being]."[50] Only through interpersonal exchange or dialogue could the face of the other emerge from behind the veil of ideological prejudices, stereotypes, and even, as Rengstorf put it, "painful memories." In was in response to this appeal that Buber agreed to come to Münster and to hold "a discussion with a small group of specifically invited people." In a reply to a letter, now lost, in which Buber apparently discussed the difficulty of achieving a mutual understanding that would allow Jews and Germans to surmount the barrier of viewing each other as a faceless other, Rengstorf had protested: "What can help in these matters is not understanding but love. Therein reside the failings of the past as well as the roots of German guilt and the ultimate reasons why we have lost our faces."[51]

Writing from Jerusalem, Buber again confirmed his agreement to speak to a small group of Rengstorf's colleagues and students, adding, "It is as you say: man cannot live without love — not truly, not as a human being. But more than ever before, love seems to be grace today — felt and received by virtue of grace. Thank God I recognize it wherever I encounter it."[52]

It may have been such a graced moment that led Buber to reverse his policy not to lecture before a "faceless" German audience (as opposed to meeting with a small group of individually selected Germans). In November 1952 the Italian-born German Catholic priest and scholar Romano Guardini sent Buber a forty-four-page booklet of a lecture he had recently delivered at the University of Tübingen, "Responsibility: Thoughts on the Jewish Question."[53] Gratefully acknowledging receipt of the booklet, Buber wrote Guardini a brief three-sentence letter signaling a dramatic volte-face: "While reading it I noticed that something had changed for me: It was once again possible for me to speak publicly in Germany."[54] Buber did not expand on this declaration. It was surely not only the content of Guardini's lecture but also the person who penned it that had moved Buber to reverse his position. Guardini was already widely regarded as one of the most eminent Catholic theologians of the twentieth century; his many intellectual disciples would include Joseph Ratzinger (later Pope Benedict XVI) and Jorge Mario Bergoglio (later Pope Francis).

Buber had known Guardini before he had attained pre-eminence in Catholic intellectual life. Upon reading Guardini's first published monograph, *The Spirit of the Liturgy* (published in 1918), Buber wrote him to express his admiration of his phenomenological analysis of liturgical worship.[55] The correspondence that followed continued throughout the years of the Weimar Republic, and resumed after World War II when Guardini sent Buber a copy of his lecture on the Jewish Question.[56] With a clarion, unambiguous voice, Guardini made an impassioned plea for Germans to acknowledge the evil perpetuated in their name at Auschwitz and other death camps, and to repent by accepting moral responsibility for the decimation of European Jewry. It is not, he emphasized, a question simply of admission of guilt, but also of an ethical responsibility incumbent on each and every German to "make amends" for the Holocaust in "whatever way it is possible and appropriate. Wrong can only be overcome in this way." Hence, the ethical responsibility of which Guardini spoke could not be discharged by the political act of the state or public institutions. Genuine ethical responsibility had to be assumed by each individual; indeed, what Hitler sought was to obliterate "the basis and beginning of every ethical judgement, namely the person."[57] What was at stake was the restoration of not only the personal dignity of the Jews, but also that of the Germans themselves; in Buber's (and Rengstorf's) terms, doing so would restore the face of both the Jew and the German.

A month after he had written to Guardini, Buber informed Snell that he would be honored to attend the Goethe Prize award ceremony in Hamburg and to deliver a lecture.[58] He did not, however, write a lecture especially for the occasion, which took place on June 24, 1953. Rather, he read a lecture on "The Validity and Limitations of the Political Principle" that he had actually written in 1947 and had presented in the summer of 1953 at various German universities.[59] He regarded the lecture as a "radical critique" of the German concept of "the political principle"—the centralization of power in governmental institutions at the expense of human fellowship—which he believed had abetted the horror from which Europe had just emerged. He was therefore surprised at how well his lecture was received, not only at the Goethe Prize ceremony but also, with the exception of Bonn, at the universities where he delivered it.[60]

In the lecture, Buber took as his point of departure a critique of what he deemed to be a grievous misreading of Matthew 22: 21 ("Render to Caesar the things that are Caesar's; and to God the things that are God's") as sanctioning the unfettered independence of the political principle. He traced in philosophy the mistaken and ultimately pernicious tendency, inaugurated by Hegel, to assign to history an ontological autonomy—that is, to regard the dialectical unfolding of history as an ethically self-validating process. The consequent understanding of historical time and its political manifestations, Buber argued, leaves no "room for a suprahistorical [divine] reality that sees history and judges it."[61] In a parenthetical remark, Buber alluded to his own relationship with Zionism: "I believe that it is possible to serve God and the group to which one belongs if one is courageously intent on serving God in the sphere of the group as much as one can."[62]

A week before the ceremony in Hamburg, Buber was notified that he was to be awarded the fourth annual Peace Prize of the German Book Trade.[63] The previous recipient was no less than Guardini (who had been preceded by Albert Schweitzer and the German-Jewish writer Max Tau). Buber happily accepted the award in person. On this occasion, he delivered an original paper appropriate to the theme of the prize: "Genuine Dialogue and the Possibility of Peace." The award ceremony took place on September 27, 1953, at Saint Paul's Church (Paulskirche) in Frankfurt am Main; ever since 1848, when the church served as the seat of the Frankfurt Parliament, the first freely elected German legislative body, it had symbolized the birth of German democracy. Destroyed in 1944 in an Allied bombing of Frankfurt, it was the first public structure to be rebuilt after the war, as a symbolic tribute to Germany's rededication to democracy. Reopened on the centennial of the Frankfurt Parliament, the imposing building served no longer as a church, but as a venue for cultural events of a decidedly humanistic bent—a fact that was ignored by or unknown to some of Buber's Israeli critics, who excoriated him for speaking in a church.

The ceremony had great symbolic significance, and not only in its setting in the cradle of German democracy, whose first vice-president, Gabriel Riesser, had been an indomitable advocate of Jewish emancipation. Among the more than one thousand individuals who attended the event was the president of the Federal Republic of Germany, Theodor Heuss. Buber was introduced by Albrecht Goes, a Lutheran theologian who had served as a chaplain in Hitler's Wehrmacht (the united Nazi armed forces). With poetic pathos, Goes spoke of "Martin Buber as our support"—the support not of "a dictator and his preceptors," but of "the concern of an I for its Thou," and "for bringing together what is falling apart. . . . But concern is trust. And this trust includes the readiness to be sad with others and to keep silent for a long time, because we are united by the insight that it is hard really to love one's fellow men, because, in the words of Sasov Rabbi, frequently enough we do not know what ails the other fellow."[64]

In his address Buber did not hide his pain as "a surviving arch-Jew" (*Erzjude*).[65] A decade before, he solemnly noted, "a considerable number of Germans—there must have been thousands of them—under the indirect command of the German government and the direct command of its representatives, killed millions of my people in a systematically prepared and executed procedure whose organized cruelty cannot be compared with any other historical event." These henchmen of Hitler's diabolic madness "have so radically removed themselves from the human sphere, have so transposed themselves into a sphere of monstrous inhumanity inaccessible to my comprehension that not even hatred, much less an overcoming of hatred, was able to arise in me.—And who am I that I could here presume to 'forgive'!"[66]

And yet—as perhaps Guardini's essay brought home to him—there were other Germans. One cannot allow "the concrete multiplicity" of a people "to be obscured by the leveling of a totality constituted and acting in just such a way and no other." It is precisely this invidious leveling that blurs the face of the other. There were Germans and there were Germans; they did not act monolithically. To be sure, many knew of Auschwitz and Treblinka, and despite whatever feelings they had, did not oppose "the monstrous event." But, Buber exclaimed, at the same time, "my heart, which is acquainted with the weakness of men, refuses to condemn my neighbor for not prevailing upon himself to become a martyr." There were certainly the masses that consciously chose to remain ignorant of the horror perpetrated in their name. "When I have these men in mind, I am gripped by the thought of the anxiety, likewise known to me, of the human creature before a truth which he fears he cannot face." And yet, Buber noted—reportedly in a voice trembling with emotion—there "appears before me those who refused to carry out the orders and suffered death, and those who learned what was taking place and because they could do nothing to stop it killed themselves. Reverence and love for these Germans now fills my heart."[67]

Turning to the generation of Germans who came of age after the war. Buber called upon them to join with him in the struggle of "*homo humanus* against *contrahumanus.*" As a "Jew chosen as a symbol I must obey this call of duty even there, indeed precisely there when the never-to-be effaced memory of what has happened stands in opposition to it." It was thus incumbent upon Jews and Germans to express the solidarity "of all separate groups in the flaming battle for the rise of a true humanity." That solidarity was not a matter of reconciliation or a pretense to cauterize the wounds of memory, but the duty mandated by that very memory for "peoples to engage in dialogue with one another if the great peace is to emerge and the devastated life of the earth to renew itself."[68] As a testament to his understanding of this calling, Buber contributed the monetary award attached to the Peace Prize (as he had done with the earlier Goethe Prize) to an organization in Israel promoting Arab-Jewish coexistence.

Some six months after the ceremony at the Paulskirche, Buber received an invitation from the president of the Bavarian Academy of Fine Arts to deliver a lecture at the prestigious forum on art on "the problem of man."[69] Buber gratefully accepted, and in November 1954 gave a lecture at the academy on "Man and His Image." The visit to Munich also occasioned a lively discussion on language with Clemens Count Podewils, the general secretary of the Bavarian Academy. Buber and Count Podewils subsequently conducted an intense correspondence between Jerusalem and Munich on the nature of the German language and the problem of language in general. At one point in their exchange, Buber broached the idea of a conference on language, and suggested that, should Podewils be amenable to the proposal, he should consider inviting Martin

Heidegger to participate. (One can only conjecture why Buber was eager to include Heidegger, the unrepentant Nazi, in the conference. Since the 1930s, in his philosophical writings he had recurrently "debated" with Heidegger, questioning his exclusion of anthropological and hence ethical considerations from his ontological existentialism. As we shall see, he was bent on engaging Heidegger in a dialogue on these issues, especially as they pertained to his endorsement of National Socialism.) The count responded enthusiastically to the proposal and immediately wrote Heidegger, who was "very impressed by [Buber's] readiness to collaborate with him."[70] A preliminary organizational meeting was arranged.

Buber and Heidegger would meet in the late spring of 1957 in the township of Altreuthe, on the pastoral grounds of a castle that belonged to Prince Albrecht of Schaumburg-Lippe, the brother-in-law of Count Podewils.[71] The two septuagenarian philosophers strolled for hours in animated conversation. Years later, recalling their meeting, Buber would humorously muse that they must have appeared "à la Rumpelstiltskin like two dwarfs, gnomes with disproportionate large heads" — neither stood more than five foot two inches in height — Heidegger setting the cadence of the conversation, fervidly gesticulating with both hands.[72] They were joined by Carl von Weizsäcker, a physicist and philosopher of science, and Count Podewils, in order to confer on the organization of the proposed conference on language.

Between their meetings, Buber and Heidegger would take long, rambling walks on the nearby Island of Mainau. "We were able," Buber relates, "to laugh about ourselves, two elderly, contentious men, full of prejudices and resentment, less about our own than about the prejudices and resentments of our environment — here against the Jews, and there against the Nazi Rector" — that is, against Heideigger, who had joined the Nazi Party ten days after being elected rector of the University of Freiburg.

Buber parenthetically added, "many are offended that I mention [in my writings] in one and the same breath Kant, Hegel and Heidegger. But since this meeting [with Heidegger], I know that [my critics] are inane or baseless to have contested placing Heidegger on the same rung as these other thinkers."[73] These reminiscences were solicited by a young theologian, Hans A. Fischer-Barnicol, who had learned that Buber's "friendly, indeed [allegedly] conciliatory meeting with Heidegger" had led to a "very vehement debate" among Buber's circle of "friends in Jerusalem."[74] When Fischer-Barnicol queried Buber about the controversy, however, Buber dismissed any suggestion that the meeting with Heidegger was an expression of reconciliation:

> No, our discussion was purely matter of fact. The past remained un-mastered—God be praised, for we must also allow ourselves to speak bluntly about guilt, about forgiveness, also about the guilt of thought (*Schuld des Denkens*). We spoke fully impartially with one another, and without defensiveness. First we spoke for a long time about philosophical questions, then ever more openly about initially suppressed theological matters—which, as you know, is for me an alien language. I do not know whether Heidegger had confused this exchange with a religious dialogue, which it was not. A religious dialogue must emerge from [concrete, historical] experience (*Erfahrung*) and be addressed out of experience—and not only out of the experience of thought (*Da muß aus Erfahrung gesprochen werden—und nicht nur aus Erfahrung des Denkens*).[75]

At the conclusion of their meeting, Heidegger extended to Buber an invitation to visit him at his *Hütte* (cabin retreat) in the Black Forest to continue their conversation, but Buber declined the invitation. "A struggle between two elderly men is not good. And we were in agreement that this struggle could not be avoided. . . . Because a religious dialogue cannot be avoided."[76] What constitutes a religious dialogue—and what kind of self could truly participate in such a dialogue, as opposed to another kind of philosophical or theological exchange—would, in fact, be the implicit theme of Buber's contribution to the envisioned conference on language. Crucial for Buber would be the distinction "the experience of thought—that is, the experience of the thinking 'I,'" which Heidegger sets apart from the apperceptive self that is conscious of itself in relation to a reality external to oneself. In Heidegger's terms, the apperceptive self (Buber's dialogical self) is defined by the experience of ontic entities (*Seiende*) as opposed to ontological meditations detached from the existential imperatives of concrete existence. The divide between Buber and Heidegger was precisely due to their divergent conceptions of the self that they deemed to be the proper focus of philosophical analysis. Indeed, for Buber, only a self in dialogical relationship with other persons could participate in genuine existential and religious dialogue.

Despite—but also perhaps because of—their studious avoidance of the difficult questions attendant to Heidegger's Nazi past, Buber recalled his meetings with Heidegger warmly, noting that in person Heidegger is "more to my taste than his writings."[77] In the interview with Fischer-Barnicol, Buber even took the opportunity to defend Heidegger from the widespread view that he lacked a sense of humor. He gleefully recounted that "one evening [at Prince Albrecht's castle] Heidegger read aloud" a selection of poems by the German satirical poet Johann Peter Hebel. It was, Buber recalled, "an enchanting, artful, indeed, enrapturing comic rendition."[78] Buber's defense of Heidegger's sense of humor was made in response to a comment by the French philosopher Gabriel Marcel (reported to him by Fischer-Barnicol) that neither Marcel nor Heidegger were suitable candidates to participate in a series of radio broadcasts on "great living philosophers" that Fischer-Barnicol was then preparing. Marcel concurred with Heidegger that popular publicity is not appropriate for a philosopher. "Even if it were,"

Marcel noted, "we would not have the slightest chance of competing with Brigitte Bardot for popularity." Buber found the prospect of such popularity not particularly appealing, since, as he conceded, he had been somewhat of a "star" from early on, and found it to be a "nuisance." With some amusement, he attributed his ambiguous status as a celebrity to his beard (which, as noted earlier, he had originally grown to cover a crooked lower lip). As the beard gained fullness, people took him for a prophet. "Believe me," he told his interlocutor, "I would shave this wonderful beard off, but then I would destroy my image. Hmmm. So I am after all akin to Brigitte Bardot?!"[79]

Curiously, when Heidegger was interviewed by Fisher-Barnicol and asked about his acquaintance with Buber, he responded as if he knew of him by name only.[80] This feigned ignorance of Buber is quite confusing, given (among other things) the reported intensity of the two-and-a-half-day meeting at Lake Constance, which was followed by several organizational meetings toward the conference on language. Moreover, Heidegger was apparently an avid reader of Buber's writings.[81] Upon his initial meeting with Buber at Prince Albrecht's castle, he gave Buber a copy of his recently published *Hebel—Der Hausfreund* with the dedication, "For Martin Buber with sincere admiration, Martin Heidegger, Altreuthe, May 19 [19]57."[82] With this copy of his book on the writer Johann Peter Hebel, which was a meditation on the debasement of language through modern "calculative" (I-It) thinking, Heidegger undoubtedly sought to signal that he shared some of Buber's fundamental concerns.

Heidegger was also eager to solicit, if not Buber's friendship, then at least his public acknowledgment. Toward the preparation of a Festschrift marking his seventieth birthday, Heidegger specifically requested that the publisher ask Buber for a contribution.[83] Buber declined, claiming that poor health would not allow him to meet the stipulated deadline—though he continued to publish apace until his death some six years later. On another occasion, in the summer of 1959, Heidegger wrote Wilhelm Hoffmann, director of the State Library in Stuttgart, requesting that he inform Buber, who was then visiting Germany, of a lecture on Hölderlin he was to deliver under the library's auspices.[84] His eagerness to court Buber's acknowledgment stands in sharp contrast with his distancing himself from Buber when asked by third parties about their relationship. At a discussion in 1964 with a small group of philosophers in Heidelberg, Heidegger was asked rather insistently by "a young American professor" how he regarded Buber's thought. Palpably perplexed by the question, Heidegger hesitantly replied: "Buber hardly dealt with [my] basic question," quickly adding that he "was however not sure."[85] It is not clear if Heidegger's hesitation to confirm publicly his relationship with Buber or familiarity with his writings was due to his reluctance to engage in the kind of dialogue demanded by Buber, or if, beyond that, he was confused, if not offended, by Buber's own resolute refusal to continue their conversation on terms other than those Buber deemed appropriate.

In a conversation with Heidegger in the early winter of 1964, Fischer-Barnicol had the feeling that Heidegger was still deeply troubled by his failed relationship with Buber, and accordingly wrote Buber: "I am again and again moved to believe that it might, indeed, be correct and good were you to grant Heidegger's wish to have [another] talk with him. Perhaps it will help him?"[86] Buber seems not to have replied.[87] He was eighty-six when he received this last appeal to renew his "dialogue" with Heidegger. Frail and in poor health, he certainly was not in a position to visit Heidegger in Germany, and though he remained intellectually active, the pace and extent of his correspondence had also diminished in what was to be his last year of life. Buber's reluctance to sustain or renew a relationship with Heidegger may be traced back to the protracted organizational meetings for the conference on language, in which it became increasingly clear that Heidegger not only did not share his understanding of dialogue, but also adamantly refused to acknowledge that a dialogue between a Jew and a German (and unrepentant supporter of National Socialism), if it were to be existentially genuine, would perforce take place in the shadow of the Holocaust.

Heidegger, was, it seems, eager all along to engage Buber—as a representative of Jewry—in a dialogue, but a dialogue not burdened by discussion of ultimately irresolvable issues. As Heidegger himself said in the lecture he eventually gave at the conference on language, "one may speak endlessly, and all the time say nothing. Another person may remain silent, not speak at all and yet, without speaking, say a great deal."[88] To speak—and silence may be as resonant as the spoken word—is to say something, that is, to point to the "clearing" or the life-world in which one's being unfolds. Language, spoken or otherwise, is as the German Romantic author Jean Paul put it, potentially "the spiritual index finger."[89] Heidegger had clearly come to Prince Albrecht's castle with the expectation of engaging Buber in just such a dialogue beyond speech and confession. In August 1952, he had read an article by Buber, "Hope for This Hour."[90] As he wrote to his wife about it:

> The essay by M. Buber [in which he speaks of the exigent need of the postwar generation to reestablish existential trust] is excellent. . . . The diagnosis is farsighted and of great wisdom—but the healing must start even deeper than he [Buber] suggests. And there remains a question of whether we mortals address our eternal Thou (B. means God) *through* our mortal Saying-Thou to one another, or whether we aren't brought into correspondence to one another only through God's address. . . . The final sentence of [Buber's essay] is beautiful and essential: "Reconciliation effects reconciliation." [*Versöhnung wirkt Versöhnung*]. . . .
>
> Mere forgiving and asking for forgiveness are not

enough. Reconciliation belongs with "atonement" & "to atone" really means: to be still—to bring one another the stillness of belonging to one another in essence. The genuine & fruitful & fundamentally ceaseless dialogue [*Gespräch*] is one where those conversing [although] *different* in kind intuitively recognize their *Wesenszugehörigkeit* [belonging to one another], and neither out of mere indifferent acceptance nor according to a single yardstick & its doctrine.[91]

In light of Heidegger's own reflections here on the existential ground of reconciliation, it would seem that the failure of the two men to achieve the dialogue that both manifestly sought was fundamentally due to their different conceptions of what Buber called a religious encounter. Buber likely had had similar expectations to the poet Paul Celan, who on a visit to Heidegger's cabin retreat in July 1966, described in the philosopher's guestbook his dashed "hope for a word coming from the heart."[92] Heidegger was disinclined to utter the "word" that Buber and Celan had hoped for, deeming it to be only a surface gesture, and believing that the genuine act of atonement is to be expressed and attained beyond words, in the stillness in which an existential bond is forged between individuals, even in the face of incommensurable, or conflicting, primordial and historical positions.

The seemingly insurmountable divide between Buber and Heidegger may have been specifically, even primarily, theological; more precisely, their divergent horizons of expectation reflected very different conceptions of grace and atonement. Heidegger, who in his youth initially had studied for the Catholic priesthood, articulated his own position in his letter to his wife: Divine address and its protection [*Geheißes und seines Schutzes*] are the ontological ground of any possible human reconciliation; God's word bears within it a protective grace that empowers one to trust in the promise of reconciliation— independent, it would seem, of any specific conciliatory words or actions.[93] His eagerness to engage Buber in dialogue may have been prompted by a desire (that Buber may have in turn intuited) to receive exculpation from him (however implicitly)—or as Celan bitterly put it when he first heard of Buber's meeting with Heidegger, a *Persilschein*, a clean bill of health, a whitewash for his Nazi past.[94] Buber's (and conceivably also Celan's) opposing vision of reconciliation was undoubtedly shaped by a Jewish theological sensibility that there can be no divine pardon for offenses against others until one has turned to one's fellow human beings whom one has offended, and not only asked their forgiveness, but also adequately repented for the wrongs done to them.

To be sure, the failure of Buber and Heideigger to engage in a genuine dialogue was surely also due to what Buber called a Vergegnung—a mismeeting—born of divergent expectations of what constitutes dialogical reconciliation. Although surely disappointed, Buber had met with Heidegger with duly guarded expectations, and for him, mismeetings inhere in the very quest for dialogue, which thus entails an existential risk. Buber's faith in the importance of dialogue was paradoxically born precisely of the painful realization that life is invariably punctuated by such mismeetings. The autobiographical fragments he recorded toward the end of his life, and others scattered throughout his writings and correspondence, attest to his painful appreciation of the human vulnerability to mismeetings in the quest for dialogue.

Buber had found in Paula, with whom he had bonded in his twenty-first year, a buffer from the many mismeetings that he would experience over a lifetime. As he poignantly expressed in one of the many poems he addressed to her:

> To Paula
> The Abyss and the Light of the World,
> The Pressure of Time and the Yearning of Eternity,

Vision, Event and Poem:
Dialogue it was and is with you.[95]

Their dialogue was to come to an abrupt end in August 1958.
On the first of that month, Paula and Martin boarded a ship
in Venice that was to take them back to Israel after a lecture
tour in America and a vacation in Europe. Upon occupying
their cabin, the robust eighty-one-year-old Paula suddenly collapsed and was rushed by gondola to the hospital on the Lido di
Venezia, where she was diagnosed with a blood clot. She died,
on August 11, with her husband and their two children (who had
rushed to Venice to be with their mother) at her side.

The following day, Paula was buried in the thirteenth-
century Jewish cemetery on the Lido. Accompanied by Eva
and Rafael, a profoundly bereaved Buber returned to Jerusalem, uncertain how he would proceed after the loss of his wife
and most intimate partner of nearly sixty years. "The structure
of my life," he bemoaned, "has been broken up so thoroughly"
that he could not contemplate giving lectures or writing.[96] Yet
he gradually returned to his writing desk, affirming that "one
must continue to live; one learns obediently to accept if not to
understand."[97] He found solace in work, although he regarded
it is as "walking against the wind." The outpouring of sympathy helped sustain him, as he put it, "in the darkest hour of
my life."[98] Writing from New York City, Hans Jonas, who had
been close to Buber and his wife when he taught in the 1940s at
the Hebrew University, told Buber that he and Paula exemplified in his eyes a life of dialogue:

> I have never seen a more perfect community of two who
> remained what they were while affirming the other. That
> youthful choice can prove itself in this way and become ever
> truer in the course of time—such a success is the highest
> tribute to those to whom this possibility was entrusted by the
> *tuche* [Greek: chance] of the original encounter. . . . It was

always beautiful every time to see you together. The blessing
of that infinite community has to extend into your present,
finite loneliness.[99]

Thanks to such comforting words, Buber felt that "though
alone," he was "not abandoned."[100]

It was especially his family in Jerusalem who served to sustain his spirits. With the passing of Paula, their granddaughter Barbara took charge of the home that she and her family
had been sharing with *Nonna* Paula and *Vater* Martin. Under
Barbara's stewardship, the dynamic of the household changed
perceptibly. While Paula had shielded her husband from all that
might disturb his "peace and quiet," and accordingly had organized the living space and even eating schedule to guard his autonomy (she and Martin generally ate alone), Barbara sought to
integrate her grandfather into the life of her family. She did this
not only by reconfiguring the bedroom assignments, but also
by insisting that Buber eat together with her and the rest of the
family, her husband, Zeev, and their two children, Tamar, then
eight, and Gideon, who was six. Vater Martin seemed to enjoy the new arrangement, especially the more intimate contact
with Tamar and Gideon. Schalom Ben-Chorin recalled visiting
Buber as a guest on the holiday of Sukkot (the Feast of Taber-
nacles) and found him patiently helping Tamar and Gideon
decorate a *sukkah*. Buber greeted his guest by observing, "One
does not understand one's children, and one's grandchildren a
bit better. But one understands one's great-grandchildren undoubtedly best."[101]

When Buber resumed lecturing abroad, his granddaughter
Barbara accompanied him, assuming Paula's role as a traveling
companion. It was, however, his daughter Eva who went with
him on the first trip abroad after Paula's death. In July 1960, he
participated in a small symposium intended as a follow-up to
the conference on "The Word and Reality," which had taken

place in January 1959—with Heidegger, but without Buber. Count Podewils sent Buber a copy of the handwritten text of Heidegger's address, and Buber had evidently studied the text carefully in preparing his lecture the following year. Delivered on July 11, 1960, at the University of Munich, the lecture— "The Word That Is Spoken"—was for the eighty-two-year-old Buber not just another occasional lecture or intellectual exercise. Although written with a controlled cadence, and articulating a fastidiously crafted conceptual dialectic, it was animated by a palpable existential earnestness.

To Buber's mind, Heidegger's understanding of the ontological structure of language ignored the intersubjective dimension of the spoken word—the fact that language is used when real and specific human beings talk to and meet one another. The ontological character of language-qua-speech act "would be completely missed," Buber averred, "if one regards [it] as existing outside of [the] personal texture of language or speech. ... Every attempt to understand and to explain [the ontological structure] of language as accessible only when detached from the context of its actual speakers must lead us astray."[102] For the "ontological presupposition of conversation" is "the otherness of one's partner in a conversation"—and that otherness is manifest "in the moment of surprise."[103] One can never anticipate, nor should one anticipate, what the other might say, for the other is a particular, autonomous subject. Thus "the human truth of which I speak opens itself only in one's existence as a person. This [other] concrete person—in the life-space allotted to him—answers with faithfulness to the word that is spoken by him."[104]

With this affirmation, Buber concluded his lecture and brought to a full crescendo his critique of Heidegger as betraying the humanistic tradition of German philosophy and letters; the essence of his critique was that Heidegger neglected the interpersonal responsibility of one individual to the other, even to a stranger who bears no name, allowing for the excessive celebration of "superpersonal" social and political institutions in our "disintegrating human world."[105] This was not only an indictment of Heidegger, but also consistent with Buber's long-standing critique of the modern ethos that had detached the spiritual realm from the quotidian everyday world—a process in Western thought that had come to a head in Weimar Germany, with its attendant radical separation of the political from the ethical.

In his address upon receiving the Erasmus Prize in Amsterdam in July 1963, which would be his final lecture abroad, Buber spoke of the exigent need for a "believing humanism" to heal the breach between the spiritual and the everyday life of humanity. Before an audience that included Dutch royalty, he ascribed that breach to a mistaken conception of "the modern question of man concerning himself."[106] We have been led astray, he said, by "a powerful stream in German philosophy from Hegel to Heidegger, [which] sees in man the being (*das Wesen*) in whom Being (*Sein*) attains consciousness of itself."[107] According to this worldview, one should chiefly turn inward and reflect on oneself in order to attain "self-consciousness." But that focus on "the relation of the human person to himself," in effect, severs the question of the human, the life of the spirit, from "the lived life of the human person, in the life lived by each of us between birth and death."[108] In contrast, the "believing humanism" that Buber offered recentered the question of the human and the life of the spirit in the lived life of the person.

> Here humanity and faith do not appear as two separate realms each of which stands under its own signs and under its special laws: they penetrate each other, they work together, indeed, they are so centrally related to each other that we

may say our faith has humanity as its foundation, and our humanity has our faith as its foundation.[109]

The Erasmus Prize lecture concluded a career of lecturing and teaching in Europe and Israel that had spanned nearly six decades—a career that toward the end also included many lectures and other significant teaching stints in the United States. Buber first came to the United States in 1951. Accepting an invitation to deliver the annual Israel Goldstein Lectures at the Jewish Theological Seminary in New York City, he boarded a flight (accompanied by Paula) on October 31, 1951, from Tel Aviv to London, where he stayed for five days (meeting, among others, the poet T. S. Eliot, who years later recalled "the strong impression that I was in the company of a great man") before continuing his journey to New York. Along with the talks at the Jewish Theological Seminary, delivered between November 8 and December 21, Buber lectured to Jewish communities in Cleveland, Chicago, and Detroit, and at Dartmouth College, Haverford College, Brandeis University, Yale University, Columbia University, the University of Wisconsin, and the University of Chicago. At each venue he drew enormous audiences. At the University of Chicago, more than two thousand people filled the Rockefeller Memorial Chapel to hear him lecture on Heidegger and Sartre.

Learning of the throngs that were assembling to greet Buber, Gershom Scholem, writing from Jerusalem, related to Hannah Arendt that he was told that "since Pepsi-Cola hit America there was nothing like Buber!" Scholem also asked Arendt "whether Buber already succeeded in making himself incomprehensible."[110] In fact, many did have difficulty following him, not only because of his heavily accented English—he consistently pronounced "Thou" as "Vow"—but also due to what they found to be his overly academic, ponderous exposition. The arcane Germanic inflection of his lectures, however, did not diminish the aura that surrounded his visit, but paradoxically seemed to enhance it. While in Chicago he arranged to meet with Gustav Landauer's grandson, the actor and Oscar-winning film director Mike Nichols, who at the time was a premed student at the University of Chicago.

In a preface to the published version of the three Israel Goldstein Lectures, which he gave in November and December 1951, Buber requested that "the reader bear in mind, that a Jew speaks here [in these lectures] to Jews, in the center of the Diaspora, in the hour when the deciding crisis begins to become manifest."[111] Held at Columbia University's capacious Horace Mann Auditorium in order to accommodate an overflowing audience, the first of the seminary lectures, "Judaism and Civilization," delineated what Buber held to be the crisis faced by Jewry both in the Diaspora and the State of Israel. Contrary to prevailing popular opinion, for Buber the crisis was not that of a conflict between civilization and religion—rather, it was the retreat from the founding principle of Judaism "to actualize the divine truth in the fullness of everyday life," and, hence, "the whole life of a people—economy, society, and state."[112] Accordingly, civilization "must incorporate the whole of the individual, his life at home and in the market place, in the temple and in the popular assembly. That is to say, it means the wholeness and unity of civilization."[113] In the long years of the Diaspora, Jewry understandably had tended to shield itself from the torments of history by withdrawing to "purer spheres" of inner spirituality.[114] But "when at last we stepped out of the ghetto into the world, worse befell us from within than had ever befallen us from without: the foundation, the unique unity of people and religion, developed a deep rift, which has since become deeper and deeper."[115]

The establishment of the State of Israel and the return of the Jews as a nation to history had not healed the rift; the political culture of the fledgling state resisted "fulfilling the de-

mand for the integral fulfillment of divine truth and justice."
But while for the infant Jewish state, confronted as it was by an
imminent danger to its very existence, urgent pragmatic concerns would seem to demand immediate attention, in the Diaspora "the question of the survival of the principle of Jewish
being" confronts us in its "nakedness."[116] Nowhere in the Diaspora, Buber lamented, "as far as one can see, is there a powerful
striving to heal the rift and to hallow our communal life." He
concluded his inaugural address to American Jewry with a challenging question: "Are we still truly Jews? Jews in our lives? Is
Judaism still alive?"[117]

In the second Goldstein lecture, "The Silent Question,"
Buber argued that given its failure to affirm the founding principle of its divine calling, contemporary Judaism was bound
to fail to satisfy those Jews who seek a spiritually and ethically meaningful existence. In the third, "The Dialogue between Heaven and Earth," he discussed the communal and
political significance of the biblical injunction for Israel to regard itself as addressed by God and accountable to Her in "the
totality of its life." Ideally, he said, Jewry should then be in
the position to resist the modern ethos that allowed for a distinction between private and public morality, lamenting that
"what is thought reprehensible in the relations between persons is [often] thought commendable in the relations between
peoples."[118] Yet, Buber conceded, there are times in which "it
is difficult for the individual, and [all] the more [so] for the
people, to understand themselves as addressed by God; the experience of concrete answerability recedes more and more . . .
in a seemingly God-forsaken space of history."[119]

The imponderability of God's apparent retreat from history is described "in a picture of startling cruelty" in Psalm
82, with its vision of God as impotent Judge—an image that
so haunted Kafka while writing *The Trial* that he impulsively
boarded a train from Prague to Berlin to discuss the psalm with

Buber.[120] "In our own time," Buber comments, the psalmist's cry is ours:

> How is a Jewish life with God still possible in a time in which there is an Oswiecim [Auschwitz]? The estrangement has become too cruel, the hiddenness [of God] too deep. One can still "believe" in Him who allowed these things to happen, but can one speak to Him? Can one still hear His words? Can one as an individual and as a people, enter at all in a dialogic relationship with Him? Dare we recommend to the survivors of Oswiecim, the Job of the gas chambers: "Call to Him, for He is kind, for His mercy endureth forever?"[121]

For the survivors of Auschwitz—indeed, presumably all Jews—the harrowing mystery of God's hiddenness remained inscrutable. But distinguishing them from "the tragic hero of the Greeks before a faceless fate," Buber counseled his American audience to continue "despite everything" the struggle to redeem the world, appealing for God's help. And should God's voice be heard again, it would "resemble no earlier one," but "we shall recognize it" as that of "our cruel and merciful God."[122]

Shortly after delivering this lecture, which may have been the first to broach the question of faith after Auschwitz, Buber flew to Los Angeles to assume a visiting professorship for the spring semester 1952 at the University of Judaism, the West Coast institution of Conservative Judaism and sister institution to the Jewish Theological Seminary. During this period he and Paula visited the Grand Canyon, the grandeur of which enthralled Paula in particular. Over the course of the next four months, he gave more than forty lectures (sixty in total since arriving in the United States).[123] Before returning to Israel in late April 1952, Martin and Paula visited Albert Einstein at the Institute for Advanced Study in Princeton, New Jersey. Buber and Einstein had been friends since serving together on the committee overseeing the founding of the Hebrew University of Jerusalem, which they had both hoped would not become another "Diplomfabrik," a mere factory for the production of diplomas. Einstein's son-in-law reported to Buber that "Einstein gave me a very enthusiastic account of your visit."[124]

Buber's visits to the United States were in many ways an outgrowth of his relationship with Maurice S. Friedman, who was then a young assistant professor at Sarah Lawrence College. Friedman had written a doctoral dissertation on Buber, which he submitted to the University of Chicago in 1950.[125] In a letter he wrote to Buber, delivered personally by Friedman's mother who was at the time on a visit to Israel, Friedman asked Buber whether he would read the dissertation, which Friedman was preparing for possible publication.[126] Buber readily agreed to do so, and having learned about Friedman's personal problems from his mother, also offered his psychological counsel: "I will read [your dissertation] and send you my remarks. Another thing may prove more important yet. I want you to write down your life experience for me—not thoughts about your life, but the tale itself. It must be done of course in utter frankness, but without self-analysis. It will not be easy, but you must overcome the difficulties. I shall read it attentively; I shall not tell you about any impression of it, but the knowledge will show me what I may be able to do for you."[127] So began an exceedingly fruitful relationship. Inspired by Buber's counsel (which was shaped by Buber's long-standing interest in psychology and psychiatry), Friedman made seminal contributions to the development of dialogical psychotherapy. He also edited and translated a number of Buber's works into English, which together with the revised version of his dissertation served to promote Buber's thought in the English-speaking world, creating a demand for Buber as a speaker and teacher.

Through his growing interest in adapting Buber's principle of dialogue to psychotherapy, Friedman befriended Leslie Farber, director of the Washington School of Psychiatry, which promoted a non-Freudian "existential psychology." At the behest of Farber, Friedman wrote Buber to inquire whether he would accept an invitation to come to Washington, D.C., and address Farber and his colleagues. In his reply, Buber candidly noted that although he did not quite see himself "in such an institute," it would be an opportunity for him and his wife to visit America again: "But the fact is that a few days before receiving your letter my wife said to me: 'We did not see enough of the grand wild nature of America.' (We saw only the Great [*sic*] Canyon that impressed us very much, but the course of the Hudson [River] we saw only from the railway window), and I answered: 'Who knows—we may see more of it yet.'"[128] He thus indicated that he would accept Farber's invitation if the trip would "enable us to see the scenery more intensely"; and would not "renew the absorbing and tiring experience of the [previous] American lecture-tour."[129]

In May 1956, Buber received a formal invitation from Farber to give the William Alanson White Memorial lectures, centered on the contribution of "philosophical anthropology to psychiatry." In March 1957, a month after his seventy-ninth birthday, Buber and his wife arrived in the United States. Over the next month, he delivered four public lectures and concurrently led a seminar of seven sessions on dreams and the unconscious in which some thirty psychiatrists and a few philosophers participated. The lectures were later included in a 1965 volume *The Knowledge of Man*, comprising his essays on philosophical anthropology.[130]

Learning of Buber's lectures in Washington, D.C., the coordinator of religious affairs at the University of Michigan, the Reverend DeWitt C. Baldwin, invited Buber to Ann Arbor for a conference on his philosophy of dialogue. The high point of the three-day conference was on Thursday evening, April 18. Before an audience of four hundred, Buber engaged in an hour-and-a-half conversation with the American psychologist Carl

Rogers, who was among the founders of the "humanistic," or client-centered, approach to psychology. At the time a professor of psychology at the University of Chicago, Rogers initiated the unscripted conversation (which Buber reluctantly agreed to be tape recorded) with what he acknowledged might be construed as an impertinent question, but also an understandable one: "I have wondered: How have you lived so deeply in interpersonal relationships and gained such an understanding of the human individual, without being a psychotherapist? . . . And so, um, if it is not too personal, I would be interested in knowing what were the channels of knowing that enabled you to really learn so deeply of people and of relationships?"[131]

Though taken aback by Rogers's question, Buber replied with autobiographical candor. In a verbatim transcript of his reply, he gropes at times for the right words, occasionally pausing to collect his thoughts:

> It's rather a biographical question. Eh, eh, I think I must give instead of one answer, two. I am not entirely a stranger in, let me say, psychiatry, because when I was a student—it's long ago—I studied three terms psychiatry, and what they call in Germany "Psychiatrische-Klinique." I was just, eh I was most interested in the latter. You see, I have studied psychiatry not in order to become a psychotherapist . . . I studied it three terms . . . I was also very young, inexperienced, and not a very understanding young man. But I had the feeling that I wanted to know about man, and man in the so-called pathological state. . . .
>
> But what *mainly* constituted what you ask, was something else. It was a certain inclination to meet people, and as far as possible to, just to change if possible something in the other, *but also* to let me be changed by him. At any event, I had no resistance, I had no resistance—I put no resistance to it [to being changed by the other]. I already then as a young man—I felt I have not the right to want to change another

[person] if I am not open to be changed by him as far as it is legitimate. Something is to be changed and his touch, his contact, is able to change me more or less.[132]

Buber then referred for the first time publicly, either orally or in print, to the impact that the "barbaric" assassination of a "great friend" — Gustav Landauer — had on him and his understanding of the encounter with the other: "Just when it [the war] was finished, it finished, eh, by a certain episode in uh May 1919 when a friend of mine, a great friend, a great man [Gustav Landauer], was killed by uh, anti-revolutionary soldiers in a very barbaric way, and I, now again once more — and this was the last time — I was compelled to imagine just this killing, but not in an optical way alone, but may I say so, just with my body." (Rogers: "With your feelings.") "And this was the decisive moment, after which, after some days and nights eh in this state, I eh felt, 'Oh, something has been done to me.'"[133]

> And from then on, eh, eh, these meetings with people, particularly with young, young people um were the, eh — became in a somewhat different form. I had a decisive experience, experience of four years, a very concrete experience, and eh from now on, I had to give something eh more than just eh eh my inclination to exchange thoughts and feelings, and so on. Eh, I had to give the fruit of an experience. (Rogers: "M-hmmm, mhmmm. Sounds as though you're saying the knowledge, perhaps, or some of it, came in the twenties, but then some of the wisdom you have about uh interpersonal relationships came from wanting to meet people without wanting to dominate. And then — I see this as kind of a threefold answer — and the third, from really living the World War, but living it in your own feelings and imagination.")[134]

Responding to Rogers's intervention, Buber replied: "Hmmm. Just so. Because this latter [experience] was really, I cannot eh-eh say it in another language, it was really living *with* those people. People wounded, killed in the war." (Roger: "You felt their wounds.") "Yes. But feeling is not sufficiently strong."[135]

Although Buber did not elaborate on the autobiographical significance of "the decisive experience" of the World War—of "imagining the real" of the wounds and brutal death of others as his own experience, it may be viewed as a seminal moment in the crystallization of his interest in dialogue, in attentive listening and a fully engaged response to the life-experience of others.

Immediately after the conference, Buber and his wife flew to New York City, where he would meet with two of his friends from Germany: the Protestant theologian and colleague at the University of Frankfurt Paul Tillich, and Abraham Joshua Heschel, who had taught for a while at the Freies Jüdisches Lehrhaus when it reopened in the 1930s under Buber's directorship. Buber also led a seminar on biblical faith, organized by Jacob Taubes, then a professor at Columbia University. The seminar was restricted to faculty from various universities in the New York City area; among the participants were the theologian Reinhold Niebuhr, the scholar of mythology Joseph Campbell, and the philosopher Walter Kaufmann, who in 1970 would publish a new translation of *I and Thou*.

Buber and his wife returned to the United States less than a year later, as guests of the Institute for Advanced Study. They arrived several weeks after Martin had celebrated his eightieth birthday in Jerusalem, and in conveying his birthday greetings, one of Buber's admirers, writing from London, imagined "a vast procession of young (mainly young) and old people is on its way to Jerusalem—Jews, Christians, Muslims, Buddhists, heathens. Everyone has a letter addressed to Martin Buber in his hand, on which is written in large letters: Thanks, Health, Love, Peace, Humanity."[136] Buber, indeed, received many greetings. Theodor Heuss, president of the Federal Republic of Germany, prefaced his birthday wishes by recalling the speech Buber gave upon receiving the Peace Prize of the German Book Trade:

> I believe many of your fellow citizens in the State of Israel watched you embark on your journey from Jerusalem to Frankfurt with feelings of displeasure. You ignored these, for you have always been an inwardly independent person. You came and spoke. We were grateful that you were there, and when you, who have called yourself an "arch-Jew," spoke with clear, distinct definitions and without any inherently impossible attempt to gloss over anything but with the discrimination of a spiritually free nature about the tragedy of the Jewish fate and about [my people's] compliance with a brutality that will forever be connected with the darkest chapter of German history, all of us who listened to you were profoundly moved.[137]

The novelist Hermann Hesse, who in 1949 had nominated Buber for a Nobel Prize in literature, congratulated him on his "noble work and life," and expressed his wishes that he "continue to be a loving teacher and admonisher to your people and the world."[138] From his hospital in Lambaréné, French Equatorial Africa, Albert Schweitzer penned a rather somber birthday missive: "Actually, condolences are in order for an eightieth birthday, because from that time on everything becomes harder every year. One can only express one's wishes that in this situation the person celebrating an anniversary might fare as well as possible."[139]

In contrast to his lugubrious friend of five decades, Buber greeted his eightieth year with exultant gratitude. In a printed text in German and Hebrew, sent to each of his many well-wishers, he wrote:

> It is necessary time and again to thank one's fellow man, even when he has not done anything especially for one. For what, then? For the fact that when he met me, he had truly met

me, that he opened his eyes, and did not confuse me with anyone else, that he opened his ears and reliably heard what I had to say to him, yes, that he opened what I addressed, his well-closed heart. This hour in which I write is an hour of great thanks; *before me*, in a beautiful huge box made by my granddaughter [Barbara], are all the greetings received on this milestone day of my life's path from people who have physically and spiritually met me on the way, and *in my memory* are all the greetings [said to me] directly. The gratitude that I express here to all is not directed to a totality but each individual.[140]

Buoyed by the cornucopia of birthday greetings, Buber would have surely applied to himself what he had admiringly said of a venerable colleague, "Old age is a glorious thing when one had not unlearned what it means to begin anew."[141] The three-month fellowship at the Institute for Advanced Study allowed the eighty-year-old Buber not only to complete projects, but also to begin several new ones. "Princeton means for me quiet and work with few and short interruptions."[142] One exception was a lecture he gave in New York City on April 30, 1958, to the American Friends of Ichud. A transcript of the lecture, "On Zionism and Modern Israel," was published in the organization's newsletter.[143] In this memorial lecture marking the tenth anniversary of the death of Judah Magnes, Buber reviewed the divergent paths to the realization of Zionism, those who pursued realpolitik as well as the advocates of Arab-Jewish cooperation. In the course of the lecture, he mentioned in passing that among the former there were those who had adopted the tactics of Hitler by putting their trust in power rather than in the spirit. Widely cited in the American Jewish and Israeli press, this comment was severely criticized. Initially stunned by the opprobrium, he soon acknowledged that he was at fault:

I have seen now—too late, this is my own fault—that the text in the Newsletter is somehow misleading. . . . In my notes I find the following sentence: "In the days of Hitler the majority of the Jewish people saw that millions of Jews have been killed with impunity, and a certain part [of the Jewish people] made their own doctrine that history does not go the way of the spirit but the way of power."[144]

In a letter to the editor of the Tel Aviv daily, *Haaretz*, he asked that his clarification be published, and noted, "I must yet add that this part of the Jewish people has not after the defeat of Hitler changed its view. I now oppose as I did then with all my might those who uphold and act in accord with the doctrine that 'not through spirit but power.'"[145] He subsequently published in both the Hebrew and English press an elaboration of his position.[146] In a letter to Maurice Friedman, whom he asked to have the article translated into English and to find an appropriate forum in which to publish it, Buber apologized for "the confusion I have caused concerning the Hitler passage. I do not exactly understand how I did it. My heart cannot recover from it, because here, as far as I can see, is the first negative sign of my advanced age, of which I had hoped to be spared. I like being old. I like the strange experiences of old age. I like even its burden and difficulties, but I hate causing confusion."[147]

In early June 1958, at the end of his fellowship at the Institute, Martin and Paula left the United States for Europe in early June by ship for a relaxing voyage, followed by a vacation in Italy—which would come to a sad conclusion with Paula's death in Venice.

# 11

*Not to Belong*

WITH HIS HOPE of living out the rest of his life with Paula now buried with her in the ancient Jewish cemetery of Venice, Buber faced his declining years largely ensconced in his study. In reply to a query from friends in Tübingen, Germany, about how he coped with the inevitable ills and loneliness of old age, Buber offered a glimpse into a routine that allowed him to carry on and contend with lingering bereavement:

> This is what things are like here: one doesn't really "feel" sick, but if one behaves as though one were well and ventures to go out some evening to hear [the cellist Pablo] Casals play, one has to pay for it the next day. Thus, one sits at one's desk, sits away and reads the last proofs of the last volume of the Bible [translation]—and in between sits on the terrace and breathes one's fill. In doing so, one does, thank God, have one's faith on one's right, but one could not get along without humor on one's left. There are all sorts of things

to think about, and people keep showing up with questions, among them not a few young people from Germany (including Tübingen), and one imparts information to the best of one's ability. And in the midst of this, again and again one feels memories touching one's forehead, and the living friends with whom one shares them are not anywhere but here [in Jerusalem], all here at this moment. This is what things are like.[1]

In his twilight years, Buber increasingly cherished friendships and visits, particularly by youth from abroad and Israel. To be sure, as he had mused on the eve of his seventieth birthday, "I sometimes close the door to my room and surrender to a book, but only because I can open the door again and see a human being looking up at me."[2]

In mid-February 1961, Buber opened the door of his home in Jerusalem to friends who had come to celebrate the completion of his German translation of the Hebrew Bible. Five of the guests, all but one of whom had known Buber in Europe, read short tributes.[3] Gershom Scholem was the first to speak (in Hebrew). "My dear Martin Buber, somewhat like a traditional *syyum* marking the completion of the course of study, we have gathered today in your home to celebrate the completion of your German Bible translation. It provides us with a significant opportunity to look back on this, your work, its intent, and its achievement. Some of us have witnessed and followed the development of this work from its inception and we can well understand the feeling of satisfaction, which must accompany its conclusion. You are a man who has always brought great perseverance and endurance to his tasks. . . . If I am not mistaken, thirty-five years have now passed since we received the first volume of the translation by you and Rosenzweig."[4] Scholem proceeded to review in nuanced detail what he lauded as the monumental achievement of the translation. He then paused to note that Buber and Rosenzweig had undertaken the daunting project with the intent of prompting German Jewry to return to the original Hebrew of the Bible, with the concomitant objective of retrieving largely forgotten semantic and lexical registers of language in order to enrich contemporary German. There was thus a "utopian element" in Buber's and Rosenzweig's conception of the *Verdeutschung der Bibel.* In historical perspective, Scholem observed, the translation could be viewed as "a kind of *Gastgeschenk*"—a gift given by a guest to one's host—of German Jewry to the German people, "a symbolic act of gratitude *upon departure.*" But, alas, the "departure" was hardly a cordial farewell. Accordingly, Scholem felt obliged to pose a question that he acknowledged was provocative: "For whom is this translation now [just fifteen years after the Holocaust] intended and whom will it influence? Seen historically, it is no longer a Gastgeschenk of the Jews to the Germans but rather—and it is not easy for me to say this—the tombstone for a relationship that was extinguished in unspeakable horror. The Jews for whom you translated are no more. . . . And what the Germans will do with your translation, who could venture to say?"[5]

The other friends of Buber who were there, having assembled to congratulate him on completing the project he had commenced with Rosenzweig thirty-five years earlier, were aghast at Scholem's suggestion that Buber had labored on the translation in vain. They were painfully cognizant of the tragic shift in the significance of the translation (as undoubtedly Buber himself was), but they found Scholem's remarks inappropriate for the occasion.[6] Moreover, Scholem did not seem to take into account that Buber had continued the translation after Rosenzweig's death in December 1919 in memoriam for his deceased friend.

Characteristic of their always rocky relationship, Scholem had no inhibition about questioning the aging Buber's intellectual legacy. Later that year, upon learning of a lecture Scholem had given in London criticizing Buber's interpretation of Hasidism, the editor of *Commentary* invited Scholem to publish his critique in the respected monthly magazine, sponsored by the American Jewish Committee. Scholem unhesitatingly accepted the invitation; his trenchant critique of what he held to be Buber's tendentious presentation of Hasidism (which Scholem felt was of questionable scholarly merit) appeared in the October 1961 issue of *Commentary*.[7]

Though generally averse to public polemics, Buber reluctantly felt he had no choice but to respond to Scholem's critique. As he told Maurice Friedman: "I must clarify the difference between a scientific and religious approach to a great fact in the history of religion."[8] Due to illness and the mounting infirmities of advanced age, he could not muster the concentrated effort to reply to Scholem until just after his eighty-fifth birthday. Buber's rebuttal, published in the September 1963 issue of *Commentary*, began by noting that there are "two ways in which a great tradition of religious faith can be rescued from the rubble of time and brought back into the light." The first is historical scholarship, and the other is an "essentially different" way of "restoring a great buried heritage of faith to the light." The latter approach seeks "to recapture a sense of the power that once gave it the capacity to take hold of and vitalize the life of diverse classes of people." The intent of this (that is, Buber's) approach is "to convey to our time the force of a former life of faith and to help our age to renew its ruptured bond with the Absolute." Historical scholarship, Buber contended, is inherently incapable of inspiring this renewal, even should it succeed in "unearthing a forgotten or misunderstood body of teaching." To effect the desired renewal, one must "convey the reality of the way of life that was once informed by these teachings."[9]

Buber failed to appease Scholem. The divide between them, as Buber made clear, was not just a question of methodology, but more fundamentally, a matter of divergent conceptions of Judaism and Zionism. Like many of his generation of German Jews, Scholem had been initially enthralled by Buber's portrayal of Hasidism, although he already had doubts then about the authenticity of his sources and their exposition. In 1932, he visited Buber at his home in Heppenheim, and in the course of their conversation, he expressed his hope that Buber would write a comprehensive study of Hasidic theology. Buber assured him that he would, but only after Scholem, then a young lecturer in Jewish mysticism at the Hebrew University, had written a compendious work on kabbalah. Recalling that exchange, Scholem observed, "At the time I did not yet understand that [Buber] was unable to maintain a scholarly attitude toward this topic." He came to realize that some ten years later when he visited Buber, this time in Jerusalem, to give him a copy of Scholem's recently published *Major Trends in Jewish Mysticism*. It was also an occasion to explain to Buber his "fundamental doubts about [Buber's] interpretation of Hasidism; doubts which have grown during the long years of continuous study of the texts."[10] Buber listened attentively.

> When I was done he was silent for a very long time. Then he said slowly and stressing every word: "If what you are now saying is true, my dear Scholem, then I have worked on Hasidism for forty years absolutely in vain, because in that case, Hasidism does not interest me at all." It was the last conversation I had with Buber about the substantive problems of [his interpretation of] Hasidism. Words failed me. I understood that there was nothing more to be said.[11]

Buber was undeterred by Scholem's criticism. In 1946, his long-awaited comprehensive anthology of Hasidic legendary anecdotes, *Or ha-Ganuz* (The hidden light), was published in Hebrew (it would also be issued later in English and German).[12] In the preface to the Hebrew volume, he noted that it represented work largely done after his immigration to the Land of

Israel, the air of which, as the rabbinic sages taught, "makes one wise," and by virtue of which he gained "the strength to begin anew." As a result, he had rejected his earlier approach of poetically adapting Hasidic tales and anecdotes, for when he revisited them in his later years, he was "shocked by the pathetic lightheartedness" of his youth.[13] He then sought to adhere to the spirit of the original texts. In an autobiographical essay published a decade later, he spoke of his earlier representation of Hasidism as that of an "immature man" who could not "hold in check my inner inclination to transform poetically the narrative material." An ill-conceived need to render Hasidism palatable to Western aesthetic sensibilities had "led me to pay all too little attention to its popular vitality." The transformation of his relationship to the "inner reality" of Hasidism was incremental, and eventually led him to focus on the exemplary lives of the Hasidic masters. He now understood his task as reconstructing the "life-event" (*Lebensvorgang*) they exemplified. This gave life to the literary form that Buber called the "legendary anecdote"—a genre that "enabled me to portray the Hasidic life in such a way that it becomes visible as at once reality and teaching."[14]

Scholem had never voiced in print his criticism of Buber's interpretation of Hasidism until the *Commentary* article of 1961, on which he subsequently elaborated in a feuilleton in the *Neue Zürcher Zeitung* in May 1962. Less than a year after Buber's death in June 1965, Scholem expanded the scope of his critique to include Buber's conception of Judaism and Jewish renewal. Before an audience of leading scholars of religion, who were gathered at the shores of Lake Maggiore, Switzerland, for the annual Eranos Conference, Scholem's critique of Buber resonated as an ideological polemic that extended well beyond scholarly issues. At the very outset of his lecture, it became clear that he harbored a personal ambivalence toward Buber. "No one who knew Buber," he confessed, "could avoid the strong radiance emanating from him and making an intellectual engagement with him doubly passionate. To engage Buber intellectually meant to be tossed hither and yon between admiration and rejection, between the readiness to listen his message and disappointment with that message and the impossibility of realizing it."[15]

Scholem's disappointment lay in Buber's ambivalence about the Zionist project, which, as Scholem saw it, was evidenced by Buber's failure to honor his own call for the renewal of Judaism to be realized through the reconstruction of Jewish national life in the land of Israel. Scholem still perceived as a betrayal Buber's apparent earlier reluctance to join a generation of European youth who had been inspired by his message to immigrate to Palestine, such as Scholem had done in 1923. Moreover, Buber's consciously and defiantly "heretical" vision of Jewish renewal proved to be exasperatingly utopian, given its nearly exclusive focus on spiritual sensibility and its lack of normative content.[16] Thus, Scholem depicted as a tragic paradox that while Buber's teachings enjoyed a receptive audience among non-Jews, he failed to speak to his own people.

Buber did not exercise the level of influence in the Jewish world that he might have wished. But in the years prior to World War II, especially in the Nazi period, he was indisputably a leading voice within the Jewish community of Central Europe. And in the post–World War II years, he was feted by non-Jews with honors, receiving honorary doctorates and prizes in Austria, France, Germany, and the Netherlands. In the United States, he was likewise a figure celebrated by both the non-Jewish and Jewish public. Nor was he by any means utterly irrelevant on the Israeli scene, even though he often took unpopular positions that would, he knew, cast him as an outsider—as an outsider, he had his constituency. His consistent call for Israel to acknowledge its responsibility for both the Arab refugees of Palestine and the abuse of the rights of the

Arabs who remained within the boundaries of the state found resonance, especially among the radical Left, which nominated him to be the third president of the State of Israel.[17] But it was also Buber's post-traditional conception of Judaism that increasingly spoke to youth raised with the secular values of socialist Zionism. Typical was a letter Buber received in May 1956 co-signed by two teenagers—one of whom was the sixteen-year-old daughter of Moshe Dayan, the Israeli war hero:

> After having read your writings and attempting to understand them, and because we are dissatisfied with our environment, with its scientific creed, and the conventions of the society in which we live, we have decided to turn to you. The central problem we face is basically simple: is it possible for human beings, young people like ourselves, fully recognizing the need to have faith, the need to feel life, to attain self-perfection based on faith and feeling, on knowledge and love of Jewish culture and the Bible? We were raised in a secular, non-religious environment that deified science and its laws. This year we shall graduate secondary school with a rather considerable store of scientific knowledge and general knowledge, but where do we go from here? . . . We would be grateful to you if you could give us an appointment for a conversation or write to us how it is possible to escape the fetters of our environment.[18]

Buber duly extended to his two young correspondents an invitation to visit him. "He received us two sixteen-year-olds," Yael Dayan reported, "like friends his same age, and conducted a serious conversation with us for two hours in the study and garden of his home. He explained that the road to faith was intuitive and that love of our fellow men and creative work would also bring us to faith. He answered our surely naïve and childish questions patiently and lovingly, as though we were the first who ever struggled with these questions."[19]

In his waning years, Buber's counsel was sought particularly by young, Israeli-born members of kibbutzim. Most of those kibbutzim had been created as an expression of a socialist ethos and a radically new Jewish culture and identity, free of the seemingly self-abnegating religious values and practices that were seen as debasing the life of the Jews in the galut. Beginning in 1960 and until a year before his death, Buber received regularly in his home delegations of youth from various kibbutzim. The meetings were largely organized at the initiative of Avraham "Patchi" Shapira, a twenty-four-year-old member of a kibbutz in the Jezreel valley. In his memoirs, Patchi recalls that he and his comrades were at first puzzled by Buber's adamant refusal to entertain abstract, theoretical questions, insisting that "I am not an idealist and I do not know what ideas are. I know only matters that are tangible and emerging." To a young *kibbutznik*, who sought advice on a personal problem, he explained that there "are things we must do—here and now. I have no principles, only a direction and sense, and an act to fit the situation."[20] As he later explained to Patchi, "People want me to provide them with generalities, to spare them from having to make the personal decisions which are required of them." Buber was aware that the young *kibbutznikim* came to him with the hope that he would be their "rabbi," but he consistently refused to accept the pastoral mantle or serve as a theological oracle, insisting that he was at most a teacher. "Whoever expects of me a doctrine, something other than teaching, will invariably be disappointed."[21]

Although the kibbutz youth who turned to Buber for guidance were, indeed, often disappointed by his failure to provide more concrete instruction on how to face the imponderables of communal life, they found his writings on Judaism more inspiring and formed reading groups to study them. A journalist who joined one of the sessions organized by Patchi at his kibbutz, in which they read Buber's *Gog and Magog*, published a vivid description of their deliberations:

A simple, wooden hut, guests sitting for many hours on hard wooden chairs. Only a few of those gathered had dealt many hours in their lives with spiritual matters. Most of them were enveloped with a certain, imperceptible smell of dealing with concrete, real things—the land to be ploughed; the cows to be milked. . . . I was astonished to see the extent to which this secular group transcended its normal categories of thought and agreed to the symbolic mixing together of the higher worlds and the lower ones. . . . The group in which I was sitting understood the meaning of the book [*Gog and Magog*] to the full and adapted it to their own quest, their own struggles. . . . They understood the full meaning of this struggle [portrayed in Buber's novel] between strong forces, at its base ideological, and this so-human a quest laden with passions of desire for power, jealousy, and religious zeal. Within all this they perceived the tiny voice of the human.[22]

Buber also enjoyed a measure of public recognition in Israel. In April 1953, he received the Israel Prize for the Humanities, in a ceremony presided over by Prime Minister David Ben-Gurion. In a brief address on behalf of the other recipients of that year's Israel Prize, Buber pointedly spoke (in oblique criticism of Ben-Gurion) about the relationship of the state to culture. There are, he noted, two principal understandings of this relationship; one is that culture is to be mobilized in the service of the state and its interests; the second is that the state must view culture not as an instrument to further its political agenda, but as an autonomous and independent dialogical partner.[23] In 1959, he was elected the first president of the Israel Academy of Sciences and the Humanities. (There had been only one objection to his appointment—which was widely speculated to have been by Scholem.) In December 1961, the city of Tel Aviv awarded him the Bialik Prize for his contribution to Jewish studies. Other prizes and honorary degrees in Israel and abroad followed.

There were also nominations that never came to fruition. In 1946, Hermann Hesse had recommended Buber to the Academy in Stockholm for the award Hesse himself had received three years earlier in 1946. In January 1959, Shimon Halkin, professor of modern Hebrew literature, on behalf of the senate of the Hebrew University, nominated Buber for a Nobel Prize in literature. In September 1961, Swedish diplomat and secretary general of the United Nations Dag Hammarskjöld was about to nominate Buber for the Nobel Prize when Hammarskjöld died in an airplane crash, en route to negotiate a cease-fire between contending parties in Katanga, Africa. Among his charred belongings, a draft of the Swedish translation of *I and Thou* was found. Although the Nobel Prize ultimately eluded Buber, he was especially gratified to receive the Erasmus Prize, which had been established in 1958 at the initiative of Prince Bernhard of the Netherlands to recognize individuals and institutions that have made seminal contributions to the spiritual and cultural life of Europe and humanity at large. It is one of Europe's most distinguished awards.

After the July 3, 1963, Erasmus Prize ceremony in Amsterdam, Buber vacationed in Switzerland. Upon his arrival at Hotel Sonnmatt, a sanatorium nestled in the Swiss Alps, overlooking Lake Lucerne, he was greeted by Naemah Beer-Hofmann. The youngest daughter of his late friend, the Austrian Jewish poet and playwright Richard Beer-Hofmann, Naemah was an American-trained physical therapist who had come to Jerusalem the previous summer in order to accompany a frail Buber to Sonnmatt. She had stayed in Jerusalem for over a month, visiting him daily, before traveling with him to Switzerland. During this period she, in her early fifties, and the eighty-four-year-old Buber developed a warm, mutually affectionate relationship. Rumors in scandalous tones circulated and eventually reached the Israeli press, but they were fed more by the imagination than genuine knowledge.[24] In the correspondence between them, initiated by Naemah in September 1961, she allowed herself as a "family friend" to address Buber endearingly as "Mein Lieber" (my dear) but with the formal third-person pronouns "Sie" and "Ihnen"). It was only after her visit to Jerusalem in August 1962 that she and Buber addressed one another with the informal second-person pronouns "Du" and "Dir." Indicative of the depth of the relationship is that, from 1961 until his death in June 1965, Buber wrote her some sixty letters, and she a similar number to him. The correspondence, however, does not suggest anything romantic or erotically intimate. What Naemah seems to have provided Buber is a nurturing feminine, if not a maternal, presence, which he had lost with the passing of Paula.[25]

Naemah's visit to Buber in Jerusalem coincided with his preparations for an introduction to an edition of her father's collected writings. The tone and analytical thrust of the introduction may also reflect his experience of his relationship with Naemah. Buber identified the overarching theme of Beer-Hofmann's poetry, plays, and novels as an ongoing "struggle for the answer to death."[26] With his own death closing in on him, Buber identified Beer-Hofmann's ultimate answer to be "love—the gracious love of God for men and the active love of man for his fellow men, indeed, for all existing beings, but above all for those who are dependent upon him and are thus entrusted to him." This is, he said, "the central message" of Beer-Hofmann's final and most mature work, *Jacob's Dream*— that loving God and one's fellow creatures "signifies the ever renewed overcoming of death." One hears in this exhortation Rosenzweig's identification of a passage in the Song of Songs as the heart of biblical faith: "Love is strong as death" (2:8)—love does not conquer death, but it removes its sting by affirming the bond of mutual care and affection between human beings.[27]

Another woman with whom Buber bonded in his last years was the Austrian Jewish writer and psychotherapist Anna Maria

Jokl. In 1959, she first visited Buber in Jerusalem in order to express her gratitude for his Hasidic stories and their image of man, which had served to establish the foundations of her approach to psychotherapy. She had the impression that Buber, who had sequestered himself behind his big mahogany desk as if it were a "wall," was hardly listening. "I soon wanted to leave 'mission accomplished,' since he made it clear that he sought to shield himself from being run over by idolizing visitors from all the world." As Jokl was about to leave, however, she said something that piqued Buber's interest and immediately changed the tone of the conversation. "As if he were liberated from the isolation of a monument," he stood up and came from behind his desk, opened his arms and "pressed me against his heart and offered me his great friendship"—a friendship that eventually led to her decision to move from Berlin to Jerusalem (though sadly, she arrived shortly after Buber died).[28]

In their great appreciation of Buber, Anna Maria and Naemah were joined by Grete Schaeder. The widow of the esteemed Orientalist and Iranologist Hans Heinrich Schaeder, she wrote to Buber in 1961 to express her interest in coming to Jerusalem to consult with him regarding a monograph she had hoped to write about his philosophy. Perhaps to make amends for her husband's Nazi sympathies, she was eager to present to the German public a portrait of Buber's "Hebrew humanism."[29] Over the next four years, she would become a frequent visitor at Buber's home. A friendship blossomed between them, as attested to by the nearly 120 letters they exchanged. In October 1964, Buber handed Schaeder a poem in his study and left the room for a few minutes to allow her to read it alone. It was dedicated to her and entitled "The Fiddler":

> Here on the world's edge at this hour I have
> Wondrously settled my life.
> Behind me in the boundless circle

The All is silent, only the fiddler fiddles.
Dark one, already I stand in covenant with you,
Ready to learn from your tones
Wherein I became guilty without knowing it.
Let me feel, let there be revealed
To this hale soul each wound
That I have incorrigibly inflicted and remained
    in illusion (*Schein*).
Do not stop, holy player, before then![30]

Grete Schaeder recalled that upon reading this poem, she "felt only a wave of sadness rise up in me over the fact of how close [Buber] felt himself to death."[31] When Buber returned to his study, Grete said to him, "Your relation to death has changed." And then, "half reflecting, half asking," she said "illusion" (Schein). Buber merely nodded. She did not discuss the poem further with him, "out of shyness before the nearness of death that was expressed in it."[32] Schaeder understood Schein here in light of Buber's interpretation of Psalm 73, in which he read its "music of death" as revealing whether one has unknowingly committed acts that make one "guilty towards one's fellow men"—and is thus without ethical blemish only *im Schein*, in appearance.[33] But she concurred with Maurice Friedman that Schein also refers to Buber's distinction between "seeming" (Schein) and "being" (Sein)—two contrasting modes of interpersonal life.[34] One may project an image of how one would like others to perceive oneself. "Seeming" engenders mutual mistrust and "existential guilt"; in contrast, "being" is a mode of meeting others, a mode free of the obfuscations of Schein and thus one that allows for bonds of mutual trust.

While Buber's female friendships late in life did encourage him, as Anna Maria Jokl observed, to emerge from the "isolation of a monument," he was also aware that they came to him in the first place because of the image they had of him.[35] The friendships that unfolded, then, may have softened his ambiva-

lence about his celebrity status. This is suggested by an undated, unpublished poem, in which he muses:

> Fame is a hollow nut,
> It cracks whom it must crack!
> Nevertheless, once cracked, it creates
> For you at times much that is agreeable.[36]

Buber's international fame, however, did not soften his
public image in Israel, even in his final years. His misgivings
about the direction the Zionist project had taken remained un-
diminished. He continued to protest in the press and in correspondence what he regarded to be the persistent abuses of
Palestinian rights and dignity. His concern for the ethical character of the State of Israel came to a head with the trial of Adolf
Eichmann. One of the principal architects of the extermination of Jews in German-occupied Eastern Europe, Eichmann
was captured in 1960 in Argentina by Israeli secret agents and
brought to Jerusalem to stand trial for crimes against the Jewish people and humanity. At the conclusion of the eight-month
trial, the court of three judges announced their verdict on
December 13, 1961, sentencing Eichmann to death by hanging.
In May 1962, a panel of five supreme court justices rejected the
appeal of Eichmann's lawyer to stay the execution. On May 30,
a petition to commute the death sentence, among whose signa-
tories were Buber, Hugo Bergmann, the poet Leah Goldberg,
and Gershom Scholem, was sent to then-president of Israel
Yitzhak Ben-Zvi. He rejected the petition, and on the night of
May 31, 1962, Eichmann was executed.

From the very beginning of the trial, Buber had questioned
both its participants and its intent. Eichmann, he held, should
be tried in an international court, for as victims of Eichmann's
heinous crimes, the Jews should not cast themselves as judges,
but rather as his accusers. When the Jerusalem district court,
which had tried Eichmann, announced its verdict, Buber tele-

phoned Ben-Gurion and requested to speak to him urgently about the court's decision and its ethical and political consequences. The prime minister replied that since he was younger than Buber, he would come to his home. They spoke for two hours. Although he listened attentively and with a measure of sympathy to Buber, Ben-Gurion indicated that he did not have the prerogative to intervene in the court's decision; nor, undoubtedly, did he have the desire to do so. Buber related the gist of the conversation to Aubrey Hodes, a young Israeli who was among Buber's most frequent visitors.[37] Buber, an opponent of the death penalty on principle, told Hodes: "I remember [publicly objecting to it] in 1928 in Germany. And I cannot now agree to it because it would be my own people that would carry out the sentence in its own country. . . . It is more than a question of Eichmann and what I think of his horrible crimes. Anyone who thinks that I wish us to be lenient to Eichmann does not understand my basic position."[38]

If Eichmann is not to be executed, Hodes asked, what then should be his punishment? "Buber sighed. 'This is a very difficult. He should be sentenced to life in prison. But we must remember always he is a symbol of the Nazi Holocaust, and not an ordinary criminal.'" Shaking his head, Buber paused as if groping for a precise formulation of what he had in mind. He then continued, emphatically declaring: "He should be made to feel that the Jewish people was not [utterly] exterminated by the Nazis, and that they live on here in Israel. Perhaps he should be put to work on the land—on a kibbutz. Farming the soil of Israel. Seeing young people around him. And realizing every day that we have survived his plans for us. Would not this be the ultimate and most fitting punishment?"[39]

In interviews in the Israeli and foreign press, Buber's position was given wide coverage—and most often evoked scornful accusations that he lacked an understanding of the psychological need for retribution and Jewish pride.

Buber was disappointed that his opposition to the execution of Eichmann was, he felt, misconstrued, but he was not terribly troubled by the criticism itself, even when it was ad hominem. A self-conscious outsider in the context of pre- and post-1948 Zionism, he was by the end of his life inured to being branded unpatriotic. As Theodor Heuss had perceptively noted, Buber had always "been an inwardly independent person." A conversation Jokl had with him may have elicited an acknowledgment of the existential consequence of his independence of mind and, when he deemed appropriate, his voicing his dissent. Jokl recalled visiting Buber one summer at Hotel Sonnmatt (likely just after the execution of Eichmann, in June 1962), sitting on the terrace overlooking the majestic Alpine summit Jungfrau. Sipping espresso, Buber asked her what she, as a psychotherapist, believed is the source of angst, for "Freud says that angst stems from terrible childhood experiences. I do not believe so. I do not have angst and I had a terrible childhood." Anna was initially at a loss for how to reply, but suddenly blurted out, "I believe angst is *not to belong*." Buber was silent, reflected, and repeated slowly "*not to belong*," and then said: "Yes—that may be—*not to belong*."[40]

At the age of eighty-four, Buber had long reconciled himself not to belong, at least not to belong fully. Within the political culture of the Yishuv and later the State of Israel, it had been precisely his attention to the ambiguities of the Zionist project that had pushed him to the margins of society. Yet in his later years, his voice found increasing resonance (albeit still limited) among those, especially of the younger generation, who shared his concerns for the unfolding ethical character of the country. As he approached his eighty-fifth year, he was duly honored as a venerable forefather of the Zionist movement—even if the tributes occasionally had a note of ambivalence, such as the cable Ben-Gurion sent Buber on February 8, 1963, his birthday: "I honor and oppose you."

Other tributes were unequivocally gracious. At a banquet in Buber's honor, the Hebrew University announced the forthcoming reprint of a German pamphlet, with a Hebrew translation, that he had coauthored and published in 1902, calling for the establishment of Jewish university, preferably in Palestine.[41] The tribute that perhaps moved him most was a nocturnal serenade by some five hundred Jewish and Arab students of the Hebrew University. On the night of his eighty-fifth birthday, bearing flaming torches, they marched from a student cultural center in Jerusalem to Buber's home. Beckoning him to exit his home, a delegation of seven students climbed the stairs to the veranda where Buber stood and placed a garland of flowers around his neck. All those gathered before his house sang the Hebrew equivalents of "For he is a jolly good fellow!" and "Happy birthday, dear Martin." The president of the student association then made a short speech: "When we were born you were already a legend. We are only sorry that we were too late to be your students at the Hebrew University and that we did not have the honor, the pleasure, and the privilege of being taught by you." He concluded by conferring on Buber honorary membership in the student association.[42] As Buber held the membership card he had been given, he made a short speech thanking the students for the honor that they had bestowed upon him: "There was a Dutch professor [Johan Huizinga] who wrote a book about the *Homo ludens*—someone who enjoys playfulness as an expression of freedom." Buber then suggested that analogously one might recognize what he called "the naturally studying person"—someone for "whom learning and study are an expression of human freedom." Such a student is "someone who aspires to know truth, in order to build upon it a structure worthy for people to inhabit. If this is your aspiration, I am delighted that you have made me a partner in it, and by accepting me as a student in your association.[43]

In response to these appreciative words, the students

chanted the traditional Jewish birthday salutation, "Until a hundred and twenty!" Buber interjected to ask, "Don't you think that's a little too much? Well, perhaps we can reach a compromise." One of the students shouted a query, "Professor Buber, when you were young did you ever take part in a midnight serenade such as this?" With a twinkle in his eyes, he replied, "Yes, I did—in Germany, where this was often done for popular professors. But I only went along a few times. And for a very good reason: I didn't like most of my professors."[44]

Buber's spirits were lifted by this exuberant tribute, which concluded after midnight, long past his usual bedtime. His body, however, was in rapid decline. Already in April 1962, there had been troubling lapses of memory, which progressively worsened.[45] Finding it difficult to conduct his demanding correspondence, he became ever more dependent on his secretary Margot Cohn, who had worked for him since Paula's passing. Despite his poor health, his physicians agreed to allow him to spend that summer in Sonnmatt, presumably on the condition that someone would accompany him.[46] (This is when Naemah Beer-Hofmann entered the picture, since Buber's granddaughter Barbara, who usually accompanied him abroad, was traveling in Europe with her husband that summer.) In his last years, Buber would rarely leave his home, even for a brief walk as his doctors had recommended. He nonetheless sought to keep up his spirits, at least externally. As was his wont, he confined his deepest feelings to poetry. In January 1964, he penned a verse while contemplating the engraving by the German Renaissance master Albrecht Dürer, *Melencolia*, which features an hourglass showing time running out. Entitled "Beside Me" (*Zuseiten mir*), the poem reads:

> Beside me sits melancholy
> (Thus once the master had seen her).
> She does not speak to me, she never whispers.

Only the hesitant stirrings of her breath
Carry to me, unto my innermost ear.
The lament of the spirit which—when then? How?—
Lost the power of the soul.[47]

For Buber the life of the soul, as Grete Schaeder explained in commenting on this poem, "was the power of relationship." Failing health and the strain of maintaining relationships—the "original spontaneity of the heart"—drew him to Dürer's hourglass.[48]

Time began to make its last run for Buber when on April 26, 1965, he fell as he undressed to go to bed, and yelled for help.[49] Barbara and her husband lifted him from the floor and summoned his personal physician. Upon examining Buber, Dr. Otto Strauss had an ambulance rush him to Hadassah Hospital, where they operated on him that night for a fractured right hip. He would stay in the hospital for nearly a month. Although he had long ago mastered Hebrew, he requested a German-speaking nurse. He was released from the hospital on May 23, but after three days at home he was hospitalized once again. When the patient next to him suddenly died, he insisted that he be taken back home. Although the fracture was healing satisfactorily, the fall had aggravated a chronic kidney inflammation, which quickly led to acute kidney failure and uremic poisoning.

While Buber battled to hold on to life, the mayor of Jerusalem, Mordechai Ish-Shalom, a member of the Labor Party, was in the midst of a struggle to have the city council grant Buber honorary citizenship of the city. The right-wing members of the council adamantly refused, citing Buber's "reprehensible" opposition to the execution of Eichmann, whereas the ultra-orthodox councilors argued that Buber's heretical view of Judaism disqualified him for this honor. By a slight majority, the proposal passed, whereupon the mayor, accompanied by Agnon, rushed to inform Buber that he had been named "Yakir Yerushalayim" (worthy citizen of Jerusalem). Sadly, Buber was at that moment too weak to acknowledge the award. He managed soon after, however, to request that a substantial sum allocated in his last will and testament for scholarships for Arab students at the Hebrew University be doubled.

Life steadily slipped from him. He passed away on Sunday, June 13, 1965, at 10:45 in the morning. When fifteen-year-old Tamar came rushing home from school to see her beloved great-grandfather, she found him dead, with Agnon sitting at his side. The Hebrew novelist was soon to be joined by another of Buber's oldest friends, Zalman Shazar, president of the State of Israel. Despite his fears, the "power of the soul," of which he wrote in "Beside Me," was not lost with the approach of death. As he had mused in a meditation on the existential significance of scholarship: "I knew nothing of books when I came forth from the womb of my mother, and I shall die without books, with the hand of another human hand in my own."[50]

After paying a condolence call to Buber's family, Ben-Gurion said on Israeli national radio that Buber's passing was "a great loss to the country's spiritual life." Prime Minister Levi Eshkol asked the members of his cabinet, which met that Sunday for its weekly meeting, to stand in memory of Buber. Afterward he delivered a brief eulogy and sent a message to Buber's family expressing the government's sympathy at their loss.

In accordance with Jewish custom, the funeral took place the next day. Before the burial, Buber's body, wrapped in a tallit, a black and white prayer shawl, was brought to the Hebrew University campus for a funeral service. Classes were cancelled in order to allow students to attend the ceremony, at which Prime Minister Eshkol was the first to speak. He eulogized Buber "as the most distinguished representative of the Jewish people's reborn spirit. Today the people of Israel mourn a light and a teacher, a man of intellect and action, who revealed the soul of Judaism with a new philosophical daring. Humanity as a whole mourns together with us one of the spiritual giants of this century." The prime minister was followed by Buber's friend of sixty-three years, Professor Hugo Bergmann. Turning to the students, he beseeched them to learn from Buber that Judaism does not mean only "performing existing, static commandments. It means struggling for Judaism, fighting for it, each one of us in his own life. Buber knew how to fight for Judaism and even how to be unpopular. But he was able to defend his kind of Judaism courageously, both inside Jewry and outside it."

Bergmann referred to two instances in which Buber felt the need to go it alone. The first was when "we, his friends" were troubled by his decision to go to Frankfurt in 1953 to accept the Peace Prize of the German Book Trade. "We were not sure the time had come to be in Germany again. Buber went. But he did not touch the money. He donated it to [organizations] working for peace with the Arabs." Bergmann also lauded, in retrospect, Buber's readiness to be virtually alone in his opposition to Eichmann's execution, "the stand of a great teacher." Addressing the body of his deceased mentor and friend, a tearful Bergmann declared: "I take my leave from you. You were a blessing to us. May your memory be a blessing to us, and a guide to the coming generations. You have done your share. We shall try to follow in your footsteps and to realize the meaning of Judaism, each of us according to his ability. We thank you, dear Martin Buber."

# NOTES

Unless otherwise noted, all translations are mine. Works frequently cited are identified by the following abbreviations:

*Briefwechsel*    Martin Buber, *Briefwechsel aus sieben Jahrzehnten*, ed. Grete Schaeder and Ernst Simon, 3 vols. (Heidelberg: Lambert Schneider, 1972–1975)

*Letters*    Nahum N. Glatzer and Paul Mendes-Flohr, eds., *The Letters of Martin Buber: A Life of Dialogue*, trans. Richard Winston, Clara Winston, and Harry Zohn (New York: Schocken, 1991)

Martin Buber Archive    Martin Buber Archive, National Library of Israel (formerly Jewish National and University Library), Jerusalem, ms. varia 350

*Meetings*    Martin Buber, *Meetings: Autobiographical Fragments*, ed. Maurice Friedman (London: Routledge, 2002)

## Introduction

*Epigraph:* Buber to Hermann Levin Goldschmidt, October 7, 1948, cited in H. L. Goldschmidt, "Erinnerung, Begegnung, Auseinandersetzung," in *Martin Bubers Erbe für unsere Zeit*, ed. Werner Licharz (Frankfurt a.M.: Haag & Herchen, 1885), 57.

1. Hannah Arendt, "What Remains? The Language Remains: A Conversation with Günther Gaus," in Arendt, *The Last Interview and Other Conversations* (Brooklyn: Melville House, 2013), 34.

2. Philip P. Wiener, "Some Problems and Methods in the History of Ideas," *Journal of the History of Ideas* 22, no. 4 (1961): 533.

3. Bellow is cited in Wayne C. Booth, *The Rhetoric of Fiction* (Chicago: University of Chicago Press, 1961), 137–144. Cf. J. W. Worthy to Goethe: "For me, the entire fascination of your work, Your Excellency, arises from the personality, I find there—or from the personality I *think* I glimpse there." From *The Correspondence of J. W. Worthy with Ancients and Moderns*, available online at http://lettersfromthedustbowl.com/worthy.html (accessed June 25, 2018).

4. Buber to Maurice Friedman, August 1956, Martin Buber Archive, file 217a.

5. Janet Malcolm, *The Silent Woman: Sylvia Plath and Ted Hughes* (New York: Vintage, 1994), 154.

6. More than a hundred of Buber's German poems have recently been published with commentaries by Bernd Witte in *Martin Buber Werkausgabe*, vol. 7: *Schriften zu Literatur, Theater und Kunst* (Gütersloh: Gütersloher Verlagshaus, 2016).

7. *Meetings*, 21.

8. Cf. Martin Buber, "Replies to My Critics," in *The Philosophy of Martin Buber*, ed. Paul A. Schilpp and Maurice Friedman (LaSalle, Ill.: Open Court, 1967), 691–695.

9. Buber to Mitchell Bedford, December 26, 1952, in *Letters*, 572.

10. Buber to Franz Rosenzweig, September 28, 1922, in

Rosenzweig, *On Jewish Learning*, ed. Nahum N. Glatzer (New York: Schocken, 1955), 110 f.

11. Edward W. Said, *Reflections on Exile and Other Essays* (Cambridge, Mass.: Harvard University Press, 2000), 462.

12. Arthur A. Cohen, *The Natural and the Supernatural Jew: An Historical and Theological Introduction* (New York: McGraw-Hill, 1962).

13. Buber, *Hasidism and Modern Man*, introduction by David Biale (Princeton, N.J.: Princeton University Press, 2015), 42.

14. Hannah Arendt, *Das Private Adressbuch*, ed. Christine Rischer-Defoy (Leipzig: Koehler & Amelang, 2007), 84.

15. Buber, *Eclipse of God: Studies in the Relation between Religion and Philosophy* (New York: Harper and Row, 1979), 6.

16. *Meetings*, 38.

17. Ibid., 40.

18. Ibid., 38 f.

19. Wiener, "Some Problems and Methods," 533.

20. Gershom Schocken, "Gossiping about Buber," *Haaretz*, September 30, 1988 (Hebrew).

## Chapter 1. A Motherless Child

1. In an interview with Hans A. Fischer-Barnicol, Buber ironically attributed his stature as a celebrity to his beard. As the beard gained fullness, he bemusedly observed, people took him for a prophet. "Believe me," he told his interlocutor, "I would shave this wonderful beard off, but then I would destroy my image. Hmmm." See Fischer-Barnicol, "Spiegelungen—Vermittlungen," in Günther Neske, ed., *Erinnerung zu Martin Heidegger* (Pfullingen: Verlag Günther Neske, 1977), 89 f.

2. Reported to Aubrey Hodes, who "maintained a close relationship" to Buber during the last twelve years of his life. See Hodes, *Martin Buber: An Intimate Portrait* (New York: Viking, 1971), 43. For a slightly different articulation of this account, see *Meetings*, 22.

3. *Meetings*, 18.

4. Buber, "Die Kinder," *Jüdische Rundschau*, May 30, 1933; also "The Children" (1933), in William Rollins and Harry Zohn, eds., *Men of Dialogue: Martin Buber and Albrecht Goes* (New York: Funk and Wagnalls, 1969), 225, 228.

5. Buber to Franz Rosenzweig, August 2, 1922, in *Letters*, 269.

6. Martin Buber to Paula Winkler Buber, October 15, 1901, in *Letters*, 79. In an unpublished jotting, titled "For You," dated 1902, he tells Paula, "You came and gave me a soul. Therefore is not my soul merely this: your child." See *Letters*, 10 f.

7. Letter to the son of Ina Britschgi-Schimmer on the occasion of his bar mitzvah, cited in Ina Britschgi-Schimmer, "Der junge Martin Buber. Erinnerungen," *Jüdscher Rundschau* 33, no. 11 (February 2, 1920): 76. Expressing his condolence to a friend on the death of his mother, Buber wrote: "I participate in your mourning. I scarcely knew my mother, and this is perhaps why I know in a special way what it means to a person to lose one's mother." Buber to Lambert Schneider, July 23, 1955, in *Letters*, 591 f.

8. As noted in Hodes, *An Intimate Portrait*, 43. In his published autobiographical memoir, Buber explains a mismeeting as "the failure of a real meeting between men." The depth of the pain of a mismeeting was experienced for Buber when, in his thirties, his mother "had come from a distance to visit me, my wife, and children." It was the first time he had seen her since he was three years old, but "I could not gaze into her still astonishingly beautiful eyes without hearing from somewhere the word 'Vergegnung' as a word spoken to me." See *Meetings*, 22 f.

9. Buber, *Meetings*, 22.

10. Buber, *Ich und Du* (Leipzig: Insel-Verlag, 1923), 18; Buber, *I and Thou*, trans. Ronald Gregor Smith (New York: Scribner's, 1958), 11.

11. Jules-Amédée Barbey d'Aurevilly, "La vengeance d'une femme," in d'Aurevilly, *Diaboliques: Oeuvres Romanesques Complètes* (Paris: Gallimard, 1966), 2: 231.

12. Buber, "What Is Man?" in Buber, *Between Man and Man*, trans. R. G. Smith (London: Routledge, 2002), 237.

13. Rafael Buber, "Die Buber-Familie. Erinnerungen," in R. Buber, *Dialog mit Martin Buber*, ed. Werner Licharz (Frankfurt a.M.: Haag & Herchen, 1982), 352.

14. See Moshe H. E. Bloch, "Martin Buber and His Ancestors," *Ha-Doar* 44, no. 34 (1965–1966): 629–632 (Hebrew).

15. Ibid.

16. In the German edition of Buber's correspondence, his grandfather's letters are given in German, without noting that they were originally in Yiddish.

17. *Meetings*, 19; Werner Kraft, "Martin Buber über Sprache und deutsche Sprache," *Hochland* 60 (August/September 1958): 520.

18. *Meetings*, 31 (emphasis added).

19. Martin Buber, "Reminiscences," in Buber, *A Believing Humanism. My Testament: 1902–1965*, trans. M. Friedman (New York: Simon and Schuster, 1967), 30.

20. See Helit Yeshurun Raviv, "A Conversation with Dr. Moshe Spitzer," *Chadarim* (Winter 1982–1983): 53 (Hebrew).

21. Under the pressure of a deadline, Buber solicited Paula's assistance to rework some of the tales included in his second collection of Hasidic lore, *Die Legende des Baalschem* (Frankfurt a.M.: Rütten & Loening, 1908). He would provide her with a literal translation of a saying by the Baal Shem Tov, which she then elaborated freely. See the correspondence between Martin and Paula from early December 1906, in *Briefwechsel*, 1: 249–252. The letters between Paula and Martin indicate that he would send her excerpts of a Hasidic text he had translated, which she would then not only elaborate but also stylize (*Briefwechsel*, 1: 250).

22. Haim Gordon, *The Other Martin Buber: Recollections of His Contemporaries* (Athens: Ohio University Press, 1988), 40. Buber also consulted his future son-in-law, Ludwig Strauss, a highly accomplished German poet. Cf. their correspondence of May 1922. Buber sent Strauss the manuscript of a forthcoming

book on Hasidism to review. Strauss returned the manuscript with several dozen corrections of diction and syntax, all of which Buber accepted with gratitude. See *Briefwechsel Martin Buber–Ludwig Strauss: 1913–1953*, ed. Tuvia Rübner and Dafna Mach (Frankfurt a.M.: Luchterhand Literaturverlag, 1990), 79–83.

23. Theodor Lessing, *Einmal und nie Wieder. Lebenserinnerung. Gesammelte Schriften* (Prague: Heinrich Mercy Sohn, 1935), 1: 291 f.

24. Cf. Omar al-Raschid Bey, *Das hohe Ziel der Erkenntnis. Aranada Upanishad*, ed. Helene Böhlau al-Rashid Bey (Munich, 1912). Originally Friedrich Arndt-Kürnberg, al-Rashid Bey was born in Saint Petersburg to German-Jewish parents. In 1888, he traveled to Constantinople with Helene Böhlau, where they both converted to Islam, whereupon they married and he took on his Arabic name. Helene would gain fame in her own right as an acclaimed novelist.

25. Lessing, *Einmal und nie Wieder,* 294.

26. Ibid.

27. Buber's Israeli passport (No. 16890, issued in 1952) gives his height as 157 centimeters. At about the time he met Paula, he made the acquaintance of another woman, who in a memoir described him "as an utterly delicate, pale person with a high, broad forehead, dark, piercing inward eyes with feminine small, ethereal hands." Ina Britschgi-Schimmer, "Der junge Martin Buber. Erinnerungen." *Jüdischer Rundschau* 33, no. 11 (February 2, 1920): 75.

28. Cf. the couple's marriage certificate: "Beschieinigung der Ereschließung Martin Buber und Paula Winkler," Friedenau, April 20, 1907, Martin Buber Archive, file A:1d. Paula's religion is noted as "mosaisch," as is Martin's. Upon her conversion, Paula took on the Hebrew name Yehudit (Judith). The conversion was apparently performed by a liberal rabbi, for on March 26, 1934, she underwent an orthodox conversion in Berlin. See Chapter 8.

29. Ibid.

30. *Teffilin* are phylacteries worn by observant Jewish men (and in contemporary times, by some Jewish women) during the weekday morning prayers.

31. Buber to Franz Rosenzweig, October 1, 1922, in Rosenzweig, *On Jewish Learning*, ed. Nahum N. Glatzer (New York: Schocken, 1955), 110.

32. The extant correspondence between Buber and his grandparents is in the Martin Buber Archive and the Salomon Buber Archive, both housed at the National Library of Israel (formerly the Jewish National and University Library), Jerusalem.

33. During a visit to his grandparents in October 1902, he wrote to Paula: "Here it is dungeon-like narrow (*kerkermäßig eng*)." See *Briefwechsel*, 1: 177.

34. The English rabbi Simeon Singer recalled visiting Salomon Buber in Lemberg and "found him in his study at five in the morning." Such men, he commented, "seem to need no sleep." "Salomon Buber: Obituary," *Jewish Chronicle*, January 4, 1907, 13.

35. Ibid.

36. See Nisson E. Shulman, "The Responsa of 'Masat Benjamin,'" Ph.D. diss., Yeshiva University, 1970; "Slonik, Benjamin, Aaron b. Abraham," *Encyclopedia Judaica*, 2nd ed. (Stamford, Conn.: Thomson Gale/Macmillan, 2006), 18: 675–676.

37. Obituary in the Hebrew journal *Ha-Magid* (May 11, 1870): 139–140.

38. Buber's grandmother was also from a wealthy Galician Jewish family, and she too counted among her relatives esteemed rabbis and scholars.

39. Martin Buber to Adele Buber, December 17, 1899, in *Letters*, 69.

40. Martin Buber to Salomon and Adele Buber, January 31, 1900, in *Letters*, 70 (emphasis added; translation modified).

41. "Karol Buber of Blessed Memory," *Chwila* 5776 (June 20, 1935).

42. The original German dedication is "Meinem Grossvater Salomon Buber dem letzten Meister der alten Haskala bringe ich dies Werk der Chassidut dar mit Ehrfrucht und Liebe."

43. Carl Buber to Martin Buber, February 6, 1908 in *Briefwechsel*, 1: 260 f.

44. Paula Buber to Martin Buber, October 9, 1901, in *Letters*, 21.

45. Paula Buber to Martin Buber, October 18, 1901, in *Letters*, 20.

46. Paula Winkler, "Betractungen einer Philozionistin," *Die Welt* 36 (September 9, 1901): 4–6.

47. Paula Winkler to Martin Buber, August 16–17, 1899, in *Letters*, 67–69; see also *Briefwechsel*, 1: 149 f.

48. Martin Buber, *A Believing Humanism: My Testament, 1902–1965*, trans. Maurice Friedman (New York: Simon and Schuster, 1967), 48; the original German is given on the facing page, 47.

## Chapter 2. Herald of a Jewish Renaissance

1. For a translation of the essay, see William M. Johnston and Robert A. Rothstein, "Martin Buber's Literary Debut: 'On Viennese Literature' (1897)," *German Quarterly* 47, no. 4 (November 1974): 556–566.

2. Ibid., 559.

3. Ahron Eliasberg, "Aus Martin Buber's Jugendzeit," *Blätter des Heine-Bundes* 1, no. 1 (April 1, 1928): 1.

4. The essay is now published in *Martin Buber Werkausgabe*, vol. 1: *Frühe kulturkritische und philosophische Schriften, 1891–1924*, ed. Martin Treml (Gütersloh: Gütersloher Verlagshaus, 2001), 105.

5. Ibid., 103.

6. Ibid., 107.

7. Ibid., 106.

8. Ibid., 108, 113 f.

9. Ibid., 104. Although he would eventually publish mostly in German (and later in Hebrew), Buber relished every opportunity to express his abiding attachment to the Polish language and culture. In 1943, for instance, he eagerly addressed in Polish the troops of the Polish Army in exile, stationed in Haifa, Palestine, on the occasion of the four hundredth anniversary of the death of the Polish mathematician and astronomer Nicolas Copernicus. In 1939 he gave a series of lectures in Poland on behalf of the Hebrew University. See Chapter 9.

10. Witold Olschewski to Buber, July 27, 1962, in *Letters*, 648 (original in Polish).

11. For the quotation, see Buber, "Zarathustra," in *Martin Buber Werkausgabe*, 1: 107.

12. Eliasberg, "Aus Martin Buber's Jugendzeit," 4.

13. Ibid.

14. For a German translation of the address, see Buber, "'Glaube, Hoffnung, Liebe' (Ewige Jugend)," in *Martin Buber Werkausgabe*, 1: 99–102. As indicated in a note he appended to the text, Buber wrote the address on November 15, 1892.

15. "Rede gehalten von Martin Buber an seiner 'Barmizwah'-Feier am 8. Februar 1891," in *Martin Buber Werkausgabe*, 1: 93–98. An article in the Hebrew journal *Ha-Maggid* (February 1891) reported that at a festive reception—"attended by the leaders and nobility" of the Jewish community—in his grandfather's home, Martin apparently gave yet another bar mitzvah speech in which he concluded with a pledge "to observe all his life and with all his heart the precepts and ethical teachings of the Holy Torah." This report is cited in an article, "Toward the History of Martin Buber," *BeTzaron* (June 1965): 145 (Hebrew). Founded in 1840 as a "progressive" synagogue, the Lemberg "Temple," as it was popularly called, had a choir and encouraged its rabbi to give sermons in German.

16. "Rede gehalten von Martin Buber," 94; Friedrich Schiller, "Gedichte-Kapitel 97," available online at http://gutenberg.spiegel .de/buch/gedichte-9097/97 (accessed June 29, 2018).

17. Buber, "Glaube, Hoffnung, Liebe," 100.

18. Werner Kraft, *Gespräche mit Martin Buber* (Munich: Kösel-Verlag, 1966), 129.

19. Ibid., 4.

20. The late Ernst Simon, one of Buber's closest friends, related to me that Buber defiantly claimed to have no knowledge of the Talmud. Yet, as reported by Buber's research assistant in the early 1930s, on the occasion of his sixtieth birthday Abraham Joshua Heschel gave Buber as a gift a set of the Babylonian Talmud. With palpable gratitude, he told Heschel, "All my life I

wanted the Talmud." See Heit Yeshurun Raviv, "A Conversation with Dr. Moshe Spitzer," *Chadarim* (Winter 1982–1983): 54 (Hebrew).

21. In his correspondence, he occasionally cites the Mishnah. In a letter to Paula of October 1902, for instance, he quotes Mishnah Hagigah 2:1, cautioning one not to probe the mysteries of existence. *Briefwechsel*, 1: 177.

22. Raviv, "Conversation with Dr. Moshe Spitzer," 54.

23. *Meetings*, 8.

24. Eliasberg, "Aus Martin Bubers Jugendzeit," 4.

25. Mathias Acher, *Jüdische Moderne. Versuch einer modernen Lösung der Judenfrage* (Vienna: M. Breitenstein's Verlags-Buchhandlung, 1896).

26. Jacob Burckhardt, *Griechische Kulturgeschichte*, ed. Jakob Oeri (Berlin: W. Spemann, 1898), vol. 1.

27. Eliasberg, "Aus Martin Bubers Jugendzeit," 5.

28. Buber also wrote the foreword to the Hebrew translation of Jacob Burckhardt, *The Civilization of Renaissance in Italy*, trans. J. Steinberg (Jerusalem: Mosad Bialik, 1949).

29. See Alfred V. Martin, *Nietzsche und Burckhardt. Zwei geistige Welten im Dialog*, 3rd exp. ed. (Basel: Ernst Reinhardt Verlag, 1945).

30. "Die Kunst im Leben," *Organ der Kunstwissenschaften Abteilung der Berliner Finkenschaft* 1, no. 1 (December 1900): 12–13.

31. Ibid., 13.

32. Buber, "Jüdische Renaissance," *Ost und West* 1, no. 1 (January 1901): cols. 7–10. For an English translation of this seminal essay, see "Jewish Renaissance," in Gilya G. Schmidt, ed. and trans., *The First Buber: Youthful Zionist Writings of Martin Buber* (Syracuse, N.Y.: Syracuse University Press, 1999), 30–34. I have modified Schmidt's translation.

33. Buber, "Jewish Renaissance," 30.

34. Ibid.

35. Ibid.

36. Ibid., 32.

37. Buber, "Feste des Lebens: Ein Bekenntnis," *Die Welt* 5,

no. 9 (March 1, 1901): 8–9; for an English translation see "Festivals of Life: A Confession," in Schmidt, *The First Buber*, 18–20.

38. Ibid., 18.

39. Ibid., 19 (emphasis added).

40. Ibid., 18. (I have modified Schmidt's translation.)

41. Ibid. *Erleben* denotes an emotionally affective experience.

42. Ibid., 19.

43. Buber, "Feste des Lebens," 9.

44. Buber, "Festivals of Life," 20.

45. Buber, "Zwei Tänze aus dem Zyklus Elisha ben Abuja, genannt Acher," in *Junge Harfen. Eine Sammlung jungjüdischer Gedichte* (Berlin: Jüdischer Verlag, 1903): 31–33. Translated in Schmidt, *The First Buber*, 128–132.

46. Buber, "Das Zion der jüdische Frau. Aus einem Vortrag." *Die Welt* 5, no. 1 (April 26, 1901): 4, reprinted with commentary in Martin Buber, *Frühe jüdische Schriften: 1900–1922*, ed. and introduced with commentary by Barbara Schäfer in *Martin Buber Werkausgabe*, vol. 3 (Güterlohr: Güterlarher Verlagshaus, 2007), 71–81; Buber, "The Jewish Woman's Zion," in Schmidt, *The First Buber*, 111–118. The lecture, held in Vienna on April 21, 1901, was delivered before the Verein jüdischer Mädchen Hadassah.

47. Ibid., 117.

48. Ibid., 113; Buber, "Das Zion der jüdische Frau," 76.

49. Buber, "The Jewish Woman's Zion," 113.

50. Ibid., 115; Buber, "Das Zion der jüdische Frau," 78.

51. Ibid.

52. Buber, "The Jewish Woman's Zion," 115.

53. Ibid., 117.

54. Ibid., 116–117.

55. Ibid., 118 (I have modified the translation). Buber's partner (later wife), Paula Winkler, wrote a lengthy essay supporting his call for Jewish women to resume their role as the pillar of the family. Significantly, although she had yet to convert, she spoke in the name of Judaism. Turning to her "fellow" Jewish women, she beseeches them to acknowledge that "Your people calls upon you,

the best of your people." Paula Winkler, "Die jüdische Frau," *Die Welt* 46 (November 8, 1901): 4, and *Die Welt* 46 (November 15, 1901): 6 f.

56. Addressing the Third Zionist Congress (1899), Buber declared, "Zionismus ist keine Partei-Sache, sondern eine Weltanschauung" (Zionism is not a matter of party politics, but a worldview). Cited by Hans Kohn in his *Martin Buber. Sein Werk und seine Zeit, eine Beitrag zur Geistesgeschichte Mitteleuropas, 1880–1930*, 2nd ed. (Cologne: Joseph Melzer Verlag, 1961), 27. Also see Buber's lecture of 1914, "Zionismus als Lebensanschauung und als Lebensform," in *Martin Buber Werkausgabe*, 3: 134–142.

57. Cf. the Basel Program, which outlined the objectives of Political Zionism and was adopted by the First Zionist Congress held in Basel, Switzerland, in 1897.

58. Cited in Gilya Gerda Schmidt, *Martin Buber's Formative Years, from German Culture to Jewish Revival, 1897–1909* (Tuscaloosa: University of Alabama Press, 1995), 58.

59. Paula Winkler, "Betrachtungen einer Philozionistin [Reflections of a Philo-Zionist]," *Die Welt* 36 (September 6, 1901): 5; passage cited by Grete Schaeder in her introduction to *Letters*, 10.

60. Buber to Theodor Herzl, August 11, 1901, in *Letters*, 74.

61. Theodor Herzl to Buber, August 13, 1901, in *Letters*, 75.

62. Theodor Herzl to Buber, August 24, 1901, in *Letters*, 77.

63. Buber, "Mountaintop Bonfires: On the Occasion of the Fifth Congress," translated in Schmidt, *The First Buber*, 15.

64. Ibid., 16.

65. Cf. Buber, "Die Congresstribüne," *Die Welt* 5, no. 36 (September 6, 1901); reprinted in Martin Buber, *Martin Buber Werkausgabe*, 1: 88–89; Buber, "The Congressional Platform," in Schmidt, *The First Buber*, 26–28. As was his wont, Buber often signed his early articles as "Baruch," that is, Baruch ben Neriah, the Prophet Jeremiah's scribe and devoted friend. In the medieval tradition he was known as a priest and prophet.

66. Buber, "The Congressional Platform," 26; Buber, "Die Congresstribüne," 88.

67. Buber, "The Congressional Platform," 27 (I have modified the translation); Buber, "Die Congresstribüne," 88 f.

68. Ahad Ha'Am, "Nachahmung und Assimilation (Part One)," trans. Israel Friedländer, *Die Welt* 38 (September 20, 1901): 9–10; Ahad Ha'Am, "Nachahmung und Assimilation (Part Two)," *Die Welt* 39 (September 27, 1901): 4–6.

69. Herzl to Buber, September 28, 1901, in *Letters*, 77.

70. The resolution stated that "the Congress considers the cultural amelioration (*culturelle Hebung*), that is to say, the national education of the Jewish people, as one of the most important aspects of the Zionist program and obliges all fellow Zionists (*Gesinnungsgenossen*) to participate in this endeavor"; see Buber, "Ein Wort zum fünften Congreß," *Jüdische Volksstimme* 3, no. 2 (February 15, 1902): 2. A few days prior to the congress, a group of thirty-seven *Jungzionisten*, as they called themselves, met to organize as a "study circle" to strategize how to remedy what they regarded as the "neglect of cultural work within the Zionist movement. They convened at the initiative of Chaim Weizmann, who would forty-five years later serve as the first president of the State of Israel. At the congress they had no formal name, although as explained above they were ironically known as the Democratic Fraction. See Buber, "A Word Regarding the Fifth Congress," in *The First Buber*, 95 f.; Buber, "Ein Wort zum fünften Confreß," *Jüdsche Volksstimme* 3, no. 2 (February 15, 1902), reprinted in *Martin Buber Werkausgabe*, 3: 92–106.

71. Buber, "Ein Wort zum fünften Congreß," 3.

72. Buber, "A Word Regarding the Fifth Congress," 95 f.

73. *Stenographisches Protokoll der Verhandlungen des V. Zionisten Congresses, Basel. 26. bis 29. Dezember, 1901*, 395, cited in Michael Stanislawski, *Zionism and the Fin de Siècle: Cosmopolitanism and Nationalism from Nordau to Jabotinsky* (Berkeley: University of California Press, 2001), 108 f.

74. Cited in Buber, "A Word Regarding the Fifth Congress," 91.

75. Ibid., 99.

76. Buber, "Address on Jewish Art," in Schmidt, *The First*

*Buber,* 46 f. I have modified the translation according to Buber, "Referat über jüdische Kunst," *Die Welt* 6, no. 3 (January 17, 1902): 9.

77. Buber, "Address on Jewish Art," 47.

78. Ibid., 51.

79. Ibid., 48 (I have modified the translation).

80. Ibid., 49.

81. Ibid., 59.

82. Ibid., 63 f.

83. Ibid., 64.

84. Buber to Paula Winkler, January 1, 1902, in *Letters,* 81; *Briefwechsel,* 1: 171. In a letter to Paula, written on the eve of the session of the Congress at which he delivered his address on "Jewish Art," Buber reported that "a group of modernists has formed [namely, the Democratic Fraction], and I am one of their intellectual leaders—to phrase it modestly. The ancients (die Alten) are terribly scared of us, for the present more so than is justified. But today we achieved an important agenda victory, which was due chiefly to a very fiery speech by me. . . . Only this one thing more, dearest: This Congress is a turning point. We youngsters are beginning to take things under control." Buber to Paula Winkler, December 26, 1901, in *Letters,* 81.

85. See, among other places, Buber to Herzl, July 24, 1902, in which Buber solicits a contribution to the forthcoming *Jüdischer Almanach,* the inaugural publication of the Jüdischer Verlag: "You cannot be absent from this first modern Zionist anthology" (*Letters,* 83). In his reply, dated August 10, 1902, Herzl tells Buber, "I need not tell you how glad I would be to send you a decent contribution" (*Letters,* 84).

86. While it had been Herzl's wont to address his letters to Buber as "Dear Friend," in response to a letter in which Buber announced that the Democratic Fraction was to organize a conference on Jewish culture in protest of how the Zionist Organization had handled the issue, Herzl would now simply open his letters to Buber with the salutation, "My dear Fellow Zionist." See April 14, 1903, in *Letters,* 91.

87. Nordau, "Ahad Ha-am über Altneuland," *Die Welt* 7, no. 11 (March 13, 1903): 1–5.

88. Ahad Ha'am, "Yalkut Katan," *ha-Shiloah* 10 (December 1902): 566–578; German translation: Ahad Ha'am, "Altneuland," *Ost und West* 3, no. 4 (April 1903): cols. 227–244.

89. Herzl to Buber, May 14, 1903, in *Letters*, 92.

90. Buber to Herzl, May 26, 1903, in *Letters*, 97.

91. Herzl to Buber, May 28, 1903, in *Letters*, 97.

92. Buber to Herzl, May 29, 1903, in *Letters*, 98.

93. In private, Herzl dismissed Buber's conduct as puerile. In a letter to Gershom Scholem, the scholar of Hasidism Joseph Weiss, then living in London, reported that he heard "from people in-the-know and the most veteran Zionists in Vienna, that when a dispute arose between the older Herzl and the young Buber, Herzl angrily said the Buber is not a surname, but rather a 'Komperativ.'" The meaning of *bub* in German is "boy" or "youth," hence "Buber signifies someone who is 'more a boy,' in other words 'childish' or 'childlike.'" Weiss to Scholem, January 6, 1957, in *Gershom Scholem–Joseph Weiss Correspondence, 1948–1964*, ed. Noam Zadoff (Jerusalem: Carmel, 2013).

94. See Barbara Schäfer, "Zur Rolle der 'Demokratischen Fraktion' in der Altneuland-Kontroverse," *Jewish Studies Quarterly* 2 (1995): 292–308.

95. Buber, "Der Jünger," in *Jüdischer Almanach* (Berlin: Jüdischer Verlag, 1902), 168; Buber, "The Disciple," in Buber, *A Believing Humanism, 1902–1965*, trans. and with an introduction by Maurice Friedman (New York: Simon and Schuster, 1967), 40. (I have modified the translation.)

96. On Herzl being someone he had hoped to love, see Buber, "The Magi" in Buber, *A Believing Humanism*, 43.

97. Buber, ed., *Jüdische Künstler* (Berlin: Jüdischer Verlag, 1903). Particularly noteworthy are Buber's introduction to this volume and his essay on the German-Jewish Impressionist painter Lesser Ury. See also his translation from the Yiddish of David Pinski, *Eisik Scheftel. Ein jüdisches Arbeiterdrama* (Berlin: Jüdischer Verlag, 1905).

98. Buber to Weizmann, October 10, 1903, in *Letters*, 103.

99. Buber, "My Way to Hasidism," in *Hasidism and Modern Man*, trans. Maurice Friedman (Atlantic Highlands, N.J.: Humanities Press, 1988), 49.

## Chapter 3. On the Open Seas

*Epigraph:* Buber, *Legend of the Baal-Shem*, trans. Maurice Friedman (London: Routledge, 2002), 23.

1. *Meetings*, 13.

2. Buber to Paula Winkler, August 4, 1900, in *Letters*, 72; *Briefwechsel*, 1: 156.

3. Cf. "Ich tauge nicht zum Stundenmenschen," in ibid.

4. Buber to Paula Winkler, July 26, 1901, in *Letters*, 73; *Briefwechsel*, 1: 159. I have modified the English translation of this letter.

5. Friedrich Nietzsche, *Unzeitgemäße Betrachtungen. Erstes Stück: David Strauss der Bekenner und der Schriftsteller*, ed. Giorgio Colli und Mazzino Montinari, vol. 1, pt. 2 (Munich: De Gruyter, 1999), 169.

6. Buber to Hugo Bergmann, June 29, 1933, in *Letters*, 406.

7. Richard Rorty, *Philosophy as the Mirror of Nature* (Princeton, N.J.: Princeton University Press, 1979), 60.

8. Buber, "Das Problem des Menschen" (1947), in Buber, *Werke Schriften zur Philosophie* (Munich: Kösel, 1962), 1: 317.

9. Cf. Wilhelm Dilthey, "The Understanding of Other Persons and Their Life-Expressions," trans. J. J. Kuehl, in Patrick Gardiner, ed., *Theories of History: Readings in Classical and Contemporary Sources* (New York: Free Press, 1959), 213–225.

10. Buber to Karlfried Gründer, n.d., cited in Gründer, "Wilhelm Diltheys Tod vor fünfundsiebzig Jahren," in *Dilthey-Jahrbuch für Philosophie und Geschichte der Geisteswissenschaften*, vol. 4, ed. Frithjof Rodi (Göttingen: Vandenhoeck & Ruprecht, 1987), 226. I wish to thank Meike Siegfried for bringing this essay to my attention.

11. Wilhelm Dilthey, *Die Entstehung der Hermeneutik (1900)*,

in Dilthey, *Gesammelte Schriften* (Stuttgart: B.G. Teubner, 1987), 320. See also Steven Kepnes, *The Text as Thou: Martin Buber's Dialogical Hermeneutics and Narrative Theology* (Bloomington: Indiana University Press, 1992).

12. Wilhelm Dilthey, *Der junge Dilthey: Ein Lebensbild in Briefen und Tagebüchern, 1852–1870*, ed. C. Misch (née Dilthey), 2nd ed. (Göttingen: Vandenhoeck & Ruprecht, 1960), 140.

13. Ibid., 289.

14. Ibid., 290.

15. Gründer, "Wilhelm Diltheys Tod vor fünfundsiebzig Jahren," 226f; H. P. Rickman, *Wilhelm Dilthey: Pioneer of the Human Sciences* (Berkeley: University of California Press, 1979), 41.

16. Katharina Dilthey to Buber, December 5, 1911; cited in Gründer, "Wilhelm Diltheys Tod vor fünfundsiebzig Jahren," 227.

17. *Buch des Dankes an Georg Simmel. Briefe, Erinnerungen, Bibliographie*, ed. Kurt Gassen and Michael Landmann (Berlin: Duncker & Humbolt, 1958), 233.

18. Hans Simmel, "Auszüge aus den Lebenserinnerungen," in ibid., 256.

19. There are 78 extant letters between Buber and Gertrud Simmel, dating from her husband's death in 1916 to her passing in 1938. See Martin Buber Archive, file 729.

20. Margarete Susman, *Ich habe vielen Leben gelebt. Errinerungen* (Stuttgart: Deutsche Verlags Anstalt, 1962), 53.

21. Ibid., 78.

22. Judah Magnes, "The Seer of Reality in Its Fullness: For Professor Buber on His Seventieth Birthday," *Ner* 15, nos. 10–11 (1948): 20–21 (Hebrew).

23. On Simmel's range of publications, see "Of the 180 articles published in his lifetime in various journals, newspapers, and reviews, only 64 were published in scholarly journals, while 116 appeared in non-scholarly publications destined for a wider cultivated public," Lewis A. Coser, "The Stranger in the Academy," in Coser, ed., *Georg Simmel* (Englewood Cliffs, N.J.: Prentice-Hall, 1965), 34.

24. Georg Simmel to Buber, November 20, 1905, in *Brief-wechsel*, 1: 234.

25. Buber, "Geleitwort," introduction to Werner Sombart, *Das Proletariat* (Frankfurt a.M.: Rütten & Loening, 1906), vol. 1 of *Die Gesellschaft. Sammlung sozialpsychologischer Monographien*, 1: v–vii.

26. Buber, "Elemente des Zwischenmenschlichen," in Buber, *Die Schriften über das dialogische Prinzip* (Heidelberg: Verlag Lambert Schneider, 1954), 276.

27. Georg Simmel, *Die Religion. Die Gesellschaft*, vol. 2 (Frankfurt, a.M.: Rütten & Loening, 1906).

28. Personal communication by Buber's son, Rafael Buber, ca. 1985.

29. Landauer, "Durch Absonderung zur Gemeinschaft," *Das Reich der Erfüllung* (Journal of the Neue Gemeinschaft) 2 (1901): 48.

30. Buber, "Alte und neue Gemeinschaft." The text of this lecture was to be published in the never-realized third issue of *Das Reich der Erfüllung*. It is now available in *Martin Buber Werkausgabe* vol. 2.1: *Mythos und Mystik* (Gütersloh: Güterslohrer Verlagshaus, 2013), 61–66.

31. Ibid.

32. Ibid.

33. Gustav Landauer, *Skepsis und Mystik. Versuche im Anschluss an Mauthners Sprachkritik* (Berlin: F. Fontane, 1903), 69, 78.

34. Erich Mühsam, *Unpolitische Erinnerungen* (Berlin: Aufbau, 1961), 44.

35. *Gustav Landauer. Sein Lebensgang in Briefen*, ed. Martin Buber in collaboration with Ina Britschgi-Schimmer (Frankfurt a.M.: Rütten & Loening, 1929), 1: vi f.

Chapter 4. From Publicist to Author

1. Buber's record of studies at Nationalen Universitäts-archiv, Vienna, is cited in Margaret Olin, *The Nation without Art: Examining the Modern Discourse on Jewish Art* (Lincoln: University of Nebraska Press, 2001), 105.

2. The letter is cited in Hans Kohn, *Martin Buber. Sein Werk und seine Zeit, eine Beitrag zur Geistesgeschichte Mitteleuropas, 1880–1930*, 2nd ed. (Cologne: Joseph Melzer Verlag, 1961), 306. This envisioned volume was never realized.

3. Buber to Chaim Weizmann, December 12, 1902, in *Letters*, 86.

4. Cited in Kohn, *Martin Buber*, 309.

5. Buber, "Die Duse in Florenz," *Die Schaubühne* 1, no. 25 (December 14, 1905): 422–424. Partially translated in Maurice Friedman, *Martin Buber and the Theater* (New York: Funk and Wagnalls, 1969), 10. The "threat of the infinite" so haunted Buber as a lad of fourteen that he contemplated suicide. Cf. Buber, *Between Man and Man*, trans. Maurice Friedman (New York: Macmillan, 1967), 136.

6. Buber to Hugo Bergmann, April 16, 1936, in *Briefwechsel*, 2: 589.

7. Riegel and Wickhoff served as the examiners of Buber's initial and ill-fated doctoral oral in art history. Wickhoff and the classical archaeologist Emil Reisch administered the repeat exam. See Olin, *Nation without Art*, 104 f.

8. The priority he gave to completing *Die Geschichten des Rabbi Nachman* may have also been prompted by a desire to see the volume in print before his gravely ill grandfather passed away.

9. Cited in Kohn, *Martin Buber*, 309 f.

10. Buber to Franz Rosenzweig, May 28, 1925, in *Briefwechsel*, 2: 221. He specifically referred to his foreword to *Die Geschichten des Rabbi Nachman* (1906) and his preface to volume one of *Die Gesellschaft* (1906) as inaugurating his career as an author.

11. Ibid.

12. See Rafael Buber, "Die Buber-Familie. Erinnerungen," in R. Buber, *Dialog mit Martin Buber*, ed. Werner Licharz (Frankfurt a.M.: Haag & Herchen, 1982), 347. Before finding this spacious apartment, Buber and his family lived for a time near Landauer, in the Hermsdorf district of Berlin.

13. A. Frommhold, ed., *Hundertundzehn Jahre Verlag Rütten und Loening: 1848–1954* (Berlin: Rütten und Loening, 1954), 60 f.

14. R. Schmützler, *Art Nouveau*, trans. E. Roditi (New York: Abrams, 1964), 276.

15. Buber to Hugo von Hoffmannstahl, March 15, 1906, in *Letters*, 109 f. (emphasis added).

16. Buber to Horodetsky, July 7, 1906, in *Briefwechsel*, 1: 104 (emphasis added). On Landauer's "translation," see Chapter 3.

17. Dubnow to Buber, February 17, 1907, in *Briefwechsel*, 1: 253.

18. Buber, "My Way to Hasidism," in Buber, *Hasidism and Modern Man*, ed. and trans. Maurice Friedman (Atlantic Highlands, N.J.: Humanities Press, 1988), 53–55.

19. Buber, "Hasidism and Modern Man," in Buber, *Hasidism and Modern Man*, 14.

20. Ibid., 16.

21. "Weisst Du es Noch . . . ?" was inscribed in the copy of *Erzählung der Chassidim* (Zürich: Manesse-Bibliothek der Weltliteratur, 1949) that Buber gave Paula. Translated in Buber, *A Believing Humanism: My Testament, 1902–1965*, ed. Maurice Friedman (New York: Simon and Schuster, 1967), 50–51.

22. Cited without noting to whom it was addressed, in Kohn, *Martin Buber*, 310 (emphasis added).

23. Introduction to *The Legend of the Baal-Shem*, trans. M. Friedman (New York: Schocken, 1955), 13.

24. Buber, ed., *Jüdische Kunstler* (Berlin: Jüdischer Verlag, 1903), 5.

25. Ibid.

26. David Pinski, *Eisik Schafter. Ein jüdisches Arbeiterdarma in Drei Akten: Autorisierte Übertragung aud dem jüdischen Manuskript von Martin Büber* (Berlin: Jüdischer Verlag, 1903), 1 f.

27. Ibid.

28. Buber, "My Way to Hasidism," 48–49.

29. Buber to Paula Winkler, May 14, 1900, in *Briefwechsel*, 1: 155 f.

30. Ibid.

31. See, for instance, Salomon Buber to Martin Buber, November 26, 1906, in *Briefwechsel*, 1: 248.

32. Moshe Hayyim Ephraim Bloch, "Martin Buber and His Fathers." *Ha-Doar* 45 (August 20, 1965): 632 (Hebrew).

33. Salomon Buber to Martin Buber, February 5, 1905, translated from Yiddish in *Briefwechsel*, 1: 229.

34. Ibid.

35. Carl Buber to Martin Buber, February 6, 1908, in *Letters*, 114.

36. Buber to Eugen Diederichs, June 16, 1907, in *Briefwechsel*, 1: 256.

37. Buber to Eugen Diederichs, June 20, 1907, in *Briefwechsel*, 1: 257.

38. Cf. "Das Ganze hat für mich einen durchaus episodischen Charakter und kann ebensogut warten oder ganz unterbleiben." Buber to Eugen Diederichs, June 20, 1907, in *Briefwechsel*, 1: 257.

39. Cited in Paul Mendes-Flohr, *Ecstatic Confessions: The Heart of Mysticism*, trans. E. Cameron (San Francisco: Harper and Row, 1985), 1–11.

40. Georg Simmel, *Verhandlungen des ersten deutschen Soziologentages von 19–23 Oktober 1910* (Tübingen: Schriften der deutschen Gesellschaft für Soziologie, 1911), 206–207.

41. Editor's "Foreword," in Buber, *Pointing the Way: Collected Essays*, trans. and ed. Maurice S. Friedman (New York: Schocken, 1957), ix.

42. Buber, *The Legend of the Baal-Shem*, 11.

43. Ibid.

44. In 1910 the volume was published in Leipzig by Insel Verlag.

45. Reminiscence of Rafael Buber related to me in a personal conversation, ca. 1985. See also Jonathan R. Herman, "The Mysterious Mr. Wang: The Search for Martin Buber's Confucian Ghostwriter," *Journal of Chinese Religions* 37 (2009): 73–79.

46. The Chinese ghost and love stories were published in 1911 in Frankfurt by Rütten & Loening.

47. Buber to Landauer, September 1912, Martin Buber Archive, file 62d.

48. Cited by Martin Treml in his commentary to the critical

edition of *Daniel*, in *Martin Buber: Frühe kulturkritische und philoso-phische Schriften, 1891–1924* (Gütersloh: Gütersloher Verlagshaus, 2001), 319.

49. Cited by Treml in his introduction to Buber, *Daniel*; ibid., 66.

50. Buber, *Daniel*, 56 (emphasis added).

51. Ibid., 53 f. (German text: 186).

52. Ibid., 54 f.

53. Ibid., 59 (German text: 190).

54. Ibid., 133.

55. See Chapter 1.

56. Buber, *Daniel*, 134.

57. Ibid., 135.

58. *Annale de l'Université de Paris, 28 Année* 4 (1958): 503 f.

59. Gustav Landauer to Buber, July 27, 1912, in *Briefwechsel*, 1: 306.

60. Friedrich Nietzsche, *Die Geburt der Tragödie* (N.p., 1872), paras. 17 and 23.

61. "Martin Buber," *Neue Blätter des Festspielhaus Hellerau* 3, nos. 1–2 ("Buber Heft") (1913): 90–107; reprinted in *Gustav Landauer. Werkausgabe*, vol. 3: *Dichter, Ketzer, Außenseiter. Essays und Reden zu Literatur, Philosophie, Judentum*, ed. Hanna Delf (Berlin: Akademie Verlag, 1997), 165.

62. Ibid.

63. Rainer Maria Rilke, *Briefe an seine Verleger* (Leipzig: Insel, 1934), 180, 182.

64. Gershom Scholem to Erich Brauer, November 3, 1917, in Gershom Scholem, *Briefe*, vol. 1: *1914–1917*, ed. Itta Schedletzky (Munich: C.H. Beck, 1994), 122 (emphasis added).

## Chapter 5. Prague

1. Quotations in this and the following paragraph are from Leo Herrmann to Buber, November 14, 1908, in *Letters*, 118 f.; *Briefwechsel*, 1: 268 f.

2. Letter, dated Christmas 1905, cited without noting to whom it was addressed by Hans Kohn in his biography *Martin*

*Buber. Sein Werk und seine Zeit, eine Beitrag zur Geistesgeschichte Mitteleuropas, 1880–1930,* 2nd ed. (Cologne: Joseph Melzer Verlag, 1961), 309.

3. Buber, "My Way to Hasidism," in *Hasidism and Modern Man,* trans. M. Friedman (Atlantic Highlands, N.J.: Humanities Press, 1988), 20 f.

4. Buber, "Drei Stationen (1929)," in Buber, *Kampf um Israel. Reden und Schriften, 1921–1932* (Berlin: Schocken Verlag, 1933), 223 f. On the third stage, see Chapter 7. The third stage would be marked by the affirmation of a transcendent God whom one "meets"—as opposed to "experiences"—in response to His address.

5. Buber's note to Hermann, "Forty-Five Years Ago," in *Prague and Jerusalem: A Book in Memory of Leo Herrmann,* ed. Felix Weltsch (Jerusalem: Keren Ha-Yesod, n.d. [1955]), 143 (Hebrew).

6. Ibid.

7. Gershom Scholem, "Martin Buber," *Haaretz,* February 6, 1953; reprinted in *Dvarim be-Go,* ed. Avraham Shapira (Tel Aviv: Am Oved, 1976), 456 f. (Hebrew).

8. Buber, "Forty-Five Years Ago."

9. Ibid.

10. Ibid., 78.

11. Kafka to Felice, January 16 and 19, 1913, in *Letters to Felice,* ed. Erich Heller and Jürgen Bore (New York: Schocken, 1973), 157, 161. In the letter to Felice, Kafka was actually referring to a lecture, "Myth in Judaism," that Buber delivered after the publication of *Drei Reden,* which he also attended.

12. *Martin Buber Werkausgabe,* vol. 3: *Frühe jüdische Schriften, 1900–1922,* ed. and introduced with commentary by Barbara Schäfer (Gütersloh: Gütersloher Verlagshaus, 2007), 415.

13. Hermann, "Aus Tagebuchblättern," *Der Jude. Sonderhaft zu Bubers 50. Geburtstag* (special edition for Buber's fiftieth birthday) (1928): 161.

14. Buber, "Erneuerung des Judentums," in *Martin Buber Werkausgabe,* 3: 240.

15. Ibid., 244; Buber, "Renewal of Judaism," in Buber, *On*

*Judaism,* ed. Nahum N. Glatzer, trans. Eva Jospe (New York: Schocken, 1967), 34 f.

16. Buber, "Renewal of Judaism," 34.

17. Buber, "Erneuerung des Judentums," 3: 238.

18. Buber, "Renewal of Judaism," 35; ibid.

19. Buber, "Judaism and Mankind" (second of the three addresses), in Buber, *On Judaism,* 27.

20. Buber, "Renewal of Judaism," 36; Buber, "Erneuerung des Judentums," 3: 239.

21. Buber, "Judaism and the Jews" (first of the three addresses), in Buber, *On Judaism,* 17.

22. Ibid., 19.

23. Cited ibid. Heimann was the leading spirit of Berlin's *Donnestagsgesellschaft,* an open discussion group which met on Thursday mornings at a café on Berlin's fashionable Kurfürstendamm. In addition to Buber, its members included, among others, the Hebrew writer Micha Joseph Berdyczewski; the artists Emil Orlik and E. R. Weiß; the writers Gerhard Hauptmann, Emil Strauß, and Alfred Mombert; and Walter Rathenau. See Kohn, *Martin Buber,* 313.

24. Buber, "Judaism and the Jews," 19.

25. Richard Beer-Hofmann, *Gesammelte Werke* (Frankfurt a.M.: Fischer Verlag, 1963), 654 (emphasis in original).

26. Buber, "Judaism and the Jews," 13.

27. Buber, "Renewal of Judaism," 39.

28. Ibid.

29. Buber, "Judaism and Mankind," 31.

30. Buber, "Judaism and the Jews," 19–20 (emphasis in original).

31. The lectures were, namely, "Myth in Judaism" (January 16, 1913) and "Jewish Religiosity" (May 3, 1914). See Buber to Elijahu Rapperport, May 6, 1914, in which Buber cites the latter as the most important of his Prague lectures; in *Briefwechsel,* 1: 359. Cf. "Buber's connection with the Bar Kochba Zionist Student Association of Prague lasted over many years and was for both of utmost significance. . . . For the thoroughly assimilated West Euro-

peanJewish youth who joined the Bar Kochba, Buber became their guide to Judaism, a teacher who broadened their spiritual life and spurred them to [plumb] its depth." Kohn, *Martin Buber*, 90.

32. Hans Kohn, "Geleitwort," in *Vom Judentum. Ein Sammelbuch vom Verein Jüdischer Hochschüler Bar Kochba in Prag* (Leipzig: Kurt Wolff Verlag, 1913), viii.

33. Ibid., vi.

34. Ibid., viii.

35. The essay was first published posthumously in Franz Rosenzweig, *Kleinere Schriften* (Berlin: Schocken Verlag, 1937), 278–290.

36. Kohn, *Martin Buber*, ch. 2.

37. Buber, "Elements of the Inter-Human," trans. R. G. Smith, in Buber, *Knowledge of Man. Selected Essays*, ed. Maurice Friedman (New York: Harper and Row, 1965), 86 f.; Buber, "Elemente des Zwischenmenschlichen," in Buber, *Das dialogische Prinzip* (Heidelberg: Verlag Lambert Schneider, 1979), 295 (I have emended the translation slightly).

38. Buber to Frederik van Eeden, April 3, 1930, in *Briefwechsel*, 2: 369 f.

39. Excerpt from Frederik van Eeden's diary cited in *Praemium Erasmianum, MCM-LXIII, Inveniemus Viam Aut Faciemus* (Amsterdam, 1963), 86 f.

40. "Dialogue," in Buber, *Between Man and Man*, trans. R. G. Smith, introduction by Maurice Friedman (New York: Macmillan, 1965), 5 ff.

41. Ibid.

42. Florens Christian Rang to van Eeden, August 24, 1914, cited in Christine Holste, "Menschen von Potsdam—der Forte-Kreis (1910–1915)," in *Der Postdamer Forte-Kreis. Eine utopische Intellektuellenassozation zur europäischen Friedenssicherung*, ed. Richard Faber and Christine Holse (Würzburg: Königshausen & Neumann, 2001), 23.

43. Florens Christian Rang to Buber, September 18, 1914, continued September 21, 1914, in *Letters*, 157–159 (I have emended the translation).

44. Buber to Hans Kohn, September 30, 1914, in *Letters*, 160.

45. Georg Simmel to Margarete Susman, September 21, 1914, cited in *Auf gesplatenem Pfad. Ein Festschrift zum neunzigsten Geburtstag Margarete Susman*, ed. Manfred Schlösser (Darmstadt: Erato-Presse, 1964), 308 f.

46. Frederik van Eeden sent, in fact, two circular letters, dated August 10 and September 19, 1914, respectively. To the latter, he attached a German-language article that he had published in a Dutch newspaper: "Offener Brief an unsere deutschen Freunde," *De Amsterdammer: Weekblad voor Nederland*, September 1, 1914.

47. Buber to Frederik van Eeden, October 16, 1914, in *Letters*, 164.

48. Buber, *Daniel: Dialogues on Realization*, trans. Maurice Friedman (New York: Holt, Rinehart and Winston, 1964), 115 f.

49. Buber to van Eeden, October 16, 1914, 165.

50. Ibid.

51. Ibid., 163.

52. Ibid., 165.

53. Ibid.

54. Ibid., 164.

55. Buber, "Richtung soll kommen," *Masken* 10, no. 11 (1915): 173.

56. Buber, "Bewegung: Aus einem Brief an einen Holländer," *Der neue Merkur* 1, nos. 10–11 (1915): 491.

57. Buber to Frederik van Eeden, October 16, 1914, in *Letters*, 165.

58. Ibid.

59. Buber to Gustav Landauer, October 18, 1914, in *Letters*, 167.

60. Gustav Landauer and Buber to Forte Circle, end of November 1914, in *Letters*, 167–168.

61. Buber to Frederik van Eeden, September 8, 1915, in *Letters*, 177–178.

62. Martin Buber to Paula Buber, September 8, 1915, in *Letters*, 177.

63. Martin Buber to Paula Buber, September 10, 1915, in *Letters*, 178 f. (The translation has been slightly modified.)

64. Gustav Landauer to Buber, May 14, 1916, in *Letters*, 188–192.

65. Buber, "Der Geist des Orients und das Judentum," in *Vom Geist des Judentums* (Leipzig: Kurt Wolff, 1916), 47–48. In the second edition of this volume, published after the war in 1919, this passage is deleted.

66. Landauer to Buber, *Letters*, May 14, 1916, 189 (emphasis added).

67. Gustav Landauer to Hedwig Lachmann (Landauer), April 3, 1915, in *Landauer: Sein Lebensgang in Briefen*, ed. M. Buber (Frankfurt a.M.: Rütten & Loening, 1929), 2: 63 f.

68. Buber, "Zum Gedächtnis" (1915), in Buber, *Jüdische Bewegung. Gesammelte Aufsätze und Ansprachen, 1900–1915*, 1st ed. (Berlin: Jüdischer Verlag, 1916), 1: 248.

69. "Tempelweihe," in *Jüdischer Rundschau* 10-11 (January 1915): 73–74; reprinted in Buber, *Jüdische Bewegung*, 1: 232.

70. Ibid., 1: 236 f.

71. Ibid., 1: 242.

72. Ibid., 1: 241.

73. Ibid., 1: 238.

74. Ibid., 1: 240.

75. Ibid., 1: 241.

76. "Die Losung," *Der Jude* 1, no. 1 (April 1916): 2; reprinted in Buber, *Jüdische Bewegung*, 2: 7-15.

77. Gustav Landauer to Buber, May 12, 1916, in *Letters*, 190.

78. Ibid.

79. Ibid., 191.

80. "An die Prager Freunde," in *Das Jüdische Prag. Eine Sammelschrift* (Prague: Selbstwehr Verlag, 1917); reprinted in Buber, *Jüdische Bewegung*, 2: 74.

81. Ibid.

## Chapter 6. Heir to Landauer's Legacy

1. Buber to Moritz Goldstein, February 4, 1917, in *Briefwechsel*, 1: 207.

2. Stefan Zweig to Buber, undated but presumably at the end of January 1918, in *Briefwechsel*, 1: 524 f.

3. Buber to Stefan Zweig, February 4, 1918, in *Briefwechsel*, 1: 525 f. (emphasis added).

4. Buber to Hugo Bergmann, February 3, 1918, in *Briefwechsel*, 1: 526 f.

5. Ibid.

6. Shmuel Yosef Agnon, *Me'Atzmi el'Atzmi* (Tel Aviv: Schocken, 1965), 271 (Hebrew).

7. Ibid., 272.

8. On the concept of the *Endziel* and its role in the ideological discourse of the pre-state Zionism, see Ben Halpern, *The Idea of the Jewish State*, 2nd ed. (Cambridge, Mass.: Harvard University Press, 1969).

9. Buber, "Begriffe und Wirklichkeit. Brief an Hermann Cohen," *Der Jude* 1, no. 5 (August 1916), reprinted in *Martin Buber Werkausgabe*, vol. 3: *Frühe jüdische Schriften, 1900–1922*, ed. Barbara Schäfer (Güterslohr: Güterslohrer Verlaghaus, 2007), 300 (emphasis in original).

10. Ibid., 303 (emphasis added).

11. Gustav Landauer, "Sind das Ketzergedanken?" in *Vom Judentum: Ein Sammelbuch* (Leipzig, 1913): 250–257.

12. Buber to Gustav Landauer, October 15, 1916, in *Letters*, 200.

13. Buber, "Unser Nationalismus," *Der Jude* 2, nos. 1–2 (April/May 1917): 3.

14. Cited in Hans Kohn, *Martin Buber. Sein Werk und seine Zeit, eine Beitrag zur Geistesgeschichte Mitteleuropas, 1880–1930*, 2nd ed. (Cologne: Joseph Melzer Verlag, 1961), 46.

15. See Eleonore Lappin, *Der Jude, 1916–1928. Jüdische Moderne zwischen Universalismus und Partikularismus* (Tübingen: Mohr Siebeck, 2000), 22–30.

16. Personal communication by Rafael Buber, ca. 1985.

17. Gershom Scholem, "Jüdische Jugendbewegung," *Der Jude* 1, no. 20 (June 1916): 822–825.

18. Walter Benjamin to Buber, July 1916, in *Letters*, 197.

19. Cf. "Scholem remembers that 'Buber made an angry remark about [Benjamin's] letter . . . when we once met in the winter of 1916." Cited in Howard Eiland and Michael W. Jennings, *Walter Benjamin: A Critical Life* (Cambridge, Mass.: Harvard University Press, 2014), 689, n. 15.

20. Franz Kafka to Buber, November 29, 1915, in *Letters*, 182.

21. Franz Kafka to Buber, May 12, 1917, in *Letters*, 217. The two stories—"Jackals and Arabs" and "A Report to the Academy"—appeared respectively in the October and November 1917 issues of *Der Jude*.

22. "Kulturarbeit," *Der Jude* 1, no. 12 (March 1917): 792–793 (emphasis added).

23. Buber, "Gustav Landauer," *Die Zeit* (Vienna), June 11, 1904, 127 f.

24. Gustav Landauer to Buber, January 1917, Martin Buber Archive, file 184/1.

25. Lotte, as Landauer affectionately called her, was the offspring of his first marriage. See Buber, "Gedenkworte zu Charlotte Landauer-Kornstein," August 16, 1927, Karlsruhe, and "16 August 1927," Martin Buber Archive, both in file *bei* 70.

26. Julius Bab, *Gustav Landauer. Gedächtnis eines einsamen Revolutionäre* (Leipzig: Rütten & Loening, 1929), 10.

27. Gustav Landauer, "Die Legende des Baal-Schem," *Das literaratische Echo* 13, no. 2 (October 1, 1919): 148.

28. Gustav Landauer to Buber, May 10, 1918, in *Letters*, 231.

29. For the anthology, see Hedwig Lachmann, *Gesammelte Gedichte: Eigenes und Nachdichtugen* (Potsdam: Gustav Keipenheuer Verlag, 1919).

30. Gustav Landauer to Hans Franck, August 29, 1918, in *Gustav Landauer. Sein Lebensgang in Briefen*, ed. Martin Buber (Frankfurt a.M.: Rütten & Loening, 1929), 2: 261.

31. Cf. Gustav Landauer to Auguste Hauschner, July 22, 1918, in *Gustav Landauer. Sein Lebensgang in Briefen*, 2: 252.

32. Gustav Landauer to Fritz Mauthner, October 22, 1918, in *Gustav Landauer. Sein Lebensgang in Briefen*, 2: 286.

33. Kurt Eisner to Landauer, November 11, 1918, in *Gustav Landauer. Sein Lebensgang in Briefen*, 2: 296, fn. 1.

34. Gustav Landauer to Buber, November 15, 1918, in *Letters*, 232.

35. Gustav Landauer to Buber, November 22, 1918, in *Letters*, 234.

36. Buber, "Recollection of a Death," in Buber, *Pointing the Way. Collected Essays*, trans. Maurice Friedman (New York: Harper and Brothers, 1957), 119.

37. Buber to Ludwig Strauss, February 22, 1919, in *Letters*, 242.

38. Ibid.

39. Bab, *Gustav Landauer*, 15.

40. Else Eisner to Ina Britschigi-Schimmer, March 27, 1927, cited in Ulrich Linse, "'Poetic Anarchism' versus 'Party Anarchism': Gustav Landauer and the Anarchist Movement in Wilhelmian Germany," in Paul Mendes-Flohr and Anya Mali, eds., in collaboration with Hanna Delf von Wolzogen, *Gustav Landauer: Anarchist and Jew* (Berlin: Walter de Gruyter, 2015), 58.

41. Buber, "Landauer und die Revolution," *Masken: Halbmonatschrift des Düsseldorfer Schauspielhauses* 14, nos. 18–19 (1919): 291. The frontispiece of this edition of the journal reproduces a full-color photograph of the Brescia mural.

42. From an undated conversation between Grete Schaeder and Buber; introduction to *Letters*, 24.

43. Gustav Landauer's unpublished testament, dated February 22, 1918, can be found in the Martin Buber Archive, file 432/169.

44. Ibid.

45. Gustav Landauer, *Der werdende Mensch: Aufsätze über Leben und Schriftum*, ed. M. Buber (Potsdam: Kiepenheuer, 1921); Gustav Landauer, *Beginnen: Aufsätze über Sozialismus* (Köln: Marcan-Block, 1924); Gustav Landauer, *Sein Lebensgang in Briefen*, ed. M. Buber in collaboration with Ina Britschgi-Schimmer, 2 vols. (Frankfurt a.M.: Rütten & Loening, 1929).

46. See Martin Buber, *Der heilige Weg* (Frankfurt, 1919);

"Landauer und die Revolution," *Masken* 16, nos. 28–29 (1919): 282–291; "Der heimliche Führer," *Die Arbeit* 2, no. 6 (1920), 36–37; "Erinnerung an einen Tod," *Neue Wege* 23, no. 2 (1929): 161–165; and the chapter on Landauer in Buber, *Paths in Utopia* (London: R. F. C. Hull, 1949). Buber also published several essays on Landauer in Hebrew. On Landauer's philosophy, see also Ruth Link-Salinger (Hyman), *Gustav Landauer: Philosopher of Utopia* (Indianapolis: Hackett, 1977), 52–54; and Eugene Lunn, *Prophet of Community: The Romantic Socialism of Gustav Landauer* (Berkeley: University of California Press, 1973), 251–252, 271–273.

47. Martin Buber, *Der Heilige Weg. Ein Worter an die Juden und an die Völker* (Frankfurt a.M.: Rütten & Loening, 1919).

48. Buber, "The Holy Way," trans. in Buber, *On Judaism*, ed. Nahum N. Glatzer (New York: Schocken, 1967), 112.

49. Ibid., 113.

50. Ibid., 108 f.

51. Ibid., 110.

52. Ibid.

53. Ibid., 134–135.

54. Ibid., 136.

55. Ibid., 141.

56. Buber to Siegmund Kaznelson, July 9, 1917, in *Briefwechsel*, 1: 502.

57. Buber to Robert Weltsch, June 14, 1920, in *Letters*, 254.

58. Buber to S. H. Bergmann, January 21, 1919, in *Letters*, 241 f.

Chapter 7. A Reverential *Apikoros*

*Epigraph:* Adele Rosenzweig to Martin Buber, February 2, 1928 (on the occasion of Buber's fiftieth birthday), Martin Buber Archive, file 635.

1. Franz Rosenzweig, *Zeit ists. Gedanken über das jüdische Bildungsproblem des Augenblicks* (Berlin, 1917); Franz Rosenzweig, "It Is Time: Concerning the Study of Judaism," in Rosenzweig,

*On Jewish Learning*, ed. Nahum N. Glatzer (New York: Schocken, 1965), 27–54; see Rosenzweig to Buber, undated, in *Letters*, 247.

2. Franz Rosenzweig, *Kleinere Schriften*, ed. Edith Rosenzweig (Berlin: Schocken Verlag, 1937), 278–290.

3. Franz Rosenzweig to Buber, undated, presumably at the end of August 1919, *Letters*, 247 f.

4. Ibid.

5. Ernst Simon to Buber, October 18, 1921, in *Letters*, 260 f.

6. Franz Rosenzweig to Rudolf Hallo, beginning of 1922, in Rosenzweig, *Briefe und Tagebücher* (The Hague: Martinus Nijhoff, 1979), 2: 864.

7. At the time, "conservative Judaism" referred to orthodox congregations in Germany that remained in the organized Jewish community and did not follow those that withdrew to establish a separate orthodox community, the so-called *Austrittsgemeinde*.

8. Rosenzweig to Hallo, beginning of 1922.

9. Ibid.

10. Ibid., 865.

11. Buber to Franz Rosenzweig, December 8, 1921, in *Letters*, 262.

12. Franz Rosenzweig to Buber, January 25, 1922, in *Letters*, 264.

13. Ibid.

14. Buber to Franz Rosenzweig, September 28, 1922, in *Letters*, 288; Rosenzweig, *Briefe und Tagebücher*, 2: 830 f.

15. Buber to Franz Rosenzweig, September 29, 1922, in Rosenzweig, *Briefe und Tagebücher*, 2: 831.

16. As Rosenzweig put it, "Das Sprechen werde ich ihn in Frankfurt richtig lehren." See Franz Rosenzweig to Edith Rosenzweig, January 1, 1922, in Rosenzweig, *Briefe und Tagebücher*, 2: 737.

17. The comments by Simon here and in the next paragraph are from Ernst Simon to Buber, November 2, 1923, in *Letters*, 306–310.

18. Buber to Franz Rosenzweig, November 14, 1923, in *Letters*, 310.

19. Franz Rosenzweig to Buber, November 20, 1923, in Rosenzweig, *Briefe und Tagebücher*, 2: 930 f.

20. Buber to Rosenzweig, September 14, 1922, in *Letters*, 280.

21. Rosenzweig to Buber, undated letter, in *Letters*, 280.

22. Buber, "Religion as Presence," trans. Esther Cameron, in Rivka Horwitz, *Buber's Way to "I and Thou": The Development of Martin Buber's Thought and His "Religion of Presence" Lectures* (Philadelphia: Jewish Publication Society, 1988), 31.

23. Ibid., 51, 33.

24. Ibid., 31.

25. Ibid., 32.

26. Ibid., 131.

27. Franz Rosenzweig, *The Star of Redemption*, trans. William Halloin (New York: Holt, Rinehart and Winston, 1970), 205. On the underlining of Buber's copy, see Horwitz, *Buber's Way to "I and Thou,"* 131, fn. 17.

28. Buber and Rosenzweig, *Die Schrift und ihre Verdeutschung* (Berlin: Schocken, 1936), 64.

29. Buber to Gustav Landauer, August 9, 1913, *Letters*, 150.

30. Buber, "Religion und Gottesherrschaft," *Frankfurter Zeitung*, April 27, 1923; "Religion in God's Rule," in Buber, *A Believing Humanism: My Testament, 1902–1965*, trans. M. Friedman (New York: Simon and Schuster, 1967), 110 f.

31. "Preface to the 1923 Edition" of Buber's "Early Addresses on Judaism (1909–1918)," in Buber, *On Judaism*, ed. Nahum N. Glatzer, trans. Eva Jospe (New York: Schocken Books, 1967), 3–10.

32. As Buber explained it, the concept of meeting (or encounter) arose "on the road of my thinking out of criticism of the concept of *Erlebnis*, to which I adhered in my youth, hence out of radical self-correction. '*Erlebnis*' belongs to the exclusive, individualized psychic sphere. . . . The psychological reduction of being, its psychologizing, had a destructive effect on me in my youth because it removed from me the foundation of human reality, the 'to-one-another.' Only much later . . . did I win a reality that cannot be lost." See Buber, "Replies to My Critics," in *The Philosophy of Martin Buber*, part of the *Library of Living Philosophers*,

NOTES TO PAGES 143–150

vol. 12, ed. Paul Arthur Schlipp and Maurice Friedman (La Salle, Ill.: Open Court, 1967), 711 f.

33. Buber, "Religion as Presence," 112.

34. Buber, "Preface of 1923," 6.

35. Buber, "Religion as Presence," 89.

36. Buber, "Replies to My Critics," 693.

37. J. L. Borges, *This Craft of Verse: The Charles Eliot Norton Lectures, 1967–1968* (Cambridge: Harvard University Press, 2000), 31 f.

38. Franz Rosenzweig, "The New Thinking" (1925), cited in *Franz Rosenzweig: His Life and Thought*, ed. Nahum N. Glatzer, 3rd ed. (Indianapolis: Hackett, 1998), 199 f.

39. Ibid., 197.

40. Franz Rosenzweig, diary entry, December 9, 1906, cited in ibid.; Rosenzweig, *Briefe und Tagebücher*, 1: 67.

41. Franz Rosenzweig to Gertrud Oppenheim, August 29, 1922, cited in *Franz Rosenzweig*, 116 f.

42. Buber, "Rosenzweig und Existenz," *Mitteilungsblatt des "Irgun Olej Merkaz Europa"* (Tel Aviv), December 28, 1956.

43. Franz Rosenzweig to Buber, August 19, 1922, in *Letters*, 271.

44. Franz Rosenzweig to Eugen Mayer, January 23, 1923; Rosenzweig, *Briefe und Tagebücher*, 2: 883.

45. Franz Rosenzweig to Buber, January 12, 1923, in Rosenzweig, *Briefe und Tagebücher*, 2: 878–881 (partially translated in *Franz Rosenzweig*, 127 f.).

46. Ibid.

47. Ibid.

48. Buber to Rosenzweig, undated, but before January 18, 1923, in *Letters*, 296.

49. Buber, *Reden über das Judentum* (Frankfurt a.M.: Rütten & Loening, 1923).

50. Gershom Scholem, September 10, 1916, in Scholem, *Tagebücher, 1913–1917*, ed. K. Gründer and F. Niewöhner (Frankfurt a.M.: Jüdischer Verlag, 1995), 1: 397 f.

51. Buber, "Jüdisches leben," *Jerubaal* 1, nos. 1–2 (April 1918):

NOTES TO PAGES 151–157

1–8, 45–49, reprinted in *Martin Buber Werkausgabe*, vol. 8: *Schriften zu Jugend, Erziehung und Bildung*, ed. Juliane Jacobi (Gütersloh: Gütersloher Verlaghaus, 2005), 93–103.

52. Buber, "Herut: On Jewish Youth and Religion," trans. in Buber, *On Judaism*, ed. Nahum N. Glatzer (New York: Schocken, 1967), 149–174.

53. Ibid.

54. Ibid.

55. Babylonian Talmud, *Brakhot*, 64.

56. Franz Rosenzweig, "Die Bauleute," *Der Jude* (August 1924). The essay was actually written the previous summer. In the fall of 1925 it was published as a brochure.

57. Ibid.

58. Ibid.

59. See Buber, "Offenbarung und Gesetz," *Almanach des Schocken Verlag auf das Jahr 5697* (1936/1937). The correspondence is translated in Rosenzweig, *On Jewish Learning*, 109–118.

60. Buber to Franz Rosenzweig, October 1, 1922, in *Letters*, 290.

61. Ibid.

62. Buber to Franz Rosenzweig, June 3, 1925, in *Letters*, 327.

63. Published in serial form in the Hebrew daily *Davar* from November 23, 1941, to January 10, 1942.

64. Buber, *For the Sake of Heaven: A Chronicle*, a translation of the German version of *Gog and Magog* by Ludwig Lewisohn (Philadelphia: Jewish Publication Society, 1953), x.

65. Ibid., 101.

66. Ibid.

67. Ibid., 102.

68. Ibid., 103.

69. Ibid.

70. Lambert Schneider, "Meine erste Begegnung mit Martin Buber," in *75 Jahre Sachse & Heinzelmann. Ein kleiner Almanach zum 1. November 1955*, ed. Margarete Jockush (Hanover: Buchhandlung Sachse & Heinzelmann, 1955), 21–24.

71. Ibid.

72. Ibid.

73. Cited in *Franz Rosenzweig*, 149.

74. Ibid.

75. Nahum N. Glatzer (1903–1990) served as Rosenzweig's and Buber's research assistant in identifying and collecting the classical Jewish commentaries on given biblical passages. Personal communication, spring 1985.

76. Buber to Franz Rosenzweig, September 21, 1925, in Glatzer, *Franz Rosenzweig*, 151.

77. Undated letter, cited in Buber, "Aus den Anfangen unserer Schriftübersetzung," in Buber and Rosenzweig, *Die Schrift und ihre Verdeutschung* (Berlin: Schocken Verlag, 1936), 328.

78. Franz Rosenzweig to Buber, September 29, 1925, in *Letters*, 334.

79. Cf. Buber's translation of Psalm 40:8 ("zu deinen Willen, mein Gott, begehre ich, deine Weisung ist mir drinnen im Eingeweid") to Luther's: "Deinen Willen, mein Gott, thu ich gerne, und deinen Gesetz hab ich in meinem Herzen."

80. Franz Rosenzweig to Buber, "end of December 1926," cited in *Franz Rosenzweig*, 155.

81. Wilhelm Michel, *Martin Buber. Sein Gang in der Wirklichkeit* (Frankfurt a.M.: Rütten & Loening, 1925), 12.

## Chapter 8. The Tragic Grace of Everyday Reality

1. Buber, "Drei Stationen," *Judisk Tidskrift* (Stockholm) (June 27, 1929): 20; reprinted in Buber, *Kampf um Israel: Reden und Schriften, 1921–1932* (Berlin: Schocken Verlag, 1933), 223.

2. Ibid.

3. Wilhelm Michel, *Martin Buber: Sein Gang in die Wirklichkeit* (Frankfurt a.M.: Rütten & Loening, 1925), 12.

4. Registered November 26, 1935. Private archive of the Martin Buber Literary Estate.

5. Buber to Thomas Mann, September 30, 1941, in *Briefwechsel*, 3: 47–49.

6. Thomas Mann to Buber, December 14, 1941, in *Briefwechsel*, 3: 55.

7. It was subsequently published in German in 1953 by Lambert Schneider Verlag of Heidelberg.

8. Ernst Bloch, *Geist der Utopie*, 2nd ed. (Berlin: Paul Cassirer, 1923), 330.

9. Martin Buber Archive, file *heh* 22.

10. Rosenzweig to Buber, March 19, 1924, in *Letters*, 311.

11. Rosenzweig, "Apologetisches Denken," *Der Jude* 7 (1923): 460.

12. Of the ninety classes held at the Lehrhaus from 1920 to 1926, approximately one-third were on Christianity.

13. Buber, "Bericht und Berichtung," *Der Jude*, special edition: *Judentum und Deutschtum* (1926): 87.

14. Franz Rosenzweig to Buber, July 27, 1925, in *Briefwechsel*, 2: 232.

15. Buber, "Dis Schrift und ihre Verdeutschung," in Buber, *Werke*, vol. 2: *Schriften zur Bibel* (Munich: Kösel, 1964), 1182.

16. Buber, "Die Mächtigkeit des Geistes," lecture delivered at the Frankfurt Lehrhaus, available in English as "The Power of the Spirit," in Buber, *Israel and the World: Essays in a Time of Crisis*, trans. Olga Marx et al. (New York: Schocken, 1948), 180 ff.

17. Cf. Howard Eiland and Michael W. Jennings, *Walter Benjamin: A Critical Life* (Cambridge, Mass.: Belknap, 2014), 155.

18. Florens Rang to Buber, March 14, 1924, in *Briefwechsel*, 2: 187 (emphasis in original).

19. Lambert Schneider to Buber, June 19, 1925, in *Briefwechsel*, 2: 223 f.

20. Viktor von Weizsäcker, "Begegnungen und Entscheidungen," in *Gesammelte Schriften*, ed. P. Achilles et al. (Frankfurt a.M.: Suhrkamp, 1986), 1: 213.

21. "Vorwort," *Die Kreatur* 1, no. 1 (1926). Although composed by Buber, the editorial preface was signed also by Wittig and Weizsäcker.

22. Buber, "Zwiesprache," *Die Kreatur* 3, no. 3 (1929): 222.

23. Walter Benjamin to Buber, February 23, 1927, in *Letters*, 350.

24. Walter Benjamin to Buber, July 26, 1927, in *Letters*, 351 f.

The article was Walter Benjamin, "Moskau," *Die Kreatur* 2 (1927–1928): 71 ff.

25. Buber, "The Spirit of Israel and the World of Today," in Buber, *Israel and the World*, 192.

26. K. L. Schmidt and M. Buber, "Kirche, Staat, Volk, Judentum: Zwiegespräch im jüdischen Lehrhaus in Stuttgart am 14. Januar 1933," *Theologische Blätter* 12, no. 9 (September 1933): 257–274.

27. The director of Stuttgard Lehrhaus, Leopold Marx, conducted a voluminous (unpublished) correspondence with Buber on the activities of the Lehrhaus. See Martin Buber Archive, file 478.

28. Ibid.

29. All quotations from this dialogue, here and in the following paragraphs, are from Schmidt and Buber, "Kirche, Staat, Volk, Judentum."

30. "Der jüdische Mensch von heute," *Almanach des Schocken Verlags auf das Jahr 5694* (1933–1934): 5.

31. Buber gave the following title to a collection of his speeches and articles from the first three years of the Third Reich: *Die Stunde und die Erkenntnis. Reden und Aufsätze, 1933–1935* (Berlin: Schocken Verlag, 1936).

32. Judith Buber Agassi, "Nachwort," in Georg Munk (Paula Judith Buber), *Muckensturm. Ein jahr im Leben einer kleinen Stadt* (Berlin: LIT Verlag, 2008), 651–657.

33. "Die Kinder," *Jüdische Rundschau* (May 30, 1933); "The Children," trans. Harry Zohn, in William Rollins and Harry Zohn, eds., *Men of Dialogue: Martin Buber and Albrecht Goes* (New York: Funk and Wagnalls, 1969), 225–228 (I have modified the translation).

34. Ibid., 227; Buber, *Schriften zu Jugend, Erziehung und Bildung. Martin Buber Werkausgabe*, vol. 8, ed. Juliane Jacobi (Güterslohr: Gütersloher Verlagshaus, 2005), 235–237, translated in Rollins and Zohn, *Men of Dialogue*, 225–228. (I have modified the translation.)

35. Ibid.

36. Ibid.

37. Ibid.

38. These comments were made by Buber at a conference of Jewish educators in May 1934. Cited in Ernst Simon, *Aufbau im Untergang. Jüdische Erwachsenenbildung im nationalsozialistischen Deutschland als geistiger Widerstand* (Tübingen: J. C. B. Mohr/Paul Siebeck, 1959), 45.

39. Ibid., 42; Rosenzweig, "It Is Time: Concerning the Study of Judaism," in Rosenzweig, *On Jewish Learning*, ed. Nahum N. Glatzer (New York: Schocken, 1955), 26–54.

40. Rosenzweig, "Bildung und kein Ende," in Rosenzweig, *Der Mensch und sein Werk. Gesammelte Schriften*, vol. 3 (The Hague: Martinus Nijhoff, 1979), 491. Translated under the title "Towards a Renaissance of Jewish Learning," the essay is included in Rosenzweig, *On Jewish Learning*, 55–71.

41. Buber, "Ein jüdisches Lehrhaus," an announcement of the forthcoming reopening of the Lehrhaus, published in *Frankfurter Israelitisches Gemeindeblatt* (November 1933), reprinted in Buber, *Schriften zu Jugend*, 8: 249.

42. Buber, "Jüdische Erwachsenenbildung," *Rundbrief* 1 (June 13, 1934), reprinted in Buber, *Schriften zu Jugend*, 8: 256.

43. Buber, "Ein Hinweis für Bibelkurse," *Rundbrief* (January 1936), cited in Simon, *Aufbau im Untergang*, 67.

44. Buber, "Bildung und Weltanschauung," *Der Morgen* (February 1935), reprinted in Buber, *Schriften zu Jugend*, 8: 282.

45. Ibid.

46. Ibid., 283.

47. The quotation is from an unedited transcript of the lecture, apparently prepared by a stenographer, in the Martin Buber Archive. Juliane Jacobi discovered this document, and included an edited version in her volume of Buber's writings, Martin Buber, *Schriften zu Jugend*, 8: 265–278.

48. Ibid.

49. Buber, "Biblischer Humanismus" (delivered at the Frankfurt Lehrhaus in October 1933); translated in Buber, *On the Bible: Eighteen Studies*, ed. Nahum N. Glatzer (New York: Schocken Books, 1968), 211–216.

50. Ibid.

51. Buber, "Bildung und Weltanschaung," 286–287; Buber, "Biblischer Humanismus," in Buber, *Die Stunde und die Erkenntnis*, 103.

52. Buber, "Biblical Humanism," in Buber, *On the Bible*, 216.

53. E. Simon, "Jewish Adult Education in Nazi Germany as Spiritual Resistance," *Leo Baeck Institute Yearbook* 1 (1956): 90.

54. Buber, "Die Mächtigkeit des Geistes," in Buber, *Die Stunde und die Erkenntnis*, 74–87; Buber, "The Power of the Spirit," in Buber, *Israel and the World*, 172–182.

55. See the unedited typescript of the lecture: *Martin Buber Werkausgabe, Schriften zum Christentum*, ed. Karl-Joseph Kuschel (Güterslohr: Gütersloher Verlagshaus, 2011), 397–410.

56. "Drei Briefe der Geheimen Staatspolizei," in *Martin Buber: 1878–1978. Ausstellung*, exhibition catalog, Jüdische National- und Universitätsbibliothek, April 1978, 39.

57. *Königtum Gottes* (Berlin: Schocken Verlag, 1932); 2nd exp. ed. (Berlin: Schocken Verlag, 1936). This was the first volume of what was to be a trilogy, under the general title *Das Kommende. Untersuchungen zur Entstehungsgeschichte des messianischen Glaubens*. According to Buber's note in the preface to the English translation of *Kingship of God*, trans. Richard Scheinman (New York: Harper and Row, 1967), 13: "The second volume entitled *Der Gesalbte* was half finished in 1938 and had already been set in type when the Schocken Press, Berlin, was officially dissolved [by the Nazis]."

58. Buber, *Die Frage an den Einzelnen* (Berlin: Schocken, 1936); Buber, "The Question of the Single One," in Buber, *Between Man and Man*, trans. Ronald Gregor Smith (New York: Macmillan, 1965), 40–82.

59. Ibid., 51.

60. Ibid., 52.

61. Buber, "The Children," 227.

62. Cited in Lambert Schneider, *Rechenschaft, 1925–1965: Ein Almanach* (Heidelberg: Verlag Lambert Schneider, 1965), 38.

63. The letters of Paula Buber to her granddaughter Barbara are in the private archive of the Martin Buber Literary Estate.

64. Leo Baeck to Martin Buber, May 21, 1935, in *Letters*, 432.

65. Buber to Hans Trüb, October 9, 1936, in *Briefwechsel*, 2: 596.

66. This book was published in 1936 in Berlin by Schocken Verlag.

67. Buber, "Teaching and Deed," in Buber, *Israel and the World*, 140.

68. Ibid.

69. Buber to Hugo Bergmann, April 16, 1936, in *Letters*, 442.

70. Gershom Scholem to Buber, February 2, 1934, in *Letters*, 415.

71. Gershom Scholem to Buber, July 16, 1936, in *Letters*, 445.

72. D. W. Senator to Buber, January 29, 1938, in *Letters*, 463 f.

73. Hannah Arendt, "A Guide for Youth: Martin Buber" (1935), in Hannah Arendt, *Jewish Writings*, ed. Jerome Kohn and Ron Feldman (New York: Schocken, 2007), 31–33.

74. Buber to Hugo Bergmann, November 13, 1935, in *Letters*, 436.

Chapter 9. Professor and Political Activist

1. Buber to Ernst Simon, November 11, 1938, in *Letters*, 463 f.

2. Buber to Hermann Gerson, September 7, 1934, in *Letters*, 424.

3. Hugo Bergmann to Buber, February 4, 1938, in *Letters*, 464.

4. Ibid.

5. Buber to Hugo Bergmann, September 11, 1927, in *Letters*, 354.

6. Franz Rosenzweig to Buber, August 18, 1929, in *Letters*, 368.

7. Paula Buber to Martin Buber, August 17, 1929, in *Letters*, 367.

8. Martin Buber to Paula Buber, undated letter, but presumably August 15, 1929, in *Letters*, 366.

9. Judah Magnes to Buber, February 21, 1934, in *Brief-wechsel*, 2: 525 f.

10. Martin Buber to Paula Buber, September 10, 1935, in *Letters*, 433.

11. Buber to Gershom Scholem, October 10, 1935, in *Brief-wechsel*, 2: 574–575.

12. Buber to Hugo Bergmann, November 13, 1935, in *Letters*, 436.

13. Ibid. (translation modified).

14. Buber to Hugo Bergmann, April 16, 1936, in *Letters*, 441.

15. Nahum N. Glatzer to Willy Schottroff, May 20, 1985, cited in Schottroff, "Martin Buber ad der Universität Frankfurt (1923-1933)," in W. Licharz and H. Schmidt, eds., *Martin Buber: Interntationales Symposium zum 20. Todestag* (Frankfurt a.M.: Arnoldshainer Texte, 1989), 1: 52.

16. Buber to Hugo Bergmann, April 16, 1936, in *Letters*, 441 f.

17. Ibid., 442.

18. Ibid., 443 (emphasis added).

19. On the 1902 program, see Buber, Berthold Feiwel, and Chaim Weizmann, *Eine Juedische Hochschule* (Berlin: Jüdischer Verlag, 1902).

20. Buber to Hugo Bergmann, January 6, 1920, in *Letters*, 252.

21. For the description of "Dr. Magnes," see Robert Weltsch to Buber, June 1924, in *Briefwechsel*, 2: 194.

22. Judah Magnes to Ahad Ha'am, July 7, 1924 (Hebrew). Cited in English in *Judah Leib Magnes: On the Century of His Birth*, exhibition catalog, ed. Margot Cohn (Jerusalem: Jewish National and University Library, 1977), 104 f.

23. Judah Magnes, "On Mt. Scopus," *Der Jude*, special edition: *Judentum und Deutschtum* (1928): 50.

24. Ibid.

25. Buber to Hans Kohn, January 26, 1929, Martin Buber Archive, file *vav* 376:1.

26. Unpublished document, Judah Leib Magnes Papers,

Central Archives for the History of the Jewish People, Jerusalem, file 2273 (Ha-'Ol).

27. Buber, "Truth and Deliverance," *Be'ayot* (July 1947): 189 (Hebrew).

28. Ibid.

29. Ibid., 490.

30. Buber to Judah Magnes, July 5, 1947, Martin Buber Archives, file *chet* 2/46, 467a.

31. Buber, "Man's Duty as Man," in "A Centenary Gathering for Henry David Thoreau," a symposium led by John H. Hicks, *Massachusetts Review* (March 1962): 55. Also see Buber's response to the question addressed to twenty-three philosophers, writers, and politicians concerning "the principle of 'civil disobedience' in light of the threat of nuclear war," in Clara Urquhart, ed., *A Matter of Life* (London: Little, Brown, 1963), 51–52.

32. Buber's response in *A Matter of Life*, 51.

33. Buber, "Man's Duty as Man," 55.

34. Buber, *The Demand of the Spirit and Historical Reality* (Jerusalem: The Hebrew University, 1938), Hebrew pamphlet of 19 pages. English translation in Buber, *Pointing the Way: Collected Essays*, trans. and ed. Maurice S. Friedman (New York: Schocken, 1957), 177–191.

35. Buber, *Demand of the Spirit and Historical Reality*, 177 (emphasis added).

36. Ibid., 178.

37. Ibid.

38. Ibid., 180 (emphasis added).

39. Ibid., 181.

40. Ibid.

41. Ibid.

42. Ibid., 182.

43. Ibid., 187.

44. Ibid.

45. Ibid., 190.

46. *Nasz Przeglad* (March 12, 1939): 13, cited in Kzazimierz

Kryzkalski, "Martin Bubers Reise nach Poland," *Judaica* 51, no. 2 (1995): 70.

47. Ibid.

48. Jerzy Turowicz, "Martin Buber: A Philosopher of Dialogue," *Tygodnik Powszechny* 27 (1965): 3, cited in Kryzkalski, "Martin Bubers Reise nach Poland," 78.

49. Buber to Eduard Strauss, May 7, 1939, in *Briefwechsel*, 3: 24.

50. Kryzkalski, "Martin Bubers Reise nach Poland," 78.

51. Estimated according to Harold Marcuse, "Historical Dollar-to-Marks Currency Conversion Calculus," available online at http://www.history.ucsb.edu/faculty/marcuse/projects/currency.htm (accessed June 28, 2018).

52. The details of this subterfuge were related to me by Rafael Buber, ca. 1985.

53. Joseph Bentwich conducted a study circle on Judaism in Jerusalem, in which Buber participated. Buber, he said, "was in many respects only a half-Jew. After all, he married a Catholic and his entire way of life was not Jewish." See Bentwich's interview in Haim Gordon, ed., *The Other Martin Buber: Recollections of His Contemporaries* (Athens: Ohio University Press, 1988), 164.

54. The equivalent today of $2,260.

55. The quotations by Senator in the next paragraphs are from a letter archived among the papers of Hans Kohn housed at Hebrew Union College, Cincinnati, Ohio. I wish to thank Dr. Sam H. Brody for bringing this letter to my attention.

56. Max Warburg's letter of April 9, 1943, can also be found among the archival holdings of Hans Kohn at the Hebrew Union College.

57. This letter from Buber to Kohn from the archives of Hebrew Union College as well as Warburg's reply to Kohn were kindly brought to my attention by Professor Sam H. Brody. By "Palestinian friends," Buber, of course, meant in this context Jewish friends residing in Palestine.

58. Ibid.

59. It was published in *Haaretz* on November 15, 1939. An

English translation is in "They and We," in William Rollins and Harry Zohn, eds., *Men of Dialogue: Martin Buber and Albrecht Goes* (New York: Funk and Wagnalls, 1969), 236–243.

60. Ibid.

61. Buber, "What Is Man?," in Buber, *Between Man and Man*, trans. R. G. Smith, introduction by Maurice Friedman (London: Routledge and Kegan Paul, 2002), 140–244. Under the title "The Problem of Man" (ba'ayat ha-adam), the Hebrew version of the lectures was published in 1943, although excerpts were published periodically before that in the daily press.

62. Buber, "What Is Man?," 238.

63. Ibid., 239.

64. Ibid.

65. Buber, *Nitivot be-Utopia* (Tel Aviv: Am Oved, 1946), 8 (Hebrew).

66. Ibid., 17.

67. Ibid., 121.

68. Ibid.

69. Buber, Preface to *Torat ha-Neve'im* (Jerusalem: Mosad Bialik, 1942), 1–2 (Hebrew). Buber dedicated the volume to the "memory of my grandfather."

70. Buber, *The Prophetic Faith*, trans. Carlyle Witton-Davies (New York: Macmillan, 1949), 2.

71. Ibid., 135.

72. Cf. Buber, *Königtum Gottes* (Berlin: Schocken, 1932).

73. Buber, *Prophetic Faith*, 135.

74. Buber, epilogue to his *Gog und Magog. Eine Chronik*, ed. Ran HaCohen, in *Martin Buber Werkausgabe* (Güterslohr: Gütersloher Verlagshaus, 2009), 19: 273.

75. Buber to Franz Rosenzweig, January 10, 1923, in *Letters*, 300.

76. Buber to Franz Rosenzweig, March 22, 1923, in *Letters*, 303.

77. Buber, "Replies to My Critics," in *The Philosophy of Martin Buber*, part of the *Library of Living Philosophers*, vol. 12, ed.

Paul Arthur Schlipp and Maurice Friedman (La Salle, Ill.: Open Court, 1967), 739.

78. Buber, *Gog und Magog*, 82.

79. Buber, "Images of Good and Evil," trans. Michael Bullock, in Buber, *Good and Evil: Two Interpretations* (Upper Saddle River, N.J.: Prentice Hall, 1997), 65.

80. Buber, epilogue to *Gog und Magog*, 271–275.

81. Helit Yeshurun Raviv, "A Conversation with Dr. Moshe Spitzer," *Chadarim: A Poetry Journey* 3 (1982): 52–54 (Hebrew).

82. Ibid.

83. Shmuel Yosef Agnon, "My Memories of Buber," in Agnon, *Me'Atzmi el'Atzmi* (Tel Aviv: Schocken, 1976), 270–271 (Hebrew).

84. Franz Rosenzweig to Buber, June 17, 1924, in *Letters*, 314.

85. Buber to Shmuel Yosef Agnon, January 1941, in *Briefwechsel*, 2: 41. The letter, originally written in Hebrew, does not give a specific date in January.

86. The dedication appears in "Pleasant Stories of Rabbi Israel Baal Shem Tov," *Molad* 18 (August–September 1980): 357 (Hebrew), cited in Dan Laor, "Agnon and Buber: A Story of a Friendship," in *Martin Buber: A Contemporary Perspective*, ed. Paul Mendes-Flohr (Syracuse, N.Y.: Syracuse University Press, 2002): 78.

87. Shmuel Yosef Agnon, *Sippurei haBesht*, ed. Emuna Yaron and Haim Yaron (Tel Aviv: Schocken, 1987) (Hebrew).

88. Dan Laor, "Agnon and Buber," 78.

89. Buber's contribution to a volume in honor of Agnon's seventieth birthday is cited in ibid., 81.

90. Buber, epilogue to *Gog und Magog*, 275.

91. Baruch Litvin to Buber, May 2, 1951, in *Letters*, 560.

92. Buber to Baruch Litvin, May 3, 1951, in *Letters*, 561.

93. Martin Buber to Paula Buber, March 25, 1926, in *Briefwechsel*, 2: 248 f.

94. Buber's son Rafael had a bar mitzvah.

95. Related to me by Buber's granddaughter Judith Buber Agassi.

96. M. K. Gandhi, "The Jews," *Harijan* (November 26, 1938): 352-362, reprinted in Paul Mendes-Flohr, ed., *A Land of Two Peoples: Martin Buber on Jew and Arabs*, 3rd ed. (Chicago: University of Chicago Press, 2005), 108.

97. Buber, "A Letter to Gandhi"; reprinted in Mendes-Flohr, *Land of Two Peoples*, 125.

98. Ibid., 111.

99. While Buber, of course, was not so prescient as to be referring here to "the Final Solution" and its death camps, there were already concentration camps in Germany in 1939, and what was happening in them was bad enough.

100. Buber, "A Letter to Gandhi," 114-116.

101. Ibid., 119.

102. Ibid., 120.

103. Ibid.

104. Ibid.; Joshua 2:27.

105. Dina Porat, "Al-domi: Palestinian [Jewish] Intellectuals and the Holocaust, 1943-1945," *Studies in Zionism* 5, no. 1 (1984): 101.

106. Buber, "Silence and Outcry," *Be'ayot* 1, no. 1 (April 1944): 21-23.

107. Ibid.

108. Ibid.

109. Buber, "A Majority or Many? A Postscript to a Speech," *Be'ayot* 2, no. 3 (April 1945): 110-113 (Hebrew), a translation appears in Mendes-Flohr, *Land of Two Peoples*, 164-168.

110. The lectures were published in 1944 in a volume entitled "Between the People and Its Land." They were then translated from Hebrew into English under the title *Israel and Palestine: The History of an Idea* (1952), and reissued as *Zion: The History of an Idea*, with a foreword by Nahum N. Glatzer (New York: Schocken, 1973).

111. Ibid., 182.

112. Ibid., 183.

113. Anglo-American Committee of Inquiry, *Report to the United States Government and His Majesty's Government in the*

*United Kingdom* (Lausanne, Switz., 1946), chapter 1, available online at http://avalon.law.yale.edu/20th_century/angcho1.asp (accessed July 24, 2018).

114. "A Tragic Conflict?" was an unpublished lecture given at a conference of the Ichud, convened in May 1946. It was translated from the Hebrew in Mendes-Flohr, *A Land of Two Peoples*, 185–189.

115. Buber, "Zionism and 'Zionism,'" *Be'ayot ha-Zman* 7, no. 8 (May 27, 1948): 3–5 (Hebrew); Mendes-Flohr, *Land of Two Peoples*, 220–223.

116. Martin Buber, J. L. Magnes, and E. Simon, eds., *Towards Union in Palestine: Essays on Zionism and Jewish-Arab Cooperation* (Jerusalem: Ihud, 1947), Buber's contribution, 7–11, 32–36 (emphasis in original).

117. Ibid.

## Chapter 10. Despite Everything

1. Heinz Politizer, "The Social Buber," *Commentary Magazine* 22, no. 6 (December 1, 1956): 589.

2. Samuel Hugo Bergmann, *Tagebücher und Briefe*, vol. 1: *1901–1948* (Königstein: Jüdischer Verlag, Athenäum, 1985), 1: 582 f.; Martin Buber to Heinz Politizer, March 17, 1948, in *Letters*, 533.

3. Ibid.

4. The reference is to the Mishnah, according to which old age begins at the age of seventy (*Sayings of the Fathers*, 5:24). Magnes's Hebrew essay is translated in *Letters*, 529–532.

5. Hans Kohn to Berthold Feiwel, November 21, 1929, in Paul Mendes-Flohr, ed., *A Land of Two Peoples: Martin Buber on Jew and Arabs*, 3rd ed. (Chicago: University of Chicago Press, 2005), 97–100.

6. Martin Buber to Paula Buber, October 3, 1929, in *Briefwechsel*, 2: 353.

7. Buber, "Gandhi, Politics and Us" (1930), in Buber, *Pointing the Way: Collected Essays*, trans. and ed. Maurice S. Friedman (New York: Schocken, 1957), 137.

8. Shalom Ben-Chorin, *Zwiesprache mit Martin Buber. Ein Erinnerungsbuch* (Munich: List Verlag, 1966), 102.

9. Buber, "Israel and the Command of the Spirit" (1958), in Mendes-Flohr, *Land of Two Peoples*, 292–293.

10. Excerpts of Ben-Gurion and Buber's exchange are translated in Mendes-Flohr, *Land of Two Peoples*, 239–244.

11. Buber, "Facts and Demands" (January 1949), translated from the Hebrew in Mendes-Flohr, *Land of Two Peoples*, 238 f.

12. Buber, "Instead of Polemics" (1956), translated from the Hebrew in Mendes-Flohr, *Land of Two Peoples*, 270.

13. Ibid., 270 f.

14. Ibid.

15. Buber, "The Polis of God," in Buber, *Pointing the Way*, 137.

16. Translated in Michael Keren, *Ben-Gurion and the Intellectuals: Power, Knowledge, and Charisma* (Dekalb: Northern Illinois University Press, 1983), 78. (I have revised the translation slightly.)

17. David Ben-Gurion to Buber, February 5, 1963, in *Letters*, 654.

18. Buber to David Ben-Gurion, February 19, 1963, in *Letters*, 656.

19. Buber, "Transcript of Testimony at the Trial of A. Cohen," Martin Buber Archive, file *zejan/22*. Excerpts translated in Aubrey Hodes, *Martin Buber: An Intimate Portrait* (New York: Viking, 1971), 64.

20. Ibid.

21. Buber to Ernst Simon, November 11, 1937, in *Letters*, 462.

22. Buber, foreword to *Between Man and Man*, trans. Ronald Gregor Smith (London: Routledge, 1947), x.

23. This is the very first line of *I and Thou*. See Buber, *I and Thou*, trans. W. Kaufmann (New York: Scribner's, 1986).

24. Ibid., 144.

25. Buber, "On the Situation of Philosophy," in Buber, *A Believing Humanism: My Testament, 1902–1965*, trans. Maurice Friedman (New York: Simon and Schuster, 1967), 136–137.

26. Buber, "Zur Situation der Philosophie," in Buber, *Nach-*

*lese* (Heidelberg: Lambert Schneider, 1966), 138 (emphasis in original). The conference, which was to take place in August 1948, was canceled.

27. Buber to Joseph Minn, September 23, 1946, in *Brief-wechsel*, 3: 123.

28. Buber to Alfred Döblin, April 26, 1950, in *Briefwechsel*, 3: 246.

29. Buber, "Das Ende der deutsch-jüdischen Symbiose." This article was published in the inaugural issue (March 10, 1939) of the *Jüdische Welt-Rundschau*, the reconstituted version of the Berlin Jewish weekly *Jüdische Rundschau*, which had been banned by the Nazi authorities after Kristallnacht. It was edited in Jerusalem, and printed in Paris, where it was distributed to the exiled German-Jewish community in sixty countries. See Buber, "End of the German-Jewish Symbiosis," in William Rollins and Harry Zohn, eds., *Men of Dialogue: Martin Buber and Albrecht Goes* (New York: Funk and Wagnalls, 1969), 232–235.

30. Lambert Schneider to Buber, July 21, 1947, in *Letters*, 140.

31. Lambert Schneider, *Rechenschaft, 1925–1965: Ein Almanach* (Heidelberg: Verlag Lambert Schneider, 1965), 90.

32. Karl Heinrich Rengstorf to Buber, December 10, 1949, in *Briefwechsel*, 3: 229 f.

33. Buber to Karl Heinrich Rengstorf, December 21, 1949, in *Briefwechsel*, 3: 232.

34. Karl Heinrich Rengstorf to Buber, May 20, 1950, in *Briefwechsel*, 3: 252.

35. Schmuel Hugo Bergmann, *Tagebücher und Briefe*, vol. 2: *1948–1975*, ed. Miriam Sambursky (Königstein: Jüdischer Berlag bein Athenäm, 1985), 79 (entries from February 6 and 10, 1951).

36. Ibid., 105.

37. Karl Thime to Buber, January 20, 1950, in *Letters*, 558.

38. Günter Schulz, "Begegnungen mit Martin Buber," in *Kritische Solidarität. Betrachtungen zum Deutsch-Jüdischen Selbsverständis. Für Max Plaut zum 70. Geburtstag 17. Oktober 1971*, ed. Günter Schulz (Bremen: F. Röver, 1971), 377–378.

39. Ibid.

40. Bergmann, *Tagebücher und Briefe*, 1: 588 (entry for July 1942). Bergmann ascribed Buber's failure to attract students to the themes of his classes, which were not of "contemporary" intellectual interest.

41. See Bergmann's diary entry from July 20, 1949; ibid., 2: 23.

42. Personal communication by Nahum N. Glatzer, ca. 1980.

43. Buber, "End of the German-Jewish Symbiosis," 235.

44. Buber, "Goethe's Concept of Humanity," in Arnold Bergstrasseer, ed., *Goethe and the Modern Age: The International Convocation at Aspen, Colorado 1949* (Chicago: Henry Regner Company, 1950), 233; Buber, "Das Reinmenschliche," in Buber, *Hinweise. Gesammalte Essays* (Zurich: Mansesse Verlag, 1953), 212–219.

45. Buber to Bruno Snell, December 22, 1951, in *Letters*, 565.

46. Ernst Simon to Buber, December 22, 1951, in Simon, *Sechzig Jahre gegen den Strom*, ed. Leo Baeck Institute, Jerusalem (Tübingen: Mohr Siebeck, 1998), 141 f.

47. Ernst Simon to Buber, January 1, 1952, in Simon, *Sechzig Jahre gegen den Strom*, 142.

48. "Martin Buber Explains His Reasons for Accepting the Goethe Prize of the University of Hamburg," *Haaretz*, December 31, 1951, 1 (Hebrew).

49. Buber to Bruno Snell, January 25, 1952, in *Briefwechsel*, 3: 309 f.

50. Karl Heinrich Rengstorf to Buber, May 20, 1950, in *Letters*, 552 f. (The date is incorrectly given as May 5.) See also *Briefwechsel*, 3: 252.

51. Karl Heinrich Rengstorf to Buber, July 10, 1950, in *Letters*, 553.

52. Buber to Karl Heinrich Rengstorf, August 20, 1950, in *Letters*, 556 f.

53. Romano Guardini, *Verantwortung. Gedanken zur jüdischen Frage. Eine Universitätsrede* (Munich: Hochland-Bücherei im Kösel-Verlag, 1952); "Reflexions on the Jewish Question," *Dublin Review* 227, no. 459 (1953): 1–14.

54. Buber to Romano Guardini, December 12, 1952, *Brief-wechsel*, 3: 232.

55. Romano Guardini, *Vom Geist der Liturgie* (Freiburg: Herder, 1918); Guardini, *The Spirit of the Liturgy* (New York: Crossroad Publishing, 1998).

56. See Robert A. Krieg, "To Nostra Aetate: Martin Buber and Romano Guardini," in Larry V. Thompson, ed., *Lessons and Legacies IV* (Evanston, Ill.: Northwestern University Press, 1991), 81–97. My thanks to Professor Krieg for providing me with a copy of his instructive essay.

57. Guardini, *Verantwortung*, 21.

58. The receipt of this letter, dated to January 30, 1953, is acknowledged by Bruno Snell in a letter to Buber dated February 13, 1953 (in *Briefwechsel*, 3: 326).

59. Buber, "Geltung und Grenzen des politischen Prinzips," in *Gedenkschrift zur Verleihung des Hansischen Goethe-Preises 1951 der Gemeinnützigen Stiftung F.V.S. zu Hamburg an Martin Buber* (Hamburg: Stiftung, 1953); Buber, "Validity and Limitations of the Political Principle," in Buber, *Pointing the Way*, 208–219.

60. Buber to Ludwig Strauß, June 26, 1953, in *Briefwechsel Martin Buber–Ludwig Strauss: 1913–1953*, ed. Tuvia Rübner and Dafna Mach (Frankfurt a.M.: Luchterhand Literaturverlag, 1990), 274.

61. Buber, "The Validity and Limitations of the Political Principle," in Buber, *Pointing the Way*, 215.

62. Ibid., 217.

63. Arthur Georgi to Buber, June 17, 1953, in *Briefwechsel*, 3: 346 f.

64. Albert Goes, "Martin Buber, Our Support," in William Rollins and Harry Zohn, eds., *Men of Dialogue: Martin Buber and Albrecht Goes* (New York: Funk and Wagnalls, 1969), 18 f.

65. Buber, "Genuine Dialogue and the Possibilities of Peace," in Rollins and Zohn, *Men of Dialogue*, 20–27. I have revised the translation slightly.

66. Ibid.

67. Ibid.

68. Ibid.

69. See Buber to Emil Preetorius, April 10, 1954, Martin Buber Archive, file 591 a:1. In this letter to Preetorius, the president of the academy, Buber acknowledges Preetorius's letter, which is not extant.

70. Count Podewils to Martin Buber, correspondence dated February 22, 1957, and May 13, 1957, Martin Buber Archive, file 588b:1. The meeting took place over two and a half days, from May 29 to May 30, 1957.

71. Ibid.

72. Hans A. Fischer-Barnicol, "Spielgelungen—Vermittlungen," in Günther Neske, ed., *Erinnerung zu Martin Heidegger* (Pfullingen: Verlag Günther Neske, 1977), 71.

73. Ibid., 91. On mentioning various philosophers in the "same breath," see Buber, "What Is Man?" in Buber, *Between Man and Man*, ed. Maurice Friedman (New York: Macmillan, 1965), 199–220.

74. Hans Fischer-Barnicol first met Buber at a colloquium sponsored by the Evangelische Akademie, Berlin, in June 1956, and corresponded with him from then on. The interview was conducted in the summer of 1963. When asked years later by Emil Fackenheim about the controversy in Jerusalem engendered by Buber's reputedly reconciliatory meeting with Heidegger, Gershom Scholem questioned the authenticity of Barnicol-Fischer's "dreary report." He assured Fackenheim that neither he nor Buber's close friend Ernst Simon—"who privately sought fervidly to dissuade Buber from conducting such a discussion with Heidegger"—"knew anything that such a meeting actually took place." Scholem to Fackenheim, January 24, 1979, Gershom Scholem Archives, Jewish National Library, Jerusalem, ms. varia 1599.

75. Fischer-Barnicol, "Spiegelungen-Vermittlungen," 91.

76. Ibid., 92.

77. Buber to Maurice Friedman, August 8, 1957, cited in Friedman, *The Life and the Work* (New York: Dutton, 1983), 3: 116.

78. Fischer-Barnicol, "Spiegelungen-Vermittlungen," 90.

79. Ibid., 89 f.

80. Ibid., 93.

81. Otto Poeggeler, *The Paths of Heidegger's Life and Thought*, trans. John Bailiff (Atlantic Highlands, N.J.: Humanities Press, 1997), 67.

82. It was published in 1957 in Pfullingen by Günther Neske. A copy, with Heidegger's dedication, is in the Gershom Scholem Collection, Jewish National Library, Jerusalem, call no. 14632.

83. Günther Neske to Martin Buber, April 9, 1959. Buber declined, curtly explaining that due to a prolonged illness he was unable to undertake any "substantial literary obligations. . . . I cannot therefore to my great regret accede to your request" (Buber to Neske, April 16, 1959). Both letters are in the Martin Buber Archive, file 539a 1:1.

84. Martin Heidegger to Wilhelm Hoffmann, July 8, 1959. Deutsches Literaturarchiv, Marbach am Necker, Martin Heidegger Collection. A copy of this letter is also in the Martin Buber Archive, file 267c:1.

85. Hans Fischer-Barnicol to Buber, November 3, 1964, Martin Buber Archive, file 206b:4.

86. Ibid.

87. For a fuller discussion of Buber and Heidegger's relationship, see Paul Mendes-Flohr, "Martin Buber and Martin Heidegger in Dialogue," *Journal of Religion* 94, no. 1 (January 2014): 2–25.

88. Martin Heidegger, "The Way to Language," in *On the Way to Language*, trans. Peter D. Hertz (San Francisco: Harper, 1979), 112.

89. Cited in ibid., 123.

90. Martin Buber, "Hoffnung für diese Stunde," *Merkur* 6, no. 6 (August 1952): 711–718.

91. Martin Heidegger to Elfride Heidegger, August 12, 1952, in Martin Heidegger, *Letters to His Wife, 1915–1970*, selected, edited, and annotated by Gertrud Heidegger and trans. R. D. V. Glasgow (London: Polity, 2010), 225–226, and *"Mein liebes Seelchen": Briefe Martin Heideggers an seine Frau Elfride, 1915–1970*, ed.

Gertrud Heidegger (Munich: Deutsch Verlags-Anstalt, 2005), 279. Emphasis in original.

92. James K. Lyon, *Paul Celan and Martin Heidegger: An Unresolved Conversation, 1951–1970* (Baltimore: John Hopkins University Press, 2006), 165.

93. Martin Heidegger to Elfride Heidegger, August 12, 1952, in Martin Heidegger, *Letters to His Wife, 1915–1970*, 226.

94. Ibid.

95. Unpublished poem; an earlier version of the poem served as the dedication to the first printing of Buber, *Zwiesprache* (Berlin: Schocken, 1932).

96. Buber to Maurice Friedman, September 9, 1958, in *Briefwechsel*, 3: 463.

97. Buber to Erwald Wasmuth, October 4, 1958, in *Briefwechsel*, 3: 466.

98. The citation is from a printed text—marked Jerusalem, February 1959—addressed to all who expressed condolences on Paula's death, in *Briefwechsel*, 3: 475.

99. Hans Jonas to Buber, October 13, 1958, in *Letters*, 622.

100. Printed text marked Jerusalem, February 1959, in *Briefwechsel*, 3: 475.

101. Schalom Ben-Chorin, *Zweigsprache mit Martin Buber. Ein Erinnerungsbuch* (Munich: List Verlag, 1966), 127.

102. Buber, "The Word That Is Spoken," in Buber, *The Knowledge of Man: Selected Essays*, trans. Maurice Friedman and Ronald Gregor Smith (London: Allen and Unwin, 1965), 110.

103. Ibid., 113.

104. Ibid., 120.

105. Ibid.

106. Buber, "Believing Humanism," in Buber, *A Believing Humanism: My Testament, 1902–1965*, trans. and ed. Maurice Friedman (New York: Simon and Schuster, 1967), 118.

107. Ibid.; "Gläubiger Humanismus," in Buber, *Nachlese* (Heidelberg: Lambert Schneider, 1965), 114.

108. Buber, "Believing Humanism," 119.

109. Ibid., 117. Per Buber's request, two-thirds of the mone-

tary prize was donated to the Leo Baeck Institute, Jerusalem. See G. Sluizer, director of Stichting Praemium Erasmianum to Buber, July 3, 1963, archives of the Leo Baeck Institute, Jerusalem.

110. Gershom Scholem to Hannah Arendt, February 17, 1952, in Hannah Arendt and Gershom Scholem, *Der Briefwechsel*, ed. Marie Luise Knott in collaboration with David Heredia (Berlin: Jüdischer Verlag, 2010), 362 f.

111. Buber, *At the Turning: Three Addresses on Judaism* (New York: Farrar, Straus and Young, 1952), n.p.

112. Buber, "Judaism and Civilization," in ibid., 16.

113. Ibid., 17 f.

114. Ibid., 19.

115. Ibid., 23.

116. Ibid., 25.

117. Ibid.

118. Buber, "The Silent Question," in Buber, *At the Turning*, 52.

119. Ibid., 58.

120. Cf. Buber, "Guilt and Guilt Feelings," in Buber, *The Knowledge of Man: Selected Essays*, ed. Maurice Friedman (New York: Harper Torchbook, 1965), 145, fn. 1.

121. Ibid., 61.

122. Ibid., 62.

123. Buber to Kurt Singer, February 1, 1953, in *Briefwechsel*, 3: 331.

124. Rudolf Kayser to Buber, February 15, 1956, in *Letters*, 594.

125. Written under the supervision of Joachim Wach, the dissertation is entitled, "Martin Buber: Mystic, Existentialist, Social Prophet: A Study in the Redemption of Evil."

126. Maurice Friedman to Buber, March 19, 1950, in *Letters*, 550–552.

127. Buber to Maurice Friedman, April 6, 1950, in *Letters*, 553.

128. Buber to Maurice Friedman, January 30, 1956, in *Briefwechsel*, 3: 405 f.

129. Ibid., 406.

130. Buber, *Knowledge of Man.*

131. The recording of the conversation was transcribed in Rob Anderson and Kenneth N. Cissna, *The Martin Buber–Carl Rogers Dialogue: A New Transcript with Commentary* (Albany: State University of New York Press, 1997). For the quotation, see 17 f.

132. Ibid., 20–25.

133. Ibid.

134. Ibid.

135. Ibid.

136. Alfred Wiener to Buber, February 2, 1958, in *Letters,* 615.

137. Theodor Heuss to Buber, January 4, 1958, in *Letters,* 613 f.

138. Hermann Hesse to Buber, n.d., in *Letters,* 616.

139. Albert Schweitzer to Buber, March 3, 1958, in *Letters,* 616 f.

140. Buber, "Expression of Thanks," in Buber, *A Believing Humanism: My Testament, 1902–1965,* trans. M. Friedman (New York: Simon and Schuster, 1967), 225 (I have amended the translation slightly; emphasis in original). Cf. Buber, "Danksagung, 1958," in Buber, *Nachlese* (Heidelberg: Verlag Lambert Schneider, 1965), 254.

141. Buber, "Prelude: Report of Two Talks," in Buber, *Eclipse of God: Studies in the Relation between Religion and Philosophy,* trans. Maurice Friedman et al. (London: Gollancz, 1953), 6.

142. Buber to Maurice Friedman, December 8, 1957, Martin Buber Archive, file 227b.

143. Buber, "On Zionism and Modern Israel," *Jewish Newsletter* (New York) 4, no. 11 (June 2, 1958).

144. Buber to Maurice Friedman, July 11, 1958, in *Briefwechsel,* 3: 460.

145. Ibid., 3: 461 f.

146. Buber, "The Spirit of Israel in Face of Present Reality," *Haaretz,* December 30, 1958, 3–4; Buber, "Israel and the Command of the Spirit," *Congress Weekly* 25, no. 4 (September 1958): 10–12.

147. Buber to Maurice Friedman, July 16, 1958, in *Briefwechsel*, 3: 462.

## Chapter 11. Not to Belong

1. Buber to Ewalt Wasmuth and Sophie Wasmuth, November 1, 1961, in *Letters*, 642.

2. Buber, "Books and Men," in William Rollins and Harry Zohn, eds., *Men of Dialogue: Martin Buber and Albrecht Goes* (New York: Funk and Wagnalls, 1969), 29.

3. Schalom Ben-Chorin, Shmuel Hugo Bergmann, Gershom Scholem, Ernst A. Simon, and his son, Uriel Simon (born 1929 in Jerusalem).

4. Gershom Scholem, "At the Completion of Buber's Translation of the Bible," trans. Michael A. Meyer, in Scholem, *The Messianic Idea in Judaism, and Other Essays on Jewish Spirituality* (New York: Schocken, 1971), 314–319.

5. Ibid. (emphasis added).

6. Reported to me by Uriel Simon, who accompanied his father, Ernst Akiva Simon, to the event. As he put it, his father's "mouth dropped" on hearing what he found to be Scholem's untimely, indeed impertinent, criticism.

7. Gershom Scholem, "Martin Buber's Hasidism: A Critique," *Commentary* 32, no. 4 (October 1961): 304–316.

8. Buber to Maurice Friedman, July 7, 1961, Martin Buber Archive, file 227b.

9. Buber, "Interpreting Hasidism," *Commentary* 36, no. 3 (September 1963): 218.

10. Gershom Scholem, "Buber's Conception of Judaism," in Scholem, *On Judaism and Jews in Crisis. Selected Essays*, ed. Werner J. Dannhauser (New York: Schocken, 1976), 166 f.

11. Ibid.

12. Buber, *Tales of the Hasidism: The Early Masters* (New York: Schocken, 1947); Buber, *Tales of the Hasidim: The Later Masters* (New York: Schocken, 1948); Buber, *Die Erzählungen der Chassidim* (Zurich: Manesse, 1949).

13. Buber to Maurice Friedman, September 25, 1956, Martin Buber Archive, file 227b. For an example of this earlier approach, see Buber, *Or ha-Ganuz* (Jerusalem: Schocken, 1946), 13.

14. Buber, "Der Chassidismus und die Krise der abendländischen Menschen," *Merkur* (October 1956): 83–94; Buber, "Hasidism and Modern Man," part 1, in Buber, *Hasidism and Modern Man*, ed. Maurice Friedman (New York: Harper, 1958), 21–28.

15. Scholem, "Buber's Conception of Judaism," 127.

16. In 1919 Scholem translated into German the Hebrew poet Chaim Nachman Bialik's essay of 1916, "Halakhah and Aggadah," which contends that "a Judaism all of Aggadah is like iron that has been heated but not cooled."

17. "Candidate of the Presidency Professor Mordecai Buber, 'Here I am, Here I am/To a Nation That Did Not Invoke My name' (Isaiah 65:1)," *Etgar*, May 2, 1963, 1 (Hebrew).

18. Yael Dayan and Joel Hoffmann to Buber, May 5, 1956, in *Letters*, 599 f.

19. Yael Dayan to Gabriel Stern, December 31, 1971, in *Letters*, 600, fn. 2.

20. Avraham Shapira, "Meetings with Buber," *Midstream* (November 1978): 48–54.

21. Ibid., 51.

22. Rivka Gurfine, "A Literary Circle in a Kibbutz Reading Buber" (Hebrew), *Dvar Ha-Poelet* (January 1966).

23. Buber, "State and Culture" (Hebrew), *Haaretz*, April 30, 1953.

24. Cf. the Hebrew articles: "At the Age of 80 Buber Conducted a Stormy Love Affair with the Daughter of the Poet Richard Beer-Hofmann" (Hebrew), *Dvar*, September 18, 1988; and "Buber Had a Lover Aged 51 When He Was 81" (Hebrew), *Yediot Achronot*, September 19, 1988.

25. Naemah's letters to Buber are in the private archives of the Buber Literary Estate.

26. Buber, "Über Richard Beer-Hofmann," in Richard Beer-Hofmann, *Gesammelte Werke* (Frankfurt a.M.: Fischer Verlag, 1962), translated in Buber, *A Believing Humanism: My Testament*,

NOTES TO PAGES 314-318

*1902–1965*, trans. M. Friedman (New York: Simon and Schuster, 1967), 61–69.

27. Franz Rosenzweig, *The Star of Redemption*, trans. William Hallo (New York: Holt, Rinehart and Winston, 1970), 199.

28. See Jokl's recollections of her relationship with Buber in her autobiography *Die Reise nach London. Wiederbegegnungen* (Frankfurt a.M.: Jüdischer Verlag im Suhrkamp, 1999), 92–97.

29. That there was an implicit motive of penance is suggested by the dedication that she gave to the volume published after Buber's death: "For Ernst Simon, Martin Buber's friend, who accompanied him on the road to the reconciliation (Völker-ersöhnung) between peoples."

30. Buber, *A Believing Humanism*, 228–229.

31. Grete Schaeder to Maurice Friedman, February 1983, cited in Maurice Friedman, *Martin Buber's Life and Work*, vol. 3: *The Later Years, 1945–1965* (New York: E.P. Dutton, 1983), 470 f.

32. Ibid.

33. Buber would have a phrase—"I am always with you"— from this "death psalm" inscribed on his tombstone. Cf. "The Heart Determines: Psalm 73," in Buber, *Good and Evil: Two Interpretations* (Upper Saddle River, N.J.: Prentice Hall, 1997).

34. Ibid.

35. In 1962 on his way to Hotel Sonnmatt, he paid a visit to his old friend Margarete Sussman in Zurich. In her memoirs, she recalls their open, candid exchange about life, death, and evil: "In our conversation, he also commented on his own life, so surrounded with fame; he simply stripped the fame off like a golden cloak that did not belong to him." Margarete von Bendemann-Sussman, *Ich habe vielen Leben gelebt. Erinnerungen* (Stuttgart: Deutsche Verlags-Anstalt, 1964), 79.

36. Now in *Martin Buber Werkausgabe*, vol. 7: *Schriften zu Literatur, Theater und Kunst. Lyrik, Autobiographie und Drama*, ed. Emily Bilski, Heike Breitenbach, Freddie Rokem, and Bernd Witte (Gütersloh: Gütersloher Verlagshaus, 2016), 191.

37. Aubrey Hodes, *Martin Buber: An Intimate Portrait* (New York: Viking, 1971), 113.

38. Ibid., 113. On Buber's publicly objecting to the death penalty in 1928, see Buber, "Über die Todesstrafe," in F. M. Mungenast, ed., *Der Mörder und der Staat* (Stuttgart: W. Häderke, 1928), 65.

39. Hodes, *Martin Buber*, 114.

40. Jokl, *Die Reise nach London*, 94. The phrase "not to belong" is cited in English in the otherwise German text.

41. Martin Buber, Chaim Weizmann, and Berthold Feiwel, *Eine Jüdische Hochschule* (Berlin: Jüdischer Verlag, 1902). Reprint with Hebrew translation by Shaul Ash and preface by S. H. Bermann (Jerusalem: Magnes Press, 1964).

42. Cf. Hodes, *Martin Buber*, 211 f. I have supplemented Hodes's account of this tribute with recollections of Buber's great-granddaughter Tamar and of Professor Yaron Ezrahi, who as a student at the Hebrew University participated in the birthday celebration in front of Buber's home.

43. Ibid.

44. Ibid.

45. Werner Kraft, *Gespräche mit Martin Buber* (Munich: Kösel, 1966), 124–125; Hodes, *Martin Buber*, 215.

46. Cf. Buber to Walter Kaufmann, April 8, 1962, in *Letters*, 646.

47. In the selection of his shorter essays and largely unpublished poetry that he prepared in the last months before his death, Buber included this poem. Cf. Buber, *Nachlese* (Heidelberg: Lambert Schneider, 1965); Buber, *A Believing Humanism* (the poem is translated on 227).

48. Cited in Friedman, *Martin Buber's Life and Work*, 3: 415 f.

49. The account that follows of Buber's last year, his illness, and his funeral is drawn from a number of sources: personal recollections shared with me, newspaper reports, and especially the chronicle of the event in Ben-Horin, *Zwiesprache mit Martin Buber*, 237–245; and Hodes, *Martin Buber*, 213–229.

50. Buber, *Pointing the Way: Collected Essays*, trans. and ed. Maurice S. Friedman (New York: Schocken, 1957), 4.

## ACKNOWLEDGMENTS

I DID NOT KNOW Buber personally, but I have been privileged to know his son, Rafael, with whom I was particularly close. For more than a decade I would meet with him virtually daily for *Abendbrot*—a light evening meal—and convivial conversation. He also consulted with me on matters concerning his father's literary estate, which he administered. Rafael introduced me to his daughters, Judith and Barbara, and in the past several years, I have also had the joy of a friendship with Barbara's daughter Tamar, who—together with her parents and younger brother Gideon—spent her early years in the same home with Buber and his wife, Paula.

Conversations over the years with Rafael, Barbara, Judith, and other members of the Buber family—including his daughter Eva's son Emanuel and Emanuel's wife, Bella—have granted me a more intimate knowledge of Buber the person. I have also had the good fortune of knowing well four of Buber's close associates: Nahum N. Glatzer, Nathan Rotenstreich, Ernst Simon, and Gabriel Stern. I am also beholden to Margot Cohn, Buber's secretary for the last eight years of his life, and later the director of the Martin Buber Archive at the National Library of Israel. She not only led me through the byways of the Buber Archive but also brought to my attention particular details of Buber's life and thought recorded in the archive's vast holdings. My good friend Avraham "Patchi" Shapira shared with me reminiscences of the meetings he initiated and organized between members of kibbutzim and Buber, and gave me his own extensive collection of documents, especially those pertaining to Buber's reception in the State of Israel.

In clarifying my understanding of my task as a biographer, I have been immeasurably fortified by conversations with dear friends: Henry Hanoch Abramovitch, Michael "Buzzy" Fishbane, Tamar Goldschmidt, Aya Kaniuk, the late Nathan Ofek, Shalom Ratzabi, Richard Rosengarten, Christoph Schmidt, the late Arnold Schwartz, and my wife, Rita. As the reader will readily note, I have made extensive reference to memoirs of individuals who knew Buber. Finally, as the coeditor-in-chief of the twenty-two-volume *Martin Buber Werkausgabe*, the critical German edition of Buber's writings, I owe a special thanks to my coeditors—initially Peter Schaefer, and, since 2010, Bernd Witte. I must also cite with gratitude our dedicated editorial assistants: Martina Urban, Heike Breitenbach, Arne Taube, and Simone Poepl—and last but not least, the editors of each of the volumes of the *Werkausgabe*, who with their resourceful and diligent research have brought to light previously unknown material of inestimable biographical significance.

I am especially thankful to Tamar Goldschmidt and the Martin Buber Literary Estate for permission to quote from the Martin Buber Archive and the correspondence of Paula Buber to her daughter Barbara; Gütersloher Verlagshaus, for permission to quote from *Briefwechsel aus sieben Jahrzehnten*, ed. Grete Schaeder and Ernst Simon, 3 vols. (Heidelberg: Lambert Schneider, 1972–1975), and *Schriften zu Literatur, Theater und Kunst* (2016), volume 7 of *Martin Buber Werkausagbe*; and Hackett Publishing for permission to quote from *Franz Rosenzweig: His Life and Thought*, ed. Nahum N. Glatzer, 3rd ed. (1998).

This volume owes its inception to the editors of the Jewish Lives series of Yale University Press: Anita Shapira and Steven J. Zipperstein. At lunch in a lovely Tel Aviv café, Anita with her inimitable charm extended to me the invitation to write a biography of Martin Buber. I subsequently enjoyed the sapient counsel of Steve, with whom I met several times at a bucolic garden restaurant in East Jerusalem to discuss the conception of the biography. Upon my submission of the initial draft of the work, Steve noted that I had considerably exceeded the length specified in the contract. With my approval, he assigned Sue Fendrick, a seasoned editor, to review the manuscript and suggest abridgments. Her suggestions were invariably judicious and, indeed, served not only to tighten but also to lend greater coherence to the narrative. At the press, the manuscript was shepherded to publication by a conscientious and eminently collaborative team of editors. Heather Gold, assistant editor, attended with deft judgment and grace to technical issues associated with the preparation of the manuscript. Having struck gold with Heather (who will forgive me for the pun), the volume was further enriched by the masterful copyediting of Julie Carlson. Her suggested emendations were invariably voiced with a gentle, indeed dialogical, voice. I am also grateful to Susan Laity, production editor, for her careful and caring final review of the manuscript; and for their conscientious support to Sonia Shannon, senior designer; Liz Pelton, senior publicist; and Ileene Smith, editorial director of Jewish Lives. Joel Swanson meticulously prepared the index. My cherished friend, the renowned Chicago photographer Alan Cohen, insisted that he take a portrait photo of me worthy of a biography of Buber.

I am above all indebted to Martin Buber, who taught me to listen to the muted, inner voice of the Other—including one's own—before trying to understand her or his words. One might call this the hermeneutics of *Menschlichkeit*.

# INDEX

JEWISH LIVES is a prizewinning series of interpretative biography designed to explore the many facets of Jewish identity. Individual volumes illuminate the imprint of Jewish figures upon literature, religion, philosophy, politics, cultural and economic life, and the arts and sciences. Subjects are paired with authors to elicit lively, deeply informed books that explore the range and depth of the Jewish experience from antiquity to the present.

Jewish Lives is a partnership of Yale University Press and the Leon D. Black Foundation.

Ileene Smith is editorial director.
Anita Shapira and Steven J. Zipperstein
are series editors.